GREAT DIRECTORS

Cinema
Great Directors

Edited by

FRANK N. MAGILL

Derived from Library Editions
Published by Salem Press, Inc.

SALEM SOFTBACKS
Pasadena, California

LIBRARY OF CONGRESS CATALOG CARD NUMBER: 81-51770

ISBN 0-89356-312-9

This material has appeared previously in
Magill's Survey of Cinema.

First Printing

PRINTED IN THE UNITED STATES OF AMERICA

PUBLISHER'S NOTE

MAGILL SURVEYS form a series of integrated study guides designed to provide sources for augmenting classroom work in the Humanities. These guides offer ready-reference information about authors and their works and are structured with classroom requirements strictly in mind.

Magill Surveys are intended to take the student far beyond the immediate assignment. For example, if the program calls for the study of "a Dickens novel," the appropriate Survey will present to the student half a dozen or more pages on each of several Dickens novels, including a critical biography of Dickens, plot summaries and critical evaluations of the novels, individual character analyses of scores of the characters appearing in these novels, and finally an average of about twenty bibliographical references for *each* of the novels—the latter element a highly valuable resource whether for class work or term papers. Thus, the student may gain extensive background information about the author and his canon while concentrating on in-depth study of a particular work.

Great Directors surveys the film work of ten well known directors, offering essay-reviews of 104 important English language films as they appear in the Library Edition, *Magill's Survey of Cinema* (1980). This arrangement by director allows the student to compare a variety of films by one filmmaker or contrast the work of several. An alphabetical list of films reviewed appears at the end of the volume.

The original material reproduced in *Magill Surveys* has been developed through consultations with and contributions by hundreds of professors and scholars throughout the United States and abroad over a period of years. Its authoritativeness is attested by the thousands of academic and public libraries where the basic works from which this material is drawn will be found. The student who wishes to go beyond his assignment will find here ample means to satisfy his desire.

CONTENTS

vii

CONTENTS

List of Contributors

Charles Albright, Jr.
David Bahnemann
Julie Barker
Charles M. Berg
DeWitt Bodeen
Ronald Bowers
Pat H. Broeske
William H. Brown, Jr.
John Cocchi
Joan Cohen
William M. Clements
Leslie Donaldson
Daniel Einstein
Lawrence Fargo, Jr.
Daniel D. Fineman
Juliette Friedgen
Thomas A. Hanson
Larry Lee Holland
Ed Hulse
D. Gail Huskins
Julia Johnson
Timothy W. Johnson
Cheryl Karnes
Judith M. Kass
Tanita C. Kelly

Jonathon Kuntz
Elizabeth Leese
Blake Lucas
Anne Louise Lynch
Elizabeth McDermott
Carl Macek
Frances M. Malpezzi
Gregory William Mank
Mark Merbaum
Harold Meyerson
Robert Mitchell
Katherine M. Morsberger
Robert E. Morsberger
Janey Place
Dena Roth
Dan Scapperotti
Anthony Slide
Ellen J. Snyder
Maria Soule
Gene Stavis
Gay Studlar
Leslie Taubman
Don K Thompson
James Ursini
Joanne L. Yeck

GREAT DIRECTORS

FRANK CAPRA

ARSENIC AND OLD LACE

Released: 1944 (completed 1941)
Production: Frank Capra for Warner Bros.
Direction: Frank Capra
Screenplay: Julius J. Epstein and Philip G. Epstein; based on the play of the
same name by Joseph Kesselring
Cinematography: Sol Polito
Editing: Daniel Mandell
Running time: 118 minutes

Principal characters:

Mortimer Brewster	Cary Grant
Abby Brewster	Josephine Hull
Martha Brewster	Jean Adair
Teddy Brewster	John Alexander
Elaine Harper	Priscilla Lane
Jonathan Brewster	Raymond Massey
Dr. Einstein	Peter Lorre
O'Hara	Jack Carson
Lieutenant Rooney	James Gleason
Mr. Witherspoon	Edward Everett Horton
Judge Cullman	Vaughan Glaser

Arsenic and Old Lace was one of the biggest Broadway hits of the 1940's, a fast-paced, light-hearted treatment of murder exemplifying the black humor of the time. When Frank Capra bought the film rights to the play and began production in late 1941, it was with the stipulation that he would not release the film until it had closed on Broadway. Capra had hoped to use the income from the film to support his family while he earned the pay of a major in the Army. Unfortunately for Capra, the play was extremely popular and the movie could not be released until 1944. However, his good fortune lay in securing the talents of Josephine Hull, Jean Adair, and John Alexander of the original cast for his film version. Having signed Cary Grant, Hollywood's best *farceur*, for the lead role of Mortimer Brewster, Capra then chose some of his favorite character actors to round out his cast, notably Edward Everett Horton and James Gleason.

Translating hit Broadway plays to the screen has always been a problem for Hollywood, and it even proved a problem for a creative hand such as Capra. Critics complained then and still complain about the scenes that were added to the original play: a comment about the unorthodox behavior of Brooklynites is exemplified by a riot scene during a Dodgers game at Ebbetts Field; a scene with Mortimer Brewster, a drama critic, and his fiancée, Elaine Harper (Priscilla Lane), applying for a marriage license; the newlyweds' tryst in the cemetery next to the Brewster mansion; and a cabby waiting for Mortimer throughout the movie with the meter on and eventually presenting him with a $22.50 tab. But in spite of these additions, *Arsenic and Old Lace* remains as entertaining on the screen as it was on the stage.

Martha (Jean Adair) and Abby Brewster (Josephine Hull) are two wealthy, sweet old maids who live in the old family mansion where they take care of their nephew, Teddy (John Alexander). Teddy needs a great deal of care, since he thinks he is President Theodore Roosevelt. One delightful and famous feature of Teddy's behavior is that every time he goes upstairs, he yells "Charge!" and then charges up to the second floor. But if Teddy is strange, his aunts are even stranger. Very church-oriented, one of their charitable acts is to serve a special elderberry wine laced with a combination of arsenic, strychnine, and cyanide to unsuspecting lonely old gentlemen who come to inquire about the room they advertize for rent. That the ladies are disarmingly sentimental about their victims, remembering all their names, and are blissfully unaware that what they are doing is immoral, makes for a very amusing situation. The bodies are properly disposed of by Teddy, who thinks that they are all yellow-fever victims from Panama and must be buried quickly to avoid contagion. He digs a grave in the cellar, which he believes to be the Panama Canal, and then he and the sisters holds a proper Christian burial service. It is all quite tidy.

However, things take a turn when Teddy's brother Mortimer (Cary Grant) comes to tell his aunts that he has married. While there, Mortimer discovers his aunts' latest "charity case" in the window seat. At first he thinks the eccentric Teddy is responsible, but with some pride his aunts assure him that the dead man is their doing. With the revelation that this is their twelfth victim, Mortimer almost goes crazy himself. However, while he worries about what to do about the situation, he prevents his aunts from taking a thirteenth victim.

When Mortimer goes out to see about getting his aunts committed to an insane asylum, his older brother Jonathan (Raymond Massey), stealthily arrives at the house with his cohort Dr. Einstein (Peter Lorre), a plastic surgeon of sorts. Jonathan is a very cold-blooded killer who likewise boasts of twelve dead victims; he also bears a striking resemblance to Boris Karloff. Jonathan has eluded the police because Dr. Einstein has given him three different faces in five years. Unfortunately, the last time he operated, Dr. Einstein had recently seen a horror movie and was drunk when he operated; the result is that Jonathan has ended up with Boris Karloff's face. Jonathan is extremely unhappy about this and turns murderously angry whenever anyone reminds him of it. The two have come to the Brewster house so Dr. Einstein can operate again and correct his error. While Raymond Massey is made up to look like Karloff and his reaction to the allusions to his face is amusing, the humor loses some of its sharpness on the screen; the real Boris

Karloff played Jonathan in the original Broadway version.

Abby and Martha make it very clear that Jonathan's menacing presence is not welcome and that they would like him to leave. During the evening it becomes known that Jonathan also has a body to dispose of—that of his twelfth victim. However, he has decided to stay for a long time, since the quiet, respectable house is a perfect hiding place.

When Mortimer returns, we find that there is little love lost between the two brothers. Discovering a new body in the window seat, Mortimer realizes that this is his brother's victim and that he now has a hold on him. However, when Jonathan discovers his aunts' victim in the cellar, he realizes that he also has a trump card. Meanwhile, however, the fact that his aunts have accumulated the same number of victims as he has makes Jonathan jealous, and to beat them, he decides to make Mortimer his thirteenth victim. Jonathan and the doctor tie Mortimer to a chair so Jonathan can kill him by the "Melbourne method," a slow method which even gives Einstein the shivers. Just as Jonathan is about to strangle his brother, police officer O'Hara (Jack Carson) arrives. O'Hara has ambitions of being a playwright, and finding Mortimer quiet and unoccupied at the moment, he takes advantage of the situation to relate the lengthy plot of his play to the helpless drama critic. A stereotypal dumb cop, O'Hara is oblivious to the fact that Mortimer is bound and gagged. Mortimer, Jonathan, and Einstein are saved from being bored to death by the arrival of two more policemen who have come to see about putting Teddy away, as he is just too much of a neighborhood nuisance. Luckily for Mortimer, they *do* notice that he is tied up, and they become very suspicious of Jonathan because of his looks. When Lieutenant Rooney (James Gleason) and Judge Cullman (Vaughan Glaser) arrive to help commit Teddy, the lieutenant recognizes Jonathan right away from wanted posters and arrests him.

Seeking some sort of revenge, Jonathan tells the police officers about the twelve bodies in the basement, but none of them will believe him. When Teddy backs up the story, the police take that as evidence that it is a crazy story from two crazy men. Even hardboiled Rooney refuses to believe it when Martha and Abby offer to show him the graves in the cellar. When the sisters are told that Teddy has to go to Happy Dale they insist on going with him and happily commit themselves. One of the play's running jokes concerns Mortimer's worry about the insanity in his family. When he signs the commitment papers as next of kin, the sisters quietly take him aside and tell him that he is really not a Brewster, but the son of a sea cook. Instead of being upset, Mortimer is overjoyed that he is not part of this family. However, the strain of dealing with four insane people has driven him slightly crazy, and the judge wonders if he is not committing the wrong Brewster. While everyone is busy getting the papers signed, Dr. Einstein tries to sneak out of the house. He is stopped by Mortimer who asks him to sign the papers because a doctor's signature is needed. Everyone is so engrossed in the paper signing that Einstein is the only one who is aware that Rooney is concurrently getting a description of him as Jonathan's accomplice over the phone. His services over, Einstein quietly escapes, unable to believe his luck.

Teddy is persuaded to leave for Happy Dale when Mortimer tells him that his term in office is over. Teddy decides that now he can go on his African safari. After everyone else has left, and while waiting for Teddy to get his things together, the sisters strike up a conversation with Mr. Witherspoon (Edward Everett Horton), the head of Happy Dale. It turns out that Mr. Witherspoon is alone in the world and not very happy. As the movie ends, the sisters sweetly offer him a glass of elderberry wine.

Arsenic and Old Lace was a departure for Capra. His previous major films, such as *Mr. Smith Goes to Washington* (1939) and *Meet John Doe* (1941), were full of social commentary and the celebration of the common man. There is not a trace of either in this film; a fact, Capra has reported, that could not have made him happier. Critics have always thought of the film as one of Capra's lesser efforts. In fact, some analyses of his work have either glossed over it or omitted it completely. The critics felt that the additions to the original play broke up its fast pace and did little to heighten its humor. They criticized the great amount of overacting from everyone, especially from Cary Grant and Jack Carson. Capra unashamedly admits that he let his cast romp and mug to their hearts' content. With all its faults, even some of the critics had to admit that the film was and is rollicking good fun. Most of the lines and sight gags are still funny today, making the film a continuous favorite with audiences.

THE BITTER TEA OF GENERAL YEN

Released: 1933
Production: Columbia
Direction: Frank Capra
Screenplay: Edward E. Paramore; based on the novel of the same name by
  Grace Zaring Stone
Cinematography: Joseph Walker
Editing: no listing
Running time: 87 minutes

  Principal characters:
    Megan Davis .... Barbara Stanwyck
    General Yen .... Nils Asther
    Jones ....Walter Connolly
    Mah-Li .... Toshia Mori
    Dr. Robert Strike .... Gavin Gordon
    Captain Li .... Richard Loo

When one views Capra's films, *The Bitter Tea of General Yen* and *Lost Horizon* (1937) stand apart from his usual exploration of American ideology, for they have backgrounds which are diametrically opposed to the world of Mr. Deeds and John Doe. They both take place in the Orient, but whereas *Lost Horizon* is set in the best of all possible worlds, *The Bitter Tea of General Yen* takes place amid civil war, chaos, and famine. The leaders of Shangri-La believe that harmony—through goodness, truth, and beauty—prolongs life, whereas General Yen holds his great power through a complete distrust of humanity, showing no mercy and having no regard for human life. *Lost Horizon* is a story about an Occidental missionary who creates a paradise in an isolated valley in the mountains of Tibet, but *The Bitter Tea of General Yen* is about the incongruity and futility of missionaries and their work in China. To savor fully the delightful jabs at Christianity and missionaries in China, one must realize that Capra was, and is, a devout Catholic. Not only does Capra crucify the missionary, but also his story makes Christianity a fatal pill for General Yen: the first time he shows mercy to anyone it leads to his quick destruction.

The story of *The Bitter Tea of General Yen* opens in Shanghai on a scene of utter chaos: peasants flee as an army moves amidst the turbulence of the civil war. Megan Davis (Barbara Stanwyck), a newly arrived American missionary, is being carried through the screaming crowds in a rickshaw, when the "boy" pulling it is struck and killed by an ominous black limousine. Kneeling in the crowd, Megan attempts to comfort the dying boy, then vents her fury on the driver of the limousine. The driver does not understand what she is talking about, but then the smiling, sardonic figure of General Yen

(Nils Asther) emerges from the car. Speaking in English but not understanding her concern, he tells her that life is cheap in China and not to worry, for he will take her to her destination. Although he is immaculately dressed in his general's uniform and is exotically handsome, she is repelled by his lack of concern and inhumane attitude. She curtly refuses him and turns to make her way on foot, while he looks after her with an insolent smile as if to foreshadow a future meeting between them.

Meanwhile, the missionaries have gathered for the wedding of Megan to Dr. Robert Strike (Gavin Gordon), another missionary. Dr. Strike has not arrived on the scene when Megan makes her appearance. The missionaries themselves are an unchristian lot, finding nothing good in the Chinese. The house where they have gathered is completely American; there is no Oriental design about it, nor are there any Orientals gathered for the marriage ceremony. When Dr. Strike does arrive, it is to postpone his wedding to Megan, for he says he must leave at once to rescue children left in an orphanage which is dangerously near the fighting line. Megan insists, to the horror of all the ladies present, that she will accompany him. Dr. Strike is helpless to deny her and allows her to go along.

When she tells him of her strange meeting with General Yen, Strike is amazed, for Yen is not supposed to be in Shanghai. Since Yen could give him a safe conduct pass, they go to the general's headquarters. As Megan waits outside, Strike begs Yen for the pass. General Yen scoffs at him, but he sits down and writes in Chinese calligraphy what Strike believes to be a pass. Actually, however, it is a message introducing Strike as a Christian fool who prefers rescuing a band of lowly children "without ancestors" to passing the night with his bride in his arms.

Megan and Strike get an automobile and reach the orphanage, where they assemble the children for flight. But the streets are full of fighting, and a band of soldiers commandeers the automobile. In the ensuing struggle, Megan is separated from Strike and the children and is felled by a blow.

When she regains consciousness, she finds that somehow she has been transported to the secret and distant summer palace of General Yen. She is surrounded by every possible luxury, and when she steps out on her balcony, she sees the expansiveness and beauty of her prison. When Yen enters the room to inquire about her, she asks him why she has been kidnaped. He laughs and tells her that he has saved her life. Coldly, she informs him that she must return to Shanghai, but he tells her that it is impossible at this time because of heavy fighting; however, as soon as it is safe, he will send her back in a special train. For the meanwhile, he asks if she will be his guest and whether he may expect her presence at dinner that evening. Then he gallantly bows as he closes her door. Not for one moment does Megan believe Yen. She will not succumb to his charm, nor be pleasant or agreeable in any way. She is a prisoner.

Next, Mah-Li (Toshia Mori), Yen's young mistress, enters and inquires if Megan has all she needs. Megan likes Mah-Li and attempts to learn more about Yen from her. Megan refuses, however, to associate with Yen, and as the days pass, she becomes confidential with Mah-Li. One night, while the moon is full, Megan and Mah-Li watch from the balcony as Yen's soldiers romance the local ladies. A whistle from below makes Mah-Li twitter, for it is her young secret lover, Captain Li (Richard Loo), Yen's right-hand man. Mah-Li implores Megan not to tell Yen, and smilingly Megan agrees and tells her to go meet her beau. Alone, she watches the lovely setting and then falls asleep.

Megan dreams that a sinister Yen in mandarin robes is coming towards her with long claws. She cowers on the bed in fear, but there is a beating at the door as her rescuer attempts to break in. Finally, the door is smashed. Her hero enters and with one blow destroys Yen. She opens her arms to her uniformed hero, who is also Yen, and he bends down and kisses her. She awakens with a start and is troubled, pondering her dream.

Daily, Megan rejects Yen's invitations to dine with him. Eventually she changes her mind, deciding to go down to dinner to meet Jones (Walter Connolly), who is Yen's financial adviser and a wily American whom she hopes will persuade Yen to release her. At first, she lets Mah-Li dress her in Oriental attire, and puts on makeup, but then, fearing that she is succumbing to Yen, she wipes off her makeup and dresses herself in her New England attire.

At dinner, Jones tells Yen that Mah-Li and Captain Li are betraying him, and Yen indifferently decides to exterminate them. Later, a panic-stricken Mah-Li tells Megan bluntly that her guilt has been exposed and she will die for her sins. Megan implores Yen to be forgiving and let Mah-Li live; carried away with the situation, she begs him to use his God-given privilege, promising that he will know for the first time in his life what real happiness is. She breaks off in tears, realizing that she has almost confessed that she herself loves him. This does not escape Yen, who forgives Mah-Li, not in order to show that he too can display the mercy of the Christian world, but to show Mah-Li how foolish Megan is to plead on the girl's behalf, for he will let Mah-Li go only if Megan will stand as hostage for her. He is confident that Mah-Li will betray him again, and he drives the bargain, not to gain Megan's love on those terms, but to prove to her how false her Christian beliefs are; in this circumstance they simply will not work. As Yen confides to Jones subsequently, he is "going to convert a missionary."

Mah-Li does indeed betray General Yen a second time—outrageously, mercilessly, and with utter finality. Through her treachery, Yen's treasure train is stolen, his troops desert him, and no one is left in the summer palace except Megan, Jones, and General Yen.

When Megan realizes the extent of Mah-Li's perfidy, she goes to Yen, expecting him to demand payment of her honor. Instead, he gives her complete freedom; he will not take anything the heart does not freely give. She does not understand that it was her life, not her love, she pledged when she stood as hostage for Mah-Li's loyalty. Megan is frightened, and Yen scoffs at her fear of death, which she seems to fear as much as she has life. He confesses that he had intended to go to her room and kill her, after which the two would be joined in some celestial life as free lovers.

Megan runs to her room, dresses herself in Oriental garb, and paints her face. Meanwhile, Yen prepares the "bitter tea," the poison he will take to escape the world. She returns to him dressed in rich Chinese attire to affirm her love for him, which she realizes is her truest and finest emotion. She kneels at his feet weeping, and he dries her tears with a fine silk handkerchief as he slowly drinks his "bitter tea."

In the final sequence, Megan and Jones are together on a boat going back to Shanghai. Jones, who has been drinking enough to feel more than mellow, is talking about Yen, whom he characterizes as "a great guy." Yen had believed that we never die; we only change. Maybe, even now, he is the wind pushing their sail; maybe he is also the wind playing around her hair. Jones hopes that when he dies, the "guy" in charge of changing things will send him wherever Yen is; he looks at Megan, and ventures the thought that she will be there, too.

The Bitter Tea of General Yen opened New York's Radio City Music Hall as a motion picture theater, with a live prologue entertainment. New York critics had praise for the film, but in its general release it was deemed too bizarre, too esoteric for rural America. It is still one of Capra's favorites of all his films, and he was disappointed that it did not receive any Academy Award nominations. He had filmed it carefully, lovingly, and yet it was not for the masses. Almost in resignation, expecting nothing, he selected an inconsequentially light love story, *It Happened One Night* (1934), for one of his next efforts. He was lucky enough to borrow Claudette Colbert and Clark Gable from other studios for the leads, and at Academy Awards time, he swept the boards with a five-point major winner and made a great deal of money at the box office as well. Today, however, whenever there is a Capra, Columbia, or Barbara Stanwyck retrospective, *The Bitter Tea of General Yen* rates high as a favorite.

Although critics did not consider Barbara Stanwyck's role as Megan Davis to be one of her more memorable performances, today's audiences respond to her sympathetically; as a missionary who is converted to the real meaning of life, she is very believable. The picture belongs, however, to Nils Asther as General Yen. He gives a superb performance, his very best in film, although he had also played an Oriental prince in Garbo's silent *Wild Orchids* (1929), looking very handsome and rated as one of the few actors strong enough not to be emasculated by Garbo's strength. Asther makes Yen a fully dimensional character, a pagan who loved and lost, but whose loving had made life worthwhile.

The picture was denounced by Protestants as an affront to their religion and their missionaries. It was banned throughout the British Empire, making it one of the few big Capra films to have lost money.

IT HAPPENED ONE NIGHT

Released: 1934
Production: Harry Cohn for Columbia (AA)
Direction: Frank Capra (AA)
Screenplay: Robert Riskin (AA) and Frank Capra (uncredited); based on a
  story "Night Bus" by Samuel Hopkins Adams
Cinematography: Joseph Walker
Editing: Gene Havlick
Running time: 105 minutes

> *Principal characters:*
> Peter Warne .... Clark Gable (AA)
> Ellie Andrews .... Claudette Colbert (AA)
> Alexander Andrews .... Walter Connolly
> Mr. Shapeley .... Roscoe Karns
> King Westley .... Jameson Thomas
> Bus Driver .... Ward Bond

Made at a studio regarded as second-rate, with a reluctant star and script
trouble, *It Happened One Night* was an unexpected success. However, it may
have been precisely these conditions which allowed the film to become a
runaway hit at the box office and at the Academy Awards, where it won all
five major honors, a feat unduplicated until *One Flew Over the Cuckoo's Nest*
(1975) forty-one years later.

Later in his career, director Frank Capra was able to sign such stars as
Barbara Stanwyck and Gary Cooper for a film even before they saw a script,
but in 1933, when he was trying to cast a film for which he and Robert Riskin
had written a script (based on a *Cosmopolitan* magazine story by Samuel
Hopkins Adams), all the actors and actresses they contacted turned it down.
Luckily for Capra and for film audiences ever since, M-G-M at that time
wanted to discipline Clark Gable, so they loaned him to Columbia, a studio
which was then held in such low esteem that it was widely known as "Siberia"
or "Poverty Row." Gable did not want to do the film, but under the rigid
studio contracts of the 1930's, he had little choice. Claudette Colbert was
signed to play the heroine, and filming began with nearly everyone involved
thinking that the project was nothing more than a routine picture. Even
Capra, so tired from all his work to get the project started, just wanted to
get it finished. However, this very atmosphere may have, in the end, contributed a natural, unpretentious air to the film in a time when major studios
often spoiled their prestigious films by using a too-reverential approach to
both the subject and the stars.

Capra also gives credit for the quality and appeal of the film to his friend
Myles Connolly, who suggested improvements in an early version of the

script. Connolly's main suggestion was to change the hero from a vagabond painter to a newspaper reporter so that audiences could better identify with him.

The theme of *It Happened One Night* is one that was quite popular in Hollywood romantic films of the 1930's and early 1940's: love triumphing over social and economic differences. At the opening of the film we learn that Ellie Andrews (Claudette Colbert), a rich man's daughter, has just married King Westley (Jameson Thomas), a man of her own social class, but also a ne'er-do-well aviator. Her father, (Walter Connolly), opposes him and wants to have the marriage annulled. Next we meet Peter Warne (Clark Gable), a reporter who has just lost his job for sending a story to his newspaper in free verse. It might seem unlikely that these two would ever meet, much less fall in love, but when Ellie escapes from her father's yacht by diving overboard, determined to make her way from Florida to New York to join King Westley, circumstances bring them together.

They meet quarreling over a seat on the night bus to New York. Ellie has never ridden on a bus before, but is doing so to escape detection by her father; Peter is traveling on the bus because that is the only fare he can afford. Their first "conversation" ends with Peter saying, "Now listen, I'm in a very ugly mood. I put up a stiff battle for that seat. So if it's just the same to you— scram." Ellie, however, does not scram, and the two eventually travel all the way from Florida to Pennsylvania together.

During the trip a romance develops between the two without either of them quite realizing it. After discovering her true identity, Peter regards Ellie as a spoiled brat who thinks her money can get her anything she wants, and she regards him as an uncouth opportunist. However, several times circumstances force them to pretend that they are married: to discourage the amorous attentions of a traveling salesman, to save money on motels (called autocamps in the film), and to fool two detectives her father has sent looking for her.

The first night they spend together in a motel is a justly famous highlight of the film. A washed-out bridge stops the bus and makes it necessary for all the passengers to find accommodations for the night. It is a situation Ellie is completely unequipped to handle on her own. Indeed, this trip is her first attempt at doing things by herself rather than having them done for her; by contrast, Peter is used to living by his wits and quickly realizes that they must register as husband and wife to save money. When Ellie gets indignant and asks what gave him the idea she would stand for such a scheme, Peter explains that he is only interested in her as a headline. He is a newspaper reporter, he tells her, and needs to sell the story of her "mad flight to happiness" to his editor to get his job back. He will, therefore, help her reach King Westley for this reason, but if she rebels, he will turn her over to her father.

Peter then explains that he likes privacy. Stringing a rope between the two beds in their room, he hangs a blanket over it to divide the room into two parts. "The walls of Jericho" he calls it, but Ellie is dubious about the arrangement and refuses to go to her side of the wall. Peter tries to reassure her by telling her that he does not have a trumpet to bring the walls tumbling down as Joshua did in the Bible. When she still does not move, Peter begins taking off his clothes one article at a time while discoursing on the various ways men take off their clothes. When he has removed everything except his trousers, Ellie hurriedly retreats to her side, acquiescing in the arrangement.

Another highlight of the film is the hitchhiking scene. They have had to leave the bus because another passenger has also recognized Ellie, and Peter is becoming quite smug about his ability to take care of the helpless rich girl. He tells her they will have to thumb a ride and explains in great detail the technique of hitchhiking. When he tries to demonstrate his infallible methods, however, he is totally unsuccessful. After watching car after car pass without even slowing down, Ellie finally says she will try, and by lifting her skirt above the knee she stops the first vehicle. The man who picks them up later tries to steal Peter's suitcase, but Peter runs after him and returns with both the suitcase and the car, and he and Ellie continue their journey by automobile.

Finally Ellie realizes that she loves Peter and tells him so (in a conversation conducted over the "walls of Jericho"). They do not immediately get together and live happily ever after, however. When she says she loves him, Peter is taken aback, never having considered the idea. By the time he ponders and accepts the idea, Ellie is asleep. He leaves for New York to obtain some money from his editor because he does not want to be penniless when he proposes to her. After his departure, Ellie is awakened by the owner of the motel, and finding Peter gone, thinks she has been abandoned; she therefore has her father come to get her. Once they return to New York, they prepare for a large formal wedding for her and King Westley, although neither she nor her father is enthusiastic about the idea.

Shortly before the wedding Peter goes to see Ellie's father. Both her father and Ellie assume that Peter wants to collect the ten-thousand-dollar reward that was offered, but he asks for only $39.60, the exact amount of his expenses for the trip. Under the father's questioning he even admits to being in love with Ellie. "But don't hold that against me," he says. "I'm a little screwy myself." The wedding ceremony begins, but on the way to the altar her father explains the situation to Ellie and tells her he has a car waiting for her if she wants to escape. At the moment in the ceremony she is asked to say "I will," Ellie picks up the train of her wedding dress and rushes off to Peter's waiting car.

In the last scene we see the outside of a motel cabin, then we hear the sound of a trumpet and see a blanket fall to the floor as the film ends.

In *It Happened One Night* Clark Gable gives one of his best performances. His Peter Warne is tough, masculine, and cynical on the surface, but has a certain tenderness and romanticism underneath. Gable makes both facets of his personality perfectly credible. In addition, the character Gable plays does some acting of his own. For the benefit of some friends he plays the ultra tough guy, telling off his boss on the telephone, although we know that the boss is no longer on the line. Later he pretends to be a gangster to frighten off the passenger who has also recognized Ellie, and he and Claudette Colbert do a humorous scene as a quarreling married couple so that a pair of detectives will not realize who Ellie is. Capra summed it up best: "I believe it was the only picture in which Gable was ever allowed to play himself: the fun-loving, boyish, attractive, he-man rogue that was the *real* Gable.

As Ellie Andrews, Claudette Colbert perfectly complements Gable in what is arguably the best role of her career. She must show both sides of Ellie, the spoiled rich girl who expects the bus to wait for her while she has a leisurely breakfast, and the spunky woman with whom Peter falls in love almost against his will. It is not easy to make both antagonism and romance credible in one relationship, but Gable and Colbert do it to perfection.

Director Frank Capra later became famous for celebrating the virtues of the common man in such films as *Mr. Smith Goes to Washington* (1939) and *It's a Wonderful Life* (1946). It is a theme which is important in *It Happened One Night* and is particularly underscored in the final scenes in which the down-to-earth reporter can barely tolerate the elaborate and meaningless extravagance of the rich. This theme is not, however, as important as it is in later Capra pictures; instead, the film is chiefly a romantic comedy. Capra proves himself a master of the genre as, with careful pacing, he builds the characterizations upon which the comedy depends, so that *It Happened One Night* is more a comedy of character than of events or surprises. Indeed, the many imitations of the film in the 1930's and the remake *You Can't Run Away from It* (1956) are so inferior to the original that they merely reinforce one's appreciation of the artistry of Frank Capra.

IT'S A WONDERFUL LIFE

Released: 1946
Production: Frank Capra for Liberty Films; released by RKO/Radio
Direction: Frank Capra
Screenplay: Frances Goodrich, Albert Hackett, and Frank Capra, with additional scenes by Jo Swerling; based on the story "The Greatest Gift" by Philip Van Doren Stern
Cinematography: Joseph Walker and Joseph Biroc
Editing: William Hornbeck
Sound: Richard Van Hessen, Clem Portman, and John Aalberg
Music: Dmitri Tiomkin
Running time: 129 minutes

Principal characters:

George Bailey	James Stewart
Mary Hatch	Donna Reed
Mr. Potter	Lionel Barrymore
Uncle Billy	Thomas Mitchell
Clarence	Henry Travers
Mrs. Bailey	Beulah Bondi
Violet Bick	Gloria Grahame
Mr. Gower	H. B. Warner
Bert	Ward Bond
Ernie	Frank Faylan
Pa Bailey	Samuel S. Hinds
Cousin Tilly	Mary Treen
Bodyguard	Frank Hagney
Nick	Sheldon Leonard

When Frank Capra returned to Hollywood from his service in the Army during World War II, he was a colonel and had been awarded the Distinguished Service Medal. He had left Hollywood, one of its foremost directors, to make films at home and abroad for the War Department. He worked on all seven pictures in the *Why We Fight* series, including the Oscar-winning *Prelude to War*; another series beginning with *Know Your Ally* and *Know Your Enemy*; the *Army-Navy Screen Magazine*; *The Negro Soldier in World War II*; *The Battle of Britain*; *Two Down and One to Go*; and several other films which he codirected. Now, in the spring of 1945, he was a civilian once again, back in Hollywood looking for a new project. Together with three other colonels who had seen service in the war—William Wyler, George Stevens, and Samuel Briskin—he formed Liberty Films, of which he was President; and the company committed itself to make nine pictures for release through RKO/Radio.

As of yet, Capra had no film in mind to make as his first for Liberty Films.

One day Charles Koerner, head of production at RKO, came to his office to tell him about an original story, "The Greatest Gift," which he had purchased for RKO from Philip Van Doren Stern. It had been written as a Christmas card to be mailed to Stern's friends, but Koerner saw a full feature film in its few paragraphs, bought it, and had already spent a fortune hiring three writers—Dalton Trumbo, Marc Connelly, and Clifford Odets—to make a screenplay of the story. So far none of their efforts had come to fruition, and Koerner wanted Capra to read the story and see what he thought. Capra read it and was overjoyed; it seemed to him to be the story he had been looking for all his life. Liberty bought "The Greatest Gift" for the fifty thousand dollars Koerner had paid for it, and Koerner threw in the three previous screenplays as part of the bargain. Capra, however, wanted a fresh start; he hired Frances Goodrich and Albert Hackett as writers, and later wrote some scenes on his own. The new title for the venture was *It's a Wonderful Life*.

Seldom has a picture been produced with more love. Capra got his old friend James Stewart, who had also been a colonel in the Air Corps, to play the leading role and the rest of the cast fell easily into place. Three actors—Lionel Barrymore, Donna Reed, and Gloria Grahame—were borrowed from M-G-M; the others, for the most part, were enlisted from what Capra has called the Ford-Capra stock company: brilliant character actors such as Thomas Mitchell, H. B. Warner, Beulah Bondi, Ward Bond, Frank Faylen, Samuel S. Hinds, Mary Treen, Frank Hagney, plus two talented additions to the ranks—Sheldon Leonard and Henry Travers.

The hero of *It's a Wonderful Life* is George Bailey (James Stewart), who never planned to be a hometown boy. Born, reared, and educated in the typical small American town of Bedford Falls, George is a victim of circumstances. He had always wanted to travel, to see the world and develop beyond Bedford Falls; but when his father died, George was committed to keeping alive the Bailey Building and Loan Company as the only alternative to allowing Bedford Falls to fall completely under the ownership of greedy and unscrupulous Henry F. Potter (Lionel Barrymore).

George's sacrifices begin at once. He gives up a trip abroad for which his father had paid in order for his brother to go to college, while he himself goes to work for the Bailey Company. He falls in love with and marries Mary Hatch (Donna Reed), but when there is a run on the Bailey Building and Loan Company, fomented by Mr. Potter, George is forced to use his honeymoon money to bolster the dwindling assets. Ending the bank day with only one dollar left, George goes home to the dilapidated old mansion which Mary has taken over to begin their future life together.

George is doomed to stay in Bedford Falls, the best-liked man in town. He and his wife have children, and the machinations of Mr. Potter seem to have come to a halt. Then Mr. Potter, obsessed with the idea of owning the town, again starts trying to gain control of the Bailey Company. When

George's partner Uncle Billy (Thomas Mitchell) loses several thousand dollars, George is tempted to give up. It is the Christmas season, but there is no love and the spirit of giving is gone in George's soul. His town has become the wreck of an American dream, turned sour by one selfish, evil man. All George wants is out—for good.

While standing on the bridge over the river at Bedford Falls, George is thinking about something that Potter had said to him about being worth more dead than alive when a stranger calls out for help from the ice water below. George jumps to his rescue, forgetting for the moment that he had been thinking about killing himself just moments before. They are both pulled from the water by the tollhouse keeper, who takes them into the tollhouse to dry off. The stranger, whose name is Clarence Oddbody (Henry Travers) tells George that he is his guardian angel, but he is an angel who has not earned his wings, which he will get if he can keep George alive. George, however, wishes that he had never been born; so Mr. Oddbody describes how different life would have been in Bedford Falls had George never lived. For example, when George was young and worked in a drugstore, he averted a tragedy when the distracted pharmacist, Mr. Gower (H. B. Warner), accidentally put poison into a prescription he was preparing. George learns, thanks to Mr. Oddbody, that he has unknowingly become the town's most important citizen, and has been involved, directly or indirectly, in the fates of almost all the townspeople.

Later, Bert (Ward Bond) the policeman finds George on the bridge and demands to know where he has been, since the whole town is looking for him. George by now is glad to be alive. Meanwhile, the citizens of Bedford Falls, filled with good will and the Christmas spirit, want to prove their faith in George. They bring him all the cash they can scrape together so that once more George can defeat old Mr. Potter. The miracle of friendship allows him and his town to celebrate. Men who have real friends know the best there is in life. Good deeds, as Everyman learned in the old morality play, are all that follow each man beyond the span of his earthly days.

It's a Wonderful Life was Capra's own favorite film of all the features he directed, and it was James Stewart's favorite as well. It received a goodly share of praise from the critics, although some were unmoved by its moments of fantasy and earnest Americanism. The public, nevertheless, greatly admired the picture, which earned five Academy Award nominations, but no Oscar; the major share of the Oscars went to the superb *The Best Years of Our Lives*, directed by William Wyler for Samuel Goldwyn as Wyler's last film before he joined Liberty Films.

As many times as a filmgoer sees *It's a Wonderful Life*, he cannot fail to be moved by certain sequences, in particular the scenes of the high school dance held in the school gymnasium. The sequence was shot at Beverly Hills High School, and when somebody in the crew mentioned that the dance floor was movable and that underneath it was a swimming pool, Capra could not resist taking advantage of the unique circumstance. Thus was born the gimmick of the Charleston contest: one of George's rivals pulls the switch which moves the floor apart, until George and Mary Hatch, performing a hectic Charleston on the very edge of the separating floor, finally tumble down into the water, followed by nearly everyone present, including the principal.

It's a Wonderful Life is still a much-loved film, with its theme that no man is a failure as long as he has one friend, and that every man's life touches everybody he knows, so that no man ever lives alone. Many fans have made a practice of viewing it on Christmas Eve, just as Capra himself still does in his own home. It is a true holiday film, intended to spread good will and cheer, which it does liberally; it is, in fact, a kind of modern morality movie, not unlike Dickens' *A Christmas Carol*, with James Stewart playing a character similar to Bob Cratchit, a worthy hero whose faith is put to the test, and Lionel Barrymore portraying a modern-day Ebenezer Scrooge.

LOST HORIZON

Released: 1937
Production: Frank Capra for Columbia
Direction: Frank Capra
Screenplay: Robert Riskin; based on the novel of the same name by James Hilton
Cinematography: Joseph Walker
Editing: Gene Havlick and Gene Milford (AA)
Art direction: Stephen Goosson (AA)
Music: Dmitri Tiomkin
Running time: 118 minutes

Principal characters:

Robert Conway	Ronald Colman
Sondra	Jane Wyatt
Alexander P. Lovett	Edward Everett Horton
George Conway	John Howard
Henry Barnard	Thomas Mitchell
Maria	Margo
Gloria Stone	Isabel Jewell
Chang	H. B. Warner
High Lama	Sam Jaffe

"Have you ever dreamed of a place where living was not a struggle but a lasting delight?" Thus reads the opening title card to *Lost Horizon*, Frank Capra's dream of Shangri-La, the inaccessible Himalayan Utopia to which British diplomat Robert Conway (Ronald Colman) is hijacked, from which he escapes, and finally to which he attempts desperately to return.

It is not, unfortunately, one of Capra's more successful dreams. *Lost Horizon* is an exception among Capra's works, not only because it is one of the two major films of this most American of directors in which he abandons an American setting (*The Bitter Tea of General Yen*, 1933, is the other), but more precisely because Capra's vision of life is inextricably rooted in struggle. The first three parts of his four-part autobiography, for instance, are entitled "Struggle for Success," "Struggle with Success," and "The Great Struggle." The point at which struggle is suspended in favor of "lasting delight" is the point at which Capra reaches the limits of his imagination.

Accordingly, the best sequences in *Lost Horizon* are those that take place far from Shangri-La itself. Among these are the scenes that open the movie: the wartime burning of a Chinese city, from which a few huddled Europeans, shepherded by Conway, Britain's foreign secretary-designate, attempt to escape. He himself accompanies the last planeload of passengers, who barely elude the hysterical mob only to find themselves hijacked to some unknown mountainous destination beyond Tibet. After the plane crashes, a search party materializes to lead the bewildered passengers over seemingly impassable mountains to the Valley of the Blue Moon, Shangri-La. There, they discover an equable climate, a peaceable native people, a magnificent palace containing all the world's art and writings, and a two-hundred-year-old Belgian monk (Sam Jaffe) who rules as High Lama of Shangri-La. Aging is retarded in the Valley, and time itself is slowed.

The sets for *Lost Horizon* were so elaborate by the standards of the day that the film cost two million dollars, four times the cost of any other Columbia production to that time, and half of Columbia's total production budget for the year. *Lost Horizon* was, among other things, Harry Cohn's announcement to Louis B. Mayer and others that Columbia was no longer a little studio on "poverty row."

Freed from the burdens of work and time, the motley crew of Europeans with whom Conway escapes attain new levels of fulfillment. The consumptive prostitute Gloria Stone (Isabel Jewell) takes a cure and becomes a nice girl; the crooked banker on the lam, Henry Bernard (Thomas Mitchell), initiates a public works program; the fussy paleontologist Alexander P. Lovett (Edward Everett Horton) teaches the valley children; Conway and his younger brother George (John Howard) each find a young European woman on the premises and fall in love. And, in time, Robert Conway discovers why they have been hijacked to the mysterious valley: the Lama is at long last dying, and he has chosen Conway as his successor.

Upon the Lama's death, Conway is prepared to occupy the Lamasary, until his brother's girl friend, Maria (Margo), convinces them that the place is a fraud. The three flee through the mountains, where it turns out that it is she who is the fraud. On their first day out, she ages by half a century—the length of time she has been living in the valley—and dies. The crazed younger Conway hurls himself from a ledge; the elder Conway is swept away in a blizzard, from which he is rescued and returned to civilization. But civilization no longer commands his allegiance. As the film concludes, he is struggling against all odds to return through the mountains to the lost valley; and in the final shot, he reaches the elusive entrance.

Capra's Utopia is barely a Utopia at all. It is more accurate to call it a sanctuary, a negation of the world without, rather than an articulated world unto itself. It operates on an unexamined racial caste system; its system of government is benevolent despotism. The secret of its social organization, the enfeebled Lama tells the supplicant Conway, is that "We have one simple rule here: be kind." Shangri-La is neither a world unto itself nor a part of the larger world; it is, as the Lama sees it, a museum, a collection of the world's wisdom of which men can avail themselves as they emerge from the rubble of the war the Lama is certain will come.

However, sanctuary, not Utopia, is Capra's stock-in-trade (his next picture,

You Can't Take It with You, 1938, turns the Vanderhof house into a refuge from the world), and throughout his films of the 1930's, that sanctuary most often takes the form of romance. It is as much Sondra, the beautiful European schoolteacher, played by a very young Jane Wyatt in her first screen role, as it is Shangri-La to which Conway is trying to return. In the whole valley, it is only Sondra who embodies something more than negation; indeed, Shangri-La can be taken simply as a metaphor for romance. In the mid-1930's, romance is still sufficient to rouse the Capra hero from his characteristic despair, but in later Capra films, love and family are not enough to deter the heroes— John Doe and George Bailey—from attempted suicide. For that is precisely what Shangri-La is—a refuge from suicide. As the Lama's assistant Chang (H. B. Warner) explains the mysteries of the valley to the newly arrived Europeans, he alludes to worldly death as "indirect suicide"; he attributes the characteristic longevity of the valley dwellers to "the absence of struggle." It is the sudden reimmersion into the world of time and struggle that immediately provokes the suicide of Conway's brother.

Capra's is the single most suicide-ridden world of any major American artist. His characters inhabit a fiercely atomistic society where no personal or social ties can ultimately bind them to life. This atomism is the basis of Capra's cutting and composition; it explains his preference for the individual set piece over the group shot (for example, Edward Everett Horton, in one of *Lost Horizon*'s all-too-few moments of comic relief, scaring himself silly in a mirror). Capra is a master at the use of the individual reaction shot to help validate a fantastic scene. As Chang tells the Europeans of the wonders of the valley, Capra repeatedly cuts to their expressions of amazement. Their disbelief preempts that of the audience, so that their ultimate acceptance of Chang's tale makes it easier for the audience to suspend its disbelief.

In the final analysis, Shangri-La is an extremely egoistic response to the world. The Lama, after all, is asking a very capable man of the world to withdraw his considerable talents from it, to cultivate his own garden with his beautiful wife until, in time, the world must turn to him. Indeed, the very notion of Shangri-La is rooted in a despair that outweighs any countervailing optimism the valley is intended to inspire. Howard Hawks and John Ford could create groups and societies within the world where friendship and loyalty and justice prevailed; theirs are worlds of middle-distance and long shots. In the one-shot world of Frank Capra, community is an unworldly commodity, and Shangri-La an unworldly repository, not of community, but simply of refuge.

MEET JOHN DOE

Released: 1941
Production: Frank Capra for Warner Bros.
Direction: Frank Capra
Screenplay: Robert Riskin; based on the story "The Life of John Doe" by Richard Connell and Robert Presnell
Cinematography: George Barnes
Editing: Daniel Mandell
Running time: 115 minutes

Principal characters:

Long John Willoughby	Gary Cooper
Ann Mitchell	Barbara Stanwyck
The Colonel	Walter Brennan
D. B. Norton	Edward Arnold
Connell	James Gleason
Bert	Regis Toomey

During the 1930's and 1940's Frank Capra directed a series of populist melodramas, films in which an honest, ordinary man fights the corrupt and powerful, and succeeds only after near failure and public humiliation. In *Meet John Doe* Capra employs a slight variation on the pattern by presenting a hero who is not scrupulously honest, at least not at the beginning.

The situation that *Meet John Doe* establishes is an intriguing one—a wealthy man with political ambitions who owns a newspaper, a young newspaper columnist determined to keep her job, and a bush league pitcher with an injured arm all trying to use one another for their own purposes. When D. B. Norton (Edward Arnold) buys the metropolitan newspaper, *The Bulletin*, he changes its motto from "A Free Press Means a Free People" to "A Streamlined Paper for a Streamlined Age." As part of the streamlining he orders the firing of anyone on the staff who does not produce enough "fireworks" to stimulate circulation. Ann Mitchell (Barbara Stanwyck) is one of those summarily dismissed because her column is thought too tame by the new management. Rather than give in, Ann decides to fight. In her last column she says she has received a letter signed "John Doe" from a man who is so disgusted by the conditions of the world that he is going to jump from the top of the City Hall on Christmas Eve.

The letter provokes such a big reaction from the people, the politicians (including the mayor and the governor), and a rival newspaper, that *The New Bulletin* (as it is now called) is forced to do something. To get her job back Ann suggests that they hire someone to pretend to be John Doe and she will write daily stories of his protests against greed, inhumanity, and hate. The paper is forced to go along with her rather than admit it has published a phony letter, and Ann and the managing editor, Connell (James Gleason), pick out their "John Doe."

The man they choose is Long John Willoughby (Gary Cooper), a bush league pitcher with a bad arm who sees the whole scheme as a chance to obtain money for an operation on his arm so that he can once again play baseball. When the stories in the newspaper begin and are instantly popular, it is arranged for John Doe to make a speech (written by Ann) on the radio. Despite some misgivings and despite an offer of five thousand dollars from the rival newspaper to admit he is a fake, John delivers the speech Ann has written about the value and importance of the little or average man. People all over the country respond and begin to form John Doe clubs. D. B. Norton recognizes the phenomenon as one he can use to gain the political power he desires and begins organizing the John Doe movement.

The situation thus established is a confused and complex one for both Ann and John. Ann uses the ideas of her honest and idealistic father in the speeches, which persuade people to believe that "John Doe" is genuine and which—not incidentally—earn her large amounts of money from Norton. It is pointed out to John that even if he gets the money to repair his arm, he will never be able to play baseball when people find out that he is a fake. He is about to give up the whole thing when Bert (Regis Toomey), the leader of one of the John Doe clubs, comes to him and tells him a heart-warming story about how their lives have been changed and their appreciation of their fellow man deepened by what he has done. Both Ann and John at least partially believe the John Doe message, but one character has no ambivalence, no confusion of motives—D. B. Norton. He is the one purely evil figure in the film. Slightly heavy set, expensively dressed, smugly polishing his eyeglasses, he tells Ann that she will never have to worry about money if she plays her cards right.

Standing somewhat outside the action but always commenting on it is John's friend, who is called simply the Colonel (Walter Brennan). He has bummed around with John and views with disdain anything that complicates life. When first given fifty dollars, a new suit, and a hotel room, John enjoys it all, saying that even the major leaguers do not have such luxury. The Colonel, however, is contemptuous of the whole thing. As he explains it, money makes you used to things which will wreck you. You start by eating in restaurants, and the next thing you know you cannot sleep without a bed. You start with fifty dollars and end up with a bank account and with everyone wanting to sell you something. This, he says, turns everyone into "heelots," which, he explains, means "a lot of heels," who think only of how they can get money from you. The Colonel much prefers their old life when they rode freight trains and slept under bridges together.

The Colonel with his skeptical attitude provides the film with moments of humor and a refreshing counterpoint to the sometimes overly sentimental scenes. During Bert's long and emotional declaration to John, we see the Colonel looking on disgustedly; and in a delightful scene in the hotel room, John and the Colonel play a game of baseball with an imaginary ball.

The climax of the film occurs at a huge rally of John Doe club members from all over the country. Over twenty thousand have gathered in a ball park in the rain, and the event is being covered by national radio. Norton plans to have John Doe announce at the rally the formation of a third party with Norton as its presidential candidate. He and his cohorts plan a Fascist-style government to rule the people with an "iron hand." John, who is planning to ask Ann to marry him, finds out about the plot from Connell, who is cynical, but not cynical enough to let such a thing happen. When he goes to Norton's house to confront him, John finds that Ann, wearing a new fur coat and a diamond bracelet, is there together with Norton and all his cohorts. John threatens to reveal the truth to the rally, but Norton replies that he will kill the John Doe movement if he cannot use it. Completely disillusioned, John goes to the rally, but Norton outmaneuvers him. After newsboys distribute thousands of papers at the rally proclaiming John Doe a fake, Norton denounces him from the microphone and then has the wires cut so John cannot reply to the charges.

Long John Willoughby and John Doe both seem completely defeated; indeed, director Capra has admitted that he could not find a satisfactory conclusion for the film. He shot five different endings and finally settled on one in which John decides that the only way he can prove his sincerity is to jump from the top of the City Hall on Christmas Eve. Ann, Connell, and the Colonel all go to the Hall to try to stop him. When they find him, they are unable to dissuade him even though Ann tells him that the first John Doe has already died for the people. It is only when Bert, his wife, and another John Doe club member come to plead with him that John decides to live rather than die. Connell turns to Norton, who is also present, and says, "The people—try and lick that."

Perhaps *Meet John Doe* can best be characterized as a flawed masterpiece. Most of the flaws are in the last part of the film, where the pace slows drastically and the story seems to lose its bearings and drift off course. The drifting begins with John's somewhat out-of-character description, which lasts far too long, of a dream to Ann which shows his love for her. When John learns about the plot to use him to establish a third party, the pace again slows as Connell delivers a maundering, drunken harangue. And to say that the ending is overdone is to understate the obvious. It uses shameless Christian imagery as well as the characterizations of a repentant, hysterical woman who has gotten out of a sickbed (Ann) and a corrupt and powerful man (Norton) overmatched by one of the little people (Bert)—all on a cold, snowy Christmas Eve.

While it is still on course, however, the film is powerful and affecting, and most of the credit must go to the acting and directing. Ann is in many ways a typical Capra heroine—the clever, manipulative woman who finally has a change of heart and ends up on the side of the "sucker" she has been trying to manipulate. Barbara Stanwyck plays the role with enthusiasm and effectiveness. Gary Cooper is perfect as Long John Willoughby, the simple man who finds himself realizing the complexities of his situation a bit too late. He convincingly conveys the artlessness of Long John, notably in the scene in which he reads the first radio speech, which he has not seen before he goes on air. It does not slight the performances of Stanwyck and Cooper, however, to say that the Colonel as played by Walter Brennan is perhaps the most memorable character in the film.

Despite its weaknesses, *Meet John Doe* was deservedly well received by the critics and the public. Its main theme—the danger of Fascist takeover—fit well with the mood of the time (Hitler had taken most of Europe and was threatening to take over the rest of the world), and its other themes and concerns, especially the manipulation of people by the media, remain apt today.

MR. SMITH GOES TO WASHINGTON

Released: 1939
Production: Frank Capra for Columbia
Direction: Frank Capra
Screenplay: Sidney Buchman; based on a screen story by Lewis R. Foster
   (AA)
Cinematography: Joseph Walker
Editing: Gene Havlick and Al Clark
Running time: 125 minutes

> *Principal characters:*
> Jefferson Smith .... James Stewart
> Saunders .... Jean Arthur
> Senator Joseph Paine .... Claude Rains
> Jim Taylor .... Edward Arnold

While Frank Capra's critical reputation was comparatively low during the 1960's, his excellence as a director is now properly recognized. This delay was in part brought about by Capra's own withdrawal from the post-television cinema of the 1950's; in that era of director-stars he preferred retirement to the rejection of his own edict: "One man—one film." This delay also was caused by a critical and academic prejudice against popular and successful movies. In Capra's case this prejudice is exceedingly inappropriate since his populism and democratic empathy are exactly at the heart of his great creative gift. Indeed Capra, perhaps more than any other director, loves America, especially as it is embodied in its people. For him the American Dream, the Horatio Alger story of the triumphant individual, was a reality.

The youngest of a totally illiterate Sicilian family of seven children, Capra came to the United States in 1903 when he was six. By selling newspapers as a boy he both supported his family and began his involvement with the common man. Despite his education at California Institute of Technology as a chemical engineer, he continued his door-to-door contact with the proletariat as an itinerant post-World War I photography salesman. He avoided the inherent drudgery of both jobs by celebrating and even mythologizing the workaday world. It is this celebration and love which forms the kernel of his greatest films.

During the Golden Age of cinema, from the advent of sound to the on-slaught of television, Frank Capra's films between 1932 and 1939 were nom-inated six times for the Academy Award of Best Picture of the Year. The first of his Columbia comedy series, *It Happened One Night* (1934), won all five major Academy Awards (Best Picture, Actor, Actress, Screenplay, and Director) and remained the only film to have done so until *One Flew Over the Cuckoo's Nest* in 1975. By combining a small stable of attractive stars with the grand themes of the American political experiment, Capra annually brought a humane yet self-critical awareness to an enthralled public.

With the possible exception of some echoes in the somewhat anomalous and slightly pessimistic *Meet John Doe* (Warner Bros., 1941), Capra ended this series of comic Columbia successes with *Mr. Smith Goes to Washington* (1939). This picture, perhaps even more than its clear cinematic predecessor *Mr. Deeds Goes to Town* (1936), demonstrates the wonderful mixture of entertainment, social consciousness, idealism, and corruption which was the earmark of these movies. Thus, even without his talented previous script collaborator, Robert Riskin, Capra was able to re-create that delicate balance between pleasure and instruction so evident in the movie's plot.

The movie's story is fairly simple but is open enough to contain both sentiment and pathos. Following the unexpected death of his unnamed state's senator, Mr. Jefferson Smith (James Stewart) is appointed by the corrupt organization of Boss Jim Taylor (Edward Arnold) to fill the remainder of the dead senator's term in office. Taylor chooses him because he believes that Smith's naïveté (his only other leadership position was as head of the "rangers," or boy scouts) will allow the unimpeded passage of a pork barrel land bill. At first Taylor seems correct: Smith amuses the Washington sophisticates and reporters with his country manners and his well-honed duck call. However, with the typical serendipity of the local yokel, Smith proposes a national boys' camp exactly on the site of Taylor's pork barrel land deal. Now he must be dealt with.

Taylor turns to his minion, Senior Senator Joseph Paine (Claude Rains) from Smith's own state, and sets about to discredit Smith's proposal by falsifying documents to show that the camp is Smith's own pork barrel. With Boss Taylor controlling radio and newspaper, except for the Rangers' boyish publication, things look bleak for Smith. Following his secretary Saunders' (Jean Arthur) directions, Smith attempts to triumph over political adversity with a one-man, twenty-three-hour filibuster. As Smith collapses in exhaustion at the end of his heroic effort, Senator Paine, in a fit of remorse, admits his complicity and exonerates Smith and the American Way.

Obviously, such a "corny" (or, as Capra called it, "Capra-corny") plot line could not hold our attention without excellent acting, but the cast meets the challenge. Jimmy Stewart as Smith is warm, lovable, and believable; his innocence and idealism are humane, yet not maudlin. Further, Jean Arthur as his secretary Saunders shortcircuits what disbelief we might have in Smith's childish character by expressing that disbelief for us and then transforming the doubts into infatuation. Against these two, Claude Rains as Senator Paine and Edward Arnold as Boss Taylor form the perfect counterpoint. Rains's austere dignity and polished rhetorical style are perfect for the suspect political practitioner. Arnold's active style and rotund figure also seem to fit perfectly his role, that of a businessman whose power borders on the Machiavellian. However, all this talent might have gone for naught if Capra had not knitted it together with the techniques of his craft.

Aside from his usual talent for balanced composition and natural lighting, Capra applied some special skills to *Mr. Smith Goes to Washington*. The use of the Washington background, and the Lincoln Memorial in particular, added much inherent interest in a Depression era of restricted travel. This innovation was matched by the perfect duplication of the Senate Floor at the Columbia Studios. To add to the realism of the filibuster sequence, Capra had Stewart's throat painted three times a day with a substance that made him artificially hoarse and sore. Likewise in his choice of small part players, Capra gave each of them a personality which added to the fullness of the whole picture; one example is Guy Kibbee as the weak governor. Even in his rendition of legislative procedure Capra was extremely careful: James B. Preston, former superintendent of the Senate press gallery, acted as technical adviser.

Capra also used theatrical devices which keep the audience involved for more than two hours. Capra had a talent for humor which he developed while working as a gag writer for Mack Sennett and Harry Langdon. Jokes, however, are not funny unless they move, so Capra skillfully utilized montage and juxtaposition, while verbally augmenting the effect by forcing his actors to speak their lines twenty percent faster than was their natural inclination.

All these effects, however, add up to more than simply an enjoyable two hours. Capra is, perhaps above all, a social critic and a utopian idealist. As Mr. Smith's first name, Jefferson, indicates, Capra is in a long line of Jeffersonian idealists. He believes in an agrarian society of self-sufficient individuals who discover the principles of democracy in the simple freedoms of rural life. Thus, in all Capra's films it is the country "rube" who eventually embarrasses the forces of the Hamiltonian centralization of power such as Senator Paine and Boss Taylor.

Because *Mr. Smith Goes to Washington* was released just after the Nazi invasion of Poland, many powerful individuals in the industry and in politics felt the film's images of social corruption might be misused by the Axis. The other Hollywood studios were so alarmed that they offered Columbia $2,000,000 to "can" the film. Senior Ambassador Joseph P. Kennedy urged that the film not be released in Europe because it would "destroy . . . morale." Luckily, at Capra's insistence, the film was distributed and became, for the Allies, an image of the success of freedom over oppression. Thus, in occupied France one theater chose to show *Mr. Smith Goes to Washington* for thirty days straight before the film was barred by Nazi control.

STATE OF THE UNION

Released: 1948
Production: Frank Capra for Metro-Goldwyn-Mayer
Direction: Frank Capra
Screenplay: Anthony Veiller and Myles Connolly; based on the play of the
   same name by Howard Lindsay and Russell Crouse
Cinematography: George J. Fosley
Editing: William Hornbeck
Running time: 124 minutes

> *Principal characters:*
> Grant Matthews .... Spencer Tracy
> Mary Matthews .... Katharine Hepburn
> Spike McManus .... Van Johnson
> Kay Thorndyke .... Angela Lansbury
> Jim Conover .... Adolphe Menjou
> Sam Thorndyke .... Lewis Stone

The body of film work by Italian immigrant Frank Capra centers on the belief in "Life, Liberty and the Pursuit of Happiness" as set forth in the American Declaration of Independence. Often described as the principal Hollywood exponent of populism, Capra's ideologies support the individuality of the common man against the cynical world of political corruption and materialism. His films always show the triumphs of the honest man. While they have been criticized for the simplicity and naïveté of their politics and their inevitable happy endings, Capra at his best presents a heartwarming idealism which made him one of the most popular directors of the 1930's and early 1940's, with such films as *It Happened One Night* (1934), *Mr. Deeds Goes to Town* (1937), *You Can't Take It With You* (1939), *Mr. Smith Goes to Washington* (1939), *Meet John Doe* (1941), *Arsenic and Old Lace* (1944), and *It's A Wonderful Life* (1946).

It's a Wonderful Life was the first production of Capra's own company, Liberty Films, which he had formed with Samuel Briskin and directors George Stevens and William Wyler following World War II. The trademark for the company was appropriately the cracked Liberty Bell, and the first film was released through RKO/Radio, with whom Capra had arranged a deal to present nine films under the Liberty banner at a total cost of $15,000,000. However, when *It's a Wonderful Life* failed to return the profit RKO/Radio had expected, they refused to finance Liberty's next project, Capra's production of the popular Howard Lindsay and Russell Crouse play, *State of the Union*, which was budgeted at $2,800,000 and for which Gary Cooper had been discussed for the starring role.

When RKO/Radio vetoed the project, Capra became aware that M-G-M's

Spencer Tracy was interested in the role of Grant Matthews, and Capra took the project to Louis B. Mayer. He struck up a deal not unlike the one he entered into with David O. Selznick for *Gone with the Wind* in 1939. M-G-M would finance and release the production, Tracy would be the star, and M-G-M contractees Van Johnson and Angela Lansbury would join the cast. The part of the candidate's wife was to be played by Claudette Colbert.

Just three days before shooting was to begin, Colbert walked into Capra's office and informed him that a very important clause had been left out of her contract. In his autobiography, *The Name Above the Title*, Capra goes into great detail describing the scene. It seems that Colbert inserted into each of her contracts that she was not to work past 5 P.M. According to Capra, she told him her agent, who was her brother, always included this item in all her contracts because her doctor, who was her husband, said she got too tired if she worked any longer. Capra refused to acquiesce and Colbert walked out, an unwise career move for her as this film could have bolstered her greatly diminishing box-office appeal.

Capra first called Mayer, who told him to call Tracy before he heard the news from someone else. Tracy, who had been rehearsing his role with his friend Katharine Hepburn, suggested her for the part. Capra responded by asking, "You think she'd do it?" Tracy replied, "I dunno. But the bag of bones has been helping me rehearse. Kinda stops you, Frank, the way she reads the woman's part. She's a real theater nut, you know. She might do it for the hell of it." Hepburn agreed and the picture was on.

The Tracy-Hepburn relationship goes back to 1942 when they made *Woman of the Year*, the first of their nine films together. Hepburn had sold the idea for that film to M-G-M and felt that Tracy would be perfect as her costar in the picture which cast them as sparring newspaper columnists who marry. It was the beginning of one of the longest and most popular screen teams in motion picture history as they went on to make *Keeper of the Flame* (1942), *Without Love* (1945), *The Sea of Grass* (1947), *State of the Union*, *Adam's Rib* (1949), *Pat and Mike* (1952), *Desk Set* (1957), and *Guess Who's Coming to Dinner* (1967).

Lindsay and Crouse had written *State of the Union* as a vehicle for Helen Hayes. When Hayes turned down the role it was offered to both Margaret Sullavan and Katharine Hepburn, who both refused the role. When the play opened at the Hudson Theatre in New York City on November 14, 1945, its star was Ruth Hussey. The play ran for 765 performances. Sullavan later did the television version with Joseph Cotten on November 16, 1954.

Anthony Veiller and Myles Connolly fashioned the screenplay of the film. Wealthy aircraft manufacturer Grant Matthews (Spencer Tracy), an honest, liberal American hero-tycoon, is proposed as the dark horse Republican candidate for President of the United States. He and his wife Mary (Katharine Hepburn) are estranged, but she is talked into pretending that theirs is a solid marriage in order to help his campaign. She joins him in a cross-country campaign tour to alleviate any rumors of his romantic relationship with the seductive Kay Thorndyke (Angela Lansbury). Thorndyke is Matthews' most powerful supporter. She has inherited a chain of newspapers from her father who had once lost a presidential bid. She has her sights set on backing a candidate for president and being a powerful Washington influence, hostess, and, if she can pull it off, First Lady. Matthews' campaign manager is Jim Conover (Adolphe Menjou), an astute manipulator. Another strong supporter is Spike McManus (Van Johnson), a Drew Pearson-style newspaper columnist.

As his campaign progresses, Matthews gets caught up in the corruption of the political machinery and the variety of vested interests which must be pleased; he begins to sacrifice his ideals in order to win. The title of the play and film refers to not only the country, but also to the Matthews marriage. The Tracy-Hepburn chemistry works wonders with this aspect of the plot. On the cross-country tour they have a wonderful bedroom scene together. Mary has agreed to keep up the pretense of their marriage for his career but she is very much aware of his adulterous relationship with Kay Thorndyke, an element very much played down in the film. In their hotel room she takes over the bed and fixes a pallet for him on the floor. He presumes that the bed is to be his and in a typical Tracy-Hepburn battle of the sexes, he tries to convince her that they should share a bed. But she remains adamant.

Finally, Mary can no longer overlook the corruption of the campaign, and at an important dinner party she speaks out against the deceit and corruption. This spurs Matthews on to make a radio appeal in which he admits his dishonesty with the American people, withdraws from the race, and saves his marriage.

The play had relied upon sparkling Lindsay-Crouse topical political satire and jokes. Capra used the best of the play, adding and updating the political jibes to include many against Harry S Truman (the cross-country trip was not unlike the one Truman made) and Communism. The plot, in typical Capra style, takes on many facets of American political life—big business, agriculture, labor, the judiciary—all shown to wield considerable power over political aspirants. Some critics felt Capra's updating of the political satire weakened the script. For the most part it is a criticism which does not hold up when the film is viewed today with the retrospective knowledge of political corruption of the 1970's. While the politics may be oversimplified, as is the happy ending, the film packs a solid satirical punch at the business of politics, which is as valid today as ever.

The acting throughout is excellent. Tracy and Hepburn are ideal in their parts and a perfect screen team. Adolphe Menjou is properly cynical and unctuous as the unscrupulous campaign manager, and even Van Johnson gives an acceptable performance as the newspaper columnist. But the acting honors go to Angela Lansbury, whose icy bitchiness as Kay Thorndyke is a joy to watch. It is even more impressive when one realizes that at the time Lansbury was only twenty-two years old, depicting a woman in her mid-forties.

While the script makes numerous digs at Harry S Truman, he happily attended the Washington premiere of the film and found it so much to his liking that he ordered a print for the presidential yacht and showed the film repeatedly.

One additional note regarding *State of the Union* is the volatile political mood in Hollywood at the time the film was made, at the height of the House UnAmerican Activities Committee's investigation which led to hundreds being blacklisted and thus prevented from working in Hollywood. Adolphe Menjou was a rabid Communist hater and Hepburn was a known liberal. Capra says in his autobiography, however, that, while the two hated each other, there was never any hint of that animosity during the making of the picture.

GEORGE CUKOR

ADAM'S RIB

Released: 1949
Production: Lawrence Weingarten for Metro-Goldwyn-Mayer
Direction: George Cukor
Screenplay: Ruth Gordon and Garson Kanin
Cinematography: George J. Folsey
Editing: George Boemler
Running time: 101 minutes

Principal characters:
Adam Bonner .... Spencer Tracy
Amanda Bonner .... Katharine Hepburn
Doris Attinger .... Judy Holliday
Warren Attinger .... Tom Ewell
Kip Lurie .... David Wayne
Beryl Caighn .... Jean Hagen

Billed as the hilarious answer to the age-old question "Who wears the pants?," *Adam's Rib* was years ahead of its time in its portrayal of a marriage of equals. The battle between the sexes theme which dominates the film gives director George Cukor the opportunity to explore the potential conflicts and possibilities for growth in a relationship in which the husband and wife are intellectual equals. *Adam's Rib* is also notable for being the sixth in the series of nine motion pictures made by Spencer Tracy and Katharine Hepburn, considered to be one of the screen's great couples, and it is one of their best.

The story contrasts the views of attorneys Adam and Amanda Bonner and compares their relationship with that of philandering Warren Attinger (Tom Ewell) and his scatterbrained wife, Doris (Judy Holliday). Adam and Amanda Bonner move from mutually supportive husband and wife to competitors when district attorney Adam confronts defense attorney Amanda, who seeks to defend the woman (Doris Attinger) whom Adam has been drafted to prosecute for the attempted murder of her husband. Their battle soon moves out of the courtroom and into their home as each staunchly defends his or her contrasting point of view. As the trial progresses, their marriage is shaken, but eventually each learns from the experience, and the two reach a mutual understanding.

As the story opens, the audience sees Doris Attinger follow her husband Warren from his office to the apartment of his mistress, Beryl Caighn (Jean Hagen). In one of the movie's funniest scenes, Doris stands outside in the hallway holding a revolver which she has purchased that afternoon. She is so inept that she is unable to release the safety catch without consulting the instruction manual, and she seems more likely to shoot herself than anyone else. She finally shoots the lock and bursts into the apartment to find a surprised Beryl and Warren nestled together on the couch. She fires several rounds, finally wounding her husband in the shoulder. When she runs out of bullets, Beryl runs for help, while Doris looks down at Warren tenderly.

The main theme of the film, the double standard of conduct for men and women, is established when Adam and Amanda read about the incident the next morning. Amanda takes the strongly feminist stand that Doris has done exactly as any man might have done in that situation, but that social conditioning will cause her to be convicted of a crime for which a man would go free. Adam, a strict believer in law and order, believes that crime must be punished, not condoned. Complications arise later when Adam, much to his chagrin, is assigned Doris' prosecution in what seems to be an open and shut case. When Amanda hears this, she rushes to offer her services to Doris. That night, when Amanda tells Adam she has taken the case, he tries to dissuade her and they begin to bicker. Each day their feud intensifies, until it becomes all-out war. In court, they progress from friendly competitors who drop pens in order to blow kisses to each other under the table, to arch enemies, when Amanda humiliates her husband in public.

Adam and Amanda both fight the case on the basis of principle, he believing in the sanctity of the law, she defending the idea of equal justice. Adam has little sympathy for philandering Warren while Amanda has great sympathy and understanding for simpleminded Doris. We see their overreaction to this case during Amanda's initial interview with Doris. Amanda, prepared to defend equal rights, is aghast at Doris' willingness to plead guilty, and refuses to let her do so. The actual details of the trial become less and less important to the attorneys, while the principals of the case, Doris and Warren, become mere rallying points in the battle of the sexes between Adam and Amanda.

As part of her defense, Amanda calls a succession of successful women whose professions prove that they are intellectually and physically equal to men. In the movie's most farcical scene, Amanda turns the courtroom into a circus by having a female weightlifter lift a protesting Adam up over her head to demonstrate a woman's potential strength. Adam, although shaken, remains professional in the midst of this debasing treatment. It is clear that Amanda's passionate desire to win has both clouded her judgment and seriously damaged her marriage. That night, Adam moves out.

During her summation the next day, Amanda illustrates for the jury how different their reactions would be if Doris' and Warren's positions were reversed. At this point the camera shows the action through the jurors' eyes, as Amanda urges them to picture Doris, dressed as a faithful husband seeking to protect his home, and Warren, pictured as a blond woman, lured away by Beryl, the predatory male wolf. Adam's stance that every crime should be punished stands no chance against Amanda's theatrics. Doris is acquitted.

That night an ambivalent Amanda seeks companionship next door with her neighbor Kip Lurie (David Wayne). While he tries to seduce her, Amanda can think only of Adam. Just as Kip is about to kiss her, Adam bursts into the room, pointing a gun at them and declaring he has the right to defend his marriage. Panic-stricken, Amanda blurts out that no one has the right. Adam, with a triumphant smile, agrees and then places the gun to his mouth. Kip and Amanda are horrified until Adam bites off the barrel of the licorice pistol.

When Adam and Amanda meet in their law office the next day, they begin recalling times spent in their country home. Amanda is greatly touched when tears well up in Adam's eyes; they are reconciled and drive to the country house for the weekend. That night, Adam demonstrates that men can effectively use women's wiles when he shows Amanda how easy it is for him to concoct those tears. She claims that his demonstration proves there is very little difference between men and women, to which Adam replies "Vive la différence!"

Director George Cukor's use of an immobile camera during scenes containing lengthy dialogue gives the audience more of a feeling of watching a stage performance than a film. The screenplay by Ruth Gordon and Garson Kanin is lively and provides some witty dialogue, but the story is a spoof which must take the characters through some improbable antics at the end in order to resolve the plot.

The film works as well as it does primarily because of the excellence of all the performances, which met with universal praise from critics. Tracy and Hepburn have a magnetism between them which makes even the most absurdly contrived plot work. *Adam's Rib* was a box-office success which bolstered Tracy's and Hepburn's popularity and launched the film careers of Judy Holliday, Tom Ewell, and Jean Hagen. As a result of her portrayal of Doris, Judy Holliday landed her Oscar-winning role in *Born Yesterday* (1950).

BORN YESTERDAY

Released: 1950
Production: S. Sylvan Simon for Columbia
Direction: George Cukor
Screenplay: Albert Mannheimer; based on the play of the same name by Garson Kanin
Cinematography: Joseph Walker
Editing: Charles Nelson
Costume design: Jean Louis
Running time: 103 minutes

Principal characters:
Billie Dawn ....Judy Holliday (AA)
Harry Brock ....Broderick Crawford
Paul Verrall ....William Holden
Jim Devery ....Howard St. John
Eddie ....Frank Otto
Norval Hedges ....Larry Oliver
Mrs. Hedges ....Barbara Brown

In the period immediately following World War II, both cinema and the stage in the United States presented stories that treated the problems and the changed conditions of the new postwar era. The film *The Best Years of Our Lives* (1946), for example, dealt realistically with such issues as the new social forces, readjustment to peacetime economic trends, and safeguards for democracy. In the same year, the play *Born Yesterday* opened on Broadway; the underlying concern of its comic, although equally valid, treatment is the issue of adherence to democratic principles and vigilance to see that democracy is not thwarted. After the play enjoyed a successful run of 1,642 performances, the movie version of *Born Yesterday* appeared in 1950, with only minor changes made to accommodate the story for the screen.

The movie opens with junk tycoon Harry Brock (Broderick Crawford) arriving in Washington. Included in his entourage is his blonde companion-mistress Billie Dawn (Judy Holliday). Paul Verrall (William Holden), a Washington journalist, observes their arrival and goes to Harry's hotel suite to get an interview concerning the latter's business interests and political connections in Washington; his initial attempt at uncovering information, however, is unsuccessful. Meanwhile, Harry has been consulting with his Washington lawyer Jim Devery (Howard St. John), who suggests that Billie must acquire some polish and education so that Harry will not be ashamed of her in their contact with important people in Washington. In the course of the story it is revealed that Harry has been using Billie as an unwitting accomplice in his suspect business ventures. Harry has placed his empire of interlocking junkyard businesses in Billie's name so that, even though Harry is actually controlling things, legally he cannot be held responsible for any of the activities of the business.

It transpires that Paul is hired as a tutor to give Billie the polish necessary to meet with congressmen and other influential people as a part of Harry's Washington dealings. Paul has his own reasons for accepting the assignment of educating Billie: he is secretly interested in exposing Harry's nefarious Washington maneuverings, and this position would give him a chance to find out more about the Brock operations. After some persuasion by Paul, Billie embarks on her education; Paul assigns a list of books she is to read and guides her around the monuments and public buildings of the capital. As she begins to acquire some education and social grace, the fundamentally bright Billie becomes imbued with a social consciousness and a respect for democratic views. Along with her enlightenment, Billie rebels against Harry's blatant corruption and arrogance. Harry now represents to her the menace of acquisitive power and greed against which democratic people must be alert. Billie refuses to sign any more of the papers involved in Harry's attempt to form a scrap iron cartel, and she tells Harry that she is leaving him. In order to prevent Harry from continuing to circumvent the democratic process, she will keep the companies in her name and release them back to him at the rate of only one per year; this means that it would take about eighty years for him to regain complete control of his companies. Meanwhile, Paul and Billie have fallen in love, and the story ends with the two married.

The serious moral of *Born Yesterday* is not slighted, but it was the humorous aspects of the film that made it the triumph it was. Much credit must be given to the performance of Judy Holliday as the comically ignorant blonde chorine with the pronounced New York accent, which won for her the Academy Award for Best Actress of 1950 and established her film career. The film gave Holliday the opportunity to demonstrate her great versatility as an actress. Particularly memorable is her voice, which can range from a plaintive squeak to a scream. There are several scenes in the film which have become "classics" because of her genius for comedy. One involves a gin rummy game between Billie and Harry in which Holliday combines quick manipulation of the cards with outrageously loud humming. In another scene, while Harry and Paul are trying to convince her to take lessons in culture, she defines the word peninsula as "the new wonder drug" so defiantly that the audience almost accepts her definition.

Broderick Crawford, who had recently won an Oscar for Best Actor for his performance in *All the King's Men* (1949), seems to parody his previous performance. His scenes with Billie are particularly noteworthy because he changes from a buffoon to a cold, calculating opportunist without detracting from the believability of either aspect of his character. William Holden gives a good performance, but his role does not require anything beyond a standard, journeymanlike job. The other actors in the film also give solid but unspectacular performances. The critical and financial success of the film was due to the marvelous appeal of Judy Holliday, with a large measure of assistance by Broderick Crawford and director George Cukor.

CAMILLE

Released: 1936
Production: David Lewis for Metro-Goldwyn-Mayer
Direction: George Cukor
Screenplay: Zoe Akins, Frances Marion, and James Hilton; based on the novel and play *La Dame aux camélias* by Alexandre Dumas, *fils*
Cinematography: William Daniels
Editing: Margaret Booth
Running time: 115 minutes

Principal characters:

Marguerite Gautier (Camille)	Greta Garbo
Armand Duval	Robert Taylor
Monsieur Duval	Lionel Barrymore
Baron de Varville	Henry Daniell
Olympe	Lenore Ulric
Nanine	Jessie Ralph
Prudence Duvernoy	Laura Hope Crews
Nichette	Elizabeth Allan
Gustave	Russell Hardie

For over a century the romance that Alexandre Dumas, *fils*, wrote as a novel and then as a play, *La Dame aux camélias*, has held its audiences spellbound. Its heroine, Marguerite Gautier, was based upon a real *demi-mondaine*, Marie (*née* Alphonsine) Plessis, whom Dumas knew in Paris, a youthful courtesan who had crowded a lifetime into her brief twenty-three years. Dumas made Marie immortal when he created Marguerite Gautier; and many an actress since has yearned to play her, because the role is such a challenge. In the theater, great dramatic stars such as Sarah Bernhardt and Eleanora Duse triumphed in the role. From 1915 to 1927 there were at least four well-remembered silent film productions of *Camille*, as the story was known in the English-speaking world, starring such actresses as Clara Kimball Young, Theda Bara, Nazimova, and Norma Talmadge.

In 1936, the first talking film production of *Camille* was released, starring Greta Garbo. It remains the definitive version, for it represents a perfect melding of all the talents concerned in its making. Garbo was never more moving, never so much the mistress of the camera. "She's never been so unguarded," noted Irving Thalberg, head of production at M-G-M. An actress playing the role of Camille must appear to be unguarded, for Camille slips moodily from one emotion to another, revealing every extreme, relishing every delight, tasting every sorrow. She was guided by her director, George Cukor, into sheer perfection, the realization of every nuance of her character, looking and moving always as if she had stepped directly from the mid-nineteenth century.

Paris was never so light-hearted as it was in 1847, when its citizens dictated the taste of the European world. Every night theaters were crowded with women in silks and diamonds attracting new lovers, for Paris was the city of love, and every Parisian lived for love, even though it lasted but a single night. It is in the early hours of such a night that the film's story begins. A carriage pauses at a florist's shop run by Madame Buyon, who hurries out with a handsome nosegay of camellias. A gloved hand emerges from the open window of the carriage. The old florist smiles happily and with a proud little bow presents the flowers. "For the lady of the camellias," she says—and as the carriage starts up again, the camera moves inside for a first view of the lady, beautifully gowned in fine velvets and silks, with jewels reflecting the radiance of her exquisite face. This is Marguerite Gautier (Greta Garbo), known familiarly to all in her world as "Camille," because she always wears camellias. She is with her elderly companion, Prudence Duvernoy (Laura Hope Crews), a greedy, well-dressed bawd who knows her way around. She scolds Camille for her extravagances; she should make better use of her extraordinary charms and conserve her delicate health only for those lovers who will shower her with gifts that count—a lover such as the Baron de Varville (Henry Daniell), for example, to whom Prudence intends to introduce her that night.

At the theater, Camille lingers at the head of the double staircase, looking down upon the well-dressed crowds thronging the main lobby. At the foot of the stairs a young man looks up at her with frank adoration. She is pleased and amused by his youth and sincerity, and flirts with him audaciously. She takes her place beside Prudence in the box as the entertainment begins. Prudence, directing her opera glasses over the house, is excited when she spies the Baron de Varville, middle-aged, cynical, and one of the richest and most desirable men in Paris. She gives the glasses to Camille, pointing out the Baron, but by mistake Camille focuses upon the young man she had seen in the foyer, and is both delighted and surprised that a real baron can be so young, handsome, and available. She agrees to be introduced to him, and it is only during the meeting that she realizes, with some embarrassment, that he is not de Varville but a young man recently come to Paris named Armand Duval (Robert Taylor). He is disappointed, thinking that she was interested in him only for a wealth he does not possess, but she puts him at ease and sends him to the confectioner's for some bonbons. In the meantime, Olympe (Lenore Ulric), a jealous rival of Camille, has snagged the Baron de Varville into her box; but Camille smiles enticingly at him, and by the time Armand returns breathlessly with the sweets, Camille has departed with the Baron. Armand finds a glove she has carelessly left behind and clutches it longingly as the scene fades out.

And so the stage is set, with all but one of the principal characters introduced in a single superbly written sequence. The one remaining character is Monsieur Duval (Lionel Barrymore), Armand's father, and he does not come into the action until later when his character becomes pivotal. This introductory scene is completely original, the creative device of the three screenwriters, used to establish the colorful Parisian *demi-monde* of the period. All other versions of the movie were modeled after the novel or directly upon the play. The novel begins with Marguerite Gautier already deceased and a sale of her private effects in progress to satisfy her creditors; this provides a frame for the romance itself, which is told in flashback. Some theater productions used this device in introducing Armand, who reads Camille's diary under a full-length portrait of her, as the lights dim and the first act begins. The Norma Talmadge silent screen version, modern but not stylized, used this prologue frame, dissolving into an introductory sequence wherein Camille is washing windows in the shop where she works, and as she clears a clean circle of glass, she looks out to see the Baron de Varville "discovering" her.

But in this M-G-M talking version, the entire scene is boldly played as straight narrative, with a haunting musical background, and all the characters coming into the picture as flesh-and-blood people with humors and passions of their own. They may owe their being to Dumas, *fils*, but their separate lives, personalities, and dialogue are the creation of Zoe Akins, Frances Marion, and James Hilton, who dramatized the old story with a new verve and true professional skill.

The pattern of the screen story thereafter more closely follows that of the novel and play, but even so, the approach is fresh and, above all, the romance of Camille and Armand is both accurate and believable. The story of a courtesan and the youth she loves outside the bonds of matrimony was scarcely proper film fare for the mid-1930's, when censorship ruled the screen mercilessly; but a remarkably clever device was manufactured to satisfy the Puritanical whims of those who guard the public morals. Camille and Armand realize their love in the country at her cottage, even though he is supposed to be sleeping in a nearby inn. Camille has an old friend, Nichette (Elizabeth Allan), from the days when she worked as a shopgirl, and Nichette is to be married to a respectable young man, Gustave (Russell Hardie). Camille begs to be allowed to give the wedding party in her garden. The marriage ceremony has a special significance for Camille and Armand. Later he tells her that every word the priest spoke was meant for them and that in his heart he made all the vows—to her; she responds glowingly, "And I to you." The censors chose to look the other way.

In a crucial scene that shortly follows, Armand has gone to Paris for business reasons, and in his absence, Monsieur Duval, his father, comes to the cottage to plead with Camille to give up the love she and Armand share, for that love is ruining Armand's chances for success in a diplomatic career. This has always been a crucial scene in any dramatization of *Camille*, for it allows the actress to run the full gamut of emotion, promising finally to send Armand back to his father, and then pretending convincingly to renounce her love, making Armand believe that she has wearied of him and is returning to de Varville. Garbo plays this scene with heartbreaking sincerity made all the more dramatic because the Armand of Robert Taylor is so innocently confused, so desperate with youthful unhappiness.

The story line continues after the established pattern, with the famous gambling scene wherein Armand wins a fortune from de Varville, only to throw it at Camille's feet, denouncing her as a woman who can be bought, who has a price for everything. De Varville challenges him to a duel, which Camille cannot prevent. Armand wounds de Varville, and has to leave Paris for a few months until the scandal of the affair dies.

The last reel of the Garbo picture is superb. Armand returns to Paris to find that Camille is dying. He takes her in his arms, but even as they plan a happy future together, she grows limp, saying that she has lived for love, and now she is dying for it. He puts her on a chaise longue and kneels at her side. She looks at him with ecstatic happiness, and her eyes close in death, while he buries his face on her breast, weeping.

As a film, the Cukor-Garbo version was not only an enormous success critically, but it was also well received by international audiences. The picture is constantly being revived, both as a theatrical release and as a television classic. Garbo's performance gained her a nomination by the Motion Picture Academy as Best Actress of the Year, but she lost to Luise Rainer in *The Good Earth*. Today, the name of Luise Rainer is scarcely remembered, while *The Good Earth* is a film more often read about than seen. In 1955, the Academy awarded Garbo an overdue honorary Oscar for her many unforgettable screen performances. And the one that is the most unforgettable is the one she gave in *Camille*.

DINNER AT EIGHT

Released: 1933
Production: David O. Selznick for Metro-Goldwyn-Mayer
Direction: George Cukor
Screenplay: Frances Marion and Herman J. Mankiewicz, with additional dialogue by Donald Ogden Stewart; based on the play of the same name by George S. Kaufman and Edna Ferber
Cinematography: William Daniels
Editing: Ben Lewis
Running time: 110 minutes

Principal characters:

Carlotta Vance	Marie Dressler
Larry Renault	John Barrymore
Dan Packard	Wallace Beery
Kitty Packard	Jean Harlow
Oliver Jordan	Lionel Barrymore
Max Kane	Lee Tracy
Dr. Wayne Talbot	Edmund Lowe
Mrs. Talbot	Karen Morley
Mrs. Oliver Jordan	Billie Burke
Paula Jordan	Madge Evans
Jo Stengel	Jean Hersholt

When *Dinner at Eight* opened on Broadway in October of 1932, it was an instant success. It ran for 232 performances at the Music Box Theatre, and the rights to film it were acquired by M-G-M, where Irving Thalberg, who never received screen credit on any picture he personally supervised, planned it as one of his own productions for 1933. Thalberg, however, fell seriously ill and was forced to take a vacation from filmmaking. Louis B. Mayer turned over production to his son-in-law, David O. Selznick, who gave *Dinner at Eight* preferential treatment, bringing over his friend, George Cukor, from RKO.

The two men established the film as an all-star feature presenting ten stars in the leading roles. M-G-M had done very well during the 1930's with a series of productions that were truly all-star, starting in 1932 with *Grand Hotel*. Now, with ten players featured in *Dinner at Eight*, all of whom rated top billing, even the subsidiary roles were filled by performers who were known at the box office, such as Karen Morley, Louise Closser Hale, Phillips Holmes, and May Robson. The film proved to be one of M-G-M's biggest moneymakers, although it did not earn a single Academy Award nomination, perhaps because it was slick, glamorous, sophisticated, and had almost no real heart. Selznick gave the production his own touch of glitter, and Cukor, with the help of a very smartly written screenplay, made the story move smoothly, with all episodes leading up to the final scene in the Jordan drawing-room.

Dinner at Eight is basically the story of a fashionable dinner party given by a socialite wife, Mrs. Oliver Jordan (Billie Burke). Unknown to her, not only is the Jordan Steamship Line on the verge of financial disaster, but her husband (Lionel Barrymore) is on the brink of a physical breakdown. A week before the dinner party, Mrs. Jordan has acquired Lord and Lady Ferncliffe as honored guests, and she is building her guest list around them. She is having Dr. Wayne Talbot (Edmund Lowe) and his wife (Karen Morley), and Carlotta Vance (Marie Dressler), who had once been a great star in the theater. Oliver asks her also to invite Dan Packard (Wallace Beery) and his wife Kitty (Jean Harlow). Packard, who lives somewhere out West and owns freight lines, might be able to do Jordan some good. What Jordan does not know is that Packard plans to acquire the ailing Jordan line for as small a sum as possible.

When Kitty tells her husband that they have been invited to dinner at the Jordans on the coming Friday, he says they are not going. When he learns that Lord and Lady Ferncliffe will be there, however, he admits that he has been trying for years to meet the Ferncliffes and changes his mind. He leaves his wife's boudoir before Dr. Talbot arrives. Almost at once the relationship between Kitty and Dr. Talbot is established. He is a Park Avenue doctor with a "bedside manner," and already Kitty is becoming one of his most demanding patients.

Millicent Jordan has all her guests' acceptances, but she needs an extra man because Carlotta Vance is coming by herself. She decides to invite Larry Renault (John Barrymore), a stage star who had gone into the movies and made a big hit, until he began drinking. As a result of liquor and his advancing years, he can no longer get film roles. Now he is in New York seeking a play that will put him back in circulation. What Millicent does not know is that her daughter Paula (Madge Evans), engaged to marry the socially prominent Ernest DeGraff within a month, has caught the fancy of Renault, and Paula and Renault are enjoying a secret, if somewhat indiscreet, love affair. Larry tries to talk Paula out of the crush she has developed on him, pointing out that she is nineteen, while he is in his forties and burned out; but Paula is determined that nothing shall hurt their lovely affair.

On the day of his wife's dinner party, Oliver Jordan suffers an acute heart attack and is taken to Dr. Talbot's office. The doctor recognizes that Jordan will not live more than a few months, and mildly suggests that he skip his wife's dinner party that night and get a little rest. Jordan is not fooled by the doctor's demeanor, but he also will not disappoint Millicent; he will be the host as usual.

It does not take long for Jordan to learn the worst about his failing steamship line. Although he has asked Carlotta to hold onto her stock, she has sold it that afternoon, because of her own financial problems, to a man named James K. Baldridge. Jordan learns that another block of stock has been sold by other friends to the same man. He knows that Baldridge is a front name to cover the identity of the real buyer, who is Dan Packard.

The Packards have an argument as they are dressing for the Jordans' dinner, and Dan accuses Kitty of cheating on him. Kitty denies it; she has seen no other man except the doctor, and her maid verifies that. When she threatens him with her knowledge of his crooked deals, the argument is stalemated, with Kitty forcing Dan to make good on the Jordan stock in exchange for her silence.

Larry Renault's fate is more tragic. He has insulted the one Broadway producer who might have given him a choice supporting role, insisting that he will accept nothing but the lead; this causes his hitherto faithful agent to turn on him. Alone and half-drunk, Larry realizes that he is going nowhere; he is financially broke and virtually friendless. He locks the door, stuffs pillows and clothing at the door and window cracks, turns on the gas, and sits in front of the heater in his dinner clothes, waiting.

The guests begin to arrive at the Jordans' home for dinner. At the last minute, the secretary to Lord and Lady Ferncliffe, who were the *raison d'être* for the dinner, has called to say that they are sorry, but they are in Florida and unable to attend the party. Millicent, who is distraught over the preparations for the party, has gotten her cousins to substitute at the last moment. Because Millicent is so caught up in her own petty little world, she fails to realize how ill her husband is and chastizes him for wishing to go to bed early. She also refuses to listen to her daughter as Paula tries to tell her mother of her love for Renault.

The stories are neatly wrapped up before the guests sit down to dinner. Oliver is told by Packard that his company has been saved, shortly after Millicent tearfully tells her husband that their life will be "happier than ever" when she learns of his financial and physical worries. She admits to her frivolousness and promises to change. The Jordans' daughter decides to marry her fiancé after all when Carlotta informs her that Renault has killed himself; Paula realizes the hopelessness of that love and she walks into dinner on Ernest DeGraff's arm.

Thus, all the plots and subplots of the story are resolved just before the guests sit down to their dinner. The final lines of the film are a classically funny interchange between Carlotta and Kitty. Kitty observes brightly, "I was reading a book the other day," an admission that brings an incredulous look to Carlotta's face, but Kitty goes on blithely: "It's about civilization or something. Do you know, the guy said machinery is going to take the place of every profession." Carlotta grunts to herself with a meaningful look at the sensuous Kitty, "Oh, my dear. That's something you'll never have to worry about."

Top billing went to Marie Dressler, who played her part as legitimately as she could; Cukor somehow managed to get her to soft pedal her usual mugging. Carlotta Vance, the actress played by Dressler, was supposed to have been an intimate of Somerset Maugham, Michael Arlen, and Charlie Chaplin. There are elements of famous socialite and actress Maxine Elliott in the background of Carlotta as written by Kaufman and Ferber, but there is never anything of the upper crust society woman in Dressler's characterization.

John Barrymore and Wallace Beery got second and third billing. Barrymore brings elegance to his role of Larry Renault, and Beery, who had been co-starring in several films with Dressler, manages some mugging of his own as the uncouth Westerner, Dan Packard. Fourth billing went to Jean Harlow, who positively blooms under Cukor's experienced direction. The role of Kitty Packard is so well-written as to be almost actress-proof, and Harlow plays it with the innocent but nonetheless malevolent joyousness that she first displayed in *Red-Headed Woman* (1932).

Lionel Barrymore is sympathetic as the dying Oliver, underplaying the part effectively; Lee Tracy gives one of his best performances as the faithful actor's agent, Max Kane. Edmund Lowe has just the right virility and polish for the society doctor, Wayne Talbot; and Billie Burke, who had been annoyingly saccharine in her first talking roles, is perfect as a fluttering matron unaware that her fine house is tumbling down. Madge Evans brings youthful beauty and sincerity to her role as the daughter, Paula Jordan, and Jean Hersholt is perfect as Jo Stengel, the producer willing to give the fading Larry Renault a second chance.

The play had boasted a series of subplots devoted to the servants who prepared and served the dinner, but the downstairs part of the play was cut and the upstairs emphasized in the movie version. *Dinner at Eight* marked David O. Selznick's debut as a producer at M-G-M (he followed it with another 1933 all-star production that is forgotten today: *Night Flight*, with both John and Lionel Barrymore, Helen Hayes, Clark Gable, Robert Montgomery, Myrna Loy, and William Gargan). *Dinner at Eight* remains a top favorite and is certain to be included in every retrospective of the best from M-G-M in the 1930's.

GASLIGHT

Released: 1944
Production: Arthur Hornblow, Jr., for Metro-Goldwyn-Mayer
Direction: George Cukor
Screenplay: John Van Druten, Walter Reisch, and John L. Balderston; based on the play of the same name by Patrick Hamilton
Cinematography: Joseph Ruttenberg
Editing: Ralph E. Winters
Art direction: Cedric Gibbons and William Ferrari (AA)
Interior decoration: Edwin B. Willis and Paul Huldschinsky (AA)
Running time: 114 minutes

Principal characters:
Paula Alquist	Ingrid Bergman (AA)
Gregory Anton	Charles Boyer
Brian Cameron	Joseph Cotten
Nancy Oliver	Angela Lansbury
Miss Thwaites	Dame May Whitty
Elizabeth Tompkins	Barbara Everest

Gaslight is George Cukor's classic Victorian melodrama. Nominally a murder mystery, the plot is on the skimpy side, and the murder which opens the film is solved at the end, but the "whodunit" aspects of the plot are peripheral to Cukor's real concerns. *Gaslight* is a study in induced madness, and, paradoxically, the film sustains our interest because Cukor's direction intentionally subverts the traditional elements of mystery in the plot. Cukor unmasks the villain early on; and the tension in the film comes as a result of the audience watching helplessly as the villain very methodically sets about driving the heroine insane. *Gaslight* opens with a murder on a foggy night (in contrast to his interior shots, Cukor's exteriors are rather unimaginative, consisting primarily of swirling fog). The headline on a newspaper unfolds the story: "Thornton Square Strangler on Loose." The entire sequence spans less than two minutes, and provides the backdrop for the remainder of the film.

Cukor next shifts the scene to Italy. It is a decade after the murder, and a young English voice student, Paula Alquist (Ingrid Bergman), is being courted by Gregory Anton (Charles Boyer), a French pianist. Although she is obviously in love with the man, she protests that she hardly knows him, and resolves to spend a week at Lake Como to think things over. On the train to Lake Como, Paula finds herself seated next to Miss Thwaites (Dame May Whitty), a garrulous Englishwoman addicted to murder mysteries. Elsewhere in the film, Cukor uses Miss Thwaites primarily for comic relief but here she serves as the link between the heretofore unexplained opening murder scene and the happy, if confused, Paula Alquist. The book Miss Thwaites is reading

on the train reminds her of a genuine murder that occurred in her neighborhood in London ten years earlier—the Thornton Square strangling. As
the old woman prattles on about the murder, Paula grows increasingly agi-
tated. Thus Cukor reveals that there is some sort of connection between
Paula and Thornton Square, although the precise nature of this connection
will not be clarified until later in the film.

As the train pulls to a stop at the lake, an arm is suddenly thrust through
the open window of Paula's berth. Cukor quickly defuses the sinister implications of the incident; the arm belongs to Gregory Anton, who, unable to
bear the idea of being separated from his beloved, has preceded Paula to her
destination. She is happy enough to see him, and the jarring note is temporarily forgotten. It represents, however, Cukor's first hint that Gregory is
not the perfect lover that Paula takes him to be. *Gaslight*'s story is written
largely from Paula's point of view, which will grow increasingly distorted as
Gregory's machinations progress. Cukor reveals this distortion to the audience by his choice of camera angles, lighting, and pacing, all of which will
serve notice that, whatever Paula may believe, Gregory Anton is not be be
trusted.

At Lake Como, Paula agrees to marry Gregory, who reveals to her that
he has always wanted to live in London. By a curious coincidence, the dream
house that he describes to Paula bears an uncanny resemblance to the one
that Paula herself already owns, the house at 9 Thornton Square, which she
inherited from her murdered aunt, the victim in the film's opening scene.
Although she dreads living in this, of all houses, she accedes to Gregory's
pleas: "I've found peace in loving you. You shall have your house in Thornton
Square." With his two principals safely ensconced in their new surroundings,
Cukor devotes himself to the crux of his story—the persecution and near
destruction of Paula Anton by her husband. Shortly after they set up residence, Gregory, pretending to be solicitous of Paula's health, gradually closes
her off from the outside world. He is forever nagging her about her supposed
memory lapses. One key sequence in the film illustrates both Gregory's technique and that of George Cukor in explicating it.

Immediately prior to one of their rare excursions outside their house—a
trip to the Tower of London to see the Crown Jewels—Gregory gives Paula
a brooch. With a condescending smile, he chides her for losing things, and
makes a great show of putting it in her handbag. They visit the Tower, and
upon returning home, Gregory asks to see the brooch. An incredulous and
panicky Paula empties her bag, but to no avail. To her dismay, the brooch
is nowhere to be found, and Gregory, having made his point, contents himself
with only a mild reproof.

From the dialogue in this sequence, there is no evidence to support either
Gregory or his wife on the question of the loss of the brooch. We never see
Paula lose it, but she is off camera part of the time, and could have lost it

then. Nevertheless, by the end of the scene, Cukor has made it clear that it is Gregory, not Paula, who is responsible for the brooch's being missing. He keeps the camera focused on Gregory's face longer than usual, and his lighting emphasizes his eyes, which glint strangely. By tilting the audience's sympathy in this fashion towards Paula, the director undercuts much of the script's suspense, but the removal of any doubt about Gregory's guilt permits Cukor and the audience to concentrate on the melodramatic irony implicit in the situation: whether Paula is losing her mind on her own or being driven insane by her husband becomes secondary to the simple fact that she is, indeed, going mad.

Not the least of Gregory's weapons in his effort to rob his wife of her sanity is the house at Thornton Square itself. More than a mere set, the house becomes, in Cukor's hands, a third character. 9 Thornton Square is a marvelous three-storied building, and Cukor uses each of the stories in his narrative. The first floor of the house belongs to Gregory. It is where he administers most of his admonitions to Paula about her failing mental health, and it is also where Paula is forced to deal with Nancy Oliver (Angela Lansbury), a cheeky young girl whom Gregory has hired as a maid. Nancy clearly has eyes for her employer and makes no effort to disguise her contempt for Paula. Although she is unaware of Gregory's plotting, she serves his purpose well, constantly keeping Paula in a state of agitation.

The bedrooms are on the second floor, but Paula finds no refuge in her room. Left alone every night since Gregory claims to have rented a flat elsewhere, to which he purportedly goes nightly to practice his piano, Paula is beset by flickering lights, the gaslights that give the film its title, and mysterious noises that seem to emanate from the third floor. Indeed, the third floor seems, inexplicably at first, to be the symbol of Paula's horrors because on the third floor, behind locked and boarded doors, are all of her dead aunt's furniture and other possessions, providing a constant reminder of Paula's childhood trauma.

Gregory, meanwhile, steps up his assaults on Paula's sanity. His admonitions are no longer gentle, and he begins to accuse her of theft as well as mere forgetfulness. He browbeats her in front of Nancy and forbids her to see any of her neighbors, including Miss Thwaites, the woman she had met on the train to Lake Como. Indeed, Paula leaves the house at Thornton Square only once after her visit to the Tower of London, and that turns out to be a disaster. When she insists upon attending a party, Gregory reluctantly agrees to let her go, but quickly reduces her to hysteria once they arrive, and the pair returns home immediately, where Gregory threatens to have his wife declared insane and institutionalized.

What remains to be revealed is the motive for Gregory's villainy. The mechanism for this revelation is Brian Cameron (Joseph Cotten) of Scotland Yard. Cameron, as it happens, had been a fan of Paula's aunt, and when he catches sight of Paula at the Tower during the Antons' fateful visit, he is intrigued by the resemblance between aunt and niece. He finds himself drawn to the Thornton Square neighborhood, where Miss Thwaites fills him in as best she can. His interest piqued still further, Cameron reopens the ten-year-old murder case, which occurred, we now learn, during an apparently unsuccessful attempt to steal the victim's jewelry. Cameron puts Gregory under surveillance, and the policeman assigned to the task reports that Gregory leaves home every night, walks around the block, and then climbs onto the roof of his own house, which he thereupon enters through a trapdoor. Cameron, meanwhile, learns that Gregory had also been an admirer of Paula's aunt, and a jewel thief as well.

Piecing the facts together, Cameron rushes to 9 Thornton Square. He arrives as Paula is being tormented by flickering lights and moaning noises; and, winning her confidence with the story of his affection for her aunt, he tells her his theory about all of her problems. Gregory, he says, murdered her aunt, and is currently spending his nights above Paula's bedroom methodically ransacking her aunt's possessions in search of her jewelry, as well as driving Paula mad from fear in the process. Paula hardly knows what to believe, but when Cameron, in searching Gregory's desk, discovers the long-missing brooch, she is convinced. Having revealed the ultimate solution to the mystery, Cukor brings *Gaslight* to a close. Brian Cameron arrests Gregory, ironically, just after he finds the jewels that have led him on his bizarre quest; and, in a deliciously vengeful scene, Paula declines her husband's pleas for help. She is insane, Paula taunts; how could she possibly help anyone? The film ends on a comic note as Miss Thwaites, the neighborhood busybody, walks in just as Cameron and Paula are discussing what promises to be the start of a long relationship.

Gaslight is a claustrophobic film, and Cukor makes this claustrophobia work for him rather than against him. The tension generated by the house at Thornton Square, and the increasingly suffocating relationship between the two principals, more than replace the potential plot tension which Cukor diffuses early by revealing that Gregory Anton is manipulating his wife.

None of this would have worked, however, without top actors in the starring roles. Charles Boyer, an Academy Award nominee, plays Gregory Anton as a suave sadist, nearly always under control and able to turn every situation to his advantage. In turn soothing and bullying, he is able to take the young and naïve Paula to the edge of insanity with consummate ease. Ingrid Bergman, who won an Academy Award for her portrayal of Paula, is outstanding. Her physical beauty makes Paula an attractive character from the outset, and her acting skill insures that none of the impact of her psychic disintegration is lost on the audience. In the film's minor roles, Joseph Cotten has little to do but act stalwart as Brian Cameron of Scotland Yard. More noteworthy is the acting debut of Angela Lansbury; a Cukor discovery, Lansbury plays the tarty young Nancy Oliver with the aplomb of a veteran actor; she earned an Academy Award nomination as Best Supporting Actress for her efforts.

Gaslight owes its success to George Cukor, and to the performances he elicited from his cast, particularly Charles Boyer, Ingrid Bergman, and Angela Lansbury. The film thus stands near the top of its genre, a classic of melodrama.

HOLIDAY

Released: 1938
Production: Everett Riskin for Columbia
Direction: George Cukor
Screenplay: Donald Ogden Stewart and Sidney Buchman; based on the play
   of the same name by Philip Barry
Cinematography: Franz Planer
Editing: Otto Meyer and Al Clark
Running time: 94 minutes

    Principal characters:
       Linda Seton .... Katharine Hepburn
       Johnny Case .... Cary Grant
       Julia Seton .... Doris Nolan
       Ned Seton .... Lew Ayres
       Nick Potter .... Edward Everett Horton
       Susan Potter .... Jean Dixon
       Edward Seton .... Henry Kolker

One of the best comedies of the 1930's, *Holiday* sparkles with undiminished radiance even today. Sophisticated and witty, it is a romantic comedy with serious undertones. Underlying the intelligent, urbane banter and the critical view of the rich is the struggle of two kindred spirits to overcome social and psychological obstacles.

Having met and fallen in love with Julia Seton (Doris Nolan) during a vacation at Lake Placid, Johnny Case (Cary Grant) does not know that she is a member of a socially prominent and wealthy family. A charming, clever, free-spirited soul with no social position, Johnny is attracted to Julia at once because she is sweet and intelligent; he assumes that she wants the same kind of life he does although he knows nothing much about her. When, after the vacation, he first visits the Seton house, he is astonished at all he sees as the butler escorts him through the palatial marble-floored hall with its tapestries, paintings, and statuary. When the butler leaves him gingerly perched on the edge of an antique chair, he performs a flip-flop to keep from being over-awed. Once Julia arrives, he finds that their romance is not going to be as simple as he had expected, and the audience begins to see that he and Julia may not be so well-matched after all. Johnny laughingly chides her for not telling him she is rich. "Aren't you funny to talk about it?" she responds. "Is it so sacred?" he asks, and when she tells him quite seriously that she expects him to make millions himself, he responds equally seriously that he will not be doing that. The basic conflict between them is thus established.

The atmosphere is very different, however, when he is introduced to Linda (Katharine Hepburn), Julia's sister. He and Linda like each other immediately, and beneath their light banter we can see that they are kindred spirits, although it takes them a while to recognize it.

Linda Seton is, in fact, the film's central character. As critical of the society in which she lives as Johnny Case is, she is also a product of that society. To it she owes the poise and elegance that a background of money and secure social position can provide, but her sensitivity and intelligence are always at odds with the constricted and pompous circle of family and acquaintances who surround her. Linda has tried painting, acting, and nursing without success. Her problem, as she confides to Johnny, is deciding whether she wants to be Joan of Arc, Florence Nightingale, or John L. Lewis. There are elements of self-pity and theatricality in Linda's character, but she is basically honest and sincere, although puzzled about how to break out of the life she is living. One reason she is instantly attracted to Johnny is that he is a nonconformist.

Significantly, it is to Linda that Johnny explains his philosophy of life. He wants to take a holiday for a few years to find himself and to find out why he is working—surely it is not just to pay bills and pile up more money. There are new, exciting ideas around, he says, and he wants to discover how he fits into the changing world. The catch, as he explains to Linda, is that he wants to retire young and work when he is older. There is an element of pleading in Johnny's voice as he talks to the sympathetic Linda. He almost seems to be reassuring himself at the same time that he asks for her support and confidence.

Linda is not the only Seton who does not fit into the family's marble-pillared world. Her younger brother Ned (Lew Ayres) is also unhappy; but he is less courageous. Having given in to his father's pressure to work in the family bank, he has taken refuge in alcohol to forget that he is a talented musician and wants to pursue music as a career. Their mother, they tell Johnny, "tried to be a Seton for a while and gave up and died."

Representing this nonconformist side of the Setons is a part of the mansion completely different in spirit from the echoing marble halls—the playroom. It is Linda's refuge—a warm, intimate room filled with dreams, childhood mementos, Ned's musical instruments, and a portrait of their mother over the fireplace. Linda invites Johnny up to the playroom, and she and Ned go through an amusing little charade with Johnny to prepare him for the cross-examination he can expect from their father. Julia, however, is not amused and tries to stop them. When Linda says, "Money is our God," Julia is seriously upset and tells Johnny that it is not true. Amused, Johnny responds, "I ask myself what General Motors would do and do the opposite."

Having found out that Johnny has a promising financial future, Mr. Edward Seton, the father (Henry Kolker), decides to overlook his lack of social standing and give his consent to the marriage of Julia and Johnny; but all the conflicts culminate at their engagement party. Linda is so happy that Julia has found such a good man—"Life walked into this house," she says—that she wants to give a small engagement party for them with "no white ties, no formal invitations." As she speaks these words, however, the scene dissolves to a close-up of an engraved invitation and then to a huge formal party—Edward Seton and Julia have not agreed with her idea. Because giving an intimate party was so important to her, Linda stays in the playroom and refuses to come downstairs.

The only people invited who are not connected with the Setons are Johnny's good friends, Nick and Susan Potter (Edward Everett Horton and Jean Dixon). When they appear, they are self-conscious and obviously out of place. Stared at by the butler, they nervously produce their invitations to prove that they have been invited. Seeking to escape, they accidentally end up in the playroom with Linda. An immediate rapport is established among the three, and when Ned wanders in they all begin playing and singing and laughing together.

Soon Johnny, wearing white tie and tails, appears, sent by Julia to persuade Linda to come downstairs. He joins the group after being properly chastised for allowing the marble pillars to overwhelm him. Linda and Johnny attempt an acrobatic trick and end up falling on the floor just as Mr. Seton and Julia enter. Mr. Seton, losing his temper, tells Linda that she has caused enough trouble and orders her downstairs. Turning to Johnny, he tells him how extremely pleased he is with the success of his stock market manipulations and offers him a desk at the Seton bank. Johnny chooses this moment to try to explain his idea of taking a long holiday and to turn down the offer. Neither Julia nor her father can understand him, and Julia has to persuade her father to leave to prevent an open quarrel. After an inconclusive conversation Julia leaves; but Johnny stays to talk to Linda, and they begin waltzing to a music box. It is a very quiet, tender moment in which they are drawn closer together. Then Johnny goes back to the party for the announcement of his engagement to Julia.

Johnny then spends several days vacillating between compromising his principles and leaving Julia for good. Julia will not bend; she insists that he accept her father's position. Finally Johnny tells her, "I love feeling free inside more than I love you"; and he leaves to join the Potters on a trip to Europe. When Julia admits that she does not love Johnny, Linda sees her opportunity to escape and join the man she loves. She arrives at the ship just in time to see Johnny do a flip-flop, and the film ends with their first real kiss.

Johnny's friends, Nick and Susan Potter, are very important to the development of *Holiday*. They are in the very first scene, in which Johnny comes to tell them that he is going to marry Julia; and they are in the last, when Johnny comes to the ship to tell them that he is going to Europe with them. Although they are older than Johnny and are both intellectuals (Susan is a former teacher and Nick a university professor) the film never makes them seem ridiculous. In fact, they are a human, witty, interesting couple. When they look and feel out of place at the formal engagement party, we know that their values are right and that the others' are wrong. When they meet Linda, they immediately side with her against the stuffy side of the Seton family.

Perhaps the only question we might ask is why Johnny does not realize that Linda rather than Julia is right for him long before he does. Indeed, Linda herself does not realize until near the end that Julia is, as Ned tells her, "a very dull girl." Everyone, he says, is taken in by her looks.

Closely following the play by Philip Barry, the script by Donald Ogden Stewart and Sidney Buchman artfully blends wit, feeling, and romance. Although the dialogue always seems natural, it is carefully constructed to have a certain rhythm and to be very revealing of character. Also skillful is the naturalness of the exposition. Most of the characters are just meeting each other, so we learn about them as they learn about one another. There are no scenes in which a character explains something solely for the benefit of the audience. The chief virtue of the script, however, is the creation of four interesting and believable characters: Linda, Johnny, Nick, and Susan.

Brilliantly bringing the script to life is a cast perfectly directed by George Cukor, who wisely realized that the acting had to be slightly stylized but without affectation. Katharine Hepburn as Linda ranges from playful and witty when she first meets Johnny Case and his friends, the Potters, to intense and serious as she finds Johnny a sympathetic person and unbends to him; it is one of her best performances. As Johnny, Cary Grant is also at his best in portraying the charm and spirit of a young man with his own ideas about what is meaningful in life. Edward Everett Horton and Jean Dixon as the Potters and Lew Ayres as Ned excel in crucial supporting roles; indeed there is not a weak performance in the film.

Holiday set box-office records in 1938 and has been recognized ever since as a great achievement of three artists of the cinema, George Cukor, Katharine Hepburn, and Cary Grant.

LITTLE WOMEN

Released: 1933
Production: Merian C. Cooper for RKO/Radio
Direction: George Cukor
Screenplay: Sarah Y. Mason and Victor Heerman (AA); based on the novel of the same name by Louisa May Alcott
Cinematography: Henry W. Gerrard
Editing: Jack Kitchin
Running time: 115 minutes

Principal characters:
Jo .... Katharine Hepburn
Amy ....Joan Bennett
Professor Fritz Bhaor .... Paul Lukas
Meg .... Frances Dee
Beth .... Jean Parker
Laurie .... Douglass Montgomery
Marmee .... Spring Byington
Aunt March .... Edna May Oliver
Brooke .... John Davis Lodge
Mr. Laurence .... Henry Stephenson

The fifty-year association of Katharine Hepburn and director George Cukor has produced an elegant and impressive body of work. Their ten films together extend from Hepburn's cinematic debut in *A Bill of Divorcement* (1932) to her latest *The Corn Is Green* (1979). Cukor has been able to catch this great star at crucial junctures of her career—her comeback in *The Philadelphia Story* (1940), maturity in *Adam's Rib* (1949), and old age in *Love Among the Ruins* (1975). In the same manner, *Little Women* is for both Hepburn and Cukor a masterpiece of their youth; its high spirits are the projection of filmmakers just reaching the height of their powers.

Little Women fully captures the joy and feeling of the classic 1868 novel by Louisa May Alcott, which parallel's Alcott's own family experiences on the home front during the Civil War. The story's episodic structure follows the development of the March family of Marmee (Spring Byington) and her four daughters, who are always cheerful and quick to help those less fortunate than themselves. The idyllic innocence of youth supplies much of the film's warmth, but sadly, this charm seems to slip away as the girls mature. These idealized glimpses of a cheerful family life surviving amid severe external hardships held a special significance to filmgoers of the Depression, just as they had for post-Civil War readers.

Katharine Hepburn plays Jo March, the imaginative and independent daughter who is the center of the film. In her fourth film role, Hepburn projects a vibrancy that is no doubt derived in part from the closeness of her character's situation to Hepburn's own New England upbringing. Cukor said that she was born to play the role, and in it, Hepburn captures Jo's tomboy qualities and also delicately projects the beauty and intellect of Jo as a woman and budding writer. Following directly upon her Academy Award-Winning performance in *Morning Glory* (1933), *Little Women* won Hepburn the Cannes Film Festival best actress award.

The plot of *Little Women* chronicles the maturation of the four March sisters in Massachusetts during the Civil War. While their father is at war, their mother, Marmee, holds the family together through her inspirational example of doing good deeds. The spirited Jo entertains her sisters with her imagination, helping them to weather the hardships of genteel poverty; but as the girls mature, they go their separate ways to find romance. Bemoaning this loss of innocence, Jo flees to New York, where she meets kindly but provincial Professor Bhaor (Paul Lukas), who tries to settle her down. Sisters Amy (Joan Bennett) and Meg (Frances Dee) find husbands, but Beth (Jean Parker) dies, and Jo, transformed by this event, comes to accept her new life and decides finally to marry the professor.

Little Women presents a gallery of female characters: Jo's boisterousness is complemented by Meg's straight romanticism, Amy's humorous concern with status, and Beth's quiet goodness. Supervising the little women is Marmee, even-tempered through all adversity, and crotchety Aunt March (Edna Mae Oliver), whose complaints conceal an inner strength that makes her a spiritual partner to Jo. Although the March household appears to be a matriarchy, it is the spirit of the absent father that is evoked as the basis for all activity. The men live next door, notably the playful Laurie (Douglass Montgomery), who is a match for Jo in physical exuberance and love of life, and the handsome Brooke (John Davis Lodge). In New York, Professor Bhaor appears sober, shy, and very much a man of the old world and older generation. It is ironic that the energetic Jo should end up with the demure Bhaor, while her pretentious sister Amy marries the boy next door, Laurie.

The performances in *Little Women* are felicitous matches of talent to role. A very young Joan Bennett is superb as Amy, ever scheming for the good life; Douglass Montgomery has the boundless youthful energy necessary for Laurie; and Frances Dee's beauty complements John Lodge's handsomeness. Edna May Oliver, like Hepburn, was born to play the role of the gruff but lovable Aunt March, while Paul Lukas portrays well the difficult role of Professor Bhaor.

Director George Cukor has had a long career in Hollywood. Imported from the Broadway stage by Paramount during the rush to enlist talent to make talking pictures, he began as a dialogue director, quickly advancing to full director status with *Tarnished Lady* (1931), starring Tallulah Bankhead. At RKO, Cukor worked with David O. Selznick on several projects, an association which reached its apogee with *Little Women*, and which later fell apart over the epic problems posed by *Gone with the Wind* (1939). In 1932 and 1933 at RKO, Cukor directed three vehicles for Constance Bennett and Hepburn's first film, *A Bill of Divorcement*, while completing the all-star film version of *Dinner at Eight* at M-G-M. Cukor followed *Little Women* with a series of literary adaptations at M-G-M, beginning with *David Copperfield* (1935).

The struggle of an independent, imaginative woman against the social roles and structures imposed on a female has been a central theme in other Cukor films, such as *Holiday* (1938), *Adam's Rib*, and *Bhowani Junction* (1956). An oft-mentioned Cukorian "touch" is the use of the theater and of theatricality. For example, a climactic moment during the youth of the little women is the performance of Jo's play, "The Witch's Curse," with her in both male roles, hero and villain. This exploration of the male side of the character portrayed by Hepburn prefigures the role of transvestism in *Sylvia Scarlett* (1935), as well as the Hepburn characters who take on male roles in *Adam's Rib* and *Pat and Mike* (1952).

Little Women focuses some attention on the social functions of an earlier age which are depicted in terms of their effects upon the private Jo. Jo's play, with siblings as cast and relatives for audience, places her as the star playing all of the male roles—Roderigo and Black Hugo—as well as both playwright and director. The camera captures it all with a long take of the backstage transformation of Hepburn as Jo, putting on the voice, manner, and goatee of Black Hugo with obvious glee. Later, at a social dance at the Laurence's, we again glimpse Jo in a private moment as she dances by herself in the hall, nervously refusing to mix with ordinary boys. Finally, at the marriage of Meg and Brooke, Jo is isolated from the wedding festivities, poignantly framed by the fence, a nostalgic image of a lost world of innocence frozen for a moment before slipping away.

The adult identity that each girl assumes is distinctly tamer in nature than that which each manifests earlier. Desire has been channeled into romance and legitimized through marriage. The film ends with Jo accepting the marriage proposal of Professor Bhaor; but this is not the unambiguously happy final embrace of many Hollywood romances. The earlier Jo, though headstrong, still had a radiant life force; by comparison, her proposed new life as the wife of this shy older man appears distinctly dull.

Little Women boasts a line-up of creative producers impressive even amid the richness of Hollywood's golden age. The executive producer was Merian C. Cooper, who also in 1933 produced and directed *King Kong*. He later produced a striking series of films with John Ford, including *The Quiet Man* (1952) and *The Searchers* (1956). Although only his associate, Kenneth MacGowan, gets screen credit, the legendary David O. Selznick prepared the film as producer, and his influence is felt throughout, particularly in the film's attention to period atmosphere and detail. Cukor has said that he felt *Little Women* was one of Selznick's forerunners to *Gone with the Wind*, which Cukor himself began as director. The meticulous production accounted in part for the film's great success in 1933, which included Academy Award nominations for Best Picture, Best Direction, and Best Screenplay Adaptation, winning in the latter category.

The award-winning script by the wife and husband team of Sarah Y. Mason and Victor Heerman is an unconventional narrative. Highly episodic, the film focuses on the characters without slavishly following a plot. Dialogue is expressively employed for characterization—from Jo's expletives ("Christopher Columbus!") to Amy's mispronunciations. The maturation of the girls is presented within a seasonal motif that adds richness to every scene. The story of *Little Women* is a classic for young readers, and has provided material for several film versions, including a 1919 silent with Dorothy Bernard and a 1949 M-G-M production, as well as a recent television series.

MY FAIR LADY

Released: 1964
Production: Jack L. Warner for Warner Bros. (AA)
Direction: George Cukor (AA)
Screenplay: Alan Jay Lerner; based on Alan J. Lerner's and Frederick Loewe's musical play of the same name, adapted from the play *Pygmalion* by George Bernard Shaw
Cinematography: Harry Stradling (AA)
Editing: William Ziegler
Art direction: Gene Allen and Cecil Beaton (AA); set decoration, George James Hopkins (AA)
Costume design: Cecil Beaton (AA)
Sound direction: George R. Groves (AA)
Music: Andre Previn (AA)
Running time: 170 minutes

> *Principal characters:*
> Henry Higgins .... Rex Harrison (AA)
> Eliza .... Audrey Hepburn
> Alfred Doolittle .... Stanley Holloway
> Colonel Pickering .... Wilfrid Hyde-White
> Mrs. Higgins .... Gladys Cooper
> Freddie .... Jeremy Brett
> Zoltan Karpathy .... Theodore Bikel
> Mrs. Pearce .... Mona Washbourne

The screen rights to *My Fair Lady*, the Lerner and Loewe musical that had run on Broadway for six years, cost five and a half million dollars, plus a large percentage of the film's gross profits. George Cukor was an obvious choice to direct so popular and expensive a property, whose songs already formed a part of contemporary music. Cukor's career encompassed a variety of projects including two of the strongest Spencer Tracy and Katharine Hepburn outings, *Adam's Rib* (1949) and *Pat and Mike* (1952), as well as some literate, witty adaptations from the stage: *Dinner at Eight* (1933), *Holiday* (1938), *Philadelphia Story* (1940), and *Born Yesterday* (1950). At its best, Cukor's art is the cinema of whimsy and dreams; yet *My Fair Lady* demonstrates Cukor working conservatively and often routinely, his style becoming apparent only with some bravado amidst the sheer bulk of the production values. *My Fair Lady* is foremost a producer's vehicle: the stage musical has not so much been adapted to film as it has been artfully and reverentially ossified there. The film became enormously successful, taking the Academy Award for Best Picture in that era of richly executed winners that began with *West Side Story* (1961) and continued through *The Sound of Music* (1965). *My Fair Lady* also won Academy Awards in seven other categories, including that for direction, thus belatedly giving Cukor, at sixty-five, his only Academy Award.

My Fair Lady is derived initially from the story of *Pygmalion*, first recorded by the Latin poet Ovid in his *Metamorphoses* in the opening decade of the Christian era. Pygmalion, legendary king of Cyprus and master sculptor, hated women because of what he considered their innate vices, but he made an ivory statue of a woman so beautiful that he fell in love with it, praying to Venus to give him a wife like his beloved statue. Venus brought his ivory maiden, called Galatea in later tradition, to life for him to marry. George Bernard Shaw's play *Pygmalion*, written in 1912, furnishes the immediate source for the stage musical and, in turn, for Lerner's screenplay from his own libretto. While music and lyrics displace about half of the play's dialogue, the resulting condensation follows Shaw's text practically verbatim.

Professor Henry Higgins (Rex Harrison), a phonetics expert, wagers his friend Colonel Pickering (Wilfrid Hyde-White) that within six months he can teach a Cockney flower girl, Eliza (Audrey Hepburn), to speak well enough to pass for a duchess at an Embassy ball. Without respite, Higgins drills Eliza in pronunciation and grammar, both intimidating and insulting her in the process. He gives her a trial at the Ascot Races, where she recites scarcely genteel details from her family history but does so with impeccable diction; however, she nearly spoils the masquerade when, excited by the race, she yells to her horse to move his "bloomin' arse." Her behavior, nevertheless, wins the devotion of the young fop Freddie (Jeremy Brett). At the important test, the ball, Eliza captivates all; her speech convinces a language specialist, Zoltan Karpathy (Theodore Bikel), that she cannot be English because she speaks the language too well for a native. Then Eliza, deeply hurt by Higgins' indifference toward her now that he has won his bet, flees to the home of Higgins' mother (Gladys Cooper), encountering the omnipresent Freddie on the way. Higgins tries to get her back, coming to realize his affection for her, and, although she vows to marry Freddie, she promptly follows Higgins back home.

In his play Shaw treated language as an institution that helps ensure the advantages afforded to the rich and the servility endured by the poor. *My Fair Lady* softens the play's original social criticism by using speech differences primarily as a vehicle for comedy and romance, although language, and the advantages that correct language can make available in life, still determine the action. Thus, in the beginning, Higgins, busily recording phonetic notations on "interesting" (that is, substandard) dialects of London, rightly appraises that Eliza is condemned by every syllable she utters. Because Eliza recognizes the necessity of speaking well—she wants to be a lady in a flower shop rather than a flower girl at the curb—she seeks out Higgins and then for six months submits to his harsh tutelage. At the Ascot Races, her triumph over vowels and consonants aside, her grammar and vocabulary remain that of the street: "them as pinched it, done her in" she reports to her staid audience in reference to the fate of her new hat and her aunt's death. Freddie, nevertheless, seems equally taken by Eliza's loveliness and her colorful recitations, or "new small talk," as Higgins quickly explains.

Higgins, Freddie, and Eliza come to form a love triangle unorthodox for a musical comedy, but one without a single kiss exchanged. Eliza finds herself idolized by a man she does not want while tyrannized by a man she loves. She has evidenced her love for Higgins, notably in the song "I Could Have Danced All Night," but at the end she must resort to saving face. Her magnificent performance at the ball fails to bring the changes she has hoped for: Pickering, abetted by the servants, congratulates Higgins at length on his cleverness in passing off Eliza as a lady, totally ignoring, as does Higgins, her role in the stratagem. Worse yet, Higgins shows no concern for her fate now that the game has ended; she remains simply the "squashed cabbage leaf" whom he rescued from the gutter. Although she acknowledges that she is an ignorant flower girl beneath her elegant speech and refined manners and that the differences are too great for her to expect Higgins' love, she does expect kindness and friendship and an equality within certain limits. Thus, Eliza resolutely departs in the middle of the night when she understands that Higgins will not grant even that modest demand.

Parallel to the basic story is the action involving Eliza's father, Alfred Doolittle (Stanley Holloway), a dustman whose major energies go to cadging drinks. In the manner of his daughter, he greatly improves himself through the offices of Higgins; but prosperity falls upon Doolittle without his ever having to learn even one syllable of polite English. He "sells" Eliza to Higgins for five pounds; Higgins, amused by his persuasive rhetoric and avowed lack of scruples, puts him in touch with an American millionaire who founds moral reform societies. Doolittle becomes a wealthy man when the millionaire provides for him in his will. Although he decries his entrapment in middle-class morality, he nonetheless lacks the courage to give up the money, regretfully marrying Eliza's "stepmother."

Cukor smoothly integrates the musical numbers into the story, but foregoes practically all of the strenuous dance sequences of the stage play. The majority of the numbers help advance the action, usually by further developing characterization. Higgins' songs portray him as a thoroughly case-hardened bachelor who has little patience with women ("Let a Woman in Your Life," "Why Can't a Woman Be More Like a Man?"), although he grudgingly acknowledges his attachment to Eliza in his final song, "I've Grown Accustomed to Her Face." Eliza's songs, expertly dubbed by Marni Nixon, trace her progression from fanciful waif ("Wouldn't It Be Loverly," "Just You Wait, 'enry 'iggins," "I Could Have Danced All Night") to resolute woman not to be passed over ("Show Me," "Without You"). Doolittle's two numbers mark his reversed circumstances: in "With a Little Bit of Luck," he explains his philosophy of unwedded bliss; then, prosperous and respectable, he sadly reflects on his last few hours of freedom in "Get Me to the Church on Time."

That final number by Doolittle blends Cukor's direction on Hermes Pan's choreography into superior cinema as the camera whimsically tracks the drunken antics of Doolittle and his friends. This scene, complete with its dark, sweaty colors plastered about a brightly lighted pub, looks back in contradistinction to the Ascot Gavotte sequence, where ladies and gentlemen bloodlessly parade about in the open air in blacks, whites, and grays. The Ascot Gavotte is itself the most impressive scene in the film; even though highly stylized in its extravagant costumes and decor, it creates a valid sense of that leisurely world enjoyed by the privileged class in Edwardian England. A playful bit of class satire, Ascot Gavotte details the complacency and, especially, the studied ennui of the spectators: in a freeze-action frame they watch without trace of emotion as the horses gallop by, then intone with aristocratic boredom, "'Twas a thrilling, absolutely chilling/ Running of the Ascot op'ning race."

As Henry Higgins, the role which he had originated on Broadway, Rex Harrison brings some badly needed movement to an indifferently paced screenplay. He strides through his scenes with a perceptive determination, neither singing nor speaking his numbers but declaiming them in the tone and rhythm demanded by the occasion. His bad manners, particularly regarding Eliza, confirm instead of question his masculinity and his status as a tradition-bound bachelor who prefers the company of men. For all the vigor of Harrison's performance, however, he rarely establishes any emotional cohesion with Audrey Hepburn's Eliza. Higgins and Eliza extend themselves to each other most effectively when she finally renders "The rain in Spain" elocution properly; and yet, they simply share the warm camaraderie of teacher and pupil who together have conquered an important class barrier that separates one individual from another.

Hepburn is an unfortunate choice for this Galatea-Cinderella role of the ignorant Cockney transformed into a princess beloved by her creator. Her strength has always been in her winsome but regal charm rather than in any ability to define character. She is never convincing as a potential gem awaiting the polish by the master but rather, from the start, is the elegant princess openly masquerading behind the dirt and grating accent. As Doolittle, Stanley Holloway, also repeating his part from Broadway, plays off creditably enough against Harrison and Hepburn with his mellow low comedy which, to be sure, belongs more to the English music halls than to Shaw. The usually reliable Wilfrid Hyde-White delivers an embarrassingly static Pickering, but Gladys Cooper does superbly as the matriarchal Mrs. Higgins, upbraiding her son unmercifully and correcting his social lapses in an ironic inversion of his own role with Eliza.

The love story, despite its centrality to the plot, becomes the least engaging

part of *My Fair Lady*. The audience's interests and sympathies rest mainly
on Eliza's struggles to escape the limitations of her background. The obstacle
to romantic involvement between Higgins and her is Higgins' disposition, not
her lowly origins; and that she could be anything more to him than a household
factotum seems unlikely. Eliza does return to Higgins to make the ending
a happy one, the stuff of musical comedy, since any kind of life with Higgins,
the man she loves, would be preferable to marriage to the inconsequential
Freddie. However, the real strengths of *My Fair Lady* are its very sump-
tuousness, its sets and costumes on the one hand, and its music on the other.
The film restores a lost age when flower girls could indeed become princesses,
if only for one night.

ONE HOUR WITH YOU

Released: 1932
Production: Ernst Lubitsch for Paramount
Direction: Ernst Lubitsch and George Cukor
Screenplay: Samson Raphaelson; based on the play *Only a Dream* by Lothar Schmidt
Cinematography: Victor Milner
Editing: no listing
Art direction: Hans Dreier
Song: Oscar Straus, Richard Whiting, and Leo Robin
Running time: 80 minutes

Principal characters:

Dr. André Bertier .... Maurice Chevalier
Colette Bertier .... Jeanette MacDonald
Mitzi Olivier .... Genevieve Tobin
Professor Olivier .... Roland Young
Adolph .... Charles Ruggles
Police Commissioner .... George Barbier
Madamoiselle Martel .... Josephine Dunn
Detective .... Richard Carle

Before Busby Berkeley and Fred Astaire defined the genre for decades to come, the Hollywood musical went through a number of what today would seem to be radical formal experiments. Indeed, the most interesting musicals from 1929 through 1933 are closer to cinematic opera than to the production number and dance musical that later came to dominate the field. The early 1930's musicals of Ernst Lubitsch and Rouben Mamoulian and the series of musicals scored by Richard Rodgers and Lorenz Hart (which are clearly influenced by the innovative political Gershwin shows that reached Broadway during this period) are characterized by the use of music to advance and comment upon the action, and by extensive use of rhymed dialogue that stylizes the action in a deliberately unnaturalistic manner. There is no more radically stylized or brilliant example of this type of early 1930's musical than Ernst Lubitsch's neglected masterpiece, *One Hour with You.*

The culmination of Lubitsch's musical experiments, *One Hour with You* is virtually a subgenre unto itself—the minimalist musical. The film is a remake of Lubitsch's trailblazing 1924 comedy *The Marriage Circle*, and, amazingly, it is more intimate in scale than the original. Like its predecessor, *One Hour with You* concerns the romantic permutations and peregrinations of five characters; unlike its predecessor, it constantly employs music and a host of cinematic devices to distance (yet never disinvolve) the viewer from the action. The uncluttered simplicity of the exposition is calculated to make visible both the social conventions that hold sway in the society Lubitsch depicts and the cinematic conventions by which they are conveyed. For this reason, *One Hour with You* is the quintessence of Lubitsch's career, in which Lubitsch sets out simultaneously to expose and celebrate artifice—and therefore society.

In the opening scenes, the central characters, Dr. André Bertier (Maurice Chevalier) and his wife Colette (Jeanette MacDonald), are seen flirting with each other in a Parisian park. Upon their return home, however, we discover that Colette is unsure—groundlessly, it develops—of André's fidelity. She is afforded a respite from her cares when her old girlhood friend Mitzi Olivier (Genevieve Tobin) arrives in Paris with her Professor husband (Roland Young). From the moment Colette introduces Mitzi to André, it is abundantly clear to everyone but Colette that Mitzi is interested in him. This is a welcome development for the Professor, who is having Mitzi followed by a detective in order to obtain grounds for a divorce; it is also quite all right with André's best friend Adolph (Charles Ruggles), who in a pathetic way has romantic designs on Colette and is looking for an opening to express them. Indeed, the whole weight of the action, including every misguided effort of the innocent Colette, is directed at throwing the reluctant André into an affair with dazzlingly beautiful Mitzi, to whom he finally succumbs. The Professor, delighted at finally having a case, presents the evidence to an embarrassed André who then confesses to Colette. Feeling the need to establish some parity in the matter, Colette prompts Adolph, whose advances she actually has spurned, to make a bogus confession of adultery to André. Adolph confesses with the secret encouragement of André, who thinks the affair the height of comic improbability. Their respective honors satisfied, the Bertiers reconcile happily.

Lubitsch revels in the codes and repressions of his contemporary society: passion and conflict find expression in oblique and indirect ways. Dinner guests surreptitiously rearrange their place cards for reasons of sexual ambition; Mitzi undoes André's cravat (he cannot tie ties) to raise Colette's suspicions of his infidelity and then teases that she will tie it for him if he promises to come to see her. The only character in the film who lacks all sense of the rules of the game is Adolph, the fifth wheel, who arrives at the party in costume when it is not a costume party. Upon his arrival, the camera suddenly abandons its objectivity and tracks closely with him from room to room as he seeks out Colette. It is a ludicrous plunge into the passion that the characters and the camera normally mediate with some saving distance.

This distance is ever-present for the audience as the film constantly calls attention to itself as film. Again, Adolph's ignorance of artifice provides a key sequence. In the ballroom dance that accompanies the title song, couples form and then regroup as each of the principals confides to a desired party how much he or she would "love one hour with you." Later, the party over, Adolph and Colette are alone. He begins the song again. Colette stops him cold. The number is finished, she tells him, the orchestra gone, the song unreprisable. It is as if he has forgotten the movie and she must remind him of it. It is an extraordinary moment, superficially similar to Woody Allen's hearing harp background music in *Bananas* (1971) and opening the closet to find a harpist, but ultimately more complex. This is not the comedian's traditional demolition of plot, and Lubitsch, for all his subversions, is not really asking the audience to abandon its suspension of disbelief.

It is through techniques peculiar to film and musicals, however, that Lubitsch makes artifice most visible. The opening sequence concludes with the Bertiers happily bedding down and turning out the light as the scene begins to fade toward black; only it does not fade to black. Something has piqued Colette's curiosity; a seed of doubt about André's fidelity has been planted. She turns on the light again and the scene continues, fading to black as André dims the light and beginning again as she relights it, until finally an exasperated André unscrews the bulb. Equally arresting is the use of offscreen space. More than any director, Lubitsch developed the use of objects as symbols for particular persons or emotions. In the song "Oh, That Mitzi," he uses directions. Poised in the foyer with his wife's bedroom to his left and the door to the street and Mitzi to his right, André faces the camera and confides his dilemma—his wife is terrific (glance offscreen left), but "Oh, that Mitzi!" (increasingly lascivious glances offscreen right).

The film's self-acknowlegment culminates in its acknowlegment of the audience. The most remarkable of André's soliloquy songs (of which "Oh, That Mitzi" is an example) is "What Would You Do?" The "you" in question is the audience, to whom André addresses his case after he has spent his climactic afternoon with Mitzi (although the audience does not yet know whether it was climactic). Exploiting his immense ability to charm and confide in an audience, André concludes the song by asking the spectator, having duly considered Mitzi, "What would you do?"—and then, nodding, he sings, "That's what I did, too."

The moment is breathtaking. The climactic moment of the film—the revelation of the affair—is made to come from the audience, with André merely confirming its collective judgment. Audience fantasy is incorporated directly into the action. The motif is repeated at the film's conclusion when André and Colette speak to the male and female members of the audience respectively, asking them if *they* would reconcile; and, following the audience's advice, they do exactly that.

These are more than distancing devices. The audience becomes aware not so much of its alienation from the artificial world of the film as of its commitment to and even complicity in that world. For Lubitsch is both satirist and celebrant of society, and his ambivalence goes beyond that of most American comedy. It is, precisely, the comic apotheosis of the ultimately fatal ambivalence of pre-Hitler German Jewry to the culture in which they lived, an ambivalence rooted in their desire to be more German than the Germans.

In his American comedies, Lubitsch finds a confident and delocalized expression of the uneasy mixture of disdain and need for approval with which he must have confronted German society when he began his career as a Jewish character comedian in pre-World War I Berlin.

Almost since its release, *One Hour with You* has languished in the shadow of Lubitsch's next film, *Trouble in Paradise* (1932), generally regarded as his greatest talkie. In fact, either film is a worthy claimant to the title. They are Lubitsch's first two solo collaborations with his favorite screenwriter, Samson Raphaelson, and the freshness and good feeling of the partnership enlivens both scripts. Each film boasts unnaturally perfect, almost hermetic sets by Hans Dreier and razor-sharp cinematography by Victor Milner. What may tip the scales ever so slightly in favor of *One Hour with You* is Maurice Chevalier, who offers his greatest performance. No other Chevalier film so exploits his unmatched ability to establish an intimacy, or perhaps complicity, with the spectator.

One reason for the unjust relegation of *One Hour with You* to obscurity is the fact that for years it was thought to have been directed by George Cukor from Lubitsch's plan. In fact, Cukor worked as director for only two weeks, as he himself has told Gavin Lambert in the book *On Cukor*, and during that time he followed Lubitsch's design religiously. Withal, this ambiguity over the directorial credit and the film's relative inaccessibility have diminished the picture's reputation. The time has come for its upward revaluation. *One Hour with You* is another Lubitsch masterpiece.

THE PHILADELPHIA STORY

Released: 1940
Production: Joseph L. Mankiewicz for Metro-Goldwyn-Mayer
Direction: George Cukor
Screenplay: Donald Ogden Stewart (AA); based on the play of the same name by Philip Barry
Cinematography: Joseph Ruttenberg
Editing: Frank Sullivan
Running time: 112 minutes

Principal characters:

C. K. Dexter Haven	Cary Grant
Tracy Lord	Katharine Hepburn
Macaulay (Mike) Connor	James Stewart (AA)
Elizabeth (Liz) Imbrie	Ruth Hussey
George Kittredge	John Howard
Uncle Willie	Roland Young
Dinah Lord	Virginia Weidler
Sidney Kidd	Henry Daniell
Seth Lord	John Halliday

Set in the world of high society, *The Philadelphia Story* is a sophisticated romantic comedy about an arrogant young woman who learns some things about who she is and what she really wants during a hectic twenty-four-hour period before her second wedding. Macaulay (Mike) Connor (James Stewart), a writer for the scandal sheet *Spy*, and his photographer Elizabeth (Liz) Imbrie (Ruth Hussey), are assigned to cover the Philadelphia society wedding of Tracy Lord (Katharine Hepburn) to George Kittredge (John Howard). Connor, who is a serious writer and has published an unremunerative volume of short stories, considers the assignment degrading and has to be coaxed into accepting it by the more practical Liz, who is in love with him. They are able to get into the Lord's house because Tracy's ex-husband, socially prominent C. K. Dexter Haven (Cary Grant), introduces them as friends of Tracy's brother who is in South America. What they do not know is that Haven has promised this exclusive inside story on the wedding to Sidney Kidd (Henry Daniell), the publisher of *Spy*, to keep him from printing a scandalous story about Tracy's father, Seth (John Halliday), and his affair with a dancer.

When Haven explains the scheme to Tracy, she is outraged but agrees to let them stay because she does not want the scandal about her father to be published. For the benefit of Connor and Liz, who do not realize she has been told their true identities, Tracy and her young sister Dinah (Virginia Weidler) put on an act. They speak French to each other and English to Liz and Connor in an artificial manner, parodying the *Spy* magazine conception of high society. After this act Tracy immediately assumes command of the situation and turns the tables by interviewing Connor and Liz. Her astuteness and interest upset Connor's preconceived idea of her as a "rich, rapacious American female."

After lunch, Connor goes to the public library to do some research on the Lords and discovers Tracy reading his book of short stories. As they walk together back to the Lords's estate, they become increasingly interested in each other. At the Lords's pool, they are joined by Haven, who proceeds to dissect Tracy and his marriage to her while Connor watches and listens. Tracy's self-confidence is a little shaken by his reproaches, and later it is further undermined when her father also takes her to task for her intolerance and priggishness. That evening at a party given by her Uncle Willy (Roland Young), Tracy begins to drink champagne quickly to hide her uncertainty; drinking is something she does not normally do and usually condemns.

At the same party Connor becomes drunk enough to lose most of his inhibitions, and he goes off to Haven's mansion to discuss Tracy with him, revealing to Haven and to the audience his growing infatuation with her. He also reveals his knowledge of a scandalous story concerning Kidd that would stop the publisher from printing the gossip about her father. At this moment Liz arrives with Tracy to pick up Connor and is persuaded to stay to type the story. This allows Connor to drive off for a private conversation with Tracy, who has now revived from her inebriation. Although he accuses her of arrogance and tries to persuade her not to marry Kittredge, it quickly becomes apparent to both of them how much he admires her. Tracy, self-conscious and slightly overwhelmed by his effusive compliments, tries to lighten the mood by suggesting a moonlight swim.

Later that evening, Haven brings Liz back to the Lords's mansion in time to see Connor carrying Tracy back from the pool and up to her room. Kittredge, worried because Tracy has failed to answer her telephone, also arrives in time to witness the scene and becomes incensed with both Tracy and Connor, imagining the most compromising explanation for the scene although Connor assures him they have just gone for a moonlight swim. Kittredge is about to hit Connor, but Haven knocks him down first because, as he says apologetically to Connor, "He's in better shape than I am."

The next morning, Tracy, with a terrible hangover, totters onto the terrace where Haven and Dinah are talking. At first she remembers nothing about the previous evening, not even the swim, but Dinah tells her about a "dream" in which she saw Connor carry Tracy across the lawn and upstairs to her room. Already alarmed by the implications of what Dinah (who, of course, has seen everything from an upstairs window) is saying, Tracy is even more upset when Connor arrives and calls her "darling."

She is now handed a letter from Kittredge in which he demands a full explanation of the night's happenings before he will go through with the wedding. As she is reading it, Kittredge himself arrives in a belligerent mood. When Connor repeats that nothing compromising happened, Kittredge is pleased, but Tracy is upset. "Was I so unattractive?" she demands. She is placated by Connor's reply that he did not want to take advantage of her while she was drunk.

Kittredge is satisfied and wants to go ahead with the wedding, but Tracy now realizes they are not suited for each other and tells him good-bye as nicely as possible. Connor then offers himself as the bridegroom in Kittredge's place, but after a moment's hesitation and a glance at Liz's stricken face, Tracy gently declines his offer. She then turns to Haven, who offers to extricate her from her embarrassing predicament by marrying her himself, a contingency for which he has obviously been hoping and waiting. Tracy now realizes it is Haven she really loves and happily accepts his offer. The film ends with Kidd taking snapshots of the dismayed wedding party.

At the heart of *The Philadelphia Story* is Tracy Lord. When we first see her, she seems to be an ideal woman, beautiful and intelligent. As the film progresses, however, we learn about her less attractive qualities and ultimately discover that the "goddess" has feet of clay. Her ex-husband, C. K. Dexter Haven, calls her a "virgin goddess," so secure in her sense of "inner divinity" that she cannot tolerate weakness in others. Her contempt for him and her intolerance of his drinking has led him to drink even more, he tells her.

Tracy's father accuses her of much the same thing. He places part of the blame for his philandering on Tracy because she did not give him enough warm, uncritical affection. She is intelligent and beautiful, he says, but lacks an understanding heart.

Tracy's three romantic entanglements are with men of quite different social and intellectual characteristics who involve different facets of Tracy's character. C. K. Dexter Haven is a man of her own class, wealthy, socially prominent, and charming, but Tracy divorced him because she could not tolerate his weakness and alcoholism. He resents Tracy's assumed superiority and aloofness but appreciates her beauty, her strength, and her intelligence.

Mike Connor is a product of a middle-class family with little money. He thinks he despises the idle rich, and he has dreams of eventually supporting himself as a writer. At first antagonistic and wary of Tracy, he is soon dazzled by her beauty and magnificence of spirit; but he is always outside of Tracy's world and serves as a detached commentator on the society in which she moves. As he tells Tracy, his philosophy is based on an old Spanish peasant's proverb: "With the rich and mighty, a little patience." Connor ironically sums up his view of Tracy's world: "The prettiest sight in this fine, pretty world is the privileged class enjoying its privileges." His conversations with Tracy provide an opportunity for some witty exchanges in which each accuses the other of snobbery.

George Kittredge is given a cursory treatment and is not an interesting or sympathetic character. He is a self-made man who has worked for his wealth and social position, but his riches have not enlarged his mind or made him anything other than a conventional, self-important, suspicious man with commonplace ideas. When he sees Connor carrying Tracy back from the pool, he immediately thinks the worst. "I have eyes, I have imagination," he exclaims angrily to Haven. His error is in believing that Tracy is no different from any other woman when both Haven and Connor have taken great pains to point out how unusual she is.

Philip Barry wrote the play *The Philadelphia Story* especially for Katharine Hepburn, tailoring it to her mannerisms and acting style. As a play it was a hit on Broadway, and as a movie it revived Hepburn's film career. The actress had astutely bought the film rights from Barry before the play opened and was thus able to choose her director and costars.

Director George Cukor deliberately chose not to do the film in the frenetic style of the screwball comedies. He felt that "the material determined the tempo" in this literate comedy in which conversation is an art for the people involved. "They say witty things, and they're witty about serious things," Cukor has said. In order to give full value to the language of the film, he chose to be somewhat deliberate and to take time to build up character and detail.

Even though dialogue is the mainstay of the film, one of the best scenes has no dialogue at all. The opening scene shows Haven, with an angry expression on his face, carrying his suitcases out of his house. A moment later Tracy, in her nightgown, appears at the door with his bag of golf clubs. Her face is imperiously cold as she extracts one club from the bag, throws the bag after him, and then deliberately breaks the club over her knee, smiling contemptuously at him all the while. Enraged, he marches up to her and starts to hit her in the face but cannot quite bring himself to do it. Instead, he shoves her back through the door. The scene quickly and deftly establishes the personalities of the two as well as their relationship to each other. Much of the credit for devising this scene, which was not in the play, apparently belongs to Cukor, who felt some "reconstruction" of Tracy and Haven's marriage was necessary but did not want a long scene with a great deal of dialogue. Cukor's approach to the film was much the same as that of the screenwriter, Donald Ogden Stewart: to add something new and fresh without violating the structure or tone of the original play.

To say that the film is dominated by Hepburn's performance is not to detract from the excellence of the rest of the cast, particularly Cary Grant as C. K. Dexter Haven and James Stewart as Mike Connor. Grant's role is not as colorful or as demanding as that of Stewart, but with a lift of an eyebrow or a quizzical grin he can command the attention of everyone. He holds his own in his scenes with both Hepburn and Stewart although he is playing a less flamboyant character than either. James Stewart received an Academy Award

for Best Actor of the year for his delightfully humorous and appealing performance as the bedazzled, sardonic reporter; he is a perfect foil to both
Hepburn and Grant. Indeed, the cast and direction were so excellent that a
remake was bound to suffer in comparison. M-G-M nevertheless remade the
story in 1956 as *High Society*, a musical featuring Grace Kelly, Bing Crosby,
and Frank Sinatra. The film made money but failed to achieve the special
qualities of *The Philadelphia Story*.

A STAR IS BORN

Released: 1954
Production: Sidney Luft for Transcona Enterprises; released by Warner Bros.
Direction: George Cukor
Screenplay: Moss Hart; based on the screenplay for the 1937 film of the same
   name
Cinematography: Sam Leavitt
Editing: Folmar Blangsted
Running time: 154 minutes

> *Principal characters:*
> Esther Blodgett/
> Vicki Lester .... Judy Garland
> Norman Maine .... James Mason
> Matt Libby .... Jack Carson
> Oliver Niles .... Charles Bickford
> Danny McGuire .... Tommy Noonan

"Inside Hollywood" stories have provided the material for many filmmakers' products over the years, and few variations on this theme have been repeated more often or more successfully than that of *A Star Is Born*. No than three films with this title have been made, the first by William Wellman in 1937, and the latest by Frank Pierson, who in 1976 made his protagonists rock stars instead of actors. The best of these films, however, is arguably the 1954 version, directed by George Cukor and starring Judy Garland and James Mason.

Like its predecessor, Cukor's *A Star Is Born* is the story of Norman Maine (James Mason), a talented but alcoholic movie star who discovers young Esther Blodgett (Judy Garland), propels her to stardom under the stage name of Vicki Lester, marries her, and finally commits suicide when he realizes that his alcoholism is ruining her career. Into the midst of this drama, however, Cukor inserts musical comedy of the highest order. It is a tribute to the talent of the director, and his two stars, Garland and Mason, that the two apparently conflicting genres mesh and complement rather than detract from each other.

A Star Is Born is at least nominally about Hollywood, and Cukor uses three official Hollywood ceremonies, strategically placed at the beginning, middle, and end of the film, to comment on the Hollywood scene as well as to advance the plot. The first of these ceremonies is a concert for a benefit known as "The Motion Picture Relief Fund," the proceeds of which go to out-of-work actors. "Hollywood never forgets its own," boasts the Master of Ceremonies, but Cukor underscores the irony of this statement throughout the picture as he chronicles the downfall of Norman Maine. Although Norman is sufficiently self-destructive to ruin his own career, the way is made easier for him by his studio, most notably by Matt Libby (Jack Carson), the mean-spirited publicity man.

As the film opens, however, Norman has just begun his descent from the top. He arrives at the benefit late and obviously drunk. After disrupting things backstage and insulting Libby, he lurches onstage into a performance by the Glenn Williams Orchestra. Esther Blodgett, the orchestra's singer, cleverly incorporates Norman into their song and dance routine, saving everyone from major embarrassment. Even in his inebriated condition, Norman is aware of what an extraordinary gesture Esther has made; for her part, Esther is more amused than offended. "Mr. Maine is feeling no pain," she quips, but later adds "drunk or not, he's nice." A sullen Libby sees to it that Maine gets home safely. By showing the evident hostility between the two men, Cukor lays the groundwork for a time when the worm will turn.

Later that same night, Norman awakens and, haunted by the memory of the girl in the Glenn Williams Orchestra, tracks Esther down at an afterhours club where she and her fellow musicians hang out. In this scene, Cukor makes effective use of the soundtrack by playing a very quiet orchestral reprise of one of Esther's songs to suggest that she is in Norman's thoughts. As Norman enters the club, he is transfixed by Esther's rendition of "The Man That Got Away." After witnessing this performance, both Norman and the audience realize that Esther Blodgett is not simply a cute and talented singer; there is a spark of genius in her, a rare star quality just waiting to be discovered. "The Man That Got Away" scene is one of the keys to the believability of the film. Garland's performance of the Harold Arlen-Ira Gershwin song has been justifiably praised as one of the classics of the Hollywood musical film. We do not have to take Esther's potential on faith—Garland makes it abundantly obvious.

Norman is happy to sponsor Esther's entry into show business, and he cajoles the reluctant head of the Oliver Niles Studios (Charles Bickford) into giving her a screen test. She passes the test and becomes a part of the studio. Cukor emphasizes, however, what a minor part she is in a hilarious sequence in which Esther, now renamed Vicki Lester, is shuttled from person to person, each of whom, from the wardrobe lady to the head of the studio, greets her with a cordial "Glad to have you with us," and then promptly proceeds to ignore her. Finally, again through the good offices of Norman, she gets a chance at a starring role in a musical comedy. Cukor shows us a long sequence from this film at a special screening at which Norman's new film is also being previewed. The sequence is an exquisitely staged musical "biography" of Vicki Lester's character. She opens and closes with "Born in a Trunk." In between, interspersed with her ironic commentary on being a "ten-year-overnight sensation," come such classics as "I'll Get By," "You Took Advantage of Me," "Melancholy Baby," and "Sewanee." The screening is a sensation; the title of the film has become a reality. Vicki Lester has become a star.

Norman has mixed feelings about his protégé. His own film has been ignored in the fanfare that greeted Esther's smash debut. He knows himself well enough to be aware that he destroys everything to which he gets close; nevertheless, he loves Esther, and she persuades him to give marriage a try. After losing the frustrated Libby, who has hoped to get some publicity mileage out of their elopement, Norman and Esther are married by a sleepy country justice of the peace under Norman's real name, and become Mr. and Mrs. Ernest Sidney Gubbins.

Despite an idyllic honeymoon, both Norman and his marriage soon begin to unravel, and Cukor uses another Hollywood ceremony to demonstrate this fact. It is Oscar night, and Vicki Lester has won an Academy Award. She is about to make her acceptance speech when Norman once again lurches drunkenly onstage. He makes a rambling, self-pitying speech about his inability to get work; and, gesturing wildly, accidentally slaps Vicki. As the audience gasps in shock, Vicki somehow manages to get offstage. However, the damage is done: Norman Maine's career is finished.

Norman makes an effort to adjust to his new circumstances, and even has himself committed to a sanitarium in an effort to dry out; but the lure of alcohol proves to be too strong. When his old adversary, Matt Libby, provides him with an excuse to go off the wagon by picking a fight with Norman at a racetrack and beating him, the humiliated Norman responds by going on a monumental drunk, ultimately turning up in a local drunk tank and bringing more scandal down upon himself and his wife. Esther, for her part, feels helpless. She loves Norman, but admits that she hates him as well. Torn between her husband and her career, she tells Oliver Niles that she is quitting her career to stay with Norman at their Malibu home. Norman, who has been in a drunken sleep in the next room, overhears the conversation; a look of agonizing self-loathing crosses his face, followed by a look of grim determination. After Niles leaves, Norman, with a huge smile, comes to Esther, wearing swimming trunks. He is turning over a new leaf, he vows, and will begin his healthy new life at once by getting in some swimming. He stops short, however, and looks wistfully at his wife for a long moment. As Esther goes inside to prepare dinner, Norman runs into the ocean and drowns. Although his death is officially ruled an accident, it is obvious that he has sacrificed his own life for the sake of Esther and her career.

Cukor closes the film with a third Hollywood ceremony; it is another benefit and a grief-stricken Esther is persuaded to come out of mourning in order to perform. When an excited announcer introduces her as Vicki Lester, she corrects him emphatically: "Hello everybody. This is *Mrs.* Norman Maine!" As the audience applauds ecstatically, the camera pulls back slowly, and the film ends with a long shot of Esther, smiling through her tears.

In 1932, George Cukor directed his sixth film, *What Price Hollywood?*, which traced the rise and fall of a young actress whose film career was masterminded by an alcoholic director. This film provided the inspiration for William Wellman's original *A Star Is Born* in 1937, which Cukor, in turn, remade seventeen years later. It was through this circuitous path that George Cukor produced the film that has been acclaimed by some as Hollywood's greatest musical. Among a host of first-rate actors, three performances stand out. James Mason's thoughtful, unmannered portrayal of Norman Maine won him an Academy Award nomination. Because Mason has no illusions about Norman, neither does the audience, but Mason is a good enough actor to show us the talent and the warmth beneath Norman's dissipation. We can understand why Esther loves him, and his demise, though inevitable, is thus genuinely tragic. In a supporting role, Jack Carson is similarly effective as Matt Libby, Norman's chief antagonist. Libby is the film's only real villain, and Carson's performance is appropriately mean-spirited. His Libby is a classic today, a man who despises those whom he serves. As good as Mason and Carson are, however, *A Star Is Born* belongs to Judy Garland; she does not so much overshadow her colleagues, however, as illuminate them. She performs with such an intensity that at times she almost seems to glow. It is not inconceivable that actors other than Mason and Carson could have handled the roles of Norman Maine and Matt Libby; it is almost impossible to imagine anyone other than Judy Garland as Esther Blodgett. Her performance lifts *A Star Is Born* into the first rank among Hollywood musicals.

WHAT PRICE HOLLYWOOD?

Released: 1932
Production: David O. Selznick for RKO/Radio
Direction: George Cukor
Screenplay: Jane Murfin, Gene Fowler, Rowland Brown, and Ben Markson;
    based on a screen story by Adela Rogers St. John
Cinematography: Charles Rosher
Editing: Jack Kitchin
Running time: 91 minutes

     Principal characters:
       Mary Evans .... Constance Bennett
       Maximilian Carey .... Lowell Sherman
       Lonny Borden .... Neil Hamilton
       Julius Saxe .... Gregory Ratoff

    Hollywood has always liked to portray itself on the screen; the mood of such self-portraits ranges from the nostalgic *Singin' in the Rain* (1952) to the sardonic *Sunset Boulevard* (1950). Affectionately satirical, *What Price Hollywood?* falls somewhere between these two extremes. Its theme, the contrast between two careers, is a popular one, but seldom has it been so well realized.

    While working as a waitress at the Brown Derby Restaurant, Mary Evans (Constance Bennett) meets Max Carey (Lowell Sherman), a famous and successful movie director. While he is tipsy he invites her to accompany him to a Hollywood premiere, and afterwards she sees him safely home. As a reward he gives her a bit part in one of his films. Though she has only one line of dialogue ("Hello, Buzzy, you haven't proposed to me yet tonight"), her performance is seen by an important producer, Julius Saxe (Gregory Ratoff), who realizes she has some talent and decides to make her a star. As Mary's career blossoms (she is publicized as "America's Pal"), Carey's declines because of his alcoholism. Saxe has tried to persuade him to quit drinking and has given him jobs but now he can no longer rely on Carey's work. Finally, Saxe's patience is exhausted, and despite Mary's pleading, he refuses to hire Carey again. Through all this Mary remains loyal to him, remembering that it was he who gave her a chance for stardom.

    Meanwhile, Mary meets a wealthy polo player, Lonny Borden (Neil Hamilton), and after a stormy courtship, they are married despite Carey's gloomy prediction that a movie star's marriage never lasts. Saxe sees the wedding as a chance for more publicity for Mary and arranges for it to be a big media event. As a result, Mary is mobbed by the crowd as she and Lonny attempt to leave the church, and she has to be rushed back inside, torn and disheveled. Lonny and Mary are tired and overwhelmed by the photographers, the reporters, and the crowd, but Saxe is happy because the wedding "broke all

house records for this church." He then tells Mary that her honeymoon will
have to be postponed to film more scenes for her latest picture.

During the shooting of Mary's film we see a busy set with every member
of the cast and crew active. Only Lonny, sitting on the sidelines reading a
magazine, has nothing to do. When Carey finds Mary talking to Lonny instead
of listening to his directions, he becomes very irritated and tells him to "let
me direct Miss Evans, and you be Mr. Evans." At a script conference Lonny
is again the outsider. His advice is ignored, and as Saxe, Mary, and Carey
argue heatedly, he walks away from the group, unnoticed.

In the most effective satirical scene in the film, a gossip columnist comes
to interview Mary and Lonny about their marriage. Mary has to cajole an
embarrassed and uneasy Lonny into talking to the columnist, who overhears
their heated argument. As Mary clings closely to Lonny, the columnist asks
them several impertinent questions about their love life—"Do you have separate bedrooms?" "How far should a wife go to keep her husband's love?"
Lonny is outraged and he replies sarcastically to all of her questions, finally
stalking out of the room.

The film deftly but affectionately mocks Hollywood, yet makes it plain that
its inhabitants are loyal, compassionate, and kind. These qualities are contrasted with those of Lonny's friends, whom Mary calls "stuffed shirts" (although we never see any of them). Lonny, on the other hand, thinks Mary's
professional friends are cheap and vulgar and does not want her to associate
with them socially.

Mary and Lonny's marriage slowly disintegrates, and its end is hastened
by the appearance one night of a drunken Carey at their house. Upset and
disgusted by this intrusion into their private life, Lonny wants Carey to leave,
but Mary refuses to make him go, saying she cannot let him down. Angrily,
Lonny leaves and goes ahead with divorce proccedings, not knowing that
Mary is pregnant.

We next see Mary a year later playing with her son, Jackie, and refusing
to share custody of the child with Lonny. Her career continues to be successful
(she has even won an award for Best Actress) while Max Carey's sinks lower
and lower. Carey is reduced to hanging around the set on Mary's pictures.
Finally she gets word that he is in jail and immediately goes to bail him out.
She takes him to her house, determined that this time she will persuade him
to remain sober; but Carey has declined too far to be rehabilitated, and in
self-disgust he shoots himself. In the ensuing scandal, Mary is questioned by
the police, vilified by the public, and hounded by reporters; her films are
even banned. Finally, she flees to France because she is afraid Lonny will try
to get custody of their son. All of this is conveyed by a quick montage of
newspaper headlines which give the impression that Mary is being crushed
by relentless forces beyond her control. The film ends quickly and happily,
however, as Mary is reunited with Lonny. He also delivers a message from

Saxe saying that he has a new story that will make a great comeback vehicle for Mary.

The film's major limitation is the divided focus of its second half. After establishing that Lonny and Mary live in two different worlds, the film, instead of concentrating on their marriage and its problems, concentrates on the declining career of Max Carey and his relationship with Mary. David O. Selznick, the producer of *What Price Hollywood?*, has said he wished he had been able to spend more time on the script. The shifting back and forth between Carey and Lonny leaves Lonny's character somewhat undeveloped, and his relationship to Mary is merely sketched in, although it is done cleverly and deftly. Despite this problem, director George Cukor handled the script's limitations and his actors so expertly that *What Price Hollywood?* became his first major screen success.

There are numerous clever touches in the way Cukor treats some significant scenes. In the first of these, we see Mary rehearsing over and over the line she has been given in Carey's picture until she finds the right note of brittle sophistication. Later, when Saxe and Carey are watching the daily rushes, Mary blunders into the projection room, is thrown out by Saxe, and watches her scene from the projectionist's booth. She is as amazed as Saxe at her image on the screen, and when he tells her he is going to make her a star, her dazed reaction is, "I'm in pictures." Quickly and adroitly it shows how this particular star is born.

Cukor nicely balances such lighter moments as these with the more dramatic scenes. The suicide of Max Carey is particularly well handled. In the hands of Cukor and actor Lowell Sherman, Carey is a sympathetic, witty alcoholic who never asks for pity, and especially not for Mary's pity. After Mary rescues him from jail and takes him to her house, he tells her he is dead inside, no longer the man she once knew, and that his career is finished. After she leaves the room, he accidently discovers a revolver in a desk drawer. He then sees his reflection in the mirror over the desk and flinches at the sight of his haggard, unshaven face. Underscoring the contrast with his former debonair, robust appearance is an old photograph of him on the desk below the mirror. As he stares at himself in the mirror with an expression of revulsion on his face, he hears a whirring sound like angry bees, and, his brain bursting, he shoots himself. As he falls, quick glimpses of his past life flash before his eyes.

The outstanding performance of the film is Lowell Sherman as Max Carey, but Constance Bennett as Mary Evans is also remarkable. As a waitress she is bright and vivacious and pretty enough to make her break in pictures credible. As a movie star she is the epitome of glamorous sophistication and elegant chic. She makes us believe that she does indeed have that certain "something."

Sometimes *What Price Hollywood?* is remembered merely as the inspiration for the original *A Star Is Born* (1937), and sometimes too much emphasis is given to the fact that the Max Carey character is supposedly based on the careers of silent film director Marshall "Mickey" Neilan and actor John Barrymore. While these are interesting sidelights, the film endures as a well-directed, well-acted work that stands on its own merits.

THE WOMEN

Released: 1939
Production: Hunt Stromberg for Metro-Goldwyn-Mayer
Direction: George Cukor
Screenplay: Anita Loos and Jane Murfin; based on the play of the same name
   by Clare Boothe
Cinematography: Oliver T. Marsh and Joseph Ruttenberg
Editing: Robert J. Kern
Running time: 134 minutes

> *Principal characters:*
> Mary Haines .... Norma Shearer
> Crystal Allen .... Joan Crawford
> Sylvia Fowler .... Rosalind Russell
> Miriam Aarons .... Paulette Goddard
> Countess DeLave .... Mary Boland
> Peggy Day .... Joan Fontaine
> Mrs. Moorehead .... Lucile Watson

From the time of its first Broadway performance on December 26, 1936, Clare Boothe's comedy about the humors and manners of the female sex, *The Women*, was an enormous hit, but it still came as something of a surprise when Hollywood's top studio, M-G-M, acquired the film rights. It is a comedy with an acid wit; of the all-female cast, only one character, the lead, is sympathetic; she is a good although uninteresting woman. The rest of the women are stupid, idle, unscrupulous "bitches" who do nothing but gossip, talk dirty, and play bridge. Their preoccupation is men, although no man ever appears onstage. As movie material, it seems to have many strikes against it.

Producer Hunt Stromberg and director George Cukor, however, were not fazed in the least. They hired Anita Loos to give the play more bite as she wrote the screenplay, and they teamed her with Jane Murfin, who contributed warmth and humanity to several of the backbiting characters. Many of the lines in the play would never have passed the censor; others were markedly vulgar albeit truthful. The two screenwriters substituted dialogue which was far more witty and only verged on the naughty.

Stromberg and Cukor decided to cast the film, as the producers of the play had done, with an all-female cast. Norma Shearer, first lady of M-G-M, was cast in the lead of Mary Haines, the wife and mother who discovers that her world and her sex are predatory, and that she must be willing to fight for her happiness. Joan Crawford went to the studio's front office and asked to play the "other woman," Crystal Allen, an unsympathetic although glamorous role. Rosalind Russell was assigned to play Sylvia Fowler, the meanest woman in Manhattan.

A novel means of introducing the women was devised. As the cast credits were listed, a picture of each actress dissolved into a closeup of an animal whose nature is analogous to that of the character played by the actress. Thus the young and innocent Joan Fontaine, playing Peggy Day, is shown as a wistful, frightened sheep, and the other women become, in turn, tigers, cows, does, and other animals representative of each woman's character.

The ladies meeting for lunch at Mary Haines's well-appointed home are either married or about to be, or are separated and about to divorce. Their most exciting gossip is about their hostess, Mary Haines, for her husband is known to be philandering. Sylvia, who has been to her manicurist, got the information about Mary's husband because the manicurist knew the husband-stealing woman. Sylvia none too subtly suggests to Mary that she go to the new manicurist at Michael's salon named Olga, who gave her this gorgeous "Jungle Red" nail color. Mary divines that Sylvia is trying to tell her something about her marriage when Sylvia insists that "A woman's paradise is always a fool's paradise," and she decides to go to Michael's to get her nails done by Olga.

It does not take much time for Mary to hear the current gossip from Olga, who seems to be sharing it with every customer. The girl who is being kept by Stephen Haines calls herself Crystal Allen; she is a seductress who works behind the perfume counter at "Black's" Fifth Avenue.

Mary tells her mother, Mrs. Moorehead (Lucile Watson), of her husband's infidelity, and her mother gives her some wise advice: she should say nothing. It is something that happens to most wives, and it does not necessarily mean that her husband is tired of her. He may simply be tired of himself and wanting something new; everything would change if he realized that he already has what he wants and could lose it. Mary bides her time and only confronts Crystal when they occupy adjoining booths at a dress salon. Crystal tells Mary that she may be a saint but that she is a very dull woman, and that it is no wonder her husband is roaming.

Mary tries to maintain her calm with her husband, but although he does not want a separation, it is arranged, and Mary leaves for Reno to get a divorce. Meanwhile, others in Mary's circle are unhappy in their own marital lives. The divorce roundelay begins, and Mary meets some of her Manhattan friends in Reno — Sylvia, her archenemy, in particular, has been thrown out by her husband, who is even willing to make a large financial settlement in order to be rid of her. Sylvia learns that Miriam Aarons (Paulette Goddard) is the other woman in her husband's life, and the two women engage in a hair-pulling, kicking and screaming tussle.

The gentle Peggy Day (Joan Fontaine) has had a falling-out with her husband as well and has joined the women in Reno, where she discovers that she is pregnant. Mary advises her to phone her husband at once and acquaint him with the good news. This Peggy does, and there is a reconciliation over the phone, after which she leaves joyfully for Manhattan and her husband. Mary also gets a call from her husband, and for a moment allows herself to hope, but Stephen is only calling to see if the divorce has come through, because he has married Crystal that morning.

Mary sadly returns to New York a divorced woman. Although Crystal and Stephen are married, she is soon having an affair with a cowboy named Buck Winston, a Western radio star whom the silly Countess DeLave brought back from Reno as her new husband. Mary learns from her own young daughter that Stephen is disenchanted with Crystal and is really still in love with Mary; she also learns that Crystal is cheating on Stephen with Buck Winston. With that knowledge and a little bold faking, she blackmails Crystal. The last shot of Mary is when she goes to rejoin her husband, and his shadow appears on the stair wall as he comes to meet her. She has fought to regain the man she loves and won; there is a radiant, triumphant smile on her face.

As a movie, *The Women* enjoyed the same kind of success as the play. George Cukor, who had gained a reputation as a "woman's director," enjoyed working with his all-star cast. Norma Shearer probably had the most difficult role she ever played onscreen, in making a good woman interesting. *The Women* is one of her last outstanding features. The role of Crystal Allen was also one of Joan Crawford's final important films at M-G-M. She worked well with Cukor and respected him. She was to work with him twice again at M-G-M, in *Susan and God* (1940) and *A Woman's Face* (1941), both departures from the kind of glamour roles that had made her the shopgirl's delight. Rosalind Russell took a rare delight in throwing herself into the bitchy role of Sylvia, a prelude to the career woman comedies that were to be her specialty as a star.

Two younger actresses just beginning their careers as important players especially distinguished themselves in *The Women*. Joan Fontaine was charming, wistful, and appealing among all these cannibalistic females. Her next role after *The Women* was opposite Laurence Olivier in Hitchcock's first American film, *Rebecca* (1940), which made her a star. Similarly, Paulette Goddard, after Charles Chaplin's *Modern Times* (1936) and David O. Selznick's *The Young in Heart* (1939), shone with a luster in her wise-cracking role of Miriam, the girl who knows her way around and finally tangles with the wife whose husband she has stolen. After this film, Goddard went to Paramount, to whom Selznick sold the contract he held with her, and for the next six years she was a Paramount star, reaching her greatest popularity in the big Technicolor spectaculars of Cecil B. DeMille.

A fashion show staged in Technicolor with gowns by Adrian was another attraction of *The Women* and helped make it an unqualified box-office hit. It did not, however, gain a single Oscar nomination; 1939 was a year crowded with big hits, all potential Academy Award winners, such as *Gone with the Wind*; *Goodbye, Mr. Chips*; *Stagecoach*; *Wuthering Heights*; *Ninotchka*, and

The Wizard of Oz. In any other year *The Women* might have earned some Oscars. It was not an easy film to make, but good taste, wise showmanship, and stars in abundance supervised by a director in perfect control prevailed to make the film a hit.

Seventeen years later, in 1956, M-G-M remade *The Women* as *The Opposite Sex*, a Joe Pasternak production. The studio would have done better to reissue *The Women*, which was still remembered, liked, and considered definitive. As *The Opposite Sex*, it was no longer a stylish and scorching comedy but a tame, second-rate marital drama that featured musical numbers and men in the cast, neither of which helped. The actors were negligible, and among the actresses only Ann Sheridan and Joan Blondell managed to shine. As many times as *The Women* has been restaged as a play, only once did it have any of the glitter of its original Broadway production, and that was during World War II when it toured the European Army bases as an all-male USO production, with men in women's clothes playing the female characters. That, at least, was original and hilarious.

JOHN FORD

DRUMS ALONG THE MOHAWK

Released: 1939
Production: Raymond Griffith for Twentieth Century-Fox
Direction: John Ford
Screenplay: Lamar Trotti and Sonya Levien; based on the novel of the same
  name by Walter D. Edmonds
Cinematography: Bert Glennon
Editing: Robert Simpson
Running time: 130 minutes

> *Principal characters:*
> Gilbert Martin ....Henry Fonda
> Lana (Magdelana) Martin .... Claudette Colbert
> Mrs. McKlennar .... Edna May Oliver
> Caldwell ....John Carradine
> Reverend Rosenkrantz .... Arthur Shields
> General Nicholas Herkimer .... Roger Imhof
> Adam Helmer .... Ward Bond
> Blue Back ....Chief Big Tree

In the twelve-month period from March 2, 1939, through March 15, 1940,
John Ford released four films: *Stagecoach* (1939), *Young Mr. Lincoln* (1939),
Drums Along the Mohawk, and *The Grapes of Wrath* (1940). There is general
agreement among film scholars that *Stagecoach*, *Young Mr. Lincoln*, and
The Grapes of Wrath are major achievements in Ford's fifty-year film career.
It is generally conceded that *Drums Along the Mohawk*, does not quite
match the astonishing creativity of the other three films of this highly productive period; this is not to suggest, however, that the film is not without
significant merit. It is an exciting and vivid film—Ford's first in color—and
is directly concerned with a theme which Ford would examine many times
in the next thirty-five years—that of Americans settling the frontier.

The film begins in Albany, New York, just before the Revolutionary War
at the wedding of Lana Borst (Claudette Colbert) to Gilbert Martin (Henry
Fonda). Lana, the daughter of a wealthy Dutch burgher, is accustomed to
the comforts and pleasures of a settled town; her husband, a yeoman farmer,
will take her to his frontier homestead in the Mohawk Valley. After the
wedding, they leave her father's home in a wagon leading a cow and proceed
west into the wilderness. They spend their wedding night at an inn, where
they have a troubling encounter with a sinister man named Caldwell (John
Carradine) who is most interested in Gil's political views on the crisis between
the colonies and England.

The next evening they arrive at the cabin Gil has constructed for his bride.
It is a small, stark hovel compared to her father's brick mansion in Albany,

and Lana is shocked, thoroughly frightened, and drenched by the fierce thunderstorm through which they have driven; but when an Indian invades the cabin, she collapses in total hysteria. Gil slaps her back to sensibility, and when Lana calms down, he introduces the Indian as Blue Back (Chief Big Tree), a friend and "a better Christian than you or I."

In a series of short scenes, Lana is shown slowly adjusting to the life of a farm wife. Gil takes her to the fort, which is the center of community life; here she meets the other farm wives and watches the men drill as militia in order to defend themselves against a possible attack by the English and the Indians. That attack comes swiftly, and Lana and Gil are forced to abandon the farm and flee to the fort. The Indians are driven back by the militia at the fort, but in the process, the Martins have lost everything including the baby Lana was carrying.

Without either home or money, Gil hires himself out to work the farm of Mrs. McKlennar (Edna May Oliver), a robust and willful woman who is steadfast in her love for her late husband, Barney. She is also kind and motherly and soon looks upon Gil and Lana as her children. She waits with Lana when Gil is called to go off to fight with the militia, and when the soldiers finally return, she sets up a hospital in her kitchen. Gil, however, does not return with the militia, and Lana sets out to search for him, finding him ultimately in a ditch, unable to walk. Lana manages to bring him back to the house to tend to his wounds. As Gil awakens after a recuperative period, Lana tells him that she is expecting another child. Meanwhile, downstairs in the kitchen, General Nicholas Herkimer (Roger Imhof), the leader of the successful campaign, dies of his wounds.

In the spring, amid much drunken celebration by the father's friends, Gil and Lana's baby is born. Just as life seems to be improving for the Martins, the Indians attack once more, led by Caldwell, the Tory agent whom the Martins had met on their wedding night. During this attack, the Indians invade Mrs. McKlennar's bedroom, and in a comic battle of wills, she forces them to carry her bed out of the house which they have set on fire. Although the Martins manage to escape to the fort with the feisty widow, Mrs. McKlennar is killed in the ensuing attack on the fort.

With the fort in grave danger and the women helping the men defend it, a farmer volunteers to go for help by night. When he is quickly captured and tied to a burning haywagon by the Indians, Reverend Rosenkrantz (Arthur Shields), a militant minister, shoots him to save him from the more painful death by fire. Gil, volunteering to run for help, gets away from the fort, but is soon discovered by three Indians who start pursuing him in an epic foot race that lasts past daybreak. Gil finally is victorious in outdistancing his pursuers and returns with the soldiers, who break the siege and enter the fort to raise the new American flag—a symbol which seems to promise the settlers a new era of peace in which they can raise their families in the fertile valley.

John Ford would never again be quite so positive about the settling of the American continent; in his very next film, *The Grapes of Wrath*, he would deal with the failure of America to care for all her people, and World War II would further challenge his belief in the morality of America's past. But in 1939, he was convinced that taking the land from the Indians was both necessary and proper, and the Indians in the film are portrayed as truly savage, with no evidence of humanity. They are more like demons than men, with the only good Indian being a Christian, an emasculated comic figure who has no real function in the community.

The white settlers are portrayed as decent, moral people who yearn only for peace in order to farm their rich valley and to rear their families; they are the people who will make America great, and there is no sense that they have committed any wrong in driving the Indians from the land. Ford here presents good and evil only in shades of black and white whereas in his later films, the grays would predominate. *Drums Along the Mohawk* was Ford's last film in which everything was simple and clear-cut.

Ford was always to prefer the look of black-and-white cinematography to color, but he worked easily with color from the beginning, and his sense of color composition in *Drums Along the Mohawk* is superb. He uses color to enhance the mood of the story; the Indians, for example, are associated with fire, like demons from hell. In the foot race sequence, while the Indians seem strongest at night, Gil grows stronger as day breaks, and the arrival of a glorious Technicolor dawn signals his triumph.

Henry Fonda starred in three of the four films Ford directed during this period, but there is very little similarity in the three characters Fonda plays: Abraham Lincoln in *Young Mr. Lincoln*, Tom Joad in *The Grapes of Wrath*, and Gil Martin in *Drums Along the Mohawk*. Fonda demonstrates the depth and power of his skill and talent in all three roles, and his Gil Martin characterization portrays a stalwart young farmer sure of himself and his young country as he and his wife begin their life together. The scene in which Gil holds his newborn child for the first time is a model of acting as Fonda conveys excitement, awe, pride, embarrassment, and the burden of responsibility, in a charmingly comic manner. Edna May Oliver was nominated for Best Supporting Actress in her role as Mrs. McKlennar; her superb performance is full of nuance as well as the bolder strokes of an endearing and broadly comic character. Arthur Shields is memorable in his small role as the fighting parson, a character Ford would return to again in *The Searchers* (1956). Although Ford would return to the theme of settlers confronting the wilderness many times during his career, he never again would view their efforts with quite the same equanimity as he does in *Drums Along the Mohawk*.

THE GRAPES OF WRATH

Released: 1940
Production: Darryl F. Zanuck for Twentieth Century-Fox
Direction: John Ford (AA)
Screenplay: Nunnally Johnson; based on the novel of the same name by John Steinbeck
Cinematography: Gregg Toland
Editing: Robert Simpson
Running time: 128 minutes

Principal characters:
Tom Joad ....Henry Fonda
Ma Joad .... Jane Darwell (AA)
Pa Joad .... Russell Simpson
Grandpa Joad .... Charley Grapewin
Rosasharn .... Dorris Bowdon
Casy ....John Carradine
Muley .... John Qualen

The Grapes of Wrath, based on John Steinbeck's widely read novel about the plight of migrant workers during the Great Depression, is director John Ford's most famous work. It bears the characteristic stamp of many of his classic films; it is the story of a hapless society told with strong visual narrative technique. In this case, the microcosm of migrant workers is represented by a single family, the Joads from Oklahoma.

The film opens with the view of a small figure walking down the road against an expansive Oklahoma landscape. It is Tom Joad (Henry Fonda), recently paroled from prison. He is returning after four years to the home of his family, who are tenant farmers. Things have changed during his absence. The dust bowl conditions, combined with the advent of mechanized farming, have caused their ruthless landlords to force the Joads, as well as hundreds of their neighbors, off their lands. Tom rejoins his family just as they are preparing to leave for California, where handbills have proclaimed that there is plenty of work harvesting fruits and vegetables. The Joads—Tom, Ma (Jane Darwell), Pa (Russell Simpson), Grandma and Grandpa (Charley Grapewin), Uncle John, Tom's sister Rosasharn (Dorris Bowdon) and her new husband, and other brothers and sisters—set off in an overloaded, dilapidated truck for the "promised land" of California.

The trip itself takes its toll on the family: the elder Joads, first Grandpa, then Grandma, die en route, and pregnant Rosasharn's husband deserts her. Moreover, once in California, they find that the working conditions there in no way compare with the glowing accounts of the handbills. Thousands of migrants like the Joads have answered the call, and jobs are scarce. All are forced to live in squalid transient camps and work for starvation wages, when indeed any work is to be had. Eventually, the Joads find jobs on a ranch where some of the workers are on strike and are attempting to organize a union. During an altercation between the striking workers and a band of deputies, Casy (John Carradine), a friend of the Joads who traveled west with them, is killed. In retaliation, Tom kills one of the officers. The family flees, ending up at a clean, democratically run government camp. Contrasted with all the other places they have stayed, this camp seems almost like paradise. However, as a fugitive who has broken parole, Tom realizes the inevitable. He must leave the family and strike out on his own. In one famous scene, he bids farewell to Ma, promising to fight for social justice. As the film ends, the family continues its ever-moving search for work.

As with any film adaptation of a popular literary work, one of the first questions raised is that of the film's fidelity to its source. From the first, *The Grapes of Wrath* was praised for its faithfulness to Steinbeck's book. Indeed, despite the careful pruning of curse words from the dialogue and the compression necessary to reduce a six-hundred-page novel to standard feature length, Steinbeck's characters and events come to life on the screen with remarkable vitality. Nunnally Johnson's screenplay, which has retained Steinbeck's themes concerning human dignity and the fundamental importance of the family, along with the performances of an outstanding cast, constitute the major achievement of the film. The screenplay, however, does deemphasize some of Steinbeck's material. The angry political message of the novel, as well as its religious satire, are considerably muted on the screen. In addition, by means of a single omission and transposition the screenplay has fundamentally altered the structure of the novel and the artistic vision of its author. This was accomplished by deleting in its entirety Steinbeck's controversial ending involving the death of Rosasharn's infant and by reversing the order of two major episodes in the novel: the government camp sequence and the strike sequence in which Tom kills Casy's assassin. By concluding with the comparatively upbeat government camp episodes, the film tends to imply an optimism—not present in the novel—about the power of the American government to solve the deplorable socioeconomic problems illustrated by the odyssey of the Joads. This faith in democracy is also implicit in Ma Joad's final speech in the film: "We're the people that live! We'll go on forever because we're the people!"

The acting by the major players in *The Grapes of Wrath* is superb. Henry Fonda's portrayal of Tom Joad, who angrily insists on decency and human dignity, is one of the memorable achievements of his career. Jane Darwell's performance as the courageous Ma Joad, who struggles to preserve the family unity as the key to its survival, is sensitive and compassionate—among the strongest in the film. One of her most effective scenes is that which takes place in the predawn darkness while the family prepares for their journey

West. Ma is seen sorting through a small box of mementos. In this wordless solo scene the actress conveys a sense of the human dimensions of the past now irretrievably lost as the family leaves the farm, never to return. Charley Grapewin is effective as Grandpa Joad, who first bubbles with enthusiasm at the prospect of being able to pick grapes in California, but later balks at leaving home. Clutching a fistful of soil, he cries, "It's my dirt—no good, but it's mine!" The testimony of Muley (John Qualen) to the land—"We were born on it, and we got killed on it, died on it; even if it's no good, it's still ours"—is delivered with such skill that it becomes one of the most poignant moments in the film.

The success of the film is also due to its remarkable visual impact. Gregg Toland's evocative black-and-white cinematography gives the film an epic quality reminiscent of the great photographic record of rural America during the Depression sponsored by the United States Farm Security Administration. His strikingly photographed landscapes give graphic expression to the involvement Steinbeck's characters have with the land, and the documentary quality of the visual images succinctly underscores the hopeless conditions of the migrant workers. Productive collaboration between the photographer and the director has resulted in many images that linger in the memory: the inexorable progress of the house-demolishing tractors in Oklahoma; the journey west along Highway 66 with its montage of signs ("We fix flats," "Water 15¢ gal.," "Last chance for gas and water"); the nighttime reflection of the three riders in the truck's windshield through which can be seen the passing desert; and the subjective camera record of the arrival of the Joads at the first migrant camp as it tracks through the campground crowded with jobless, hungry people.

The Grapes of Wrath was a popular and critical success when it was first released. Both Jane Darwell and John Ford won Academy Awards for their contributions. Although it lost the Academy Award for Best Picture to Hitchcock's *Rebecca*, the film was named the outstanding film of 1940 by many other groups, including the New York Film Critics. It is historically important as one of the first Hollywood films to portray honestly and realistically one of the least admirable aspects of American society. Although the implications of the film's ending may seem too simplistic for modern audiences, *The Grapes of Wrath* remains a powerful dramatization in personal terms of a major socioeconomic problem, the rumblings of which were beginning to be heard in the 1930's.

HOW GREEN WAS MY VALLEY

Released: 1941
Production: Darryl F. Zanuck for Twentieth Century-Fox (AA)
Direction: John Ford (AA)
Screenplay: Philip Dunne; based on the novel of the same name by Richard Llewellyn
Cinematography: Arthur Miller (AA)
Editing: James B. Clark
Art direction: Richard Day and Nathan Juran (AA)
Interior decoration: Thomas Little (AA)
Running time: 118 minutes

Principal characters:
Mr. Gruffydd	Walter Pidgeon
Angharad	Maureen O'Hara
Mr. Morgan	Donald Crisp (AA)
Bronwyn	Anna Lee
Huw	Roddy McDowall
Mrs. Morgan	Sara Allgood
Ivor	Patric Knowles
Dai Bando	Rhys Williams

How Green Was My Valley was the last in a distinguished group of human dramas directed by John Ford during the late 1930's and early 1940's, including such films as *Stagecoach* (1939), *Young Mr. Lincoln* (1939), and *The Grapes of Wrath* (1940). This new film firmly established Ford's growing reputation as a successful commercial director. The film, like the novel on which it is based, became an instant popular success.

Richard Llewellyn's novel is a nostalgic remembrance of life in a late nineteenth century Welsh mining town. It is a first-person narrative, told by the aging coal miner Huw Morgan (Roddy McDowall) as he prepares to leave the valley that has been his lifelong home. The novel is essentially a collection of loosely related episodes in the lives of young Huw and his family, relying more on characterization and gentle humor than on a dramatically cohesive plot for its appeal.

The opening fifteen minutes of the film preserve the flavor of the novel almost perfectly. As the offscreen narrator (the adult Huw) begins to reminisce about his past, the audience is introduced in quick succession to young Huw, his older brothers and father (Donald Crisp) who work in the coal mine, his sister Angharad (Maureen O'Hara), and his mother (Sara Allgood). The skillfully assembled sequence establishes the peaceful order of this society in the past: the natural beauty of the valley and surrounding mountains, the community of miners who sing their way to and from work, the loving harmony of the Morgan family, the joyous wedding celebration for Huw's older brother Ivor (Patric Knowles) and his bride Bronwyn (Anna Lee). Employing vigorous narrative images with a minimum of dialogue, the sequence exemplifies one of the film's significant strengths.

The vision of this idyllic existence does not last, however. As the story moves forward, we see the gradual erosion and collapse of the Morgans' former way of life. Greedy mine owners begin to cut the wages of the miners, leading to disputes among them and eventually to a strike. Huw's older brothers angrily disagree with their authoritarian father about the strike and the formation of a miners' union and move out of the family home. Against this background of social and domestic upheaval, twelve-year-old Huw enters adolescence. One winter night Huw takes his mother up the mountainside to a secret meeting of the miners. On their return, mother and son become lost in a storm and nearly freeze to death. During his long convalescence, Huw finds a mentor in Mr. Gruffydd (Walter Pidgeon), the village minister who encourages him in his studies, and later, he attends the National School over the mountain in a neighboring valley. Mr. Gruffydd and Angharad fall in love, but because of his extreme poverty Mr. Gruffydd stoically declines to marry her, and Angharad consequently enters into an unhappy marriage with the mine owner's son. As the black slag heap from the mine spreads over the once-green and beautiful valley, we see the disintegration of Huw's world: his sensitive, musical brother Ivor dies in a mine accident, his other brothers emigrate to find work, his friend Mr. Gruffydd is forced from the valley by vicious gossip linking him with Angharad, and finally Huw's beloved father also dies in the mine.

Although considerable condensation and rearrangement were necessary to give the scenario a manageable length, the screenplay by Philip Dunne adheres to the episodic form of Llewellyn's novel. As a result, the film has a rather loose dramatic structure. Apparently as the result of a decision to cast a single young actor as Huw, the screenplay tends to emphasize the early episodes of the novel, which involve Huw at a younger age. The long section about Huw's difficulties at the National School—the taunting older students and his sadistic bully of a teacher—is included virtually intact in the film, and is one of the most satisfying sequences of the film. However, the young age of the actor is a minor disadvantage in a later episode when Huw as an older adolescent moves in with his sister-in-law Bronwyn in an attempt to take the place of his dead brother Ivor. This has considerable poignancy in the novel, but is merely amusing when played onscreen by a twelve-year-old.

The film benefits from very good actors who go a long way toward making the idealized simple folk of Huw's memory credible. Particularly effective are Donald Crisp and Sara Allgood as Huw's parents, the respective "head" and "heart" of the Morgan household; Crisp won an Academy Award for his performance as Gwilym Morgan. Roddy McDowall gives a memorable performance as the shy, sensitive Huw. In a smaller role, Rhys Williams gives a fine, lusty portrayal of Dai Bando, the professional boxer who teaches Huw to fight and who takes exquisite revenge on the teacher who beat Huw so mercilessly. The international nature of the cast, including as it does American, Irish, and Welsh actors, is responsible for a variety of vocal accents; as a result, the lilting Welsh speech is heard rather unevenly.

How Green Was My Valley is particularly distinguished by its richly detailed visual surface. The art direction was done with painstaking care. An entire mining village—stone houses, chapel, and colliery—were constructed at considerable expense for this film in California's Ventura hills. (This huge exterior set also appeared in several other films of the 1940's.) In fact, the memorable long view of the village, with the row of houses sloping uphill toward the mine at the summit, is the film's visual hallmark. Arthur Miller's superb black-and-white cinematography contributes much to this aspect of the film. His scenes are consistently arranged with care and with strong pictorial composition. In this film the camera itself moves only rarely, and then with clear, dramatic purpose: as Ivor's choir prepares to depart for a royal command performance, the camera pans slightly from the proud but troubled Mrs. Morgan in the foreground to capture a glimpse of two other sons who are leaving home to go abroad.

John Ford's direction of *How Green Was My Valley* confirmed his reputation as a master cinematic storyteller. His perfected narrative technique, weaving together a richly textured fabric of individual images and actions, nearly compensates for the rambling dramatic structure of the screenplay. His control seems to falter only in the film's occasional lapses into sentimentality. These can be partially justified, perhaps, as being inherent in the novel, as well as in the fact that overt sentimentality on the screen was then a more acceptable artistic convention than it is today.

How Green Was My Valley was a successful and highly honored film in 1941. It received Academy Awards in six categories, including Best Picture; but in making this last award, the Academy overlooked Orson Welles's innovative classic, *Citizen Kane*, choosing instead this more conventional and commercial motion picture. Nevertheless, *How Green Was My Valley* endures as a film of great visual beauty, nostalgic charm, and warm human feeling.

THE HURRICANE

Released: 1937
Production: Samuel Goldwyn for Goldwyn-United Artists; released by
  United Artists
Direction: John Ford
Screenplay: Dudley Nichols; based on Oliver H. P. Garrett's adaptation of
  the novel of the same name by Charles Nordhoff and James Norman Hall
Cinematography: Bert Glennon
Editing: Lloyd Nossler
Special effects: James Basevi
Sound: Thomas T. Moulton (AA)
Running time: 102 minutes

> *Principal characters:*
> Marama ....Dorothy Lamour
> Terangi ....Jon Hall
> Mrs. De Laage ....Mary Astor
> Father Paul .... C. Aubrey Smith
> Dr. Kersaint .... Thomas Mitchell
> Governor De Laage .... Raymond Massey
> Warden ....John Carradine

   The tensions that create rich and complex characters and relationships
between those characters, though internal in the greatest works of narrative,
are the external structural determinants of *The Hurricane*. They take the
form of a fundamental nature *versus* culture dichotomy, with the natives,
sexuality, passion, freedom, and beauty opposed to law, prison, repression,
duty, and honor. The film performs essentially the same ideological function
as most of the "South Seas" genre in that it extols the natives for their
"primitive" virtues and pits them against the corrupt ones of civilization. The
interworkings of the forces of nature and culture are thus externalized and
romanticized, and the critique of the white presence in the South Seas is
emasculated. It is rather at the level of myth or parable that *The Hurricane*
finds its expression, and it performs the myth's function of mediation and
reintegration with great beauty and emotional satisfaction.
   Like all myths, *The Hurricane* has a narrative past inscribed in its structure,
as well as a narrator whose relationship to the myth is both privileged because
he was there, and distanced because his involvement was primarily as observer
and mediator, rather than as an agent of action. The film opens as a ship in
the South Seas passes a desolate island upon which the wrath of God seems
to have been visited. Dr. Kersaint (Thomas Mitchell) begins his role as narrator, telling the others that it was once the most beautiful island in the Pacific.
The essential movement of the film has already been set forth. How did the
island become scorched earth? A dissolve into the past immediately sketches

the tensions which will come into conflict to produce the answer.

The European governor, De Laage (Raymond Massey), represents "the law" in his white coat and uncompromising posture. He is contrasted with the natives, Marama (Dorothy Lamour) and Terangi (Jon Hall), whose wedding is celebrated. The couple is identified with smooth freedom of movement, passion, and the trees and flowers of nature, as they run out of the church. Terangi is immediately linked with birds, an imagery which continues through the film. In the next of the series of oppositions, De Laage's wife (Mary Astor) arrives by ship. She is kinder and less formal than her husband primarily because, in terms of archetypes, women are always depicted as being aligned with the nature half of the nature/culture dichotomy, regardless of their cultural identification. Likewise, Marama displays a closer affinity to nature than does Terangi. His wish to wear a uniform cap and be "just like a white man" is the seed of their tragedy. The De Lagges' reserve is contrasted with the sensuality of the newly married couple. Further, Governor De Laage inhibits not only the natives but his own wife as well.

Once this is established, Terangi sails off to Tahiti, already nearly entirely corrupted by the influence of the Europeans, and leaves Marama behind. The best in Terangi, not the worst, will destroy him in this corrupt place. His imprisonment (building on his earlier linking with bird imagery) is determined through tensions constructed in the first sequence. Terangi's passionate nature, which cannot be suppressed, leads to a fight with a white man who disparages a present he has bought for Marama. The injustice which makes this a serious crime begins with the relationship of the governor with the native population. The governor as the agent of the law thus becomes Terangi's jailer, and the structural opposition is made concrete.

Terangi, with more libido than logic, cannot be confined. The visual depiction of the jail is dark and confining, with shadows, chains, and a sadistic warden (John Carradine). Terangi attempts to escape repeatedly, each time enduring savage beatings and suffering a lengthening of his sentence. Governor De Laage, who has more of a sense of honor and duty to the law than to his subjects, continues to carry out the cruelly mechanistic increasing of the sentence, in spite of the counsel of both his wife and the narrator. As a doctor, and because he is somewhat morally weak, Kersaint is closer to the European woman and to the natives than to De Laage. The source of Terangi's need becomes clear in the bird imagery and through a montage of dissolves between Marama and Terangi. His life and its sustenance are tied to his sensuality and to nature. He cannot do otherwise than try to escape, even as they systematically beat him down. The level of opposition and of injustice increases until Terangi escapes again, accidentally killing the sadistic guard. Upon hearing of the escape, the governor swears he will lock Terangi up again, but as the exhausted Terangi paddles his canoe to the island, he brings with him not the logic of the law, but the wrath of God. A hurricane hits the island. One of its first effects is to sweep the legal papers off De Laage's desk. The hurricane destroys everything on the island in one of the most impressive storm sequences on film.

At the same time, in a manifestation of the convergence of the forces of nature, a baby is born and Dr. Kersaint's role as mediator is best illustrated. He is able to give aid because he has not been acting on the side of the "antinature" forces. When the storm finally abates, many people are left alive, but no trees or buildings remain standing. Nature has destroyed the site of European cruelty, although the governor still retains the power of the legal system he represents. He has to give some indication of learning before the tension of the established opposition can relax. This is achieved, in accordance with the archetype, through his wife. Thinking her dead, he is so overjoyed when a canoe brings her to him that he runs into the water to greet her, and having been touched by it and by her, he says he will not pursue Marama and Terangi, who have given her back to him.

The romantic notion that Polynesians (like blacks) are closer to nature, simpler, more childlike, more sensual and musical than others is probably the least attractive aspect of *The Hurricane*. The abundance of destructive stereotypes in the film (the governor, the sadistic warden, and the unbelievably evil corruption of Tahiti) points up the archetypal level of the narrative, rendering it perhaps less dangerous, but no less savory. It is still the Europeans who can learn. They can take on some of the characteristics of the natives without losing their sophistication. The natives, who cannot learn and retain their sensuality, are destroyed by the contact with the developed culture, but not *vice versa*. A European has the role of narrator/mediator who can somehow be in touch with both poles. Further, as a doctor he is the agent of the life born of the storm. These are not agreeable aspects of the film, but at the level of myth *The Hurricane* delineates its task and performs it with amazing clarity, satisfaction, and grace. Despite the simplicity of the binary oppositions, Ford fills the space in between with life and emotional color, and the film is richly successful on that level.

A remake of the film by Dino de Laurentiis appeared in 1979, but it was not successful on either a critical or a financial level.

THE INFORMER

Released: 1935
Production: Cliff Reid for RKO/Radio
Direction: John Ford (AA)
Screenplay: Dudley Nichols; based on the novel of the same name by Liam O'Flaherty
Cinematography: Joseph H. August
Editing: George Hively
Music: Max Steiner (AA)
Running time: 91 minutes

Principal characters:
Gypo Nolan .... Victor McLaglen (AA)
Mary McPhillip .... Heather Angel
Dan Gallagher .... Preston Foster
Katie Madden .... Margot Grahame
Frankie McPhillip .... Wallace Ford
Mrs. McPhillip .... Una O'Connor
Terry .... J. M. Kerrigan
Bartly Mulholland .... Joseph Sauers
Tommy Connor .... Neil Fitzgerald
Peter Mulligan .... Donald Meek
The Blind Man .... D'Arcy Corrigan
Dennis Daly .... Gaylord Pendleton

The Informer is one of John Ford's darkest dramas both thematically and visually. He did not allow humor or light moments, which might have diluted the intensity of the story, to intrude on his tapestry. The film takes place in a single night, while shadows and fog surround the characters as they walk the streets. Even when the action moves off the cobblestones, the darkness seems to follow almost as if Gypo Nolan's brooding mind dims the lighting. Ford uses this technique to punctuate Nolan's increasing isolation induced by internal and external forces, both leading to the inevitable dead end.

The film is a single character study focusing on Gypo Nolan, brilliantly interpreted by Victor McLaglen, who was a regular of John Ford's stock company. McLaglen, almost fifty at the time, could alternately be tender and brutish, scheming and confused, running a wide range of mental attitudes. His performance was rewarded with an Academy Award for Best Actor that year.

The film is set in Dublin in 1922. It is a strife-torn city in the throes of the Sinn Fein Rebellion. Gypo Nolan, a simple-minded brute of a man, wanders the fog-shrouded streets and stops to stare at a police poster which proclaims a twenty-pound reward for information leading to the capture of Frankie McPhillip (Wallace Ford), a rebel leader and friend of Nolan. Nolan angrily rips down the notice and throws it into the street, but the poster, seeming to have a life of its own, persistently clings to his leg until he finally frees himself of it.

Later Nolan encounters his streetwalker girl friend, Katie Madden (Margot Grahame), who is being propositioned by a well-dressed man. Nolan, infuriated, throws the man to the ground, only to be condemned by Katie, who is penniless. A nearby window sign advertises passage to America for ten pounds, a sum that appears to be out of reach of both Katie and Nolan. The girl torments Nolan, reminding him that for twenty pounds they both could escape the circle of poverty and go to America. They argue and Katie walks away, exclaiming that she cannot afford his fine principles.

Fugitive Frankie McPhillip, dodging the British street patrols, breaks his six-month forced absence and returns to the city to see his mother (Una O'Connor) and sister, Mary (Heather Angel). Frankie arrives at Dunboy House, a cheap tavern, where he meets Nolan, who tells Frankie that he has been thrown out of the rebel organization. A traitor had to be silenced, he explains, and the members drew straws to determine who would carry out the execution imposed by the rebel court. Nolan had drawn the short straw but did not have the heart to kill the man when the victim pleaded for his life. His release of the condemned man disgraced Nolan with the rebels, and he was mistrusted by the British; consequently, he has been unable to find work and is poverty-stricken.

Frankie promises to try to help his friend. He asks Nolan to check and see if the Black and Tans (British soldiers) are watching his mother's home. Nolan, obsessed with getting the money to pay for passage to America for Katie and himself, sees Frankie's reward as the solution. He tells the wanted man that the route to his mother is clear, but as soon as McPhillip leaves, he goes to police headquarters and betrays his friend. Shortly after Frankie is reunited with his mother and Mary, the soldiers arrive and break down the front door. Frankie, trapped, opens fire on them and is killed in the ensuing gunfight. Nolan, waiting at police headquarters, learns of Frankie's death. He receives his reward and is ushered out the back door. Startled by a stranger, Nolan almost strangles him until he recognizes that the man is blind. As he walks through the swirling fog, Nolan begins to realize the consequences of what he has done.

He wanders into a bar and orders a drink. Katie finds him there and is surprised when the bartender brings Nolan his change. Nolan tells her that he has robbed an American sailor. Katie, who is in love with Nolan, apologizes for their earlier argument and returns to her flat to await him while he goes to the McPhillip home to attend Frankie's wake. The combination of Nolan's conscience and his drinking make him a pathetic figure when he arrives to express his condolences to Mrs. McPhillip. Some coins fall from his pocket and they arouse the suspicion of two members of the organization who are present. Bartly Mulholland (Joseph Sauers) and Tommy Connor (Neil Fitzgerald) approach Nolan and tell him that Dan Gallagher (Preston Foster), the leader of the rebels, wants to talk to him. They escort Nolan to rebel headquarters, where Gallagher asks him for his help in uncovering the identity of the informer responsible for McPhillip's death. He promises Nolan reinstatement in the organization if he will help them. Nolan seizes on the opportunity and accuses the local tailor, Peter Mulligan (Donald Meek), claiming he saw the man enter the Tan headquarters. He concocts a motivating story about McPhillip and the tailor's sister. Gallagher orders a court of inquiry for 1:30 that morning at the ammunition dump and tells Nolan to be present.

Following Nolan's departure, Mulholland and Connor express their belief that he is the informer, but Gallagher does not accept the accusation, knowing that Nolan was Frankie's friend. Mulholland follows Nolan as he goes from bar to bar, trying to erase the guilt of what he has done. A street brawl in which Nolan knocks two men unconscious, one of them a policeman, promotes him as a hero to the crowd. Reveling in this newfound admiration and spurred on by Terry (J. M. Kerrigan), an opportunistic member of the crowd, Nolan treats the assemblage to fish and chips with part of the reward money. Later, Terry and Nolan leave the pub together. Terry, mistakenly believing that Nolan has expended his resources, turns on him. Now drunk, Nolan is confused when Terry tells him that he only accompanied him because of his money and now that it is gone he has no further use for him. Nolan then pulls out his bankroll and Terry quickly changes his attitude once again, becoming Nolan's "good friend." Terry persuades Nolan to enter a high-class after-hours club. The initial reaction to Nolan and his friend evaporates when he shows the owner and guests his money.

Meanwhile, Dan Gallagher, who is in love with Mary McPhillip, visits the girl at her home to offer his sympathy on the death of her brother and to continue the investigation into who was responsible for Frankie's death. He questions her about the events leading up to the police raid and learns that Frankie had spoken only to Nolan before coming home. He then asks Mary to come to the court of inquiry later that night.

In a drunken stupor, Nolan is beginning to lose his grip on reality. He mistakes one of the other guests for Katie and eventually gives the woman part of his reward money so she can return to London. Terry is extolling the virtues of "King Gypo" and encouraging him to buy drinks for the other patrons when Mulholland, who has been following Nolan on his spending spree, arrives at the club with two other men. Mulholland tells Nolan that it is time for the court to convene. The group leaves, but they meet Katie a short distance away. Nolan gives her a five-pound note, the last of his money. Realizing that Nolan is in trouble, she lets the note fall to the gutter.

Gallagher, Mary, and the other members of the court are waiting when Nolan and his fellows arrive at the ammunition dump. Nolan is too drunk

to understand why Mulligan is present and embraces the man he has accused
before he realizes what is happening. Mulligan, a meek, mild-mannered man,
is asked to give an account of his actions from noon that day. The tailor's
story exonerates him while it punctuates Nolan's deception. Gallagher gives
Mulligan some money, apologizes, and sends him home. Mary then tells the
court that Nolan had seen Frankie at the Dunboy House that night. Gallagher
talleys a list of Nolan's expenditures, which total twenty pounds. Confused
and despondent, Nolan confesses that he betrayed his friend. Mulholland is
about to shoot Nolan, but Mary's scream prevents him. Gallagher orders
Nolan locked up while they draw straws for the man who will carry out the
sentence. Mary pleads with Gallagher that the killings should stop, but he
explains that while Nolan lives they are all in danger, because Nolan's own
fears will eventually drive him to the authorities. Young Dennis Daly (Gaylord
Pendleton) loses the draw and opens the door to Nolan's prison. Nolan,
however, through his amazing strength, manages to escape through the ceiling. Gallagher orders the other men to search the city and prevent the fugitive
from reaching the Black and Tan headquarters.

Nolan, however, seeks refuge with Katie at her apartment. He tells her
that he betrayed McPhillip so they could use the reward money to go to
America. The girl is shocked and blames herself for driving the man she loves
to betray a friend. Like a small, frightened child, Nolan falls asleep by Katie's
fireplace.

Katie goes to the McPhillip home where Dan is visiting Mary. She entreats
them to spare Nolan's life, but Gallagher must still refuse since there are
other lives at stake. Katie inadvertently tells them where Nolan is hiding and
is overheard by Mulholland. Daly and two other men arrive at Katie's flat,
guns in hand. They break in, but Nolan manages to fight them off and rushes
out the front door. Mulholland is waiting for him and empties his revolver
into the ill-fated informer. Mortally wounded, Nolan stumbles to a church
where Frankie's mother silently prays. He confesses to her that he betrayed
her son and asks her forgiveness. The old woman, tears running down her
cheeks, forgives the informer, and Nolan dies in front of the altar.

There is very little violent action in *The Informer*, and the film is almost
devoid of villains. The character of Terry, whose chameleonlike loyalties
change with the social or political spectrum of his environment, is the only
character who elicits a negative response. Ford does not even treat the British
as the brazen interlopers he could have, nor do we get to meet them on a
personal basis. The repression against which Dan Gallagher and the other
rebels are fighting is shown only in the presence of the street patrols and the
dark shadows featured in the effective silhouettes of the titles. Consequently,
all attention is centered on Nolan as villain-hero, a loyal traitor.

The trio of women who at first seem to be only peripheral characters are
actually second only to Nolan; they directly or indirectly initiate most of the

action. Two of them try to give Nolan life but gain him death, and the third offers him redemption. Katie unwittingly is the cause of Nolan's crime and, although she begs for his life, she causes his entrapment. The virginal Mary also pleads for Nolan, but only after she has given the evidence which condemns him. Only Mrs. McPhillip redeems Nolan, giving him consolation and spiritual life as he dies at her feet.

The Informer is one of Ford's most award-honored films, although it is not one of his best achievements. The film earned four Academy Awards: Ford for Best Direction, Dudley Nichols for Best Screenplay, Max Steiner for Best Musical Score, and Victor McLaglen for Best Actor. These awards helped to elevate Ford to a position of importance and gained him recognition as a major Hollywood talent.

THE LAST HURRAH

Released: 1958
Production: John Ford for Columbia
Direction: John Ford
Screenplay: Frank S. Nugent; based on the novel of the same name by Edwin O'Connor
Cinematography: Charles Lawton, Jr.
Editing: Jack Murray
Running time: 121 minutes

Principal characters:
Frank Skeffington .... Spencer Tracy
Adam Caulfield .... Jeffrey Hunter
Mave Caulfield .... Dianne Foster
John Gorman .... Pat O'Brien
Norman Cass, Sr. .... Basil Rathbone
The Cardinal .... Donald Crisp
Cuke Gillen .... James Gleason
Ditto Boland .... Edward Brophy
Amos Force .... John Carradine
Sam Weinberg .... Ricardo Cortez
Gert Minihan .... Anna Lee
Delia Boylan .... Jane Darwell

At the end of his career, John Ford directed a series of films that are similar in mood. Each film is a reexamination of plots and themes that Ford had considered in films throughout his career. For example, *Two Rode Together* (1961) and *Sergeant Rutledge* (1960) deal directly with racial prejudice, a subject Ford had touched obliquely earlier in his career, while *The Man Who Shot Liberty Valance* (1962) is Ford's final statement on the settling of the West. *Cheyenne Autumn* (1964) looks at the price of that settlement from the Indians' point of view. *The Last Hurrah*, like those films, also deals with the end of an era in which machine politics dominated by Irish-American ward bosses are supplanted by more modern politicians campaigning on television. It is an era Ford had known as a child in Portland, Maine, where his father had been a ward leader. *The Last Hurrah* is Ford's fond farewell to a past of better days.

Frank Skeffington (Spencer Tracy) is the four-term mayor of a "large, Northeastern city" (surely Boston) who is about to embark on the campaign for a fifth term. Knowing that it will certainly be his last campaign, Skeffington invites his nephew, Adam Caulfield (Jeffrey Hunter), to accompany him on his rounds and to observe the workings of the campaign. Adam is a newspaper reporter who works for one of his uncle's staunchest opponents, Amos Force (John Carradine) while Adam's father-in-law is another enemy of the Mayor. But in spite of these handicaps, Skeffington is closer to Adam than to his only son, who is a dilettante oblivious to his father's need for filial respect and affection. Skeffington is a widower who mourns his wife deeply and pays homage to her memory by placing each morning a single rose before her portrait, which dominates the grand staircase in the Mayor's residence. Although he is a sportswriter, not a political reporter, Adam accepts his uncle's offer.

Along with Adam we meet Skeffington's cronies and syncophants and learn of some of the more dubious practices of ward politics. Each time Adam expresses doubts about the deals and the chicanery, Skeffington's campaign manager John Gorman (Pat O'Brien) blithely reassures him with the most favorable interpretation of these practices. It is obvious that Skeffington is sincerely concerned for the welfare of his constituents, but the means by which he assists the voters are somewhat less than ethical in every case.

In a key scene in the film, Skeffington and Adam attend the wake of Knocko Minihan. The deceased was not a popular figure in the ward, but the Mayor's presence draws a large crowd of mourners. The Mayor congratulates the widow (Anna Lee) on the large number of people paying tribute to her husband and he also gives Mrs. Minihan one thousand dollars with the transparent explanation that his wife had left it to Mrs. Minihan in her will. Skeffington then gathers his henchmen in a back room to discuss campaign strategy, an action that discomforts Adam, but which Gorman explains with a comment that politics are a lot more cheerful than death.

Skeffington next invades the staid Plymouth Club to confront his strongest enemies, Norman Cass (Basil Rathbone) and Amos Force, in order to persuade them to lend money to the city for low-cost housing for the poor. When they refuse, Skeffington devises a plot involving Cass's idiot son. In order to avoid the embarrassment of Skeffington's plans for his son, Cass agrees to lend the money but also promises to support Skeffington's opponent, Kevin McCluskey, in the election.

With Cass's support, the effective use of television, and Skeffington's clinging to outmoded methods of campaigning, McCluskey defeats the Mayor, much to the surprise and horror of his loyal supporters. As a McCluskey victory parade passes in the background, Skeffington walks home alone through a darkened park, his last hurrah at an end. As he climbs the stairs past the portrait of his wife, the Mayor suffers a heart attack. Now confined to bed, Skeffington receives a stream of old friends and a few enemies who come to pay their last respects. He greets them all with humor and affection. His son is overcome with the imminent loss of his father, and once again is not there when his father needs him. Only Adam and his wife (Dianne Foster) are with Skeffington at the end. On their way out, Adam pauses to place a rose in front of the portrait as the old politicians file by to say farewell to their friend and leader.

The Last Hurrah is a film infused with nostalgia and affection. The sense of the past is palpable as Skeffington moves through his last campaign saying farewell to old friends, having one last fight with old enemies, and revisiting the scenes of happier days. There is affection in Ford's portrait of men who are motivated by their sense of duty to the voters and by their need to stay in office even if their methods are slightly illegal. The Protestant Bishop says that he prefers the engaging scoundrel (Skeffington) to the fool (McCluskey), and so does Ford. Ford clearly prefers the morally ambivalent men of the past with their concern for people to media manipulators unaware that the voters are people like Mrs. Minihan and not numbers on a tote board.

In addition to mourning the passing of an era, Ford touches on darker themes that intensify the conflict between Skeffington and Cass. Adam learns that his employer's grandfather had once fired Skeffington's grandmother for stealing two bananas from the kitchen where she worked as Force's maid. This evidence of racial and religious prejudice adds weight to the conflict between Irish Catholic immigrants and entrenched Puritan wealth. Ford had encountered that prejudice as a boy in Maine. He reminds us that while his politicians are not saints, they are preferable to a rigid establishment that cares little for the people Skeffington represents.

As Frank Skeffington, Spencer Tracy is the center of the film. In his portrait of the mayor we recognize a man worthy of the respect and affection the other characters have for him. Tracy is able to portray subtly a man who is aware of the coming defeat, a man drawn to the past and slowly disengaging himself from the present. His slow walk through the park is the walk of a man both defeated and relieved. In the part of Ditto Boland, Edward Brophy stands out as well-meaning but inept duplicate of the Mayor, so devoted to Skeffington that he apes his every move. But it is John Ford who is the controlling presence in the film. Like most of his films in this period, *The Last Hurrah* is infused with a sense of endings and summations. Like Skeffington, Ford was more interested in the past than the new, plastic present. The men of the past were worthy of respect even though they were all too human

THE LONG VOYAGE HOME

Released: 1940
Production: Walter Wanger for Argosy Productions; released by United Artists
Direction: John Ford
Screenplay: Dudley Nichols; based on the one-act plays *Bound East for Cardiff*, *In the Zone*, *The Long Voyage Home*, and *The Moon of the Caribbees* by Eugene O'Neill
Cinematography: Gregg Toland
Editing: Sherman Todd
Art direction: James Basevi
Running time: 105 minutes

Principal characters:

Driscoll	Thomas Mitchell
Ole Olson	John Wayne
Smitty	Ian Hunter
Cocky	Barry Fitzgerald
Captain	Wilfrid Lawson
Freda	Mildred Natwick
Axel	John Qualen
Yank	Ward Bond
Donkey Man	Arthur Shields

The fog and the storm are the main characters in this expressionistic film, Eugene O'Neill's favorite among the films made of his works. The men of the ship *Glencairn* are obsessed with (and, each in his own way, in search of) death. Set at the beginning of World War II, the surface narrative concerns of *The Long Voyage Home* are so tangential to the central obsession with death that the viewer is left with an impression of moody, sensual shots rather than the story. The dangerous journey to England on a ship loaded with ammunition, the "evidence" that Smitty (Ian Hunter) is a traitor, and the strafing of the ship by an enemy plane are incidental to the deaths of Yank (Ward Bond) and Smitty, Donkey Man's severance of his ties with land, and above all, the love/hate relationship the men have with their fate.

Death is a nearly physical presence in *The Long Voyage Home*, and is so sensually compelling that the men ignore the beautiful women who come onboard in favor of the rum they bring. Smitty especially, who has already given up a family and a commission and forsaken his homeland (England) forever for drink, moodily brushes off the girl who responds to his unhappiness and wants to be "his girl." The others grab the women the way they would pick up a football, then put them down to fight one another. Finally a man is cut with a bottle, and the Captain (Wilfrid Lawson) stops the fight and sends the women off without pay, since they incited the fight by bringing the rum. This is the first instance in which the men are seen to have virtually no control over the events of their lives. If certain events are put into motion, others will follow. Central to this, of course, is the notion that it is their fate to ship out continually when all they want most is to go "home."

Gregg Toland's dark, expressionistic, foggy, and long depth-of-field cinematography provides the sensual element for the men that the women cannot. Through its moodiness and darkness, which often reduces the men to faceless, nameless shadows, this sensuality is linked with death. The most compelling conversation is between Donkey Man (Arthur Shields)—a ghost figure, caught between the life of the land and the loss of memory he yearns for—and Smitty, when they speak of death in the soft, dark night during the dance with the women. Another compelling scene occurs when Driscoll (Thomas Mitchell) reads Smitty's letters and Ford cuts to strange and exciting close-ups of the men with half and one-quarter light on their faces. Smitty is also shot in close-up, gagged and in anguish as his living death is revealed to them all. At the end of this sequence, Driscoll turns out the light and chases the men away; Smitty returns to the deck in silhouette and answers Ole's call of "All's well."

To say that there is a strong current of homosexuality in *The Long Voyage Home* might be true. Certainly the men demonstrate stronger and more emotional attachments to one another than to any women. The exception is Smitty, who still loves his wife and family he nevertheless left forever, but Donkey Man points out that Smitty is different from the very first—something on land still has a hold on him. Yank's death scene with Driscoll could be seen as homosexual, as Yank recalls women they have known as indications of their bond to each other; but these homosexual implications fail to get to the heart of the film. The overhead shots of the men lying quietly on the deck are indeed the most sensual in the film, but more central is their yearning toward their own destruction. They are each simply going through the cycle—however many times it takes for them to be released from it—into death.

Ole (John Wayne) is the innocent. Young, healthy, and not subject to the others' passions for destruction, he functions rather like the opposite of a sacrificial lamb for the rest of the men. He does not die that they may live; rather, he lives that they might die. To get him off the ship and home to his farm is the goal of them all; it will redeem them indirectly in a way they are incapable of accomplishing for themselves. Ole is truly different and must be saved. He does not take part in the drinking, the dancing, and more importantly, in the "trial" of Smitty. Perhaps Ole can go home because he does not have the memories that plague the rest of them; the land is the home of memories and pain, and Donkey Man says it must be given up. Only Ole, through his very health and simplicity (which make him less interesting than the bitter, driven Smitty or any of the others), can actually make "the long voyage home." For the others, "home" is death.

Ole's innocence makes him vulnerable, and the skipper of the *Almindra* picks him out of the group to be shanghaied. When he is, it is the responsibility of all the men to save him, but this is not done without cost. Once Ole is delivered into the jaws of death—as indeed he would have been since the *Almindra* is torpedoed—the men must provide a substitute to free him. Driscoll takes his place when he pauses to gloat over the rescue, and sails off on the "devil ship." The interrelatedness of Ole going home, Driscoll sailing to his death on the *Almindra*, and the rest of the crew returning to the *Glencairn* is not accidental, but causal.

The men are propelled by a fate which causes them to ship out continually. They are shanghaied, they spend all their money, and however it happens, they find themselves at sea again. Only Donkey Man has given up the struggle to go back to the land, yet none of the men—except Ole, with the help of all of them—is able to return. Indeed, watching the last thirty minutes of the film, in which the men get drunk and are led around by the agent of the *Almindra* knowing full well that this is a repetition that will get them all (Ole included) back on ship, is a difficult experience. The men are too helpless— or too unwilling—to break out of this destructive pattern which will result in their deaths. It is not that they are incapable of struggle, but that the structure of the film makes such struggle useless. Death is expressed in the dark, foggy streets and is ultimately more attractive than the life of the land, contaminated by women, war, and families. They are drawn, through booze and fights, away from women and land, by the sensual expression of death in the film. Rather than struggle against their fate, they embrace it.

THE MAN WHO SHOT LIBERTY VALANCE

Released: 1962
Production: Willis Goldbeck for Ford Productions; released by Paramount
Direction: John Ford
Screenplay: Willis Goldbeck and James Warner Bellah; based on a story by
  Dorothy M. Johnson
Cinematography: William H. Clothier
Editing: Otho Lovering
Costume design: Edith Head
Running time: 122 minutes

> *Principal characters:*
> Ranse Stoddard .... James Stewart
> Tom Doniphon .... John Wayne
> Hallie Stoddard .... Vera Miles
> Liberty Valance .... Lee Marvin
> Dutton Peabody .... Edmond O'Brien
> Link Appleyard .... Andy Devine
> Nora Ericson .... Jeanette Nolan
> Peter Ericson .... John Qualen
> Pompey .... Woody Strode

John Ford repeatedly reexamined the impact of civilization on the American frontier in the many Westerns he filmed throughout his long and distinguished career. From an early belief in the value of progress, expressed in *The Iron Horse* (1924), Ford's views both broadened and grew more skeptical over the years. With the exception of *Cheyenne Autumn* (1964), in which he watches the encroachment of civilization from an Indian perspective, *The Man Who Shot Liberty Valance* is Ford's final statement on the gains and losses brought about by the taming of the West. That statement is ambiguous and nostalgic, contradictory and poignant, a multilayered work of art that is Ford's last masterpiece.

The film begins with a shot of a train moving through a pastoral Western landscape. The train pulls into Shinbone, a prosperous and substantial town, where a distinguished, elderly couple disembarks. They are met by Link Appleyard (Andy Devine), an equally aged man who, we learn, used to be the Marshal of Shinbone. The couple is Senator Ranse Stoddard (James Stewart) and his wife Hallie (Vera Miles), returning from Washington D.C. to attend a funeral.

As Link escorts the Stoddards to the undertaker's office, a cub reporter tells his editor of their presence in town. The editor rushes after the Stoddards and demands to know why Senator Stoddard has returned to attend the funeral of the town recluse and derelict, Tom Doniphon (John Wayne). At a sign of consent from his wife, Stoddard agrees to explain the reason for their trip.

As the flashback begins, a stagecoach traveling at night is stopped by bandits. The passengers are forced to climb out of the stage, and we recognize one of them as the young Ranse Stoddard. He attempts to protect one of the women passengers and is knocked to the ground by the leader of the gang. When he tells the robbers that he is a lawyer, the leader responds by telling Stoddard that he will teach him Western law; he then savagely beats him, shreds his law books, and leaves him for dead.

Tom Doniphon, a local rancher, and his black worker Pompey (Woody Strode) find Stoddard. They bring him to Shinbone, a raw frontier village, and ask Hallie, a vivacious energetic woman, and the Ericsons (Jeanette Nolan and John Qualen), owners of the town cafe, to tend to Stoddard's wounds. It is obvious that Tom is strongly attracted to Hallie, and, in spite of his injuries, so is Ranse. When he recovers, Ranse takes a job washing dishes in the Ericsons' kitchen since there is little need for a lawyer in Shinbone.

A few evenings later, Tom brings Hallie a cactus rose, the only flower that blooms in the desert surrounding Shinbone. Hallie is touched by the gift, but Ranse asks her if she has ever seen a real rose. He promises that someday real roses will bloom in the desert if a dam can be built to irrigate the land. Ranse then agrees to serve some steaks to waiting customers in the dining room, where he encounters Liberty Valance (Lee Marvin).

When Rance recognizes the handle of Liberty's whip as the one used to beat him, he knows that Liberty is the man who held up the stage. Liberty also recognizes Ranse, and laughs at his long white apron. As Ranse advances through the room, Liberty trips him, causing him to fall in a pile of steaks, potatoes, and gravy. Liberty and his cohorts continue to mock him, until Tom Doniphon announces, "That's my steak, Valance. Pick it up!" Liberty rises, faces Tom, and moves his hand towards his gun. Tom also prepares to draw if Liberty does not pick up the steak. Ranse then rises, picks up the steak, and says, "Everybody in this country kill-crazy?" thus ending the confrontation of Tom and Liberty. Back in the kitchen Tom advises Ranse to get a gun or leave the country. Ranse refuses to do either, believing in the law that he hopes to bring to Shinbone.

In order to build the foundation for a community governed by law and not by violence, Ranse opens a school in the back room of the Shinbone *Star*, the weekly newspaper written, edited, and published by Dutton Peabody (Edmond O'Brien). The first class illustrates the ethnic diversity of Shinbone's citizens. Swedish immigrant Nora Ericson, the children of Link Appleyard's Mexican wife, Doniphon's black servant Pompey, and Hallie are all eager students. A lesson on the meaning of the Constitution is interrupted by Tom Doniphon, who orders Pompey back to work and warns Ranse that Liberty Valance is headed towards town. Although Tom also orders Hallie back to the kitchen, saying that she has no business in the classroom, Hallie angrily defies Tom; this is the first indication that she is becoming less attracted to him. Later, after Ranse demonstrates his ineptitude with a pistol, Hallie forces Tom to promise her that he will look after Ranse.

Shinbone becomes sufficiently civilized to hold a town meeting in the saloon in order to elect representatives to a territorial convention. Tom Doniphon enforces both order and the closing of the bar, much to Peabody's dismay. Tom then turns the meeting over to Ranse. Liberty Valance arrives and demands to be elected so that he can represent the interests of the ranchers at the convention. Bolstered by Tom's presence, the men of the town defy Valance and elect Ranse and Dutton Peabody to represent Shinbone.

After much celebrating, Mr. Peabody returns to the newspaper office, where Liberty Valance is waiting for him. Valance brutally beats Peabody and then destroys the office. Valance next returns to the saloon where he issues a challenge for Ranse to meet him in the street for the inevitable gunfight. Hearing what Valance has done to Peabody, Ranse accepts the challenge. Ranse is immediately wounded in the arm; Valance torments him further by deliberately missing him as he advances towards the gunfighter. Valance tires of taunting his opponent and says that the next shot will be for real. As Valance takes aim, so does Ranse; both fire, and Valance falls dead.

The cheering townspeople escort Ranse back to Hallie, who dresses his wound. As they begin to express their feelings for each other, Tom enters, understands what is happening, and leaves, apologizing to Hallie for being too late to help Ranse fight Liberty Valance. He goes to the saloon and gets drunk; later, Pompey takes him home, where Tom sets fire to the room that he has been adding to the house for Hallie.

The scene shifts to the Territorial Convention. Although the ranchers of the territory are opposed to statehood, which they consider would weaken their control of the territory, the townspeople and small farmers outnumber them, and Ranse is nominated to carry the majority's hopes for statehood to Congress. Ranse, however, is very disturbed when he is nominated as the man who shot Liberty Valance; he attempts to leave the convention hall, but is stopped by Tom. Ranse tells Tom that he cannot accept an office which he has won because he killed another man. Tom, however, reveals that Ranse did not kill Liberty; he explains that he himself was across the street in an alley and had fired his rifle as Liberty had fired. He tells Ranse to accept the nomination for Hallie. The flashback ends as Ranse accepts the advice and returns to the hall as Tom leaves.

Senator Stoddard asks the editor if he intends to print the story. The editor replies that he will not; "This is the West, sir. When the legend becomes fact, print the legend." Ranse, getting up to leave the undertaker's, notices that Hallie has placed a cactus rose on Tom's coffin. The couple return to the station and board the Eastbound train. Hallie remarks on how lush the country surrounding Shinbone has become. As Ranse is about to reply, the conductor comes forward to offer his assistance to Senator and Mrs. Stoddard. After all, he says, "nothing is too good for the man what shot Liberty Valance," and the film ends.

Ford had, once before, dealt with the theme of "town-taming" in *My Darling Clementine* (1946). Unlike *The Man Who Shot Liberty Valance*, however, *My Darling Clementine* is a more positive approach to the process of bringing law and order to the West. In it, the hero is civilized along with the town, and Ford does not concern himself with the inevitable losses that such an advance entails. In *The Man Who Shot Liberty Valance*, Ford recognizes the necessity of progress. Shinbone clearly cannot function forever in the grip of the kind of violence personified by Liberty Valance. However, Ford has come to recognize that a price must be paid for the eradication of the violent past. If Liberty Valance can no longer control Shinbone, then neither can Tom Doniphon. In a past where force was law, strong men were truly free to live as they wished so long as they were brave enough to protect their freedom. But weak men suffered, and demanded the protection of the law. Tom and Liberty both knew that their way of life would end when Ranse arrived in Shinbone.

Ford also shows that, apart from the personal sacrifice of Tom Doniphon, the town also loses a sense of community as the more civilized order is introduced. Without law, the townspeople must depend on one another for help and protection; but with law, they no longer need one another's assistance. In a sense, Ranse Stoddard threatens the community with his law books as much as Liberty Valance threatens it with his guns. Ford mourns the passing of this sense of self-reliance and community spirit just as he celebrates the sacrifice of men such as Tom Doniphon—men of integrity and vision who helped to advance the civilizing of the West even though they knew that their way of life would disappear in the process.

The Man Who Shot Liberty Valance is totally dominated by John Ford. Even though John Wayne and James Stewart perform with the professional skill of artists at the peak of their careers, these actors, as well as the other familiar faces in Ford's stock company, are subordinate to the director's understanding of the impact of the events in Shinbone. Known for his expansive Western landscapes, Ford confines his actors to the studio set of a frontier town. Accustomed by 1961 to color cinematography, Ford's audience watches a black-and-white film. Whereas in the past Ford had used direct and simple shots with little camera movement, he now uses many night shots with expressionistic lighting, and many more close-ups than in most of his previous films. Ford uses his mastery of the medium to convey his dark and brooding reflection on the price America had paid to achieve the conquest of the howling wilderness.

MISTER ROBERTS

Released: 1955
Production: Leland Hayward for Warner Bros.
Direction: John Ford and Mervyn LeRoy
Screenplay: Frank S. Nugent and Joshua Logan; based on Thomas Heggen's
   and Joshua Logan's stage adaptation of the novel of the same name by
   Thomas Heggen
Cinematography: Winton Hoch
Editing: Jack Murray
Running time: 123 minutes

> *Principal characters:*
> Lieutenant Douglas Roberts ....Henry Fonda
> Ensign Pulver ....Jack Lemmon (AA)
> The Captain .... James Cagney
> Doc .... William Powell
> Lieutenant Ann Girard ....Betsy Palmer

Mister Roberts is a story about camaraderie in the South Pacific during the waning days of World War II. The film is an odd mixture of comedy and tragedy that finally succeeds because of fine performances by a veteran cast. It is a war film in which combat is conspicuous by its absence, and in which men display their courage not by fighting the enemy but by defying the tyrannical captain of an American ship.

James Cagney plays the priggish Captain of the *U.S.S. Reluctant*, a cargo ship whose function is to supply combat ships with soap, paint, toilet paper, and other extraneous amenities. Such a mission is perfectly suited to the Captain's personality, but his executive officer, Lieutenant Douglas Roberts (Henry Fonda), chafes at the ignominy of spending the war as a cargomaster. Roberts is an earnest man who yearns for the opportunity to distinguish himself in combat. He is not driven by a comic-book desire for personal glory, nor is he particularly bloodthirsty. Rather, he believes that only by risking his life can he be of proper service to his country. Roberts is the only man aboard the *Reluctant* who takes his duties seriously, and this conscientiousness makes him too valuable for the Captain to let go. Thus Mister Roberts' repeated requests for transfer to a combat ship are routinely denied.

The symbol of the Captain's tyranny is a tiny palm tree which he keeps in a bucket of soil on the deck of the *Reluctant*. The tree was awarded to him as captain of the most efficient cargo ship in the Pacific theater (thanks primarily to the efforts of Mister Roberts), and is the only mark of distinction in the Captain's otherwise lackluster record. It figures prominently in the crew's attempts to break free of the Captain's iron rule.

The other two major characters in the film are Doc (William Powell), the

Reluctant's physician, and Ensign Pulver (Jack Lemmon). Doc is an older man whose primary duty seems to be keeping the bored crew of the *Reluctant* from overflowing the sickbay with their imaginary illnesses. He also acts as a confidant to Doug Roberts. Where Doc's personality complements that of Roberts, Ensign Pulver's is its antithesis. Unlike Roberts, Pulver is the laziest man on the ship, and is delighted to spend the war in the safety of his bunk on the *Reluctant*; he is also reputedly the greatest romancer. He is forever planning (and deferring action on) numerous pranks to play on the strict Captain. Despite their differences, however, Ensign Pulver and Mister Roberts are friends.

The film turns on the efforts of Roberts, Doc, and Pulver to break the Captain's ludicrous but nonetheless tyrannical hold over the ship's crew. The focus of these efforts is twofold: Roberts' attempts to transfer to a combat ship and the crew's desire for shore leave after more than a year aboard the *Reluctant*. As the film opens, the *Reluctant* is anchored off an island. The crew is especially anxious to visit this particular island, since they have discovered, by the judicious use of a pair of binoculars, that there are nurses there. The Captain, however, insists on keeping the crew onboard, and only Roberts and Pulver are allowed to visit the island to pick up supplies.

Pulver, always the lothario, convinces one of the nurses, Lieutenant Ann Girard (Betsy Palmer), to meet him later aboard the *Reluctant*, where he hopes to ply her with scotch and seduce her. This sets the stage for a warmly amusing scene in which Pulver, Roberts, and Doc attempt to concoct a reasonable facsimile of scotch whiskey by mixing a combination of rubbing alcohol, iodine, hair tonic, and Coca Cola. The scene is an effective display of the camaraderie between the three men, but Ensign Pulver's stratagems are less effective since Lieutenant Girard arrives heavily chaperoned and departs with her virtue intact.

Meanwhile, the crew, with Roberts' tacit approval and support, is becoming increasingly insolent. In a scene that clearly reveals where their allegiance lies, the crew refuses the Captain's order to don their shirts until they are asked to do so by Mister Roberts. Furious, the Captain confines Roberts to his quarters for ten days, and the incident elevates Roberts to the status of hero.

Until this point in the film, Roberts' desire for transfer to a combat ship and the crew's desire for shore leave have not been mutually exclusive. Now, however, the plot takes an important turn, and a more serious note is injected into the film's light comedy. The crew's restiveness grows to the point of mutiny when the *Reluctant* docks at yet another island and the Captain again cancels their liberty. Roberts pleads with the Captain on the crew's behalf, and the Captain offers him a deal: shore leave for the crew in exchange for Roberts' promise both to stop requesting transfer from the *Reluctant* and to start obeying the Captain's orders to the letter. Further, he is to tell no one about the arrangement.

The scene is tense, and Roberts expresses his contempt for the Captain to his face. Ultimately, however, he swallows his pride and agrees to the Captain's demands. A predictably riotous evening ashore ensues, with the *Reluctant* ordered from port the next morning as a result of the crew's excesses. The crew, after recovering from its brief fling, is puzzled by the change in their esteemed Mister Roberts. The Captain enjoys their bewilderment and adds to it, implying publicly that Roberts' new spirit of acquiescence is motivated by a desire for a promotion in rank. Roberts grimly keeps his silence, and the crew gradually comes to hold him in the same contempt that they once reserved exclusively for the Captain.

The atmosphere aboard the ship grows increasingly turgid. Roberts, hurt by the crew's attitude and upset by the impending end of the war (for he still has not given up hope of combat duty), begins to take out his frustrations on the crew. All of this comes to a head when the news of VE Day reaches the *Reluctant*. Sensing that the time has come to act, Roberts hits upon a plan that will restore him to the crew's good graces without breaking his word to the Captain. Very quietly, he strolls across the deck and throws the Captain's beloved palm tree overboard.

The deed is discovered, and the Captain sounds a general alarm via the ship's intercom system. Roberts proceeds to the Captain's cabin and calmly confesses, whereupon the Captain flies into a hysterical rage, berating Roberts in no uncertain terms and accusing him of reneging on his promise. Unbeknownst to the Captain, the intercom has been left on, and his ploy is revealed to the crew.

Touched by the personal sacrifice Mister Roberts has made for them, the crew forges his transfer request—complete with the Captain's signature—and his new orders come through; he is immediately reassigned to a combat ship. Roberts is stunned and delighted by the news and bids everyone an emotional farewell. Ensign Pulver is promoted to Roberts' old position of cargo officer, and the Captain finds another scrawny palm to grace the deck of the *Reluctant*.

The film's final scene takes place on the deck of the *Reluctant* a few weeks later. Two letters have arrived; the first, having been delayed in the mail, is from Roberts to Pulver, and the jubilant Pulver reads portions of it aloud to the crew. In the letter, Roberts reveals that he is grateful to the crew of the *Reluctant* for showing him that courage in the face of boredom is every bit as heroic as courage under fire, and he admonishes Pulver to stick up for the crew. The second, more recent letter is opened by Doc and the stunned look on his face foreshadows the bad news: Roberts has been killed in combat. A gamut of emotions crosses Pulver's face. Suddenly he leaps to his feet, grabs the new palm tree, and pitches it overboard. He then runs to the Captain's cabin to "confess" his misdeed. The Captain, looking stricken, understands that the spirit of Mister Roberts lives on.

   Mister Roberts enjoyed considerable success as a novel and as a Broadway play, and the film version of the story did its predecessors justice. The film's gentle message is summarized in Mister Roberts' letter—that a hero is one who copes honorably with a trying situation; and that boredom can be just as trying as combat, albeit in a much different way.

   The film succeeds on the strength of its fine cast. James Cagney plays the priggishly sadistic Captain to perfection, and the veteran William Powell is equally fine as the avuncular Doc. Jack Lemmon's Ensign Pulver is the most engaging character in the film; brash and vulnerable at the same time, Pulver landed Lemmon the Academy Award as Best Supporting Actor, made him a major star, and launched his long and successful career. While the rest of the cast plays things mostly for laughs, Henry Fonda as Mister Roberts portrays a character who is primarily serious. In the hands of a lesser actor, such a dichotomy could have caused the film to founder, but Fonda, re-creating his Broadway stage role, manages to be earnest without being humorless, and his Doug Roberts is a pleasant counterpoint to the zaniness of Pulver and the rest of the crew.

   Mister Roberts had two directors, and there is some dispute as to the precise amount of responsibility each had over the final product. It is generally conceded, however, that John Ford shot most of the exteriors before being taken ill (or, according to another story, quitting after a dispute with Henry Fonda about the direction the film should take) and was replaced by Mervyn LeRoy. Under the circumstances, one might expect a series of uneven and disjointed scenes, as the two directors' viewpoints fight for supremacy. It is a credit to LeRoy that this does not happen; his scenes are combined seamlessly with those of his predecessor. Based on the story's popularity as a novel and play, *Mister Roberts* was one of the most eagerly awaited films of its day. The result exceeded everyone's hopes, and *Mister Roberts* remains a classic.

MOGAMBO

Released: 1953
Production: Sam Zimbalist for Metro-Goldwyn-Mayer
Direction: John Ford
Screenplay: John Lee Mahin; based on the play *Farewell to Women* by Wilson Collison
Cinematography: Robert Surtees and Freddie A. Young
Editing: Frank Clarke
Running time: 115 minutes

> *Principal characters:*
> Victor Marswell .... Clark Gable
> Eloise Y. Kelly .... Ava Gardner
> Linda Nordley .... Grace Kelly
> Donald Nordley .... Donald Sinden

It is probable that the considerable success of *King Solomon's Mines* in 1950 prompted M-G-M to make *Mogambo* several years later. Once again, the film utilizes extensive African locations, but unlike the earlier adaptation of H. Rider Haggard's classic novel, *Mogambo* is not essentially an African adventure story. The source is a play, set on a tropical rubber plantation, which the same studio had used in 1932 to make *Red Dust*. The story remains superficially the same, with many picturesque African details added. John Lee Mahin, who had written the screenplay for *Red Dust*, also wrote *Mogambo*, but there is nothing stale about this fine writer's work on the film since each of the characters is subtly altered. The same star, Clark Gable, once again plays the hero; he gives the impression of being even more tough and virile than when he was a much younger man, and also provides the sensitivity and depth which many actors acquire as they grow older and more experienced. The role of the woman of the world originally played by Jean Harlow is reinterpreted by Ava Gardner, while Grace Kelly replaces Mary Astor in the role of the respectable married woman. Crucially, John Ford directed *Mogambo*, and although the material is not that which he usually favors, he handles it with characteristic mastery, and the result is a film far more vivid and moving than *Red Dust*.

The story divides into two sections, the first involving the affair between Victor Marswell (Clark Gable) and Eloise Y. Kelly (Ava Gardner) and the second involving Vic's infatuation with Linda Nordley (Grace Kelly), the wife of a scientist, Donald Nordley (Donald Sinden), for whom Vic is serving as a guide. In the first section, there is virtually no melodramatic plot development; Kelly is heading downriver and circumstances force her to stay with Vic. In spite of her warm humor, great beauty, and honest affection, Vic does not take her seriously this early in the film. For him, her apparently loose morals disqualify her as a permanent partner, and he considers the affair to be nothing more than a pleasant interlude for both of them. When the Nordleys arrive, the polished manners and feminine vulnerability of Linda make an immediate impression on Vic. Kelly remains, but Vic treats her with little regard. Although she is deeply in love with him, she must watch with mock good spirits as he becomes increasingly drawn to Linda, who finally responds. Vic ultimately realizes that he is a fool, and he and Kelly cleverly conceal his relationship with Linda from her husband after the hysterical Linda has shot and wounded Vic in a fit of anger. Although this section of the film is melodramatic it does not present a classic triangle. Kelly gives the appearance of being sporting about Vic's troubled love for Linda, and her character is looked at independently from the main thrust of the narrative, which appears to center on Vic and Linda.

What is so interesting about Ford's interpretation of this story is that it reveals something very unexpected about his attitude toward women. The prim Linda would seem to be a type of woman not too remote from many of his heroines, and he might be expected to show her greater sympathy than Kelly. Instead, he favors Kelly throughout, admiring her independence and perceiving that her waywardness leaves her fundamentally moral character untouched. Whereas Linda eventually becomes a victim of her passions, Kelly is shown to be self-reliant throughout and to have an understanding of her actions. In one of the best scenes in the film, Kelly approaches a priest whose confessional is rather primitive. As Kelly begins her confession, the priest lets down a bamboo curtain to separate them. The scene reveals Kelly to be a Catholic, as much in harmony with her surroundings as the priest is, and to be in touch with her spiritual values far from the civilization which has superficially corrupted her.

The first section of the film, in which Kelly is at the center of the action, is directed in a relaxed and charming manner. Ford captures on film Ava Gardner's free and easy rapport with the animals, and also conveys his quiet certainty that she is the perfect woman for Vic. When the second section begins and the Nordleys arrive, the director sometimes seems impatient with the melodrama of scenes involving Vic and Linda but finds plenty of opportunities for more humor and for adding incidental touches to Kelly's character. To Ford's credit, however, the love scenes between Vic and Linda are romantically intense and charged with a feeling of sexual abandon.

Throughout *Mogambo*, Ford takes advantage of the locations in Kenya, Tanganyika, Uganda, French Equatorial Africa, and the Belgian Congo to create a pictorially appealing view of Africa that is filled with near-documentary moments which, without intruding on the story, reveal native customs, details of animal life, and the physical character of African landscapes. Fortunately Ford blends the natural beauty of Africa with the personal beauty of the two leading ladies. Grace Kelly was in the process of becoming a star when she made *Mogambo*, and the film clearly contributed to her image, which appealed to Alfred Hitchcock. Immediately after *Mogambo* Hitchcock used Grace Kelly for three films, casting the actress as the archetype of a woman whose beauty is cold on the surface but whose reserve conceals a sexuality which is unrestrained once expressed. Her character as Linda was ideal to project this archetype because she was morally forbidden to the hero as an object of love. His love for her must be understood as a flaw in his character, as it is her remoteness and inaccessibility which attract him. He is a man whose emotional responses are not truly adult until he is able to respond to a woman whose feelings are freely given.

Vic's preference for Linda over Kelly is barely overcome by his rationale, however, since it remains difficult to accept even temporarily the rejection of a woman as consummately sensual and sympathetic as Ava Gardner. It is clear from his direction that Ford found Ava Gardner enchanting, and this may partly explain why Kelly stands out as the most endearing character. Cast as a goddess in all her films during this period, Gardner has never been so natural, witty, and entertaining to watch as in *Mogambo*. In the relatively few moments in which the character is able to express her emotions directly, Gardner shows a dramatic skill for which she is almost never given credit, although it has graced a number of memorable films, notably *Bhowani Junction* (1956), *The Barefoot Contessa* (1954), *Show Boat* (1951), *The Killers* (1946), *The Snows of Kilimanjaro* (1952), and *Pandora and the Flying Dutchman* (1951). For her performance in *Mogambo* she received her only Academy Award nomination.

In a touching conclusion, after the Nordleys have departed and Kelly herself is about to leave, Vic realizes that she is his true romantic partner. She is at the river and Ford composes a characteristically beautiful long shot which finds Vic going to her and embracing her. Where other directors would feel the need to cut to a close-up, Ford is visually subtle about this happy ending, and he allows the audience to respond to the resolution of the relationship without intruding on the intimacy of the two characters, thus providing the intimacy with even greater magic. The burnished orange glow of the African sky and the subdued chanting of the natives on the soundtrack contribute to making this final scene both lovely and poignant.

THE QUIET MAN

Released: 1952
Production: John Ford and Merian C. Cooper for Republic
Direction: John Ford (AA)
Screenplay: Frank S. Nugent; based on the story *Green Rushes* by Maurice Walsh
Cinematography: Winton C. Hoch and Archie Stout (AA)
Editing: Jack Murray
Running time: 129 minutes

Principal characters:

Sean Thornton .... John Wayne
Mary Kate Danaher .... Maureen O'Hara
Michaleen Flynn .... Barry Fitzgerald
Father Peter Longergan .... Ward Bond
Red Will Danaher .... Victor McLaglen
Sarah Tillane .... Mildred Natwick
Reverend Cyril Playfair .... Arthur Shields

John Ford's love for America, as evidenced in his films, was matched only by his love for Ireland. The son of Irish immigrants, Ford looked to the Old Country through a mist of nostalgia. As he grew older, he faced squarely the failings and injustices in American history. He was less willing to examine Irish shortcomings, such as the reasons why his parents, like countless others, had decided to leave Ireland, and chose instead to celebrate the virtues and strengths of the Irish people. Returning to County Galway in 1952, the country from which his father had emigrated almost one hundred years earlier, Ford filmed *The Quiet Man*, his ultimate tribute to Ireland and to a way of life forever lost to him.

Ford called *The Quiet Man* "the first love story I've ever tried," and "the sexiest picture ever made." A romance between two passionate people is at the center of the film, unlike many other Ford films, in which the love interest is peripheral to the action. Sean Thornton (John Wayne) is an American who returns to his mother's village of Innisfree. Spurred by her memories of life in the village, Sean hopes to find a peaceful refuge from the turmoil of his American past. Escorted by Michaleen Flynn (Barry Fitzgerald), the village taxidriver, bookie, matchmaker, and drunk, Sean is introduced to the local priest, Father Longergan (Ward Bond), and sees his mother's former cottage for the first time. He also sees Mary Kate Danaher (Maureen O'Hara) and is so awed by her beauty that he doubts she is real. Flynn assures Thornton that she is a vision induced by "your terrible thirst" and drives him off to the local pub.

Once Sean has been accepted in the pub and in the Church, he is able to persuade the Widow Tillane (Mildred Natwick) to sell his mother's cottage to him, much to the dismay of Squire Red Will Danaher (Victor McLaglen), the leading landowner, the local bully, and brother of Mary Kate. When Sean moves into the cottage, he finds Mary Kate, who, out of Christian duty, has come to clean it for him. With a storm blowing wildly about them, Sean kisses her fiercely. She responds with equal passion and then tears herself away, fleeing from the cottage. The following day Sean asks Michaeleen to arrange for a formal courtship according to local custom.

When Sean and Michaeleen call on Will Danaher to ask for Mary Kate's hand, the Squire refuses to give his permission. Much to Sean's confusion and outrage, Mary Kate abides by tradition and refuses to disobey her brother. Sean releases his frustration and anger in near-suicidal rides around the county on his horse. Deeply worried by Sean's behavior, the priest, the Protestant minister the Reverend Playfair (Arthur Shields), and Michaeleen conspire to convince Danaher to change his mind. The plot is sprung during the Innisfree horse race. Michaeleen and Father Longergan lead Will Danaher to believe that the reason why the Widow Tillane will not marry him is because she does not want to live in the same house with his sister. Danaher is convinced and gives his permission for Mary Kate and Sean to wed.

At the wedding, Danaher discovers he has been tricked and refuses to give Mary Kate her dowry; Sean demands the money and is knocked out by Danaher. In a flashback the unconscious Sean remembers the prizefight in America in which he accidentally killed a man in the ring. Mary Kate does not understand Sean's reluctance to fight her brother and is deeply hurt; Sean does not understand the importance of the dowry to Mary Kate. Their wedding night is a disaster as Mary Kate refuses to sleep with Sean until she has her dowry.

As the days and weeks go by, the misunderstanding deepens. Mary Kate wants her dowry because it represents her independence from her husband, and she believes Sean's refusal to fight is due to cowardice and a lack of feeling for her. Sean believes Mary Kate is merely greedy, and he is unable to overcome his revulsion against fighting for money, as he explains to the Reverend Playfair, the only villager aware of his secret. Mary Kate talks to Father Longergan about her problems and is sufficiently chastened by the priest's reaction to her denial of Sean's marriage rights to finally sleep with her husband.

The next morning, however, she leaves Sean because she is ashamed of relenting without her dowry. Now thoroughly angry, Sean rides after her, pulls her off the train, and literally drags her the five miles back to Squire Danaher's farm. All of the villagers for miles around follow Sean and Mary Kate to the confrontation with her brother. Sean demands the dowry or the marriage is over. Danaher gives him the dowry, and Sean, assisted by Mary Kate, throws it in the furnace of the threshing machine. Mary Kate now has her rightful dowry, and Sean has retained his self-respect by destroying the money. Their marriage is at last secure. Only the fight between Sean and Danaher remains, and it is indeed an epic fight. Across hills and fields, through paddocks and into pubs the two men bash and pummel each other, pausing frequently to quench their thirst until they are both too drunk to fight anymore. Sean then brings the brother home to supper, restoring the family and the tranquility of Innisfree.

While dramatic in theme, the film is comic and warmly affectionate in mood. The only somber scene in the film is the flashback to the death of the boxer which Ford films in a stunning montage of expressionistic shots. Overall the film is a paean to the lovely Irish countryside and a gently indulgent examination of the traditions of the Irish people. Ford never patronizes his characters, but demonstrates his love of the Irish people in shot after shot of affectionate vignettes celebrating their capacity for life and love and their foibles as well as their strengths.

Surely one of the funniest films Ford ever made, *The Quiet Man* is also a sensual love story. John Wayne is fully believable as the former boxer passionately attracted to the beautiful Mary Kate. But it is Maureen O'Hara who brings fire and spirit to the love story. Physically stunning with her red hair and animal energy, we understand why Thornton wants her. O'Hara's ability as an actress lends credence to her part as a woman fiercely determined to be independent and to demand that her husband respect her as a person. Film critic Molly Haskell has said that Maureen O'Hara is one of a very small number of actresses who was not entirely overshadowed by John Wayne's presence on the screen. Nowhere is this assertion more evident than in *The Quiet Man*. Without Maureen O'Hara, the lovers would not be equals, and the love story would not be, as Michaleen says in the film, so "impetuous-Homeric."

Wayne and O'Hara are ably supported by a large cast. Ford brought many of the actors in his stock company to Galway with him and supplemented the Americans with actors from the Abbey Theatre. Barry Fitzgerald is richly comic as Michaleen Flynn, the catalyst of much of the film's action. He functions as a one-man chorus, commenting on the fate of the lovers and assisting them at every opportunity. Victor McLaglen was nominated for Best Supporting Actor for his rather unsympathetic role as the braggart and bully, Will Danaher. Arthur Shields and Mildred Natwick also stand out in their supporting roles. Under Ford's direction, every member of the large cast captures a distinctive personality regardless of the brevity of many of their appearances.

The film is dominated by the genius of John Ford, who received his fourth Oscar as Best Director for his achievement in *The Quiet Man*. He carefully creates a village and its inhabitants in a not-quite-real place which he attempts to convince us is reality itself. If we are not totally persuaded, we still want

Ford's vision of Innisfree to be the truth of Ireland, just as he does. Ford created Innisfree with the help of his cinematographer Winton C. Hoch, who won his third Oscar for his sumptuous color cinematography of the Irish countryside. Ford's scenarist Frank Nugent; the art director; the set decorator; and the sound engineer were also nominated for their work in the film, and the film itself was nominated for Best Picture. Of seven nominations, *The Quiet Man* won two Oscars.

Ford's Oscar was the last he received; he was never again nominated for Best Director, although he was later to direct several films that would match and even transcend his achievement with *The Quiet Man*. He would direct one other Irish film (*The Young Cassidy*, 1964), prepare a second film about Ireland, and also make two films about the Irish in America (*The Long Gray Line*, 1955; *The Last Hurrah*, 1958). *The Quiet Man*, however, remains his definitive statement about his nostalgic homeland, his most warmly humorous film, and his most successful examination of a love affair in all of his fifty years of filmmaking.

THE SEARCHERS

Released: 1956
Production: Merian C. Cooper and Patrick Ford for C. V. Whitney Pictures; released by Warner Bros.
Direction: John Ford
Screenplay: Frank S. Nugent; based on the novel of the same name by Alan LeMay
Cinematography: Winton C. Hoch
Editing: Jack Murray
Running time: 119 minutes

Principal characters:

Ethan Edwards	John Wayne
Martin Pawley	Jeffrey Hunter
Laurie Jorgensen	Vera Miles
Captain Reverend Clayton	Ward Bond
Debbie Edwards (older)	Natalie Wood
Debbie Edwards (younger)	Lana Wood
Lars Jorgensen	John Qualen
Mrs. Jorgensen	Olive Carey
Chief Scar	Henry Brandon
Aaron Edwards	Walter Coy
Martha Edwards	Dorothy Jordan
Look	Beulah Archuletta
Lucy Edwards	Pippa Scott

The Searchers is unquestionably the masterpiece of America's foremost director, John Ford. Ostensibly a conventional Western, *The Searchers* brings together themes that concerned Ford in his fifty-year film career, and illuminates them anew with the power and vigor of the mature artist working at the peak of his creativity. Full of the action typical of the genre, the film is also a subtle study of psychological torment. Finally it becomes an epic of the American experience which parallels Melville's *Moby Dick* in its concern with the fundamental tensions at the heart of that experience.

The plot of the film is relatively simple. A cabin door opens onto a desolate wilderness and Ethan Edwards (John Wayne) is seen approaching his brother's homestead after a long absence fighting in the Civil War. His brother Aaron (Walter Coy), his sister-in-law Martha (Dorothy Jordan), his nephew, and his nieces Debbie (Lana Wood) and Lucy (Pippa Scott) greet him and lead him into the cabin. Ford quickly establishes a tension between the brothers that resides in a long-suppressed love between Martha and Ethan. Perhaps for this reason Ethan has remained away long past the end of the war. Martin Pawley (Jeffrey Hunter), the adopted son of the Edwardses, is introduced, and we learn that Ethan rescued him as a child after his parents were killed in an Indian raid.

The Edwards' breakfast the next morning is interrupted by their neighbor Mr. Jorgensen (John Qualen), Captain Clayton (Ward Bond), and a posse of Texas Rangers pursuing cattle rustlers. Captain Clayton deputizes Ethan and Martin, and the posse rides off in pursuit. They find the cattle forty miles away killed with Comanche lances. Ethan realizes that the cattle have been driven off to lure the men away from the ranchers so that a war party can attack the settlers left behind. Ethan and Martin return to the cabin to find Aaron, Martha, and their son dead, and the girls kidnaped by the Comanches. The effort to find and ransom the girls motivates what is to become a five-year search.

Ethan and Martin soon learn that Lucy has been killed but they continue to search for Debbie. During this period, Ethan's desire for vengeance is transformed into a monomaniacal obsession. Coupled with the knowledge that Debbie has been adopted by the Indians and undoubtedly married to one of the warriors, Ethan's obsession and racial hatred approaches madness. Martin stays with the search because of his concern for Debbie and because he is fearful of what Ethan will do when he finds her.

After an encounter with a treacherous trader, a comical "marriage" between Martin and the Indian woman he calls Look (Beulah Archuletta), and a Cavalry massacre of an Indian village, the searchers at last catch up with the Comanche chief Scar (Henry Brandon) and his band. The dramatic encounter between Ethan and Scar emphasizes the similarities of pursuer and pursued. Debbie (Natalie Wood) is a member of the tribe and Scar's wife. Ethan and Martin attempt to rescue her, but when they do, Ethan wants to kill her. Martin stops him, but Ethan is wounded in the fight with the Indians and the men must return to the Jorgensens' without Debbie.

When they arrive at the Jorgensen homestead, Martin discovers that his fiancée, Laurie Jorgensen (Vera Miles), has grown tired of waiting for him and intends to marry a Texas Ranger that very evening. Martin fights his rival for the right to marry Laurie, but before the matter is resolved, a Cavalry Lieutenant arrives with the news that Scar's band has been located once more.

Ethan, Martin, Captain Clayton, and his Rangers surround the camp and prepare for the attack. Martin is permitted to attempt Debbie's rescue before the attack begins. He finds her but must kill Scar in order to effect their escape. In the ensuing battle, Ethan finds Scar's body and scalps it. He then rides down Debbie; but instead of killing her, he sweeps her into his arms. The searchers return to the Jorgensens', where Debbie is welcomed back, and Martin claims Laurie for his bride. All enter the house but Ethan. The last shot reverses the first shot of the film, showing Ethan returning alone to his wilderness as the door of civilization closes.

The Searchers is a superb example of the Western film. It draws upon the familiar conventions of the genre to present multidimensional characters in surprising and unpredictable fashion. The film transcends those conventions, however, in its subtle exploration of racial prejudice and psychological turmoil. Ethan Edwards is a man obsessed with the desire for revenge and hatred for the man who violated and killed the woman he loved. As such he is not the typical Western hero concerned with clear-cut issues, but is rather a man with very human qualities forced to deal with his surroundings in a superhuman manner.

At its most profound, *The Searchers* is an archetype of the American experience. Ethan Edwards embodies the conflicts experienced by the European settlers confronting the American wilderness and its native inhabitants. Ethan is more competent in the wilderness than his fellow settlers and more akin than even he suspects to his Indian adversary. The freedom that attracts him to the wilderness also carries with it an implicit alienation from the civilization represented by his sister-in-law and by the Jorgensens. This conflict between the freedom of the wilderness and the comfort of civilization with its attendant responsibilities, is a major conflict in American history and literature. Ethan Edwards joins Daniel Boone, Leatherstocking, Huck Finn, and Ahab in the pantheon of American heroes personifying these opposing attractions.

The theme of the wilderness in opposition to civilization in the American experience is also a major concern of John Ford which he explores in the several Westerns he made during his long career. In Ethan Edwards he creates a character whose neurotic intensity and consuming obsessions render him quite unlike any other character in a Ford film. He is a tragic hero who suffers from the conflicting attractions of the vast and empty American landscape and the need for civilized order. Committed to that wilderness, he loses his beloved Martha, first to his brother and then to the savage wilderness itself as embodied by Scar.

John Wayne described the role of Ethan as his favorite among all his roles, and he brings to it a depth of feeling and range of expression that marks it as the outstanding performance of his long career. Believable as the thoroughly authoritative frontiersman, he subtly and with economy of gesture conveys the anguish and increasing madness of a character tormented by pressures he cannot control. Ford employs many of his stock company of actors in the other roles. Ward Bond as Captain Clayton and Olive Carey and John Qualen as the Jorgensens are especially effective in small but extremely important roles.

The concern with the dynamics of racism and the more violent aspects of the American experience makes *The Searchers* all the more remarkable for a film produced in 1956. Although a financial success, the film was largely ignored by the critics and it did not receive any Academy nominations. By 1972, however, *The Searchers* had increased in critical stature to the point where, in a poll of international film critics conducted by *Sight and Sound*, it was included in the list of the top twenty films of all time. It is the only Ford film on the list. Recently film directors have consciously paid homage to the film by patterning their films on *The Searchers*. Martin Scorsese's *Taxi Driver* (1976) and Paul Schrader's *Hardcore* (1979) are two examples of this trend. *The Searchers* will stand as John Ford's masterpiece and a cinematic achievement that can serve as an example to all future filmmakers of the possibilities of the art form.

STAGECOACH

Released: 1939
Production: John Ford and Walter Wanger for United Artists
Direction: John Ford
Screenplay: Dudley Nichols; based on the short story "Stage to Lordsburg" by Ernest Haycox
Cinematography: Bert Glennon
Editing: Dorothy Spencer and Walter Reynolds
Art direction: Alexander Toluboff
Costume design: Walter Plunkett
Music: Richard Hageman, Franke Harling, John Leipold, Leo Shuken (AA)
Running time: 96 minutes

Principal characters:

Ringo Kid	John Wayne
Dallas	Claire Trevor
Doc Boone	Thomas Mitchell (AA)
Buck	Andy Devine
Curly Wilcox	George Bancroft
Mr. Peacock	Donald Meek
Lucy Mallory	Louise Platt
Hatfield	John Carradine
Mr. Gatewood	Berton Churchill
Lieutenant Blanchard	Tim Holt
Luke Plummer	Tom Tyler
Ike Plummer	Joe Rickson

Stagecoach is a landmark in the evolution of the Western genre and in the career of its director, John Ford. After the introduction of synchronized sound during the 1930's, Westerns were mostly "B" type films. There were singing cowboys, (Gene Autry and Roy Rogers), action heroes (Hopalong Cassidy and George O'Brien), serials (the Long Ranger and Johnny Mack Brown), and a stampede of cheaply made quickies from the backlots of independent studios such as Republic, Monogram, and Resolute. However, when an up-beat spirit of national optimism emerged in the late 1930's, as exemplified in *Stagecoach* and Cecil B. DeMille's *Union Pacific*, the Western became a means of transmitting themes of national progress and consequently a genre to be seriously considered. *Stagecoach* also helped reestablish the epic Western as a solid box-office commodity.

For Ford, regarded as one of the genre's seminal auteurs, *Stagecoach* marked a return to the Western after a thirteen-year hiatus. (His last Western had been *Three Bad Men*, a silent film made in 1926.) The overwhelming success of *Stagecoach* with both critics and the public brought Ford the prestige and recognition that enabled him to take a fairly independent course, at least by Hollywood standards. It also paved the way for other memorable Ford Westerns such as *My Darling Clementine* (1946), *Fort Apache* (1948), *She Wore a Yellow Ribbon* (1949), *Wagon Master* (1950), and *The Man Who Shot Liberty Valance* (1962).

Though Dudley Nichols' screenplay is based on Ernest Haycox's "Stage to Lordsburg," which first appeared in *Collier's* magazine in April of 1937, Ford has stated that Haycox's inspiration probably came from Guy de Maupassant's *Boule de Suif*, a tale of a prostitute traveling by carriage through war-torn France with important members of the bourgeoisie. The dramatic structure of *Stagecoach* is based on a time-tested convention: a group of widely varied characters is placed in a dangerous situation which, like a litmus test, reveals each individual's true character. Specifically, eight passengers are brought together from an overland stagecoach journey from Tonto to Lordsburg through the perilous American Southwest, which was terrorized by Geronimo's Apache warriors during the 1870's.

The band of travelers includes Doc Boone (Thomas Mitchell), an intoxicated man of medicine; Hatfield (John Carradine), a Southern officer-turned-cardsharp; Dallas (Claire Trevor), a prostitute driven out of Tonto by the self-righteous Ladies' Law and Order League; Mrs. Lucy Mallory (Louise Platt), the pregnant wife of a Cavalry lieutenant; Mr. Gatewood (Berton Churchill), a pompous banker in flight with embezzled band funds; Mr. Peacock (Donald Meek), a timid whisky drummer who is consistently mistaken for a clergyman; Buck (Andy Devine), the skittish driver of the stage; Marshal Curly Wilcox (George Bancroft); and his prisoner, the Ringo Kid (John Wayne). In the course of their trying adventures, these characters are manipulated by Ford and Nichols so that conventional social levels are turned upside down. As a result, it is the social outcasts—the outlaw and prostitute—who emerge as most noble, while the outwardly most "respectable" member, the banker, turns out the most despicable, a man consumed by greed and self-importance.

During the journey, two major events serve as primary catalysts for revealing character. The first occurs at the Apache Wells station where Lucy Mallory goes into labor. Doc, drunk with "samples" provided by the reluctant Mr. Peacock, realizing his professional responsibility, calls for coffee. While Ringo, Dallas, and Curly help Doc sober up, Hatfield looks on with suppressed fury: "A fine member of the medical profession! Drunken beast!" Hatfield's angry disgust is based on his concern for Lucy, a concern based on a shared Southern heritage and his chivalrous stance as her protector.

Gatewood, on the other hand, complains not about Doc, but about their situation. "A sick woman on our hands! That's all we needed!" Gatewood's outburst is totally selfish; his sole concern is getting to Lordsburg as quickly as possible. Dallas, however, proves her true worth during the childbirth by assisting Doc and then sitting up all night tending to Lucy and her baby girl.

During the evening, Dallas takes a break and strolls outside the station to get some fresh air. She meets Ringo, who explains that he must get to Lordsburg to avenge the murder of his father and brother. He then tries to tell Dallas how impressed he was with her way of handling the baby. Though his words are awkward, he proposes by stating "You're . . . the kind of girl a man wants to marry." Dallas appears nonplused and tells him not to talk like that. Rushing off, however, her tears betray her deep feelings for Ringo, her concern for his impending shoot-out with the Plummer gang, and the shame she feels over being a prostitute. The next morning, Doc suggests the stage's departure be postponed for a day to allow Lucy to regain some of her strength. In spite of the threat of Geronimo, all endorse Doc's advice except Gatewood, who vehemently protests the delay.

Back on the trail, the ongoing bickering suddenly ceases as an arrow hits Peacock in the shoulder. The group's ultimate test is about to begin. Apaches swarm down from the hills in pursuit of the stage hurtling across the broad, flat plain. Gatewood, in a mad panic, cries "Stop the stage! Let me out of here!" Doc Boone bandages Peacock's shoulder. Buck drives his frenzied team of six horses with wild yells. Curly, Ringo, and Hatfield attempt to fight off the Apaches. As their end seems near, Hatfield, with one bullet left in his chamber, points his gun toward the huddled figure of Lucy muttering prayers: he obviously intends to save her from a fate worse than death. Hatfield pauses, a gunshot is heard, his gun drops and falls to the ground. Hatfield has been hit.

Suddenly, a bugle is heard in the distance blowing the charge. The cavalry has arrived. The Apaches halt and turn in flight as the troopers charge. As the coach comes to a stop, Hatfield turns to Lucy and utters his last words: "If you ever see Judge Ringfield . . . tell him his son. . . ." The others, however, are safe and proceed without further incident to Lordsburg escorted by the cavalrymen.

The stage is met by Lordsburg's sheriff, who surprises the blustering Gatewood: "You didn't think they'd have the telegraph wires fixed, did you?" Gatewood struggles to no avail, is handcuffed and marched away to the local jail. Peacock is carried off on a stretcher for more medical attention, and Lucy is assured by a Captain sent to meet her that her husband is safe. Before departing, Lucy, whose initial scorn of Dallas has mellowed because of Dallas' unselfish help, attempts to reach out by saying, "If there's anything I can ever do for. . . ."

The film concludes with Ringo's showdown with the Plummers. Having gained the marshal's respect, Ringo is given ten minutes by Curly to take care of business. In another part of town, Dallas hears a volley of shots. Fearing the worse, she cries out Ringo's name; then a figure looms in the darkness— it is Ringo. Dallas rushes forward to embrace him; the Plummers have been vanquished. Curly directs Dallas and Ringo to a buckboard. Once seated,

Curly and Doc shoo the team of horses and shout best wishes to the pair as they head out to establish new lives on Ringo's ranch in Mexico. As the buckboard rumbles into the night, Doc comments: "Well, they're saved from the blessings of civilization." The marshal then offers Doc a drink. After a majestically grand pause, Doc replies, "Just one." It is the perfect note of irony for a film whose portrait of society is itself ironic.

Stagecoach, aside from its value as a well-told tale of the West, is an incisive comment on the virtues and limitations of society. Doc, the poet of the group and Ford's voice within the film, is a man whose training was made possible by the institutions of civilization; at the same time, because of his passion for drink, he is regarded by society's mainstream as an outcast. When the chips are down, however, Doc is equal to the tasks of delivering a baby or patching a wound. Curly also straddles the line between society and the wilderness. Though his oath as a lawman requires him to return Ringo to the prison from which he escaped, Curly responds to a higher law, the code of honor of the old West. In Curly's eyes, Ringo has proved himself and repaid his debt to society; that allows Curly to give him an opportunity to face the Plummers and, later, a fresh chance at a new life in Mexico. In these and other incidents, the values of society are shown as cold, unfeeling, and even corrupt. It is clear that Ford's values are aligned with the primitive and natural society of an old West unfettered by the stultifying pressures of civilization. The beauty and freedom of the wilderness represent the ultimate in values.

Underscoring Ford's broad theme is the magnificent landscape of Monument Valley. With his broad panoramas of weathered plains, mesas, and majestic clouds, Ford creates a universe of natural order which dwarfs the actions of the men who travel through it. There is, however, the implication that those who live by the spirit of the land instead of by society's dictates will live most nobly.

Mood and atmosphere are effectively established by an outstanding score by Hageman, Harling, Leipold, and Shuken, which incorporates seventeen American folk songs from the period. The score won an Academy Award. The performances by John Wayne, Claire Trevor, Andy Devine, George Bancroft, Donald Meek, Louise Platt, John Carradine, and Berton Churchill are all outstanding as is that of Thomas Mitchell who won an Academy Award as Best Supporting Actor for his portrayal of Doc Boone.

Today, *Stagecoach* stands as one of the brightest examples of the American Western and as one of the most mature of John Ford's films. Ford was honored as the Best Director of 1939 by the New York Film Critics for his direction of *Stagecoach*.

THEY WERE EXPENDABLE

Released: 1945
Production: John Ford for Metro-Goldwyn-Mayer
Direction: John Ford
Screenplay: Frank Wead; based on the novel of the same name by William
  L. White
Cinematography: Joseph H. August
Editing: Frank E. Hull and Douglass Biggs
Running time: 136 minutes

Principal characters:
Lieutenant John Brickley .... Robert Montgomery
Lieutenant Rusty Ryan .... John Wayne
Lieutenant Sandy Davyss .... Donna Reed
General Martin .... Jack Holt
Boats Mulcahey .... Ward Bond
Ensign Andy Andrews .... Paul Langton
Admiral Blackwell .... Charles Trowbridge

They Were Expendable is about the Philippine Campaign for Bataan and
Corregidor in 1942. Based on the experiences of Lieutenant John Bulkeley,
a personal friend of John Ford, the film chronicles the destruction of a PT
Boat Squadron as it sacrifices itself in a holding action in the Pacific. A story
of defeat and the breakdown of military, social, and even personal structures,
They Were Expendable was shot in 1944 when the war in Europe was ending
and the Allied forces were preparing for an invasion of Japan.

Ford's credit reads, "Captain, USNR," for he had been on active duty in
the Navy as Chief of the Field Photographic Branch, a unit of the Office of
Strategic Services. He had already made *Battle of Midway* (1941) and *December 7* (1943), stirringly patriotic documentaries about American service-
men overseas. He received an Oscar for both of them and a Purple Heart
for wounds received during the Battle of Midway.

Given this context, *They Were Expendable* comes as a surprise. Not only
is it not a traditional war genre film of courageous victories and brutal,
subhuman enemies, it is fundamentally about the meaninglessness of the war
for the people who fought it. Generally in the war genre, themes involve the
formation of military relationships and the bond of working toward a common
goal greater than any individual could attain. The military provides a structure
for both hierarchical and pseudofamily relationships and order in the chaos
of war. In *They Were Expendable*, however, that structure is broken down
both physically in the losing battles and psychologically through its failure to
provide the men with a reason to be fighting.

The film begins in order and regularity. The PT boats cutting through the water are graceful, and Brickley (Robert Montgomery) is established in close-up (though isolated from his background through focus) as the stable commander of the PT boat unit, with the lines of men and generals expressing the chain of command and order of the Navy. Scenes in the officers' club and at a retirement party continue in even lighting, indicating normalcy, with natural shadows and stable compositions. The announcement of war brings the beginnings of chaos and isolation and finally breakdown for the PT units. First Brickley is cut off from the regular chain of command visually by the glass doors of the war room, then he passes through a long corridor alone to rejoin his men. The unit is immediately isolated from the rest of the Navy and the meaningful war effort.

Brickley as commander maintains a degree of distance from all his men. It is a required distance; only through such distance can Brickley make decisions that will cost the lives of an unknown number of his men, and only through the distance of command can the men give the unquestioning loyalty demanded by the war effort. Brickley must become a somewhat removed figure for the men, lacking in the personal dimension and accruing the iconographic significance necessary for giving orders to men who may die for the safety of the unit. This hierarchical, increasingly impersonal structure escalates up through the ranks: Brickley occupies the same relationship to the Admiral (Charles Trowbridge) that his men do to him, and the Admiral is a more remote, lonely figure than is Brickley. General MacArthur is the furthest expression of this distance of leadership: his name alone is awesome to the men, and he is photographed like a mythical figure. We see him only from a distance. He walks in long shot alone while his family walks ahead of him and his men follow behind. It is as though his loneliness and necessary isolation are so great they cannot be bridged at all.

Death in *They Were Expendable* is neither glory-filled nor brutally meaningless, the two extremes with which it is usually depicted in war films, depending on the attitude of the filmmaker toward war. In this film, both possibilities are present, balanced in a way that denies neither. The war is abstracted in such a way as to internalize the battle: there are no enemy soldiers, just planes and boats which fill the sky and sea with action and flame, but never with the sense of a struggle between navies. The sea battles especially are so abstracted they become light shows, sensory experiences of dark boats on glistening water, moving with beauty and grace through the white shining explosions that burst around them, creating patterns of light against a black sky. The Japanese carriers go down in glorious fireworks, and the Americans who die in battle do so in silhouetted low angle against the firelit sky. The sea battles are beauty and light: it is in the hospital that death is a reality. The corridor to the hospital is revealed through dark shadow passages that are strangely lit to create an expressionistic hell. Like the sea battles, the hospital is a highly stylized canvas of light and dark, but it reveals the other side of the battles. The hospital shows the people who deal with the results of the battles—the wounded men, the doctors, the nurses. The hospital scenes are no more realistic than those of the sea battles; they simply express an interior darkness filled with people and pain instead of illuminating the vast night with fire and action. The corridor seems an underground link between the world of the living and the world of the dead, and never more so than when the men visit Andy (Paul Langton), one of their company, as he is dying. His bed is in the corridor itself, curtained off from the others. During the visit, the "small talk" sustains no one, and each man faces death alone in the person of Andy.

Death here is a lonely experience, the final isolation. Ford does not try to romanticize it, but he does stylize it in a way that abstracts its full impact and allows both for the grim reality and for the personal tragedy. The levels of Andy's larger representation for the unit and for the war, and his personal dimension to both the men and his family back home, are permitted through the visual style to exist simultaneously. It is Brickley, in the isolation of his rank, who must face it even more alone than the others as Andy entrusts him with his final thoughts and letters to home. Only with Brickley can Andy stop his comforting banter and confront his death with the honesty that is of comfort to him, but only brings pain to Brickley. He walks alone through the dark corridor to join the silhouetted figures of the rest of the men, isolated from them through light and composition as he was from Andy by the finality of facing his own death while having to go on living.

The funeral in the little Spanish church is another ritualized scene in which the structures of meaning and glory in burial are observed but fall short of their comforting possibilities. Rusty (John Wayne) cannot even stay to observe the ceremony, but runs out to get a drink to sustain him as the religious service cannot.

Like the absence of enemies in the film, the concept of home is abstracted instead of conjured through flashback or misty memory. Home becomes a larger realm than simply "The States" in *They Were Expendable*, as does the military family. The men of the unit constitute a family, and Torpedo Boat Squadron 3 is its home. From the first, the men are displaced, having no specific role to play in the Navy's fight, and the first scene is of a rejection of their possible usefulness. They function as a smooth unit, and the Admiral comments on their maneuverability, but he can see no place for them. Then comes the attack on the base, and their "home" is devastated. The squadron is continually leaving one island and going to another, until it is difficult to keep track of where they are. While it is true that in 1945 audiences had a closer knowledge of the battles of the Pacific than they do today, it seems that this constant upheaval has more to do with the impermanence of any kind of base for the men than with a disregard for details that may have been unnecessary when the picture was released. The family of men disintegrates as well, first with the loss of boats which frees two crews to go fight with the army. Men die and more boats are lost, until all that is really left is Brickley, Rusty, and the small troop of men who will be left behind on the island, certain to be killed by the Japanese. The crew members we know best are the ones who die—Cookie, Slug, and Andy.

Home is more than a place in *They Were Expendable*. It is a condition that they are fighting for and which they cannot maintain. This is the basis of the transcendent failure of meaning that underlies this film. Unlike other war films which depict men becoming a unit or family whose interests are greater than those of any individual or of the country for which they are fighting, in this film the condition of "home" does not even exist structurally, and thus the sacrifices of war cannot affirm it. The war effort becomes a meaningless exercise, with the only possibility for creating meaning existing on an individual level.

The fragile love relationship between Rusty and Sandy (Donna Reed) refers to a concept of home which must always be subordinate to the war. They try to conjure up an image of home that probably never existed when they talk of tall corn and apples, images tied to the primary desire for land and food. The dinner party attempts to establish a feeling of community and home (Sandy's pathetic and touching attempts at femininity in a harsh, hellish world), but the real meaning of the party comes from its proximity to destruction and the maintenance of fragile if schematized normalcy in the face of it. Without the war, Ford suggests, the values represented by "home" would not have such meaning. Only in the face of loss and chaos can these values even be alluded to, although they are not realized. This is the dichotomy upon which Ford so often draws for depth in his films: life can be meaningful only because there have been socially required sacrifices for its continuance through rituals like religion and war, yet that sacrifice fails to return meaning to those who must carry it out, and to whom the film gives the greatest attention and sympathy.

The smooth, graceful beauty of the PT boats performing at the beginning of the film has been destroyed by the end, as the ordering chain of command has been broken beyond recognition. Brickley and Rusty trudge through the dust and dirt, in the unorganized disarray of the Army, Marine, and Navy men and equipment, totally broken down and defeated. The smoke of the battle provides a softening texture which contributes to the utter desolation of the chaotic mass of men without any chain of command or formal order, and it expresses their inner breakdown.

In the last shots, the redeeming effects of formal abstract beauty are recruited to give a transcendent quality to the utterly despairing and hopeless ending of the men being left to die as Brickley and Rusty bitterly fly off to "do their duty." The men are abstracted visually into an emotional entity, first with the close-up of guns, then with shots of two men we do not know, and finally, simply with dark shapes on the beach as the plane flies into the distance. The men and the plane are moving to different destinies, but the beauty and stability of the compositions, along with the abstraction which takes the viewer's emotions out of the realm of response to specific individuals, relates the hopelessness of the film.

It is in the visual expression of the film that the entire concept of value is contained. The dichotomy of the formal beauty and classical composition with soft, romantic lighting of the scenes which allude to home, contrasted to the unstable, harsh, dark world of the hospital and the otherworldly character of the battles, is reconciled in the last scene of the men on the beach. No real point to the struggle is thematically offered in this last scene: the men have "laid down the sacrifice" for no reason that the film will give us; they are simply alone and cut off. The structures of the military family have broken down and all that remains is the dispersing men, who are removed from individuality through lighting. The audience feels the failure of the war on every level, with the loss of human contact and men left behind to die, and simultaneously feels the redeeming effects of the visual beauty. The despair of the film is not mitigated but rather intensified by the visual abstraction, because it generalizes the central theme of lack of meaning while leaving its specific representations intact.

THREE GODFATHERS

Released: 1948
Production: John Ford and Merian C. Cooper for Metro-Goldwyn-Mayer; released by Loew's Incorporated
Direction: John Ford
Screenplay: Laurence Stallings and Frank S. Nugent; based on the novel of the same name by Peter B. Kyne
Cinematography: Winton C. Hoch
Editing: Jack Murray
Music: Richard Hageman
Running time: 106 minutes

> *Principal characters:*
> Bob Hightower .... John Wayne
> Pete .... Pedro Armendariz
> The Abilene Kid .... Harry Carey, Jr.
> "Buck" Perley Sweet .... Ward Bond
> Mrs. Perley Sweet .... Mae Marsh
> The Mother .... Mildred Natwick

John Ford's *Three Godfathers* uses a form rarely seen in films, and seen even less in the Western genre: that of the religious parable. Although Ford had dealt in religious allegory in a previous film, *The Fugitive* (1947), it is in *Three Godfathers* that he most successfully illustrates the theme of spiritual redemption through individual commitment and sacrifice. The film is dedicated "To the Memory of Harry Carey—Bright Star of the Early Western Sky." Carey, who had died in 1947, starred in Ford's silent Western, *Marked Men*, which was the director's original film version of the same story that serves as the basis for *Three Godfathers*. The story has been filmed a total of five times, including a television version in the late 1970's.

The film begins with three outlaws planning a robbery. Ford encourages us to accept the basic decency of these three "good badmen" by having the leader of the group, Bob Hightower (John Wayne), urge the youngest to consider quitting before he becomes too deeply involved in crime. The Abilene Kid (Harry Carey, Jr.) refuses the offer, and the three men—Bob, the Kid, and Pedro (Pedro Armendariz)—ride into the small Arizona town of Welcome to rob its bank. They stop at a house and talk jokingly with a man leisurely tending his garden. The outlaws prepare to get on with the robbery when they discover that the man with whom they have been amicably chatting happens to be the town marshal. Undeterred by Marshal "Buck" Perley Sweet's hospitality, they rob the bank, but in the escape, the Abilene Kid is wounded, and Sweet and his posse pursue them.

Ward Bond's admirable portrayal of Sweet makes the character a satisfying mixture of adherence to duty combined with a keen understanding of human nature, qualities often shared by other characters in Ford films, such as the priest in *The Quiet Man* (1952) and Captain Clayton in *The Searchers* (1956). Sweet's fulfillment of the obligations of his job do not obscure or diminish his humanity. Although he has an opportunity to shoot Hightower, Sweet shoots the outlaw's water bag instead, declaring, "they ain't paying me to kill folks." Nevertheless, he is a thorough professional. In a move to divert the posse, the outlaws do not go to the railroad watering station as expected, but go into the desert toward a watering hole called Tarapin Tanks. Marshal Sweet is only momentarily deceived by the outlaws' diversionary tactic and correctly assesses what their next move will be. He deftly moves his posse into the desert in pursuit of the three men.

In these scenes of pursuit, Ford's location shooting in the Mohave Desert effectively establishes a needed sense of physical reality in a film that is largely concerned with the spiritual. As he did in *She Wore a Yellow Ribbon* (1949), in which the chance occurrence of a thunderstorm provided him with the opportunity to film one of the most breathtaking sequences in any of his films, Ford uses a natural event, an actual dust storm, to enhance the physical struggle by grounding it in a believable film "reality." The terrible dust storm causes the outlaws to lose their horses and they reach Tarapin Tanks by foot— only to discover that the waterhole is dry.

When the outlaws see a covered wagon perched eerily near the edge of the Tanks, Ford resorts to an effective device that he often uses for important emotional moments. Bob goes ahead to inspect the wagon, but the audience must wait until he returns to his companions to find out what he has discovered. Bob's account of his offscreen experience is similar to Ethan Edwards' report of finding Lucy's body in *The Searchers* and Gil Martin's exhausted retelling of his battle experience in Ford's *Drums Along the Mohawk* (1939). The emotional reaction of each of the characters to his offscreen experience increases the audience's perception of that experience. Bob relates what he found in a poignant, half-literate, half-poetic monologue that reveals his own anger and despair as well as the facts of the discovery. Because a tenderfoot emigrant dynamited the waterhole in a foolish attempt to find water, Tarapin Tanks is permanently ruined. The man, leaving his wife alone in the wagon, went off into the desert to find water. "But that still ain't the worst of it," Bob declares. "She's gonna have a baby. She's gonna have it now."

Pedro goes to care for the woman, and as he approaches the wagon, Ford adds a religious touch to the imagery by framing Pedro in the wagon cover as if he were standing under the archway of a cathedral. The woman bears a son, and, realizing that she is dying, she asks the three men to be her child's godfathers. In a masterful stroke of understatement, Ford never allows the real father to be mentioned again, although the anguish of the mother is communicated in her naming the baby not with the surname of the husband who deserted her, but after the men who found her. In one of the film's most touching scenes, each man takes a solemn oath to care for little Robert William Pedro Hightower. As the mother dies, a gust of wind extinguishes the lantern. The outlaws bury her in a funeral ceremony that echoes those in many other Ford films. Gathered around her grave, they read from her Bible, and the Abilene Kid sings "Shall We Gather at the River?"

The mother's death is significant because it thrusts upon the men the responsibility of her child. Death in *Three Godfathers* is inexorably bound to the necessity of sacrifice. A mother dies, but her hope for her child lives in the sworn promise of three thieves. Later Pedro and the Kid die trying to reach a town called New Jerusalem which they choose as a destination because the Kid reads a passage in the mother's open Bible telling of the journey of the Christ Child and his family to Jerusalem. The Abilene Kid insists on carrying the baby, but he becomes increasingly weak and finally collapses, then dies, deliriously reciting a child's prayer. Pedro steps into a hole, and to avoid falling on the baby in his arms, twists around, breaking his leg. Knowing he is doomed, Pedro gives Bob the child, says his good-byes, and takes Bob's gun, ostensibly to defend himself against coyotes. Bob walks away, and a shot is heard. He stops motionless for a moment, then starts walking again.

Bob's journey is not toward such a sacrificial death, but toward a redemption ensured by the sacrifice of others and by his own acceptance of the responsibility thrust on him by that sacrifice. Of the three outlaws, Bob is shown to be the least religious. He must go through a journey in his own spiritual desert as well as through a journey in the physical one. When, as the only outlaw left alive, he decides to give up and die, Bob turns to the Bible. The passage he reads tells of the Christ Child being carried on a donkey, and the obvious, but spiritually necessary, miracle occurs: a donkey and its colt wander into sight. Using the donkey for support, Bob carries the infant into New Jerusalem on Christmas Day. His commitment to the child is rewarded with survival, but penance is due. Marshal Sweet arrives to arrest him.

Three Godfathers is saved from maudlin religiosity by its balancing of intensely serious moments with the kind of rambunctious comic scenes one comes to expect in Ford films. The opening exchange between the outlaws and Sweet is such an instance, and another occurs when the three godfathers attempt to care for the infant with the aid of a baby book. The end of the film also returns to this lighter tone. Welcome's judge offers Bob his freedom if he will let Mr. and Mrs. Sweet adopt the baby. Bob refuses, and the judge, realizing the sincerity of Bob's commitment to the child, gives Bob the minimum sentence of one year and one day. The town gives Bob an incredibly cheerful send-off. In a final comic irony, the banker's daughter gives him a warm farewell that seems to promise Bob a future married life when he returns from prison to rear his godson.

Three Godfathers presents an effectively controlled expression of Ford's themes of responsibility to community, commitment to others, and un-ashamed need for home and family. Robert Marmaduke Sangster Hightower's journey to spiritual redemption ends with Ford's optimistic assurance that the values he expounds in *Three Godfathers* are surely worth waiting one year and a day for.

THE WINGS OF EAGLES

Released: 1957
Production: Charles Schnee for Metro-Goldwyn-Mayer
Direction: John Ford
Screenplay: Frank Fenton and William Wister Haines; based on the life and
  writings of Commander Frank W. Wead
Cinematography: Paul C. Vogel
Editing: Gene Ruggiero
Art direction: William A. Horning and Malcolm Brown
Costume design: Walter Plunkett
Music: Jeff Alexander
Running time: 111 minutes

    Principal characters:

Frank W. "Spig" Wead	John Wayne
Carson	Dan Dailey
Minnie Wead	Maureen O'Hara
John Dodge	Ward Bond
John Dale Price	Ken Curtis
Admiral Moffett	Edmund Lowe
Herbert Allen Hazard	Kenneth Tobey
Lila Wead	Mimi Gibson
Doris Wead	Evelyn Rudie

The Wings of Eagles is one of John Ford's most enduring masterpieces.
Although it is one of the most appreciated of the director's late works, it is
one of the least understood. *The Wings of Eagles* is too often looked upon
as simply an entertaining, moving, and brilliantly executed biography of the
late naval commander, playwright, and screenwriter, Frank "Spig" Wead, yet
the film is much more. Whatever its angle of vision, the film reveals with
powerful insight and steady scrutiny the emotional but detached life of Spig
Wead, who alternately personifies human frailties and strengths, failure and
achievement. Credibility is established in the restraint, disarming poignancy,
and mysterious reservoirs of strength captured by John Wayne. Wayne's role
as Spig Wead is one of the best performances of his career.

The Wings of Eagles follows *The Searchers* (1956), filmed the previous year.
To some extent, as in all the Ford-Wayne films, there are continuing patterns
of themes, thoughts, and images which can be viewed simultaneously for
their oneness and for their difference. The character of Spig in *The Wings
of Eagles* can be related to that of Ethan in *The Searchers*; it is in obvious
continuity and harmony with Ford's vision of the driven outsider. In *The
Wings of Eagles*, Ford and Wayne move into a different realm in considering
this archetype. Spig is seen as being both within and without the boundaries
of society, belonging and yet ultimately not belonging to the Navy, to his

comrades, to his beloved wife Min (Maureen O'Hara), or to his writing. Ethan is of the Old West and of the family tradition, although he is forever unsettled and apart, and there is a melancholy but satisfying conclusion to his odyssey. For Spig, however, there develops a constantly somber tone of immutability in his actions that culminates in an almost hopeless and heart-breaking feeling of alienation in the final scenes of the film.

What is truly masterful in *The Wings of Eagles* is the relatively simple execution of the story line. Ford is never heavy-handed, nor does he delib-erately engage in a deep philosophical study that obscures the more imme-diately engaging qualities of the film. The mark of a master is to render the complex and universal into the simple and comprehensible. As in his previous films, Ford never sacrifices his first priority of being storyteller and entertainer. It is a film that engages both the wise and the unsophisticated viewer with levels of interest and methods of identification which strike a responsive chord in all who see it.

The narrative structure is classically direct and uncluttered. A young naval flier, Spig Wead, is impressively adventurous and happily married both to Min and to the Navy. He is reckless and fearless, coming through many mishaps without a scratch. But the death of his baby son scars him and haunts his marriage. He seeks escape from the heartache in greater service while Min waits. After five years of duty, he returns to his wife and two daughters as a more mature man who succeeds briefly in reconciling with Min, despite the feeling of estrangement his absence had created for both of them. Then, at the happiest of moments, tragedy strikes. Spig, who had piloted a plane solo before he could fly and emerged unscathed, trips on his daughter's skate and falls, breaking his neck.

The doctor's prognosis is grim, but the indomitable Spig finds another career in writing and learns to walk with crutches through determination and the support of his friend Carson (Dan Dailey), while Min keeps a distant, loyal vigil. Years after he was established himself as the successful playwright and screenwriter of such works as *Ceiling Zero*, the couple is about to rec-oncile for a second time when Pearl Harbor is attacked. Spig returns to duty at sea and works with jeep carriers in the Pacific; there, he throws himself into his work with such energy and passion that he brings on a heart condition. In the moment of his greatest naval success, the tragic paradox of the film is revealed: that Spig views his life as a personal failure. What he values most—Min and his daughters—may be lost to him, and he is incapacitated, unfit for duty, no longer able to serve. Alone in his cabin, he recalls through flashbacks the family and home he had scorned. Finally, he is transported by a high-wire cable chair to a vessel which will carry him to shore, and the film ends.

In the great Ford films, the balance between comedy and tragedy is a characteristically essential ingredient. In *The Wings of Eagles*, this balance is perfectly modulated, and the emotional reaction of the viewer is always in appropriate response to the action, even when a humorous moment is immediately replaced by a somber image. As the movie begins, for example, high-spirited Spig challenges his army rival Herbert Allen Hazard (Kenneth Tobey) to join him in a short solo flight. This incident begins a series of comic relief episodes of interservice rivalry between Navy and Army and permits the film to open in a daringly light mood. The irrepressible Spig climbs to the cockpit with daring bravado, neglecting to inform his passenger that he has never flown solo before. Pandemonium results. Spig's beautiful wife Min, dressed in becoming blue, pulls up in a red Stutz Bearcat as the plane lifts upward. She calls after him, running hip deep in the water and waving her blue parasol, her exhortations unheard. Moments later, the plane plunges into a pool at the Admiral's garden party, resulting in official reprimands.

In this hilarious opening sequence, we have learned of Spig's penchant for hell-raising and his seeming ability to escape mishap. Ford follows this sequence with one that stands in effective counterpoint. Finding their baby hot and feverish after a stroll, Min has summoned the doctor. Darkness is falling as Spig and a companion roar up the path in the Stutz Bearcat. The interior of the house is dimly lit, foreshadowing tragedy, and Min wears a white blouse and dark skirt which contribute to the fearful mood. A slightly intoxicated Spig slams the door and rushes to the infant, then paces the floor, shocked into sober reality. The gravity of his expression, his tender handling of the baby, and the suggestion of an unspoken prayer all prepare the audience for Min's anguished cry, "Spig!"

Ford has thus established the patterns with which he will tell Spig's story. That the death of the baby has a bitter effect on this marriage is implied in the images, but it is not explicitly stated. That home for Spig will always be a precarious place is already implicit. This separates the picture from the mainstream of Fordian thought in which home has been consistently depicted as a haven, as, for example, in *How Green Way My Valley* (1941) and *The Searchers*, and as a nostalgic cradle of happiness, removed from disharmony.

Ford also exercises a different direction in his treatment of women, a divergent track begun in *Rio Grande* (1950) and *The Quiet Man* (1952), both of which costarred Maureen O'Hara as the iron-willed but vulnerable woman whose onscreen chemistry with John Wayne is invaluable to the director. With a penetrating and compassionate eye, Ford enables us to predict the turbulent course this marriage will follow. As opposed to *Rio Grande*, in which the couple is separated more by the cavalry than by emotional conflict, it is Spig's own elusive nature as much as the Navy that deepens the gap in the relationship here. Min's emotions range from indulgence, patience, and devotion to skepticism, self-rejection, and despair. At the end she emerges with mature resignation and unconditional love.

After the death of the baby, Spig flees more intently into Navy service to compensate for his loss rather than staying close to Min. Ford follows him through a long tour of duty, intercut with uproarious peccadilloes between Navy and Army, one of which is an around-the-world flight. As Min and the girls sit in the semidarkness of a movie theater, the children recognize their father in a Movietone newsreel, where he is seen receiving a cup as leader of the winning Navy team. For Min, this image of Spig gives shattering insight into the emptiness of her life. She has gone through a period of living with images, interspersed with telephone calls and unkept promises. Spig's singleminded dedication to the Navy has forced her out and obliged her to live alone with their girls with only memories of the real Spig. It is at this moment of revelation, with a flickering projection on the screen, that she recognizes the lack of fulfillment in her life.

Ironically, it is after this scene that the maverick Spig returns home, but it is his two young daughters who welcome him, not Min. The children react with casual curiosity toward the father they do not know, but Spig rapidly disarms and charms them. There are empty liquor bottles in the house and it is clear that it has been unattended and the children left to their own devices. As Min enters through a softly diffused amber light, she epitomizes the self-neglect that has resulted from Spig's ambivalent attitude toward her. A cigarette dangles from her mouth as she pushes open the front door. She carries a bag of groceries, kicks off her shoes, massages her legs and walks to the kitchen with a slight stagger, suggesting that she has been drinking.

Spig has returned at a critical moment before the loneliness and rejection she has felt for so long have begun to change her irrevocably. Spig recognizes this and assumes the responsibility to change his priorities and perspectives. There is a romantic reconciliation which delights the children and steadies Spig and Min, affirming their love just before its greatest test. For in the tranquility of Spig's first night home, one of his children calls out. Spig dashes from the bed and trips on a roller skate that sends him crashing down the stairs. He lies stricken at the foot of the stairs, his neck broken, as the anguished Min calls the naval hospital. It is one of the greatest ironies in Ford's work that the reckless daredevil and hedonist is brought down not in a plane crash or a brawl, but by something as innocuous as a child's skate in the safe confines of his home.

Although Spig is not self-pitying in the hospital scenes, he is initially in a defeatist mood. Neither the doctors, the ever-vigilant Min, nor even his friend Carson can shake him into hope. In his most generous yet ruthless gesture, he endeavors to cast Min out of his life. "Take your turn, Min," he tells her. "I took mine." Only after he has faced the other side of himself, the shattered hero who has lost everything, can he begin to see things as they are. His ever-present and faithful buddy Carson helps him tap his reserves of inner strength and draw on the will to "move that toe." With total concentration which persists late into the night, as Ford shows in one of his most dramatic images,

Spig does the seemingly impossible: he moves his toe, and, in time, he graduates to crutches and a new vocation. Like a baby, Spig has learned to walk
and to find a place in life. Unfortunately, his recovery is not complete, for
he remains embittered, once again isolating himself in his work, an iconoclast
who voluntarily locks himself out of any deep human relationship. His conquering of his physical handicap is admirable, but he cannot overcome his
self-imposed alientation—a condition which is truly tragic.

Spig's writing career takes him to Hollywood to work with the noted movie
director, John Dodge (Ward Bond), a thinly disguised version of Ford himself,
for whom the real Commander Ward wrote *Air Mail* (1932) and *They Were
Expendable* (1945). In his last role in a Ford film, Ward Bond plays the
director as a down-to-earth man of keen insight, firmness, and ambiguity who
enjoys a sip of whiskey hidden in his cane. His response to the handicapped
Spig is sympathetic, but he makes no pretense that he expects anything less
than perfection. Spig accepts his position with ease; he is accustomed to
taking orders and following through. Thus, he relaxes into the role of high-
paid screenwriter with an expansive house and the spoils of a successful
Hollywood career.

It is at this time that Spig reasons he now has something tangible to offer
Min at last, and he attempts a reconciliation. Although she has aged throughout the turbulent course of their relationship, there has never been another
woman in Spig's life. There has been, however, his passion for the Navy. As
Spig and Min meet at her San Francisco apartment, there is a mood of
renewed hope and optimism. As Spig prepares for her homecoming, however,
World War II intrudes and separates them once again. Spig goes to the Pacific
where he throws himself tirelessly into his work. He is reunited with his
friends Carson and John Price (Ken Curtis), whom he once more treats with
initial warmth and then casual indifference. When Price visits him and innocently plants the thought that Spig will turn into the jeep carrier concept,
Spig callously forgets the other's presence, only turning after Price has gone
to call after him.

Ford's use both of Price and Carson measures the depth of Spig's responses
to people and the carelessness with which he treats emotion. Carson has
always been near when needed, a source of fun, loyalty, support, and motivation. Spig's recovery was, in part, attributable to Carson's upbraiding of
him and the other's ingenuity, perseverance, and faith. Now, years later, Spig
must again depend on him, for it is Carson who saves his life during a bombing.
Although Carson is a good person and a true friend, gratitude and appreciation are not feelings Spig is able to express in words or in actions, and this
relationship reveals Spig to be more sadly crippled emotionally that physically.

The end of the film shows Spig suspended on a wire between two ships.
He is being taken, both metaphorically and actually, from a known past to
an uncertain future. In a sense, the audience is left suspended as well. The

real Spig Wead lived until 1947, but for dramatic purposes Ford wanted to end his story here, preferring to leave the impression of uncertainty with the audience to parallel the feelings of the protagonist.

YOUNG MR. LINCOLN

Released: 1939
Production: Darryl F. Zanuck and Kenneth Macgowan for Twentieth Century-Fox
Direction: John Ford
Screenplay: Lamar Trotti
Cinematography: Bert Glennon
Editing: Walter Thompson
Music: Alfred Newman

Principal characters:

Abraham Lincoln ....Henry Fonda
Abigail Clay .... Alice Brady
Mary Todd .... Marjorie Weaver
Hannah Clay .... Arleen Whelan
Ann Rutledge .... Pauline Moore
Matt Clay .... Richard Cromwell
Palmer Cass .... Ward Bond
John Felder .... Donald Meek
Stephan Douglas .... Milburn Stone

Young Mr. Lincoln won no awards for 1939, the year in which John Ford's *Stagecoach* walked off with many. In recent years, however, *Young Mr. Lincoln* has been the subject of a wealth of serious film criticism. An example of "film-as-myth" par excellence, *Young Mr. Lincoln* weaves Lincoln's youth, loss of Ann Rutledge, choice of law profession, and early cases into a mythic tapestry that resonates in our knowledge of the rest of the Lincoln history/legend.

Young Mr. Lincoln begins with the legend. The film opens with the poem "Nancy Hanks" by Rosemary and Stephen Vincent Benét, in which questions to which we know the answers are posed by Lincoln's mother. We are thus alerted that a general *awareness* of the history (not simply the history itself) is going to be incorporated into the story. The film assumes and depends on audience awareness of the legend, yet at the same time, it rewrites it according to Ford's special vision of Lincoln, his role in America's history, and the forces that directed Lincoln. The poem sets up two dynamics: one is a series of either/or questons, and the other is a limiting function, establishing that the film will act out the Lincoln myth according to some principles while opposing others: it will be a rewriting, not a retelling. What is left out or repressed in such a rewriting becomes fully as important as what is included, especially in a process as self-conscious as the one employed in this film.

Three actions occuring from the film's beginning must be separated before they can be clearly seen. First is the rewriting of the Lincoln myth, second is the creation of new values (and the negative aspect—the leaving behind of values and history that are normally part of the myth) to be affirmed by this rewriting of the myth, and third is the complex function of critiquing the first two. This third function, carried out at a formal level of visual style, is what makes the best of Ford's films so much richer than most: it both affirms and critiques the values by which we live.

In the film's opening, Abraham Lincoln (Henry Fonda) decides to study law after being given a law book in trade by a family headed West. He discusses his decision at the gravesite of his beloved Ann Rutledge (Pauline Moore), who died the previous winter. Later, as a young lawyer, Lincoln handles cases with humor and fairness. During a county fair, a man is killed and the two sons of the woman who gave Lincoln the law books are accused. Lincoln takes the case and supports the mother (who witnessed the knifing) in her refusal to name which son is guilty. In an exciting courtroom drama, Lincoln forces the real killer—who has claimed to be an eyewitness—to admit that he actually killed the man after the two boys ran away from the site.

The poem and the backward-looking structure of the film are not the only indications that knowledge of the Lincoln legend on the part of the audience is assumed. In the first scene, in which Lincoln gives a speech (both to the audience and to the characters in the film), his first line is, "You all know who I am." The comment calls upon both knowledge of history and knowledge of film, thus setting the necessary self-awareness mechanisms in the audience into motion. The characterizations of Mary Todd (Marjorie Weaver) and Stephen Douglas (Milburn Stone) also rest on a knowledge of Lincoln *outside* the film, but necessary to it. Thus the film relies on external knowledge of the legend, but through Ford's choice of the determinants of the rewriting, the values of the legend are redefined. This retelling is experienced especially powerfully because it calls upon knowledge shared by the audience but external to the film. We become implicated in its reformulation as Ford directs us to supply knowledge selectively about the characters and their history.

The creation or recruitment of values is the ideological function of the film. Following the poem, this tends to be a series of binary oppositions, either/or choices, which immediately restrict the subtlety and nuance of the values represented. This is the usual ideological operation of myth: though the conventionalized, schematized representation of narrative, complexity and ambiguity are far less important than ritual. The narrative pattern of ritual must be constant, and must be schematized or abstracted from the complications of everyday experience. Thus they are nearly binary systems in which operation masks contradiction and function often as a repressive force in a culture—the Catholic Church in Latin America, for example. Ford treats the Lincoln myth in this manner in the narrative, then critiques its ideological function formally.

In *Young Mr. Lincoln*, this operation is represented graphically in the choices he makes: they are not masked but clearly represented, and all are immediately (because of our knowledge) recognizable as being determined, or operations of fate. The first is the acceptance of the law book from the mother (Alice Brady) in exchange for supplies, which not only is fated, but sets up determined, valued relationships: the mother is the giver of the law. The second determined choice is whether he will go into law: the spirit of Ann Rutledge and a stick "decide," but since we already know the outcome, this simply functions to further implicate Ann (and sexuality) in the decision. She then becomes another inscription in the Lincoln myth: a dead first love who influences important aspects of a mythic hero is often part of the legend.

Lincoln's role as mediator is insisted upon in a series of oppositions. His first law case is handled with intelligence and finally force ("Did you fellas ever hear 'bout the time I butted two heads together?"), and all parties are satisfied in the end. The money which changes hands is exactly right for Lincoln's fee, and his unifying function has been introduced. A somewhat irrational aspect of that function has also been introduced: the case is resolved not simply "by the law," but by Lincoln's threat and ability to carry it out. At the fair, this unifying function is again illustrated: he will not decide between the two pies he is "judging," and simply keeps taking a bite of one, then another, as the scene finally fades out.

Lincoln's force and irrational character are also demonstrated, however innocently: he wins the rail-splitting and he cheats by using a mule to win the tug of war for his side. In spite of his profession, unifying fairness and calm, he is even at this point shown to be not dependent upon logical, rational, knowable precepts. He is further the unifier in the main drama of the film: he refuses to consider one son guilty and split the family, and it is here that he demonstrates his greatest insight. He does not win the case with fancy legal maneuvers but with divine inspiration via the mother, who gives him the almanac. This element of irrationality is an important aspect in the myth, but relative to history, perhaps the expected metaphor of the family for the nation is of even greater value in terms of its absence. This film about the great unifier and mediator (in harmony with Ford's vision of Lincoln) does not even mention what the majority of the audience might most easily as- sociate with Lincoln the President: the Civil War and the tearing apart of the nation. Only his unifying function is suggested in his "innocent" playing of "Dixie." The *repression* of this violent aspect in the reworking of the myth and the inscription of its opposite value—unification—describes exactly the repressive ideological function of myth, and it is reversed on the formal level in this film.

Another important aspect of the historical myth which is repressed in *Young Mr. Lincoln* is that of the work process. Not only do we see very little of the political in this film (one speech, after which we do not even know or care if he has won the election; Stephen Douglas; and a few references to his career, past and future), but also the process by which Lincoln becomes a lawyer and a politician is telescoped into the transition of a dissolve. The point is not that hours and years of hard work could have been shown, but that this repression leads to the second important variation of the myth. Lincoln is a mythological figure because of a special state of being, not a state of becoming. He is a passive, removed figure in the narrative from the first shot; he already *is* (in history, in the audience's knowledge, and in myth) at that moment and is very little different at the end. At one point in the trial he says, "I may not know much about the law, but I know what's right!"

This is the crux of the Lincoln myth: he *knows*, he *is*, he does not *learn*; that which he learns does him little good. What he *knows* on intuition, however, will take him to his fate. He has a special connection to God himself. In the Lamar Trotti screenplay (written with Ford) he actually talks with God as he walks off at the end of the film. Thus his value comes not from his culture, but from above. He is essentially a visitor, like most mythic heroes. Lincoln thus becomes less a historical myth and more a cultural one, in which the facts of history which root the character in "becoming" are repressed, characteristics of greatness are detached from their generation, and a mode of being unrelated to social processes is defined.

The narrative, then, is a standard one: the myth is rewritten to remove those problematic processes of work and failure; everything that does not affirm the values of the culture is repressed and the hero is removed from a historical context. The ideological operation offers knowledge as a divine gift, the repression of sexuality as a way to such divine gifts, mothers as handmaidens of God's word, and force as the right of those who *know*. It suppresses objection based on logic and work and teaches us that history is not a process of men and women but of larger-than-life *men* whom we can understand only on faith and acceptance. This is often the function of popular culture, to suppress and rework various myths and thereby to console, offer faith-based explanations, and repress those disruptive and sexual elements that would not fit well into a hierarchical society.

There are many reasons films fill this function, such as the huge amount of money required to make them, thus giving the power structure a real stake in their impact on people; and the ideological control exercised on both an implicit and an explicit level by the people and institutions who control the money. But there is room for protest, or subversion, and it exists at the level of the form. A director can question and critique and sometimes even condemn (as Douglas Sirk does in his melodramas of the 1950's) the values offered by the narrative of the film. In *Young Mr. Lincoln*, the critique functions through a process of abstraction which involves the audience in a constant process of "becoming aware" of the work of the narrative.

The character of Lincoln, through whom this process is carried out, is abstracted and removed from the narrative of the film first by our awareness of the myth and Lincoln's "real" place in history. Further, music, composition, focus, acting, movement within the frame, and chiaroscuro all function to remove Lincoln visually and emotionally and to create at least two levels (sometimes three) of which the audience is simultaneously aware. Lincoln seems to exist on a different level from that of the action of the film. He drops into the film to narrate his own story from time to time, but is rarely fully integrated into the narrative of the film. He illustrates and comments on the film from without, often merely "watching over" the stylized action taken from the events of his life, often "narrating" or walking through those events, but generally not belonging to the level of action.

The first view we have of Lincoln is accompanied by low music. It immediately removes what will follow from the preceding level of pompous, overacted, tongue-in-cheek speechmaking; we see Lincoln reclining in a chair carving a piece of wood. The shot is an introduction, a static shot acquainting the audience with the actor who will play the part. He rises slowly, moving with the thoughtful deliberateness which will continue to isolate him from the rest of the film by the necessary slowing down of action that his movement dictates. Throughout the film, most notably in the murder sequence and the trial scenes, Lincoln hangs nearly suspended on the side of the frame, watching the action, both to function as the determining influence which makes it possible and necessary, and to stand nearly motionless waiting for his cue. In the murder sequence he follows the crowd to the site without sharing their excitement, hangs back by the little family in his dark clothes and hat as the townspeople mill around in the background, and steps in at his cue to take his position in the narrative.

In the courtroom, Lincoln is often static, framing two sides of the shot by his dark outline. His foreground dominance is not part of the action, but determines it. In other shots, he moves restlessly on another level from the action of the trial, either above it (as when he goes up the stairs and leafs through some books with the trial going on around him, sitting down on the rail as though taking a rest from his role) or below it, sitting down on the little steps that lead up to the jury box while John Felder (Donald Meek) is giving an impassioned speech. This movement is in opposition to the general movements of the court, as well as to the expected movement of his character within the scene. There are shots which compose Lincoln to resemble a bust of himself, and one in which he is draped horizontally across the frame while questioning a witness. This deliberate failure to conform to expected visual composition calls attention to the difference in the elements of the frame. The contradiction between what the narrative would seem to demand—formal courtroom composition—and what Ford presents visually requires the audience to become aware (to varying degrees), and thus constitutes a critique.

From the day Lincoln rides into town on a mule to set himself up as a lawyer (the scene itself looking like a highly stylized reenactment) his clothes set him apart from the rest of the people through chiaroscuro: he is abstracted in black and white with no gray at all; others, even when dressed in black and white, contrast with his austerity. The costume itself is clearly a costume; the stovepipe hat no one else wears is a self-conscious prop in terms of the film. It is, however, primarily in the play of light and dark that his costume places Lincoln on a different level from the rest of the film: when he is first in his office settling a case, the white of his shirt seems to collect light and glow with it, while the black of his vest contrasts it. In the night with his coat on he is appropriately like a spirit belonging to another world.

Lincoln is played with a detachment unmatched by any other character. In the courtroom scenes this detachment is contrasted for humor (as well as for purposes of removing Lincoln from the level of action) with the overly enthusiastic and emotional investment in the case by the prosecuting lawyer. With Palmer Cass (Ward Bond), the trap is set and sprung in a manner that underscores the process of acting out that Lincoln demonstrates through most of the film. His detachment from the action of the film is a part of the scene: Lincoln already *knows*—both the answers to the questions and the entirety of the story of his life.

As the film draws to a close, Lincoln becomes totally abstracted to the level he has functioned on through most of the film, and the level of action falls away. When he walks out of the courtroom toward the door where the "people are waiting," he is already removed from the people around him, even while he speaks to them. Mary Todd cannot quite touch him, and Stephen Douglas refers to history: they will be opponents again, and he will not make the mistake of underestimating Lincoln again. As Lincoln walks on, the people do not exist. We experience them as the actor does, hearing only their cheers; but the cheers are reserved for the "real" Lincoln. They have no place on the level the film is moving toward. Only the family appears once more to take their leave of the man and the myth, and then Lincoln walks off into the storm and out of the film itself. Taking his place is a bust of himself, then the statue. The abstraction is total at this point; the "actor" Lincoln has returned to the level of statue and myth, having left it on one plane (but never moved from it on another) to narrate and illustrate this version of his story.

The constant split between Lincoln and the narrative is a self-conscious device which insists upon the necessity of becoming aware—of questioning both what is inscribed in the created myth and what is being repressed. Unlike Douglas Sirk, Ford is not clear in his denunciation of the ideology of the narrative (at least at this point in his career), but his insistence in visual terms that the viewer at least be aware of the process of mythmaking and the values affirmed and repressed is at least as powerful (if less easily articulated because it is visual) as those elements of the narrative which construct the myth. There is an unusual amount of freedom to perceive both functions simultaneously in Ford's films, and to experience them according to the subjectivity of the viewer.

HOWARD HAWKS

BALL OF FIRE

Released: 1941
Production: Samuel Goldwyn for RKO/Radio
Direction: Howard Hawks
Screenplay: Billy Wilder and Charles Brackett; based on the story *From A to Z* by Billy Wilder and Thomas Monroe
Cinematography: Gregg Toland
Editing: Daniel Mandell
Running time: 111 minutes

Principal characters:
Professor Bertram Potts .... Gary Cooper
Sugarpuss O'Shea .... Barbara Stanwyck
Joe Lilac .... Dana Andrews
Professor Oddly .... Richard Haydn
Professor Gurkakoff .... Oscar Homolka
Professor Jerome .... Henry Travers
Professor Magenbruch .... S. Z. Sakall
Professor Robinson .... Tully Marshall
Professor Quintana .... Leonid Kinskey
Professor Peagram .... Aubrey Mather
Garbage Man .... Allen Jenkins

Although Hollywood has produced a variety of characterizations of the intellectual—from Bing Crosby's crooning professor in *College Humor* (1933) to Clint Eastwood's macho, mountain-climbing art historian who is also an assassin in *The Eiger Sanction* (1975)—the image audiences seem to remember best is that of the stuffy absent-minded professor. *Ball of Fire*, directed by Howard Hawks and written by Billy Wilder and Charles Brackett, is perhaps the film which best embodies the quintessential use of that stereotype.

The film opens in the study of a group of scholars who have been living and working together for nine years. They are predominately old, white-haired, conservatively dressed, and slightly unkempt. Of the eight members, only Bertram Potts (Gary Cooper) has any youth or virility. Their housekeeper, who regards all of them as overgrown children, scolds them for sneaking into the pantry to eat the strawberry jam. The project of the group is to write all the articles for an encyclopedia financed by a rich inventor who is upset that his name is not in any other encyclopedia. Each scholar specializes in a given discipline, such as botany or history, and writes all the articles in his specific area. Potts's specialty is language.

Although the youngest of the scholars, Potts is very much the pedant. He chides the housekeeper for splitting infinitives and believes that his only concern is grammar; he is naïve, innocent, and sheltered from the world. It takes a garbage man, some gangsters, and a nightclub singer to overturn the quiet, orderly world of Potts and the other scholars. The garbage man (Allen Jenkins), having noticed that the household possesses a great many books, appears, hoping that the scholars can assist him with answers to a newspaper quiz, the only use anyone seems to have for their knowledge. Similar to all the other scholars, Potts has reached the letter "S" in his research and has just written an article on slang. Listening to the garbage man talk, however, Potts realizes that his article is very much out of date and in need of revision. Since the only place to research contemporary slang is in the outside world, he leaves the house, the only one of the scholars to do so in the nine years that they have been working on the encyclopedia. (To ensure that their script was authentic and contemporary, Wilder and Brackett made similar investigations of slang, visiting malt shops, bars, and racetracks—putting the bar bills and racetrack losses on the film's expense account.)

During his research in the outside world, Potts listens to many different people until finally he wanders into a nightclub where Sugarpuss O'Shea (Barbara Stanwyck) is singing. Potts makes careful notes on the slang she uses in her song, and after the show, goes to her dressing room to invite her to come to the scholars' house the next day to assist him in his linguistic research. Sugarpuss is totally unreceptive both to the idea and to Potts, whom she neither likes nor understands; he is totally alien to her world of nightclubs, gangsters, flashy clothes, and easy money. Later that night, however, she is forced to accept the invitation because she needs a place to hide from the police who want to question her about a murder committed by her gangster lover, Joe Lilac (Dana Andrews).

Naturally, her presence in the house completely disrupts work on the encyclopedia. Not one of the staid old scholars is immune to her vivacity and allure, and before very long she has them dancing around the room in a Conga line. Finally Potts feels he must ask her to leave so that they can continue their work: "Make no mistake, I shall regret the absence of your keen mind. Unfortunately it is inseparable from an extremely disturbing body." However, since the police are still looking for her, Sugarpuss cannot leave. In order to change Potts's mind, she stands on a stack of books to kiss him, showing she does know a good use for books.

Completely out of his realm in the world of romance, Potts falls in love with Sugarpuss, not realizing that she is merely using him until she can rejoin Joe Lilac, and a great many complications ensue. First, Lilac tricks Potts and the scholars into bringing Sugarpuss to him so that he can marry her to keep her from testifying against him. Then, when Potts learns about the deception, he is disillusioned and leaves, believing Sugarpuss wants to marry Lilac. Sugarpuss, however, now finds Lilac and his world repugnant and refuses to marry him, with Lilac responding by threatening to kill Potts if she refuses.

In the best tradition of romantic comedies, Sugarpuss comes within moments of marrying Lilac, but the scholars apply their knowledge to outwit the gangsters sent to hold them captive until the wedding is over. They use a mirror to concentrate the sun's rays in order to burn through the cord of a picture hung above one of the gangsters, causing it to fall on him. The scholars then overpower the gangsters and set off to rescue Sugarpuss. After finding out where Lilac is hiding by tickling their former captors for information, they use guns and a blackjack to capture the whole gang. In an amusing sequence Potts studies an old-fashioned book on boxing in preparation for fighting Lilac, and when the techniques in the book do not work, he tosses the book away and immediately knocks out the gangster of his own accord. He then convinces Sugarpuss that he is her man, this time by a kiss rather than reason.

The basic concepts of the film play upon caricatures—the idea that a scholar is a stodgy, ineffectual person who is isolated from ordinary concerns, and the idea that to become a "real man" it is necessary to become physically violent. Once one realizes that caricature is the style of most of the film, however, the contrasts between Sugarpuss and the encyclopedists are delightful. Picking up a book of Greek philosophy, Sugarpuss says, "I've got a set like this with a radio inside," and when she invites him to pour a couple of drinks, light the fire, and "move in on my brain," Potts can only reply, "Any hasty random discussion would be of no scientific value."

It is also a delight to watch the group (played by such accomplished character actors as Oscar Homolka, S. Z. Sakall, and Richard Haydn) progress from being stuffy pedants to "squirrelly cherubs" (as Sugarpuss calls them) to intrepid, if not very adept, heroes. Gary Cooper, who plays Bertram Potts, was usually cast as a man of action, but in this film he is completely believable as a strait-laced grammarian who is disconcerted by the sight of Sugarpuss' leg. The biggest delight of the film, however, is the performance of Barbara Stanwyck as Sugarpuss O'Shea, the worldly-wise nightclub singer who easily manipulates the scholars but does not realize that she is falling in love. Although she is appropriately flippant and cynical in her early dealings with Potts and the other scholars, she also makes the romantic scenes near the end of the film very moving.

Director Howard Hawks is noted for his films of male camaraderie, and *Ball of Fire* fits into that mold even though Hawks's men are usually men of action rather than men of thought. Two moving scenes express this camaraderie: in one, they sit around a table the night before Potts is to be married and sing songs; in the other, when they all have returned to work thinking Sugarpuss is gone forever, the housekeeper accidentally turns on the phonograph, and each pauses wordlessly and remembers the liveliness Sugarpuss had brought to the house. Hawks also paces the film well, presenting an unhurried first part to set up the quiet, orderly world of the encyclopedists in order to emphasize the later confusion when Sugarpuss is thrown into their midst.

Ball of Fire, in short, combines excellent acting, screenwriting, and directing to produce a delightful comedy. A remake of *Ball of Fire* was filmed in 1948 as *A Song Is Born*, a musical featuring Danny Kaye and Virginia Mayo. Even though the remake was also directed by Hawks, it has few of the virtues of the original, and even Hawks is said not to have cared for it.

THE BIG SLEEP

Released: 1946
Production: Howard Hawks for Warner Bros.
Direction: Howard Hawks
Screenplay: William Faulkner, Leigh Brackett, and Jules Furthman; based on the novel of the same name by Raymond Chandler
Cinematography: Sid Hickox
Editing: Christian Nyby
Running time: 114 minutes

Principal characters:

Phillip Marlowe	Humphrey Bogart
Vivian Sternwood Rutledge	Lauren Bacall
Carmen Sternwood	Martha Vickers
Eddie Mars	John Ridgely
Book Seller	Dorothy Malone
Harry Jones	Elisha Cook, Jr.
General Sternwood	Charles Waldron

The Big Sleep is a classic on many counts. It is a *film noir* that consistently appears on lists or retrospectives on the movement, even though as a big-budget, big-star production it violates the "B" film norm for *film noir*. It is a cult favorite on television, college campuses, and at art houses. The Bogart-Bacall relationship, not as outrageous as that depicted in their first film together, Howard Hawks's *To Have and Have Not* (1944), succeeded off screen as well as on. The film is a classic of the private detective genre and is the best example of the type of mystery in which no one knows or cares (including the director and writers) about the intricacies of who did what to whom. Finally, *The Big Sleep* is classic Warner Bros. and classic Howard Hawks and is generally regarded as a completely successful adaptation of a much-loved Raymond Chandler novel to film. Chandler himself liked the film, calling Bogart "the genuine article" and admiring Hawks's direction.

The Big Sleep opened to excellent reviews. Bogart and Bacall were already known as a "hot couple," which assured good box-office receipts, and both critics and the public loved the film. Bogart was considered perfect for the tough-yet-romantic character of Phillip Marlowe, and today, most people—since they see the film before reading the book—picture Bogart when they meet Chandler's Marlowe in the novel.

The plot of the film makes no real sense. Phillip Marlowe is employed by General Sternwood (Charles Waldron), a sick, rich old man, to deal with a man who is asking Sternwood to pay legally uncollectible gambling debts. The debts were incurred by Carmen Sternwood (Martha Vickers), the General's youngest daughter, who is spoiled, perhaps slightly retarded, and certainly sexually perverse. The General has another daughter, Vivian (Lauren Bacall), who tries to find out from Marlowe what her father has asked him to do. She and a lot of other people assume that his job is to find Sean Regan, who has disappeared. Sean was a friend and employee of the General who was actually a surrogate son. In the film it is fairly clear that he is dead, but who killed him, and who later killed the Sternwood's chauffeur, simply ceases to be an issue. In the novel, the murderess is the dangerously psychotic Carmen, who nearly kills Marlowe as well. Hawks explains that the Production Code officials suggested the ending upon which the film finally settled: Carmen will be put away and "taken care of," and Eddie Mars (John Ridgely), who is instrumental in her corruption, is killed by his own men, leaving Marlowe and Vivian to carry on their affair. The story is carried along with plenty of action (including Bacall singing a sexy song in a gambling club) and fast, witty dialogue, and is enhanced by the love story of Marlowe and Vivian. Chandler bemoaned Hollywood's insistence upon the "love angle," but the change of focus from the novelist's lonely detective always living up to his personal honor in a corrupt world to a love story between two strong adults provides much more than a "Hollywood" ending.

The Phillip Marlowe of Chandler's novel is tough, romantic, in control, and above all pure. He is untainted by the tawdry world in which he lives and the underworld characters with whom he rubs elbows. He is a romantic, always looking for a woman worthy of him, but (and this is a key to Chandler) every potential candidate lets him down. Chandler's Marlowe is at heart a misogynist whose fundamental purity is a direct result of being uncontaminated by women. Carmen elicits a declaration of his hatred of women when she comes to his room to trade her body for his silence. His room is soiled by her very presence: "But this was the room I had to live in. . . . I couldn't stand her in that room any longer." When Carmen leaves, he must cleanse the room: "I walked to the windows and pulled the shades up and opened the windows wide." The next morning: "You can have a hangover from other things than alcohol. I had one from women. Women make me sick."

Marlowe's neurotic fear of women, and especially of their sexuality, is the basis of his alienation in the novel; only in his room can he keep himself, his memories, and his future safe from them. The Marlowe of the film is very different: like all Hawks heroes, he is challenged by sexually aggressive women. His relationship with Vivian culminates in the kind of hopeful love of which *film noir* is capable, but only at the expense of her character. Before she acknowledges her love, she is feisty, strong, and equal to him. The camera follows her in their first encounter in her bedroom—she is clearly in control both of our attention (through the camera) and of the space of the frame in which she freely moves. In their verbal sparring, when she is "winning," she dominates the frame visually, but as she falls in love with him, he gains power over her and she becomes less and less the dynamic, interesting character she was. She is merely an observer in Joe Brody's apartment, sitting still on the couch while the men spar, and she continues to lose mobility until in the final scenes she must sit like a statue. The degree of space characters create around themselves is indicative of their control in any film, certainly, but even more so in a Hawks film, where physical space is so important in determining power relationships. Vivian's space decreases as Marlowe "conquers" her in this film. By the end of *The Big Sleep* she has been visually immobilized and confined and verbally reduced to a second-rate assistant for Marlowe, in sharp contrast to the aggressive, witty, and tough fighter she was in the beginning, and the independent, provocative woman she was in Eddie Mars's gambling club. This process of "taming" the strong, aggressive and independent woman is not as effective in *The Big Sleep* as in most examples of *film noir* because sexual fear is not at the heart of the film, as it is in the book. Vivian (and Carmen, as a symbol for women in general) is not the threat to Marlowe that she is in the book, so the need for her confinement and control is not so urgent, and it is accomplished with more subtlety. Vivian's taming is presented as important for its positive rewards rather than for its loss of mobility and independence for her. The film *The Big Sleep* is a more "healthy" male fantasy than those usually seen in *film noir*, but the process of controlling aggression and undercutting the independence and intelligence of the female is still very much present, though in the less urgent form that Hawks's less paranoid view of the world requires.

BRINGING UP BABY

Released: 1938
Production: Howard Hawks for RKO/Radio
Direction: Howard Hawks
Screenplay: Dudley Nichols and Hager Wilde; based on a story by Hager Wilde
Cinematography: Russell Metty
Editing: George Hively
Running time: 102 minutes

> *Principal characters:*
> David Huxley .... Cary Grant
> Susan Vance .... Katharine Hepburn
> Mrs. Carlton Random .... May Robson
> Major Applegate .... Charles Ruggles
> Alexander Peabody .... George Irving
> Alice Swallow .... Virginia Walker

A classic of screen comedy, *Bringing Up Baby* is a frantically funny film with a breathless pace sustained by unflagging comic invention and constant surprises. It is a creation of inspired lunacy whose comic perfection is orchestrated by director Howard Hawks and performed by a wonderfully adept cast. Although Hawks is known primarily for his action films of male camaraderie, he proved here just as he had in *Twentieth Century* (1934) that he was also an accomplished director of comedy.

Dr. David Huxley (Cary Grant) is a paleontologist who hopes to persuade wealthy Mrs. Carlton Random (May Robson) to donate one million dollars to the museum where he works. In pursuit of this goal he is playing golf with her lawyer, Alexander Peabody (George Irving). During the game when he goes to look for his golf ball, however, he discovers that madcap heiress Susan Vance (Katharine Hepburn) mistakes his golf ball for hers and will not listen to his attempted explanation. After David finally proves that the ball is his, Susan dismisses the whole issue with the remark, "It's only a game." David's troubles are not over, however, for just as he is about to resume his game, he notices Susan trying to drive off in his car. When he tries to stop her, she insists that it is her car and drives off with David standing on the running board.

Later that evening David again encounters Susan, and again the results are calamitous. Walking by her in a restaurant, he slips on an olive she has dropped on the floor. David immediately tries to get as far away from her as possible, but Susan begins to be intrigued by him. When a psychiatrist (at whose table she stops to absent-mindedly pick up some more olives) explains to her that "the love impulse frequently reveals itself in terms of conflict,"

Susan's feelings about David seem to crystallize. Always direct and candid, she immediately goes up to him and tells him that he has a fixation on her. David's supposed interest in her seems to spur Susan on to greater heights of absurd behavior, which are—from David's viewpoint—new outrages.

Bringing Up Baby builds its comic world with careful increments of absurdity. In the restaurant, for example, the series of comic happenings begins with David slipping on the olive and landing on his top hat. The progression continues as, through a mistake made by Susan, David is accused of stealing a woman's purse. Susan then accidentally rips David's coat. When he tells her to go away, refusing to listen to her apologies, it is her turn to be offended, and she starts to walk away, but as she does so, the back of her evening gown is torn away because David has inadvertently been standing on it. He sees what has happened, runs after her, and claps his battered top hat over her exposed posterior. Startled and offended, Susan, as usual, refuses to listen to his attempted explanations and orders him to leave her alone and stop his strange behavior. But when she discovers her predicament, she orders him to do something to help her. They leave the restaurant together with David walking closely behind Susan so her torn gown will not be noticed. The director and screenwriters have thus adroitly escalated a slip on the floor into a major comic scene in which David and Susan walk through the restaurant as if they were glued together, provoking laughter from all the patrons.

Later that evening, as she repairs David's torn coat, Susan learns that David is trying to see Alexander Peabody, whom she knows well. She offers to drive David to Peabody's home, overcoming his objections that he is supposed to meet Alice Swallow (Virginia Walker), whom he is going to marry the next day. Susan's plan to get David together with Peabody goes awry (as we might have expected, although the plan seems plausible at first), but she is determined not to let David disappear from her life. When she receives a tame leopard named Baby from her brother in Brazil, she telephones David for advice with the excuse that he is the only zoologist she knows. She then lures him to her apartment on the pretext that Baby has attacked her and next tricks him into accompanying her and Baby to the house of her aunt (who happens to be Mrs. Random) in Connecticut, even though it is the day he is to be married.

The accumulation of zany incidents begins to accelerate again as a further complication is now introduced. David has just received a package containing the intercostal clavicle bone that he needs to complete the reconstruction of a huge brontosaurus on which he has been working for four years. When he is tricked into accompanying Susan to Connecticut, he has no opportunity to leave the bone behind and takes it along with him.

After several misadventures during the trip to Connecticut, David and Susan arrive at her aunt's house with Baby. While David is taking a shower, Susan sees an opportunity to prevent him from returning to New York to be married by having his clothes sent to town to be pressed and cleaned. After discovering what Susan has done, David puts on the only available garment, a fur-trimmed negligee, to look for the gardener whose clothes he hopes to borrow, muttering that Susan is "spoiled, conceited, and scatterbrained." He is stopped in his search for suitable clothing by the ring of the doorbell. When he answers it, he finds himself confronting Susan's aunt, an imposing-looking elderly woman who demands to know who he is and what he is doing in such clothes. He replies despairingly that he is not quite himself, and her further questions push him past the breaking point—he leaps straight up in the air, shouting, "I just went gay all of a sudden."

Director Hawks does not, however, let this wacky sequence end here; he adds a barking dog, George, and the chattering presence of Susan to prevent David from getting in a word of explanation to the aunt. When David shouts for silence, Susan only looks at him indulgently and goes on talking to her aunt. Only after he stomps on her foot does she stop for a moment, and he stalks off to continue his search for clothes.

His departure leaves Susan's aunt momentarily overawed and Susan counting on her toes "He loves me, he loves me not," but Susan is soon brought back to reality by her aunt's questions. As she dashes off in breathless pursuit of David, she says, "If he gets some clothes he'll go away, and he's the only man I've ever loved." At this point David's feelings toward Susan are quite different: "Out of two million people why did I have to run into you?" he mutters to her as he emerges from the depths of a closet in the only clothes he can find, a too-small riding outfit. This sequence is not only one of inspired comic invention but also shows a side to David's character different from his surface conventionality which makes Susan's interest in him more believable. For the first time we realize that perhaps David and Susan are not so ill-matched after all, and for the first time we hear Susan explicitly state her love for David.

The film then reaches a new height of absurdity when David discovers that George has taken the precious intercostal clavicle and buried it somewhere on the grounds. Susan, trying to be encouraging and helpful, follows David around as he tries to persuade George to dig up the bone. "Isn't this fun, David? Just like a game," she comments brightly to a disgruntled, disheveled, and dirty David. After some time and many holes later she exclaims, "What we need is a plow."

That evening Susan and David dine with her aunt and a guest, Major Applegate (Charles Ruggles), a big game hunter. The dinner is complicated by the fact that David has learned that Susan's aunt is Mrs. Carlton Random, the prospective donor of one million dollars to his museum. He asks Susan not to reveal his identity, so she gives him a fictitious name, Mr. Bone. In addition, David is unable to concentrate on the dinner table conversation because his whole attention is centered on George, who he hopes will lead him to the intercostal clavicle.

In the middle of dinner a leopard's cry is heard, but Major Applegate, who claims to be an authority on animal cries, insists that it is the cry of a loon. Susan and David, however, realize instantly that it is Baby and that he has escaped. Susan decides that she and David will have to find Baby, but David joins in the search only after Susan threatens to reveal his identity to her aunt. Another twist to the already zany complications is added when—unknown to Susan and David—a circus in a nearby town dispatches a dangerous leopard to the zoo to be humanely killed. When Susan sees the circus truck parked by the side of the road, she assumes the leopard in the truck is Baby and releases the dangerous leopard, who promptly runs away.

After wandering around in the woods for a while Susan and David finally see Baby sitting on the roof of a house. They begin singing the leopard's favorite song, "I Can't Give You Anything But Love, Baby," which always calms him. The commotion brings to the window the owner of the house—who happens to be the stuffy psychiatrist Susan met in the restaurant. Susan calmly tells him that her leopard is on his roof and she has to get it to come down. The psychiatrist naturally think she is crazy and forces her into the house where he keeps her until the arrival of the local constable he has summoned. The constable finds David lurking outside and takes both him and Susan to jail. He refuses to believe that Susan is Mrs. Random's niece, and his suspicions seem to be confirmed when a telephone call to Mrs. Random elicits an irritated response that her niece is at home in bed.

Supported by the psychiatrist, the constable now believes he has two dangerous criminals under lock and key. Next, Mrs. Random and Major Applegate arrive, but the constable does not believe they are who they claim to be or their preposterous story that they are hunting for a leopard, and throws them into jail, too. At this point Susan, ever resourceful, assumes a nasal accent and identifies herself as "Swinging Door Susie." Saying that they are all members of a gang, she promises to reveal all their activities if she is released from her cell. During the questioning she manages to escape out the window and goes searching for the leopard just before the arrival of Peabody, Mrs. Random's lawyer, and David's fiancé Alice. Next the men from the circus come to report that their dangerous leopard is missing. The constable, now thoroughly bewildered and uneasy, realizes that these absurd people may actually be who they claim they are.

Adding to the confusion is the appearance of Baby and George, which causes everyone to realize that there are two leopards, one of them dangerous and on the loose. David's first thought is for Susan's safety. "She's in danger and she's helpless without me," he exclaims, but Susan immediately appears with the snarling, untamed leopard at the end of a rope. When it is explained to her that the leopard she is dragging along is not Baby, she momentarily panics, and it is up to David to take command of the situation, which he promptly does. Stepping in front of Susan he defends her with a chair until the leopard has been maneuvered into an empty cell. He then faints while Susan maintains her usual breathless flow of chatter.

Alice's assessment of the situation is that David is "just a butterfly" and not the man for her, thus clearing the way for David and Susan to get together. But David, although he may be in love with Susan, is also afraid of her; and when she comes to see him at the Museum, he promptly runs up a ladder to a platform behind the huge brontosaurus skeleton on which he is working. Susan climbs another ladder on the opposite side of the skeleton to tell him that the Museum will receive the one million dollar gift after all—Mrs. Random is giving the money to Susan, and she wants to give it to David. As they talk, Susan begins swaying back and forth on her tall ladder, and we can see that disaster is imminent. During the ensuing conversation David finally confesses that he has never had a better time than the day he spent with her. At the same moment Susan finally overbalances on her ladder but manages to climb onto the skeleton to save herself from falling. As the giant skeleton begins to collapse, David grabs her hand, barely rescuing her. The two embrace above the ruins as the film ends.

The charm and humor of *Bringing Up Baby* lies partly in the comic situations that result from the diametrically opposed characters and personalities of David Huxley and Susan Vance. In 1930's romantic comedies, one of the protagonists is nearly always in love with a prim, conventional partner at the beginning of the film and has to be rescued and changed by an unconventional free spirit. In *Bringing Up Baby* Cary Grant is a stiff, bespectacled, dedicated paleontologist rescued by madcap heiress Katharine Hepburn. Director Howard Hawks has commented that Grant's role was intended to be a caricature of a scientist. At the beginning of the film, David is absentminded, awkward, and over-disciplined. He has devoted four years of his professional career to assembling the skeleton of a brontosaurus, but he is so inept that he tries to put one bone in the same wrong place that he tried the day before. Near the end of the film he finds himself in jail after a series of adventures which are just the opposite of his normal way of life, including assuming a false name, wearing a woman's negligee, singing to a leopard on a rooftop, and following a dog about to find a lost brontosaurus bone. Though he complains of the chaos Susan has involved him in, he does admit that she and her way of living have some attraction for him. At one time he says to her, "During quiet moments I feel a certain attraction for you—only there haven't been any quiet moments." Grant plays the stodgy scientist to perfection, using his voice and facial expressions both to convey a wooden exterior and to suggest that underneath there is a vital, fun-loving person.

The madcap, wacky heiress was a popular character in screwball comedies of the 1930's, but seldom was it so well acted and brought to such vivid, restless life as in this performance by Katharine Hepburn. She is a study in perpetual motion—always breathlessly talking and moving. Using a different expression, pose, or walk for each scene, she gives a variety and interest to her performance which keeps it both fresh and charming. Sometimes, for example, she does not merely laugh, she winnies. In the middle of the confusion, however, there are oases of calm and feeling that contrast subtly and tellingly with the frenzied activities that surround the characters. After David tells Susan that he is engaged, a close-up of her face shows that she is momentarily taken aback and more affected than we might have expected. Indeed, director Hawks uses close-ups sparingly in the film, and most are used to emphasize a moment of tranquility or deep emotion. Susan first learns of David's engagement when she offers to drive him to Peabody's house. While her face reveals to the audience her true feelings for David, her reply to him is both flippant and revealing: "Then she won't mind waiting will she?" Susan says. "If I were engaged to you I wouldn't mind waiting at all. I'd wait forever."

Another moment of deep emotion occurs when David, tired and disheveled from wandering through the woods in search of Baby, is accidentally knocked down by Susan and breaks his spectacles. He blames Susan for the accident and for embroiling him in the whole affair, making it clear that he does not want her help. There is a close-up of Susan's face—she is hurt and crushed—and she begins to cry, saying "You mean you don't want me to help you any more—after all the fun we've had?"

Hawks's achievement in the film is the creation of a complete comic world in which the absurd becomes rational and the normal becomes ridiculous. He has also created a film of almost constant comic invention and surprise that moves rapidly toward unexpected climaxes and unforeseen twists. At the beginning of some of the zaniest scenes there is no reason to suppose that they will culminate in absolute absurdity. David does not see where his actions will lead him and neither does the audience. The deft direction of Howard Hawks, the impeccable performances of the stars, and the inspired lunacy of the script make *Bringing Up Baby* a classic comedy which remains as fresh and vivid today as when it was first released

GENTLEMEN PREFER BLONDES

Released: 1953
Production: Sol C. Siegel for Twentieth Century-Fox
Direction: Howard Hawks
Screenplay: Charles Lederer; based on the musical comedy of the same name
  by Joseph Fields and Anita Loos
Cinematography: Harry J. Wild
Editing: Hugh S. Fowler
Choreography: Jack Cole
Music: Jule Styne and Leo Robin
Song: Hoagy Carmichael and Harold Adamson
Running time: 91 minutes

Principal characters:
>Dorothy ....Jane Russell
>Lorelei Lee .... Marilyn Monroe
>Gus Esmond .... Tommy Noonan
>Sir Francis Beekman .... Charles Coburn
>Detective Malone ....Elliott Reid

Gentlemen Prefer Blondes, a brassy musical comedy, would be unexceptional were it not for the presence of Marilyn Monroe. Though some people have considered her to be an untalented product of publicity and others have maintained that she was a great actress who never had the serious roles or serious consideration she deserved, neither extreme is true. Monroe had a screen presence which overcame her technical limitations in acting and singing when she was given a role suited to her screen *persona*. With her husky, whispery voice, wide-eyed innocent stare, round baby face, and pouting mouth, Monroe was perfectly suited to the role of Lorelei Lee, a seemingly scatterbrained but not-so-dumb blonde dedicated to securing her future by marrying a millionaire.

Engaged to a young millionaire, Gus Esmond (Tommy Noonan), Lorelei takes a ship to France where Gus is to meet her later. To make sure that Lorelei does not get into trouble, Gus sends along her friend Dorothy (Jane Russell), and his father sends along a detective, Malone (Elliott Reid). During the crossing they meet a rich elderly Englishman, Sir Francis "Piggy" Beekman (Charles Coburn), whom Lorelei blackmails into giving her his wife's diamond tiara. Malone finds this out, and when the girls reach Paris, they discover that Gus has cancelled their hotel reservations and their credit. They have to get jobs as showgirls in Paris, but all ends happily when Gus and his father come over and meet Lorelei. The film ends with a double wedding: Lorelei to Gus and Dorothy to Malone.

Lorelei originated in stories by screenwriter and author Anita Loos, who created the character when she was in love with editor and essayist H. L. Mencken. When she saw herself being neglected by him for a vacuous, unintelligent blonde, Loos was hurt and bewildered and decided to sublimate her jealousy by writing a story about an empty-headed blonde flapper of the 1920's whom she called Lorelei. *Harper's Bazaar* accepted her story and asked for more adventures of Lorelei. Eventually the magazine pieces were collected in a book, *Gentlemen Prefer Blondes*, which made Loos both famous and wealthy. The book remained popular over the years, being adapted first as a play, later as a silent film, then as a Broadway musical, and finally as the Twentieth Century-Fox film with Marilyn Monroe as Lorelei.

By the time the book reached the screen, it had lost some of its sharp characterization and wit, but it is often amusing, especially when Lorelei is explaining her philosophy of life to her friend Dorothy. When Lorelei advises her to find a rich man to marry, Dorothy replies that some people simply do not care about money. Lorelei is amazed by this naïve attitude. If a girl has to spend all her time worrying about money, she asks Dorothy, how can she have time to be in love? Marriage is a serious business to Lorelei. She may not be an intellectual, but she does know that her beauty will not last forever, and she intends to provide for her future. As she explains to one of her admirers, "A kiss on the hand might feel very good, but a diamond tiara is forever."

Lorelei is a shrewd judge of men's characters. When the outraged father of the naïve young millionaire she intends to marry warns her she is not fooling him, she responds instantly that she is not trying to, but that she could if she wanted to. She explains to him, with a logic that leaves him speechless, that a "man being rich is like a girl being pretty. You might not marry her just because she's pretty, but my goodness, doesn't it help?" Sometimes Lorelei seems dumb and other times astute. As she explains to Gus's father, she can be smart when it is important, but most men do not like that.

The film gains immediate momentum from a vividly colorful and sparkling musical number, "Little Girls from Little Rock," which Dorothy and Lorelei, in red sequined gowns slit up to the thighs and with feathers in their hair, perform in front of violet sequined curtains in a nightclub. Halfway through the number the credits for the film appear, and when the credits end, Lorelei and Dorothy return to finish the song. The motions and gestures of the number are based on burlesque movements, as they are also in the film's other musical numbers, but the bumps and grinds were toned down for the movie censor.

The other eye-catching number, "Diamonds Are a Girl's Best Friend," is strikingly staged and photographed and is the film's highlight. It opens in a manner reminiscent of Busby Berkeley: girls in full pink gowns and men in white ties and tails dance around human candelabra, formed by girls in black costumes. The colors, deep red and bright pink, clash excitingly. In the midst of the swirling couples, the audience suddenly sees Lorelei, sitting with her back to the audience, in a bright pink satin sheath and long pink gloves. Diamonds sparkle from her wrists, her ears, her throat. Suddenly she turns, facing the camera, and the men offer her cardboard hearts which she spurns, trilling in an operatic voice, "No, no, no," before launching into the lyrics in her own husky, whispery voice. Marilyn Monroe's singing and dancing are surprisingly effective, although the dancing consists largely of a few modified, gyrations very much as those used in "Little Girls from Little Rock." Still, within the context of the number, it is sufficient, and Monroe as Lorelei, clasping strings of diamonds to her face and surrounded by men in formal black evening attire, presents a striking picture.

The other musical numbers are more routine, both musically and dramatically, although Monroe's "Bye-Bye Baby," which she croons wistfully to her millionaire boyfriend as she sets off for Europe, is musically and emotionally effective. "When Love Goes Wrong" is Lorelei and Dorothy's best duet, sung in a bar after they have been forced to leave their luxurious hotel suite. Gradually, as the denizens of the bar gather round, two little boys begin clapping and everyone joins in for the big finale.

"Anyone Here for Love?" is a misconceived idea for Jane Russell's solo musical number as Dorothy. More interested in sex than money, Dorothy thinks she has found a gold mine when she discovers that members of the American Olympic team are aboard the ocean liner. She is quickly disillusioned when she learns that the men spend their time working out in the ship's gymnasium and must be in bed by nine o'clock. As she strolls around the gym watching the men practicing handstands, somersaults, weight lifting, and wrestling, she wryly sings the lyrics. The men's calisthenics are as carefully choreographed as a dance, but the effect is flat and unsatisfying.

Beside Marilyn Monroe the other actors are rather flat and colorless. Tommy Noonan as Gus Esmond, Lorelei's ineffectual millionaire boyfriend who is dominated by his father, seems perfectly cast, but Elliott Reid as Detective Malone, assigned to gather evidence against Lorelei by the elder Esmond, is dull as Dorothy's love interest. Charles Coburn is better in the role of Sir Francis "Piggy" Beekman, but his performance is only a collection of his now-famous mannerisms. Even Jane Russell, the brightest star in the cast besides Monroe, is somewhat wooden, though genial.

Director Howard Hawks, whose credits include *Bringing Up Baby* (1938), *Red River* (1948), and *To Have and Have Not* (1944), is obviously out of his element in *Gentlemen Prefer Blondes*, but as a star vehicle for Marilyn Monroe the film succeeds admirably and was in the top ten at the box office in its year.

HIS GIRL FRIDAY

Released: 1940
Production: Howard Hawks for Columbia
Direction: Howard Hawks
Screenplay: Charles Lederer; based on the play *The Front Page* by Ben Hecht and Charles MacArthur
Cinematography: Joseph Walker
Editing: Gene Havlick
Running time: 92 minutes

> *Principal characters:*
> Walter Burns .... Cary Grant
> Hildy Johnson .... Rosalind Russell
> Bruce Baldwin .... Ralph Bellamy
> Earl Williams .... John Qualen
> Molly Malloy .... Helen Mack

Howard Hawks's *His Girl Friday* is a culmination of the "screwball" comedy tradition of the 1930's. Hawks had a habit of coming last to a genre; but his contribution was never the least; it was always an excellent entry. This film, a reworking of Ben Hecht's and Charles MacArthur's *The Front Page*, is charged with new life through Hawks's masterful direction and major script changes. In this version, he adds a sophisticated battle of the sexes by turning the "male" Hildy Johnson into a Hildegarde, and pitting her against her boss and former husband, Walter Burns. The new love triangle replaces the old plot of political corruption and newsroom nonsense, but the changes cause only minor discomfort. The story, like the original, is all surface and no substance. The dialogue rather than the plot gives the picture its distinction.

Rosalind Russell as Hildy Johnson turns the newsroom upside down as she throws her well-padded shoulders around. Accepted by the newsmen as "one of the boys," she is fast-talking, with a quick retort for every wisecrack. A hard competitor, she is extremely successful in a man's world. Russell's acting is always adequate and at times captivating. Her most dramatic scene, for example, is with the condemned criminal Earl Williams (John Qualen) midway through the film when, as Hildy, she builds a "story" out of Williams' use of a gun to kill, turning it into a philosophical argument about "production for use." The character of Walter Burns is made-to-order for Cary Grant. Unlike the romp through the woods that Hawks gave Grant and Katharine Hepburn in *Bringing Up Baby* (1938), the stunts in *His Girl Friday* are verbal. The insults fly like daggers, and with Hawks, Grant, and Russell throwing them, they are rarely misdirected.

The pace is sometimes frenzied, yet the film does not suffer from its weak thread of a plot. As the story opens, Hildy returns to the *Morning Post* to flash her new engagement ring in her ex-husband's face and to bid him, the newspaper business, and the city farewell. She is marrying Bruce Baldwin (Ralph Bellamy), a bland insurance salesman from Upstate New York; he represents security, stability, and a white picket fence in Albany. Nothing could be duller, unless it is Bruce himself. While Hildy staunchly insists that Bruce is what she wants, Burns and the audience believe that she desperately wants to be convinced otherwise. From the beginning, Bruce is an open challenge for Burns's mischievous mind, and it is obviously no contest.

Although Hildy is ready to leave on the next train for Albany, Burns delays her departure with a plea that she cannot refuse. His star reporter, he claims, is unavailable to cover the imminent death-row story on Earl Williams. Still desperately hoping for a pardon, Williams faces execution at dawn. Hildy, Burns argues, is the only reporter "man" enough to enter the prison and get the story.

Hildy stalls Bruce from one train to the next, promising not to miss the last one. But Burns is determined to get rid of Bruce for good. Through a series of contrived mishaps which he masterminds, Bruce lands in jail twice and is nearly killed in a car accident with his "mother," all in one night.

As the evening wears on, the Governor's pardon of Williams is intercepted and concealed by a corrupt mayor who feels that his reelection depends on the execution. Meanwhile, after an interview with Hildy, the somewhat confused Williams dramatically escapes from death row, then suddenly appears in the prison newsroom where he finds Hildy alone. True to her profession, Hildy hides Williams in a rolltop desk to protect him as well as her scoop. Complications set in when Williams' alleged girl friend, Molly Malloy (Helen Mack), is interrogated for information about Williams' whereabouts. Under the pressure, Molly breaks down and leaves through the second story window, falling to her death on the pavement below.

The film does not skip a beat as, in true Hollywood "screwball" fashion, the mayor, the criminal, the love triangle, and the mother-in-law all converge in the newsroom for the grand finale. Phones ring, guns fire, and everyone shouts at once. The corrupt mayor and his henchmen are exposed and Hildy and Burns team up for another round of marriage.

Hawks's presentation of the battle of the sexes is as old as Shakespeare, and the treatment of Hildy and Burns is typical of the egocentric type of hero that the director enjoyed. However, love and respect get the better of their self-centered interests and ultimately the two join forces against the wooden, lifeless people who, they consider, make up most of the population of the world.

The directorial style of *His Girl Friday* is as straightforward as Hawks's dialogue. His direct cuts and lack of montage keep the film from being dated and keep extraneous movement to a minimum. Time dances frantically by; the comedy is copious and varied; the gags are rapid-fire. The sarcastic banter between Hildy and Burns is the soul of the film, and it is this clever repartee that captures the audience. Representative of Hawks's comedy at its best, *His Girl Friday* is a treat not to be missed if the opportunity arises.

MONKEY BUSINESS

Released: 1952
Production: Sol C. Siegel for Twentieth Century-Fox
Direction: Howard Hawks
Screenplay: Ben Hecht, Charles Lederer, and I. A. L. Diamond; based on a story by Harry Segall
Cinematography: Milton Krasner
Editing: William B. Murphy
Running time: 97 minutes

Principal characters:

Barnaby Fulton	Cary Grant
Edwina Fulton	Ginger Rogers
Mr. Oliver Oxley	Charles Coburn
Lois Laurel	Marilyn Monroe
Hank Entwhistle	Hugh Marlowe
Little Indian	George Winslow

Monkey Business is a comedy about rejuvenation, a serious theme; however, director Howard Hawks's treatment of the subject does not emphasize this seriousness. His approach is to make the situations resulting from the premise as ridiculous as possible. It has often been observed that Hawks's comedies are the inversion of his dramas. He creates a pleasing balance in his work by alternating between disturbing comedies and warm-hearted adventure stories, sometimes in immediate sequence, as was the case with *The Big Sky* (1952) and *Monkey Business*. In his comedies, which are at their best when they are most outrageous, there is a giddiness which could make us forget that Hawks's lucidity never deserts him even in the face of lunacy. He looks on the silly antics of the characters in a film like *Monkey Business* with a straight face, observing perhaps that his adult men and women are less mature than certain children and less capable than certain monkeys.

Monkey Business is one Hawks comedy, however, that is more akin to a Hawks drama. When Hawks looks at a relationship seriously, he invariably finds some simple value which validates that relationship, such as an unselfish love which causes one friend to look out for another. In *Monkey Business*, he also validates the relationship between Barnaby Fulton (Cary Grant) and his wife Edwina (Ginger Rogers), and does so with an unmistakable warmth which gives the film's conclusion a very different feeling from that found in earlier Hawks comedies such as *Twentieth Century* (1934) or *Bringing Up Baby* (1938). Barnaby and Edwina are made to look extremely foolish during most of this film, but when they decide to accept themselves as they are, they do so in a positive spirit.

The story begins with Fulton's attempts to invent an elixir that causes rejuvenation. Although Barnaby is a scientist, he is one step away from helplessness when it comes to handling the practical details of life, and Edwina is guileless enough not to try to change him. If the artificially experienced youth which his formula makes possible has a positive effect, it is to take away a craving for a carefree existence of which they really have no need.

Actually, it is the monkey and not Barnaby who comes up with the right formula, a fact of which the principals are unaware until the final reel of the film, and which makes the entire experiment seem properly frivolous. One night when the laboratory is deserted, a monkey whose cage has inadvertently been left unlocked grabs the bars of the cage door and comes swinging out toward the camera. It follows that the monkey accidentally mixes the right formula, then expresses his contempt for it by dropping it in the water cooler.

The remainder of the film is structured around three distinct episodes of rejuvenation which successively release an increasingly wild frenzy of youthful activity. In the first episode, Barnaby takes the formula and reverts to his college days, getting a youthful haircut and buying a sports car, as well as having a lot of innocent fun with Lois Laurel (Marilyn Monroe), the sexy but not very proficient secretary of his boss, Mr. Oliver Oxley (Charles Coburn). In the second episode, Barnaby is back to normal and Edwina has seized her opportunity to drink the elixir. She drags Barnaby to their honeymoon hotel, dances the hours away until he is in a stupor, then becomes insecure and mistrustful and throws her husband out of their room. He ends up plunging down a laundry chute and sleeping with the hotel linen.

These first two episodes take place during one event-filled afternoon and the long and disturbing night which follows. The final and most elaborate episode occurs the following day. Barnaby and Edwina have renounced the formula, but not knowing it is in the water cooler, they overdose on it in the belief that they are drinking coffee. They become crazed children with no thought for morality or propriety, and the result is a series of events which rival those in *Bringing Up Baby* for sheer absurdity and abandon. Barnaby and Edwina turn Oxley's offices into a playground and cover each other with white paint on the way home. In their backyard, a group of children, who seem to have emerged from nowhere, are playing cowboys and Indians. When Edwina goes to sleep after calling Barnaby's still-hopeful rival for her affections, Hank Entwhistle (Hugh Marlowe), Barnaby joins the children, who trick the hapless Entwhistle into being bound to a stake so that Barnaby can scalp him. Discovering a baby in bed with her, Edwina believes him to be Barnaby in a state of total regression. She takes him to the Oxley company, speaking hopeful words of love to him in the backseat of a taxi. Oxley and the scientists join Edwina in singing the couple's favorite song to the baby before they themselves unwittingly drink the formula and discover the bliss of becoming uninhibited and foolish, while the savage Barnaby finally gets some restorative sleep.

Although the film is ambiguous regarding the formula's redeeming value, its invention in the script has inspired Hawks and the three individually brilliant writers who collaborated with him. The cowboys and Indians sequence alone would be enough to justify admiration of this comedy since it features the solemn and inimitable George Winslow as one of the Indians, cagily tricking Entwhistle by asking the immortal questions, "What's the matter, mister; don't you like kids?" and "Why are you mean to 'em, then?" The sequence is further elevated by Hawks's perversity in permitting Barnaby actually to scalp Entwhistle (though not fatally). The concurrent action involving Edwina and the baby makes this section even more hilarious. The spectacle of Charles Coburn and a group of mature men softly singing "Bah, bah, bah" in a circle as they anxiously regard an infant and the idiotic smile of its "wife" is an endearingly nonsensical image.

Monkey Business should not be praised immoderately. Some of its humor is strained, especially in scenes which depend on Ginger Rogers' imitation of an adolescent or child. Although she is amusing, she does not have the natural flair for these scenes that Cary Grant does. The film is most enjoyable when Grant is at the center of the comic frenzy. In all of the Hawks comedies in which he has starred, Grant manages to play the most ridiculous scenes with complete conviction and without a trace of self-consciousness.

Much of the charm of *Monkey Business* comes from Hawks's skill at composition. The shot in the lobby of the honeymoon hotel is a good example. Barnaby is in the left foreground registering with the desk clerk while Edwina, acting shy and dreamy-eyed, holds the center of the image, lingering far enough in the background to seem amusingly vulnerable. A second example is the relatively long take of Barnaby and Edwina drinking coffee in the lab. Again, Barnaby is in left foreground, staring straight ahead and not seeing that Edwina, who moves freely in the background space given to her, has already started to regress. At this point in the film, the anticipated regression might have been dull; but as a result of Hawks's staging and framing, the absence of any reaction on the part of the unsmiling Barnaby as Edwina begins to cavort once more is engagingly humorous. These compositions, characteristic of Hawks's formal assurance, demonstrate no apparent complexity or virtuosity, but prove again what a master director he is.

ONLY ANGELS HAVE WINGS

Released: 1939
Production: Howard Hawks for Columbia
Direction: Howard Hawks
Screenplay: Jules Furthman; based on a story by Howard Hawks
Cinematography: Joseph Walker
Editing: Viola Lawrence
Running time: 121 minutes

> *Principal characters:*
> Geoff Carter .... Cary Grant
> Bonnie Lee .... Jean Arthur
> Kid Dabb .... Thomas Mitchell
> Bat MacPherson .... Richard Barthelmess
> Judy .... Rita Hayworth
> Dutchy .... Sig Rumann
> Joe Souther .... Noah Beery, Jr.
> Les Peters .... Allyn Joslyn

Director Howard Hawks expertly combined adventure, drama, romance, and comedy in *Only Angels Have Wings*. His films tended to feature male camaraderie and tests of courage (*Red River*, 1948), but he was also a master of the screwball comedy (*Bringing Up Baby*, 1938). In addition, because he had flown in World War I and knew many pilots, he liked to depict the drama of flying in his films (*Dawn Patrol*, 1938). When he was asked to do a film with Cary Grant and Jean Arthur, he brought all these enthusiasms into play, and because of his sure touch and the outstanding abilities of his stars and the supporting cast, he was able to make a successful film out of what could have been mere melodrama or soap opera.

Only Angels Have Wings is about a group of American fliers in the small town of Barranca, described in the film as a port-of-call for South American banana boats. They work for a flying service owned by a Dutchman whom they all call "Dutchy" (Sig Rumann), who also owns the combination hotel, saloon, and flying headquarters where they live and work. Their leader is Geoff Carter (Cary Grant), a tough, no-nonsense pilot who commands the respect of the rest because he takes some of the toughest flying assignments himself. Because the operation is not prosperous, the pilots have to use old airplanes which cannot fly high enough to go above the Andes mountains; therefore they must use a dangerous mountain pass which is frequently shrouded in fog. Geoff's and Dutchy's hope for prosperity is a government contract to fly the mail, a contract which they will receive if they can maintain a regular schedule for six months. They are within a week of meeting this deadline at the opening of the film.

The group of fliers is close-knit, but there is an especially close bond between Geoff and Kid Dabb (Thomas Mitchell), who, despite his nickname, is probably the oldest of the group. Their affection is largely unspoken but quite clearly seen, especially in Kid's solicitous gestures such as lighting Geoff's cigarettes or taking his jacket to him when he suddenly has to rush outside.

It is through Bonnie Lee (Jean Arthur) that we are introduced to this group. Bonnie is a showgirl from Brooklyn who gets off a boat in Barranca for what she expects to be a stop of a few hours before the boat continues northward. When two of the pilots—Joe Souther (Noah Beery, Jr.) and Les Peters (Allyn Joslyn)—offer to buy her a drink, she is delighted because they are Americans. But when they take her to Dutchy's saloon and Geoff sees her, Geoff tells Joe he must leave immediately to fly the mail out and makes up an all-night task for Les, telling Joe not to worry about Bonnie; "I'll be glad to take up where you left off." When Bonnie protests that she should have something to say about that, Geoff merely turns to her and says "Chorus girl?" in a tough manner which puts her immediately on the defensive.

The flying business soon interrupts their sparring and gives Bonnie a full-scale introduction to the pilots and their world. After Joe takes off with the mail, the fog becomes too thick for him to get through the mountain pass, so he turns back. The fog, however, also obscures the landing field, so Geoff orders him to circle above it until the visibility is better. But Joe wants to keep his date for a steak dinner with Bonnie and tries to land anyway; the result is a fatal crash.

Everyone takes Joe's death stoically except Dutchy and Bonnie. Bonnie gets upset when the group begins eating and drinking in the saloon as if nothing had happened, especially when Geoff calmly begins eating the steak which had been ordered for Joe. She says that she has always hated the "fuss and bother" of funerals, but at Barranca she must learn emotionally to accept danger and death stoically as the fliers do. This becomes an important part of her relationship with Geoff, for he tells her that he avoids any entanglements with women because they want to make plans and cannot endure the anxiety involved in a pilot's life. He thinks that only a man can know and accept the life he has chosen. Nevertheless, by the time the fog lifts and Geoff leaves to fly the mail himself, Bonnie has decided to stay and try to be the kind of person he wants.

When Geoff gets back and finds Bonnie still there, he is more than a little displeased and tries to ignore her. Bonnie herself is unable to explain her action. "The girl that got off that boat is a perfect stranger to me," she tells him. Even though Geoff and Kid do not express their feelings to each other, they can admit them to Bonnie. She asks Kid what he does when Geoff does not get back from a flight when he is supposed to; "I go nuts," Kid responds. And when Bonnie talks to Geoff about how simple and undemanding his relationship with Kid is, Geoff replies, "Kid? He drives me nuts."

A further complication is introduced into the group when a new flier and his wife arrive. Although the flier is using the assumed name of Bat Mac-Pherson (Richard Barthelmess), some of the men immediately recognize that he is the man who parachuted out of an airplane and let it crash with the mechanic in it. That mechanic was Kid's brother. In a further coincidence, MacPherson's wife, Judy (Rita Hayworth), is an old flame of Geoff's. Indeed, she is the one who is responsible for his ideas about women.

Later, Geoff has to ground Kid because of his weak eyes, and as is usual in their scenes together the emotion is all underneath the surface. Geoff knows that flying has been Kid's life for twenty-two years and that he wants so badly to continue that he has memorized the eye charts, but Geoff has to tell him bluntly, "You're through flying, Kid." It is not said coldly or callously but merely simply and directly.

Geoff first gives MacPherson a job too dangerous for anyone else. He has to land an airplane on a small plateau in the mountains, pick up a mine-owner's injured son, and fly back to Barranca. The take-off from the plateau is especially risky since MacPherson has to fly straight off the edge and then gain flying speed as the airplane falls. Although he does not tell MacPherson so, Geoff is impressed with his skill and courage and offers him a permanent job—with one important stipulation: that Geoff will send him "out in any kind of weather or any kind of job."

His affection for Geoff helps Kid accept MacPherson more easily than the others can, and when Les threatens to quit rather than work with MacPherson, Kid fights Les out of loyalty to Geoff and frustration at not being able to fly again. Because Les's arm is injured in the fight, Geoff must make the flight which will meet the deadline to secure the government contract.

Meanwhile, Bonnie has decided she can love Geoff the same way Kid does. She tells Geoff that he does not have to be afraid of her anymore, that she will not make plans or get in his way. When she hears Dutchy say that anyone is crazy to fly in such weather, however, she suddenly grabs Geoff's gun, threatening to shoot him if he insists on making the flight. She cannot go through with it, of course, but when she drops the gun on a table, it goes off and hits Geoff in the shoulder, so he cannot go after all.

With all the injuries and Kid's bad eyesight, the only pilot left for the flight is MacPherson. Kid, since he has been flying nearly blind for some time, insists on going along to help guide MacPherson through the foggy pass. The plan almost works, but as the airplane goes through the pass, it collides with a flock of giant condors. The airplane's windshield is smashed, the engine is damaged and on fire, and Kid is injured and unable to move. Kid urges MacPherson to jump, but he says, "Not this time," and safely lands the damaged craft, thus redeeming himself.

But nothing can save Kid. Geoff has to tell him, "Your neck's broken,

Kid." When he knows he is dying, Kid tells Geoff he wants everyone out of the room and then he asks Geoff to leave also, not because he is afraid but because it is something new and he would, he says, "hate to pull a boner in front of you, Geoff."

The formerly hostile pilots show that they have accepted MacPherson by inviting him to have a drink with them, but Geoff has not asked Bonnie to stay, so she prepares to leave on that night's boat. One of the other men encourages her to say good-bye to Geoff, so she goes into his room, not knowing what to say. Just as she is asking whether Geoff wants her to stay or not, word comes through on the radio that the pass is clear and the airplane can make it through. Geoff and Les think that together they can fly the craft since each has one good arm. Geoff still cannot bring himself to ask Bonnie directly to stay. Instead he flips a quarter, saying that she should stay if it comes up heads. It does, but Bonnie will not stay on that basis. "I'm hard to get, Geoff," she says. "All you have to do is ask me." Geoff rushes off to the airplane leaving Bonnie with the quarter, but as she turns it over and over in her hand she sees that it has two heads. She shouts happily and runs to the door to watch the airplane take off as the film ends.

The group of men engaged in a risky and demanding task was a familiar context for director Howard Hawks, as was the dialogue in which statements of fact are made simply and directly, but sentiment is expressed only indirectly, in what Hawks called three-cushion dialogue. Hawks felt comfortable with the subject of *Only Angels Have Wings* because he knew how men in such circumstances felt and how they talked; for example, Kid's death scene had come directly from his own experience. To critics who felt that its coincidences of plot made the film false, Hawks responded that everything in the film was true; he was referring to the essentials—the feelings, reactions, and language. Hawks does not, however, simply re-create a world with which he is familiar. He uses a brisk pace and a deft mixture of comedy and drama to convey that world to the audience.

Bonnie Lee was one of the first of a type of heroine Hawks was to use many times. She is honest and direct and tries to prove herself worthy to be a part of Geoff's world. But Bonnie does not simply capitulate to Geoff and his every whim; she makes conscious choices, and she changes Geoff perhaps more than he changes her. She has learned to control some of her excess emotionalism, "the fuss and bother," but he has overcome his fear of falling in love again.

The performance of Cary Grant as Geoff is also crucial to *Only Angels Have Wings*. He conveys the depth of character as well as the surface virility and charm necessary for us to see why Bonnie falls for him even though he tries to discourage her. With a lesser actor in the role of Geoff we could see Bonnie as merely misguided or foolish. Jean Arthur is the perfect complement to Grant. She convincingly conveys the fresh, open character of Bonnie—

who is direct with Geoff in both what she offers and what she asks.

Thomas Mitchell is outstanding as Kid, perfectly suggesting the feelings which cannot be stated. The rest of the cast gives excellent support, particularly Sig Rumann as Dutchy. Rita Hayworth's Judy is less interesting than the other characters, but this is largely because hers is a two-dimensional role.

The fact that Howard Hawks was a master of comedy as well as being comfortable and familiar with the world of masculine adventure makes *Only Angels Have Wings* an engrossing blend of action, romance, and comedy.

SCARFACE: THE SHAME OF THE NATION

Released: 1932
Production: Howard Hughes for United Artists
Direction: Howard Hawks
Screenplay: Ben Hecht, Seton I. Miller, John Lee Mahin, and W. R. Burnett;
  based on the novel *Scarface* by Armitage Trail
Cinematography: Lee Garmes and L. W. O'Connell
Editing: Edward Curtiss
Running time: 99 minutes

> *Principal characters:*
> Tony Camonte .... Paul Muni
> Cesca Camonte .... Ann Dvorak
> Poppy .... Karen Morley
> Johnny Lovo .... Osgood Perkins
> Gaffney .... Boris Karloff
> Guido Rinaldo .... George Raft

For cinemagoers of the early 1930's, gangsters presented a special and perverse fascination. At a time when unemployment, soup lines, and the *ennui* of a Depression-plagued nation wracked the lives of millions of Americans, it was an exciting release to see hoodlums fondle sexy "molls," drive fast cars, swill bootleg liquor, and live lives of bloodthirsty stimulation. In 1931, Warner Bros. struck box-office gold with such plot elements: in *Little Caesar*, Edward G. Robinson plays the derby sporting Rico Bandello with all the depth and grandeur of an epic tragic hero, and in *Public Enemy* a snarling James Cagney grinds a grapefruit in Mae Clarke's face and picks up Jean Harlow with irresistible pugnaciousness. While both films feature last-reel moralizing (Robinson's plaintive "Mother of Mercy—is this the end of Rico?" as he lies dying in the streets, and Cagney's mummylike corpse taking a pratfall into the living room), there was in both gangland classics a hint of glorification of these criminals. The charisma of Robinson's acting and the humor of Cagney's personality managed to add a tinge of undesirable glamour to a breed of criminal which was proving an international shame to America's salesmanship of democracy.

Hence, the stage was set for the most repulsive, repellant cinema gangster of them all—Paul Muni in *Scarface: The Shame of the Nation*. Although the 1932 classic is seen rarely because of the legendary imbroglios of producer Howard Hughes's financial empire, both before and after his death, it remains Hollywood's definitively ugly depiction of the twisted psyche of the American gangster.

It was Alphonse Capone, of course, who provided the inspiration for the character Scarface. His sensational Chicago exploits had seared Depression newspaper front pages and moved Armitage Trail to pen the novel *Scarface* on which the film was based. The property (originally titled simply *Scarface*) appealed strongly to sensation-loving Howard Hughes, whose Caddo Corporation had produced such hits as *Hell's Angels* (1930) and *The Front Page* (1931). Shooting began in the spring of 1931 under Howard Hawks's direction at the United Artists and Metropolitan Studios, with Paul Muni as Scarface, a staff of genuine underworld figures serving as "technical advisers," and a barrage of dangerous machine gun battle sequences with real artillery (Harold Lloyd's brother reportedly lost an eye to a stray bullet while visiting the set).

Scarface: The Shame of the Nation unfolds the saga of Tony Camonte (Paul Muni), a trigger-happy madman who serves as a gunman for beer baron Johnny Lovo (Osgood Perkins, father of Anthony Perkins). Deranged with bloodlust and an incestuous passion for his sister Cesca (Ann Dvorak), Camonte swells with ambition, begins leering at Lovo's "moll" Poppy (Karen Morley), and soon causes the cautious Lovo to order his main hit man "rubbed out." However, Camonte learns of Lovo's betrayal, murders the cringing Lovo, takes over the mob, beds the platinum-haired Poppy, and terrorizes the city, winning infamy as "Scarface." Slaying his most lethal rival Gaffney (Boris Karloff) in a bowling alley, Scarface appears invulnerable until he learns that his chief lieutenant Rinaldo (George Raft) and Cesca are sharing a hotel room. Unaware that they have secretly married, the insanely jealous Scarface crashes into their lovenest, slays Rinaldo, and is cornered by a squad of policemen. Scarface and Cesca try to escape, but she is killed; and the squirming Scarface, climactically pusillanimous in the face of death, is shot down like a dog in the streets beneath a flashing sign reading "The World at Your Feet."

Completed early in the summer of 1931, the film was hit with censorship problems. Sensitivity over United States gangster problems had festered so long that the Hays Office, despite the totally unglamorous image projected by Muni, refused to pass it. The censors suggested a new ending, one puffed with sermons. Hawks refused to direct it, Muni refused to play it, and finally a ludicrous closing was tacked on: an extra representing Muni, photographed from the rear and in distant silhouette, endured a plethora of crime-does-not-pay lectures before being mercifully hanged. As a bonus appeasement to the Hays Office, the film was retitled *Scarface: The Shame of the Nation*. Finally, in May of 1932, the melodrama was released (with the emasculated ending ultimately shown only in areas of very stringent censorship) and proved a sensation. *Variety* noted that the picture ". . . bumps off more guys and mixes more blood with rum than most of the past gangster offerings combined," with Muni ". . . tough enough here to make Capone his errand boy." *Scarface: The Shame of the Nation* was ignored by the Academy but did manage to place tenth on the *Film Daily* "Ten Best" list of 1932 and to perform powerfully at the box office.

Managing to see *Scarface: The Shame of the Nation* in recent years has been no easy feat, as a result of the restrictions of Howard Hughes's estate. In 1975, a New York theater managed to rent a print and show it once before a task force of Hughes's lawyers arrived to confiscate the film. Nevertheless, those fortunate enough to be at the first showing saw a still-powerful film filled with action and a spicy gallery of explosive performances. As Scarface, Muni is magnificent, a twentieth century monster festooned with greasy hair, a scar on his left cheek, and garish suits. He creates a parade of chilling vignettes, such as his fondling of a new machine gun. There is much that is dynamic but nothing that is attractive about Muni's Camonte. When Cagney flirts with Harlow in *The Public Enemy* (1931), he is insouciant; when Muni ogles Karen Morley in *Scarface: The Shame of the Nation*, he is bestial. The actor's performance helped win him a star contract at Warner Bros., where he created some of the 1930's most famous performances.

George Raft also scored in *Scarface: The Shame of the Nation*, achieving stardom as Rinaldo, the coin-tossing, paper-doll-cutting lieutenant: his own reputed underworld flirtations were reportedly tapped by director Hawks to help create proper atmosphere. Ann Dvorak, always a splendid performer, is a fiery Cesca, while Osgood Perkins twitches his bushy moustache to perfection as the oily Lovo. As Poppy, Karen Morley is the most flat-chested "moll" ever to slink through a gangster film; and Boris Karloff, as the Bugs Moranish Gaffney, is the only motion picture mobster ever to speak with an English-accented lisp. Yet both offer such colorful portrayals that these minor flaws are easily forgiven. Hawks pulls all stops in his direction, mixing with grim *élan* the dramatics with the bullet-spitting battle spectacles, and creating three marvelous death scenes: for Raft (whose eyes roll upward as he dies), Muni (whose body lies in the filthy streets shadowed and illuminated under the flashing sign), and, most famously, for Karloff (tommy-gunned while bowling, he scores a strike, the last pin toppling as he does).

In the spring of 1979, Universal Studios obtained the rights to *Scarface: The Shame of the Nation*, as well as all the other Hughes-produced films. Thus, the film should take its place along the other frequently revived gangster thrillers of the Depression years.

Finally, it should be noted that Al Capone himself saw *Scarface: The Shame of the Nation* and enjoyed it immensely. The crime lord even paid a call one evening on Howard Hawks, anxious to learn about the making of the movie and to ask where Hawks got his idea for staging a murder of a film character who was based on an actual underworld denizen of Capone's experience. Hawks replied that he got the idea from one of his "technical advisers," who had told him he knew the story to be true. "He should know," grinned Capone. "He's the one who shot him!"

SERGEANT YORK

Released: 1941
Production: Jesse L. Lasky and Hal B. Wallis for Warner Bros.
Direction: Howard Hawks
Screenplay: Howard Koch, John Huston, Abem Finkel, and Harry Chandlee;
    based on the diary of Sergeant Alvin C. York as edited by Tom Skeyhill
Cinematography: Sol Polito
Editing: William Holmes (AA)
Music: Max Steiner
Running time: 134 minutes

      Principal characters:
          Alvin C. York ....Gary Cooper (AA)
          Pastor Rosier Pile .... Walter Brennan
          Gracie Williams .... Joan Leslie
          Michael T. "Pusher" Ross .... George Tobias
          Ike Botkin .... Ward Bond

    Sergeant York is the story of Alvin C. York (Gary Cooper), a simple farmer trying to live his own life in the Tennessee Valley in the years prior to World War I. He lives with his family, working hard to build a place of his own someday. His needs are simple. He meets and falls in love with a local girl named Gracie (Joan Leslie) and plans to marry her eventually. He gets pleasure out of winning the annual turkey shoot, and he never allows anyone to get the better of him. He has an emotional experience which gives him "religion." It is this intense yet simple religious philosophy which causes him to register as a conscientious objector when he is inducted for service in the army during World War I. It is at this point that York first becomes aware of the real issues behind this so-called "Great War." Unschooled, and unsophisticated about the issues of the war, York's point of view is simple: he does not hate the Germans and he sees no reason to fight them. Eventually, however, he comes to believe that sometimes violence is needed in order to ensure freedom.

    York is sent to France, where, in the Argonne Forest, his best friend "Pusher" Ross (George Tobias) is killed by enemy soldiers. York passionately vows vengeance; driven by anger and fueled by hate for the killer of his friend, he single-handedly kills twenty-five enemy soldiers and captures an additional 132 prisoners. This feat of unbelievable courage causes General John J. Pershing, leader of the American Expeditionary Forces, to cite York as the greatest civilian soldier of the war. He is also honored with numerous medals from both France and the United States.

    On his return to America, York's fame causes him to be bombarded by promoters and merchandizers eager to have him endorse or promote their

products. For a time, he appears to be swayed by all the glamour and attention; however, reflecting upon his roots and upon the girl he left behind, he
soon rejects the limelight and returns to the Tennessee Valley and the life he
has always known.

Gary Cooper won his first Oscar for Best Actor for his performance in
Sergeant York. Sergeant York is a tribute to the solid, down-home philosophy
which characterizes much of middle America, and Cooper portrays York with
a sensitivity and naturalness that is captivating. The film was also nominated
for eleven Academy Awards, including Best Picture, Best Screenplay, Best
Musical Score, and Best Supporting Actor and Actress. Besides Cooper's
award as Best Actor, the film received an Adademy Award for Best Film
Editing by William Holmes.

Sergeant York is interesting for its political attitudes as well as for its historical content. The early portions of the film characterize York as an individual who sees things in his own unique way. As the lengthy prelude to his
involvement in the war develops, bits and pieces of his philosophy filter
through his dialogue and that of his fellow Tennesseeans. However, once the
film begins to focus on the real dilemma of a pacifist forced to bear arms in
a war that does not affect his immediate life-style, the tone becomes more
direct. Howard Koch, one of the four credited screenwriters, was a master
at infusing a script with spirit, which he does splendidly in *Sergeant York* and
did a year later in *Casablanca*. Without being preachy or too obvious, the
tone of *Sergeant York* becomes political. The film foreshadows America's
involvement in World War II while presenting a highly romanticized vision
of army life and combat.

Much of the directness of the film can be attributed to the influence of
veteran filmmaker Howard Hawks, whose direction seems effortless and completely natural. The Tennessee sequence was filmed primarily inside a studio.
It is here, with the ability to control even the smallest detail, that Hawks
creates the proper atmosphere to present York's story. His eventual acceptance of "religion," although preposterous in implication, is presented with
such simplicity and directness that it is truly believable.

The ending in which York is sought after by numerous manipulators and
merchandizers was relatively controversial for the time; many critics felt that
it detracted from the film's authenticity. However, what this conclusion actually did was to reestablish York's set of values. *Sergeant York* can be seen
as two different movies: the Tennessee prelude and the war section. The final
confrontation with wealth and fame is York's ultimate battle. He recognizes
his simple origins as a farmer, and he is also aware of the reasons for which
he fought in the war. York is lured temporarily by the possibility of "life at
the top." The voice of reason which snaps him out of his newfound "stardom"
back to reality comes from back home; he realizes his place in the structure
of things and returns to Tennessee.

There is a humility which surrounds this film. Gary Cooper, fresh from his unusual role in Frank Capra's provocative *Meet John Doe* (1941), replaces energy with common sense. Cooper embodied the spirit of the American soldier in World War I; it was a role he played in several films prior to *Sergeant York*, and he returned to it once again in *The Court-Martial of Billy Mitchell* (1955). In all these roles Cooper infuses a quality of dignity. As Cooper is attributed to have said, "Sergeant York and I had a few things in common . . . . I liked the role because of the background of the picture and because I was portraying a good, sound American character."

TO HAVE AND HAVE NOT

Released: 1944
Production: Howard Hawks for Warner Bros.
Direction: Howard Hawks
Screenplay: Jules Furthman and William Faulkner; based on the novel of the
    same name by Ernest Hemingway
Cinematography: Sid Hickox
Editing: Christian Nyby
Running time: 100 minutes

Principal characters:
    Harry Morgan (Steve) .... Humphrey Bogart
    Marie Browning (Slim) .... Lauren Bacall
    Eddie .... Walter Brennan
    Cricket .... Hoagy Carmichael
    Captain Renard .... Dan Seymour
    Johnson .... Walter Sande
    Paul de Bursac .... Walter Molnar
    Mme. Hellene de Bursac .... Dolores Moran
    Gerard (Frenchy) .... Marcel Dalio

To Have and Have Not is perhaps best known as the film that introduced
a new young actress named Lauren Bacall to the screen. At the age of only
nineteen, she starred with Humphrey Bogart and managed to do more than
a creditable job. Bogart's role as a tough, self-reliant individual plays best
when it is up against a tough, self-reliant woman, and Bacall as Slim is perfect
for the part. Their scenes together crackle with chemistry and fire and some
of film's most memorable dialogue. The plot further engages the viewer's
sympathies because it involves a classic struggle against infringement of personal liberty.

To Have and Have Not, however, is not generally considered a classic. In
a catalogue of Bogart's films, it is not as admired as *The Maltese Falcon*
(1941), *High Sierra* (1941), or *Casablanca* (1942). Likewise, in a catalogue
of director Howard Hawks's works, this film is not as well known as Westerns
such as *Rio Bravo* (1959) or *Red River* (1948), or screwball comedies such
as *Bringing Up Baby* (1938) and *Ball of Fire* (1941). Even *The Big Sleep*
(1946), which followed *To Have and Have Not* and reunited Hawks, Bogart,
Bacall, and writers Furthman and Faulkner, is generally better regarded and
remembered, although *To Have and Have Not* is arguably the better movie.

One of the problems faced by the makers of *To Have and Have Not* was
that the film followed close on the success of *Casablanca*; in fact, Warner
Bros wanted it to be another *Casablanca*. The plot of the Hemingway novel

was manipulated to include French resistance fighters and the women who support their work. Most of the interior action takes place in a bar much like Rick's Café Americaine. And there is even the ubiquitous pianist, now named Cricket and played by Hoagy Carmichael. But the film is essentially upbeat, a restrained comedy rather than melodrama. It is *Casablanca* as Howard Hawks would have made it.

To Have and Have Not is a highly appealing movie. In a role perfectly suited to his film *persona*, Bogart plays Harry Morgan, an expatriate American living in Vichy-controlled Martinique who is menaced by the war and women and who struggles to retain his freedom and individuality. Morgan owns a fishing boat and hires it out by the day to tourists. When he is approached by a group of French patriots who want to hire the boat to rescue a fellow resistance fighter from Devil's Island, Morgan refuses to get involved at any price, saying that he has no politics, nor any use for them. "What are your sympathies?" he is asked at one point. "Minding my own business" is his answer.

Bogart meets Bacall in a rather familiar looking tropical bar. The action, however, is not so typical. Morgan has been sitting at the bar watching the pianist, Cricket, and the group gathered around him, which includes Marie Browning (Lauren Bacall). She has just arrived in Martinique, a drifter who makes her way from place to place by practicing petty larceny and accepting small presents, such as plane tickets, from admirers. As she gets up to leave the room, Morgan follows and accuses her of lifting the wallet of the gentleman who was buying her drinks. Morgan has an interest in recovering the wallet because the man, Johnson (Walter Sande), is his client, and owes him more than $800 for sixteen days of fishing. Although Johnson has promised to pay him the next day after he has a chance to go to the bank, Morgan finds more than enough travelers checks in the wallet to cover the fee. Also in the wallet is a ticket out of Martinique on that night's plane. From this Morgan deduces that Johnson had intended to leave without paying. This makes allies of Morgan and Slim, as he calls Marie, since she has done him a favor by lifting Johnson's wallet.

But Morgan's luck does not hold out. Although he confronts Johnson with the evidence and asks him to start signing over the checks, they are interrupted by a raid by the Sûreté who had recognized the resistance members leaving the bar. In the ensuing struggle, Johnson is killed by a stray bullet before he has signed over the checks. This incident sets up the rest of the action. Both Morgan and Slim are now broke. They are hauled down to the headquarters of the Provisional government where they are slapped and mistreated by a surly and contemptible officer named Captain Renard (Dan Seymour). Eventually, it is Renard's authoritarianism even more than Morgan's need for money that leads Morgan to accept the offer of the resistance fighters. However, he still refuses to be emotional about their cause. Asked why he has suddenly changed his mind, he says simply, "Maybe because I like you, and I don't like them."

The rescue from Devil's Island is an atmospheric scene involving fog and shadows, flashes from far-off lanterns, and the monotonous drone of the boat's motors. Stowed away on board is Morgan's pal Eddie (Walter Brennan), an alcoholic who is no longer any good as a ship's mate, but whom Morgan keeps around because he is loyal. The relationship adds a dimension to Morgan's character; although independent and unemotional, he is shown to value friendship and loyalty. At Devil's Island, two passengers are taken on board. They turn out to be a man and wife, Paul and Hellene de Bursac. She travels with her husband, Hellene de Bursac tells Morgan, because without her, he would be useless to the cause. He would be always worrying about having to leave her behind, wondering if she had been approached by the authorities and made to talk. This exchange expands upon the theme that a man is at his strongest when he allows himself to feel emotion.

Heading back to port, Morgan spots a government boat. He takes a shot at its searchlight and prepares to make a run for safety, telling everyone to stay down. Bursac, however, panics. Standing up, he catches a bullet in his shoulder. The Bursacs are then hidden in the basement of the hotel where Morgan and Slim both are living. The two team up to nurse Paul de Bursac back to health. Morgan acts dispassionately. He does not like Hellene de Bursac and he does not believe in their cause, but he knows how to care for a bullet wound. Slim helps out because she likes Morgan.

The relationship between Slim and Morgan, whom she calls Steve although his name is Harry, develops in a series of scenes highlighted by fast-paced dialogue, pointed enough to reveal both characters. Hawks is said to have created the character of Slim because the only way the romance could bridge the age gap between Bogart and Bacall was to have Bacall dominate and to have Bogart enjoy her extravagant performance. (Interestingly, Bogart and Bacall actually did fall in love during the making of the film.) Sexual repartee and a somewhat cynical assessment of each other's pasts give way to a partnership based on mutual understanding. Gradually, we sense, a respect grows. In a showdown scene with Renard and his thugs, the understanding between Slim and Steve is crucial to the action. "Anyone got a match?" asks Morgan, echoing a phrase Slim had used in their first meeting. He directs her to open a drawer where the matches, and a gun, are kept. With Slim's help, Morgan is able to turn the tables on the police and take control of the situation. The movie ends with Steve and Slim, accompanied by Eddie, setting off, suitcases in hand, to enjoy the future together.

Besides bringing together Bogart and Bacall, *To Have and Have Not* joined Bogart and Hawks. Harry Morgan is the perfect realization not only of the Bogart character but also of the Hawks hero. Loosely based on Hemingway's novel, the movie is more Hawks than Hemingway. The two collaborated on a treatment using the character of Harry Morgan from the novel, but almost everything else was changed. Instead of Cuba and Florida, the setting is the French West Indies island of Martinique. Morgan has been changed from a down-and-out loser to a strong, upbeat hero, and Marie, the wife, is now the single and footloose Slim (Hawks's nickname for his own wife).

Hawks preferred comedies to melodramas and action to issues. Thus, although Harry Morgan is a classic Bogart hero, tough and seemingly without loyalties other than to himself, Hawks's influence makes him more appealing than many of Bogart's other tough roles. He is a loner, not an outlaw. He makes his own decisions out of choice, not because he is pursued. The role is made compellingly believable both because of what film lovers already know of Bogart and because of what is now revealed. It adds a new dimension to the Bogart *persona*. He is softened and given humor, without losing any of his strength. Hawks can be given much of the credit for having achieved a new characterization. Unlike Hitchcock, for instance, who insists that his movies are all but made before shooting begins, Hawks leaves room for invention; he is very much a collaborative director. Hawks was also fortunate in filming *To Have and Have Not* to be surrounded by people who thought very much as he did. For the man who made *Red River* and *Rio Bravo*, a Hemingway novel was a perfect vehicle, and for the man who made *Bringing Up Baby* and *His Girl Friday* (1940), Bogart and Bacall were a perfect team of costars. Hawks also reaped the benefit of having Jules Furthman, a long-time collaborator and top-notch dialogue writer, and William Faulkner, an excellent developer of character and scene, work on the screenplay.

Hawks has often been underrated by American film critics because he was not particularly daring in his interpretation of a script. Whether he was making a comedy, a Western, an action film, or a musical, he always worked within the conventions of the genre. With what he had to work with in the case of *To Have and Have Not*, and with vigorous directing and the talent and collaboration of his writers and stars, Hawks produced a memorable, enjoyable film.

TWENTIETH CENTURY

Released: 1934
Production: Howard Hawks for Columbia
Direction: Howard Hawks
Screenplay: Ben Hecht and Charles MacArthur; based on their play of the
    same name, adapted from the play *Napoleon on Broadway* by Charles
    Bruce Milholland
Cinematography: Joseph H. August
Editing: Gene Havlick
Running time: 91 minutes

    Principal characters:
        Oscar Jaffe .... John Barrymore
        Lily Garland .... Carole Lombard
        Oliver Webb .... Walter Connolly
        Owen O'Malley .... Roscoe Karns
        Max Jacobs .... Charles Levison
        Clark .... Etienne Girardot
        Sadie .... Dale Fuller
        George Smith .... Ralph Forbes
        Mr. McGonigle .... Edgar Kennedy

    According to her second cousin, Howard Hawks, Carole Lombard was
blessed from childhood with a vibrant, energetic personality; but this lively
spirit had been largely absent in her motion pictures prior to 1934. As Hawks
bluntly stated, she was a "lousy, phoney" actress, but one nevertheless with
a potential for greatness that lay dormant within her, a greatness that he was
determined to uncover. Hawks prevailed upon Columbia's obstinate president, Harry Cohn, to secure Lombard's services, and before long, the twenty-
five-year-old starlet was contracted to appear opposite the brilliant John
Barrymore in Ben Hecht's and Charles MacArthur's adaptation of the Broadway hit, "Twentieth Century," to be directed by Hawks himself.

    As the first day of filming progressed, everyone on the set could plainly
see that the young actress was in deep trouble. Her performance was miserable, and Barrymore was so appalled at the prospect of playing opposite
such a poor performer that he began to make rude faces behind her back.
During a short break, Hawks took his struggling relative aside. After reassuring her that she was indeed working very hard, Hawks asked, "How much
do you get paid for this picture?" Lombard answered that her salary for
Twentieth Century was $5,000. Hawks then said, "That's pretty good. What
do you get paid for?" "Why, acting, of course," came the confused reply.
"Okay," Hawks continued, "supposing I tell you that you've earned all the
money. You don't owe anything." The director then asked, "What would you

do if a man said 'so and so' to you." The plain-spoken Lombard told Hawks that if any man dared to call her those horrible names, she would kick him in the groin. "Well," said Hawks, "Barrymore said that to you. Why didn't you kick him?" He then told her that if she failed to kick her costar in the pants during the next scene, he would fire her from the picture and hire another actress.

Filming resumed with Barrymore unaware of the nature of Hawks's conversation with Lombard, and Hawks playfully decided to keep him in the dark a while longer. The director placed three cameras on the set to be assured of catching every bit of what was about to unfold and called for action. When Barrymore started in on Lombard, she let out a vicious kick, catching the startled actor completely off guard. However, consummate performer that he was, Barrymore continued his dialogue without missing a beat, punctuating it by jabbing his fingers at Lombard, and dancing around the set like a boxer. She in turn, kept up the pace, lashing out with both feet while Barrymore jumped to and fro. The scene finally concluded with Barrymore's exit; he returned to the set in amazement. "She's magnificent," he told Hawks. "Were you fooling me all this time?" Then, both men looked towards Carole Lombard, who was emotionally drained and sobbing in a corner of the set, and each realized that he had been privileged to witness the birth of a star.

The plot line of *Twentieth Century* has its parallels to the true tale recounted above. It also involves the process of molding a beautiful, innocent, untrained, and unpolished actress into a star, its Pygmalion/Galatea overtones overshadowed only by the more sinister ones of a Svengali/Trilby relationship. The film is a frenetic, farcical romp that has been a pleasure to behold for over forty years. Barrymore plays Oscar Jaffe, a near-legendary theatrical figure who seems to run everything, although his exact occupation is left unclear. A combination of producer, author, director, and talent coordinator, Jaffe is an imperious, egotistical tyrant who commands his underlings as a feudal lord would his serfs. His capriciousness baffles everyone. Actors, press agents, managers, and secretaries all follow his every whim.

Jaffe decides, seemingly on the spur of the moment, that a novice actress named Mildred Plotka will, after being renamed Lily Garland (Carole Lombard), become his next star, his biggest discovery. Against all advice he sets out to mold the frightened new "Lily" into a thespian. In one of the film's most memorable sequences, Jaffe shows Lily exactly how to move on the stage, indicating every few paces where and how a line is to be delivered, drawing a maze of chalklines on the floor to help her remember, and finally poking her with a pin to get the proper scream at the proper time.

Jaffe's plot succeeds and Lily is an opening-night sensation—an instant star. The scene then quickly shifts ahead three years. We see that Lily has reached the top of the theatrical world, and has become, in the bargain, her mentor's mistress. Jaffe endeavors to control every aspect of her life, from her stage career to her day-to-day activities. Lily has endured this domination for three long and frustrating years, but finally she can stand it no longer. Her breaking point is reached when she discovers that Jaffe has tapped her telephone and has hired a detective to follow her every move. Furious, she packs her bags and leaves Jaffe once and for all.

She heads West to Hollywood. Once there she singly conquers the movie world. Before long her photograph graces the cover of every fan magazine; her name appears in lights on every movie-house marquee. During this time, however, Jaffe has fallen upon hard times. Unable to produce a decent play without his longtime star, the one-time theatrical wizard watches in stunned horror as flop after flop closes on opening night. After his last-ditch comeback attempt, "The Bride of Bagdad," fails also, he appears at the end of his financial and emotional rope. Thoroughly disheartened, he takes a train to New York only to discover that Lily is also onboard. The final results of the film now involve Jaffe's frantic attempts to win his former star and lover back onto his stage and into his arms. He miraculously accomplishes both goals as the picture ends, although he has to fake a heart attack to do so.

A Svengali/Trilby motif runs throughout *Twentieth Century*, serving as the film's underlying theme. Jaffe constantly makes reference to the "gold" and the "diamond" inside Lily which are just waiting to be mined by some Svengali. Lily is, in turn, quite aware of the unnatural nature of their relationship. At one point, she screams out, "I'm no Trilby," while behind her Jaffe enters the room in the manner of Svengali, a malevolent presence in his dark hat and unfurled cape. Jaffe creates Garland's career and her public image, but is ultimately unable to control what he has wrought. While a reconciliation is finally achieved, one gets the impression that Lily will no longer be as pliable as before. She has matured enough to realize that she can make it on her own, and he, at last, has become aware of her true strength and character.

Twentieth Century is loaded with satirical barbs aimed at the theater and its denizens. This is not surprising since screenwriters Hecht and MacArthur were among the elite of New York's theatrical society. They enlarged the scope of the film to include long scenes of rehearsals and backstage life, in contrast to the stage production in which the action was confined entirely to the transcontinental train from which the play and the film take their name. The film's characters are largely stereotyped caricatures of theatrical people. Jaffe is the archetype of the pompous, arrogant producer whose artistic vehicles are merely corny melodramas with titles such as "The Heart of Kentucky" and "Desert Love." Walter Connolly plays the much-suffering manager with a bad heart, and Roscoe Karns plays the perpetually inebriated press hack. Lily herself typifies the frightened waif-turned-obstinate prima donna, her intransigence matched only by that of her mentor.

The movies *per se* are also subject to frequent jibes. When Jaffe learns that

Lily has left him and the theater for Hollywood, he moans, "Oh, Lily. How could you do it?," meaning, on the one hand, how could she ever leave him, and on the other, how could she stoop so low as to appear in movies. The filmmakers—Hawks, Hecht, MacArthur, and Barrymore—are all poking fun at themselves and their profession when they employ these little jokes, demonstrating that while they may be getting rich by making films, and while they always try to do the best job they can, they do not take their lofty positions very seriously.

Hawks's direction of *Twentieth Century* is characteristically unobtrusive. Camera movement is minimal, with long takes serving as the dominant visual strategy. He prefers to let his players create the kinesthetics as they roam about the small sets, constantly in motion, their lines delivered at a rapid-fire pace that has become the hallmark of Hawks's comedy. Hawks steps aside to allow the performers to stand out, and as always, he draws exceptional performances from his ensemble. Lombard's emergence as a brilliant co-medienne was a surprise to everyone except her director, who, like Oscar Jaffe, knew that she had vast reserves of talent buried within her, abilities that required a firm guiding hand to bring them to the fore.

Barrymore relished his role as Jaffe since it gave him the opportunity, as Hawks told him, to play "the world's second greatest ham," Barrymore himself being the world's foremost, and he played the part with great enthusiasm, allowing his comedic range to flow naturally. He is a whirlwind of energy all through the film, and even during slow moments his imagination and verve propel the film forward. His hilarious facial contortions, double and triple takes, and pompous gesturings are a marvel to watch, a perfect combination of uncontrolled slapstick and split-second timing.

The supporting players, in particular Connolly, Karns, Etienne Girardot, and Edgar Kennedy, all have their excellent moments. Seeing them in action, one cannot help mourning the passing of the days of the great character players. These secondary actors and actresses graced and enlivened countless films of the 1930's and 1940's, and too often were the only high points of a bad picture.

Finally, due credit must be given to Howard Hawks, who chose his cast with impeccable taste and care and directed the film with unassuming style and grace. Last but by no means least, he acted as Lombard's Svengali: a benign one to be sure, but nevertheless a master manipulator who played a large role in the creation of one of America's most loved comediennes and enduring personalities.

ALFRED HITCHCOCK

DIAL M FOR MURDER

Released: 1954
Production: Alfred Hitchcock for Warner Bros.
Direction: Alfred Hitchcock
Screenplay: Frederick Knott; based on his play of the same name
Cinematography: Robert Burks
Editing: Rudi Fehr
Running time: 105 minutes

> *Principal characters:*
> Tony Wendice .... Ray Milland
> Margot Wendice .... Grace Kelly
> Mark Halliday .... Robert Cummings
> Inspector Hubbard .... John Williams
> Captain Lesgate .... Anthony Dawson

Alfred Hitchcock, the undisputed master of suspense, retains the theatrical origins of this lovely melodrama by confining most of the action to one room. The result is an intellectual chase scene for the mind rather than the body, as the audience watches the police inspector unravel the puzzle of the keys. The success of the film rests with the sound plotting of the script, the fine pacing, and the cinematography. Since there is only one action scene, a stabbing which occurs halfway through the movie, most of the tension is derived from the way Hitchcock first involves the audience in the murder scheme, and then in the efforts to entrap the murderer.

From the beginning it is clear that charming tennis pro Tony Wendice (Ray Milland), is planning to have his beautiful but unfaithful wife, Margot (Grace Kelly), murdered. Tony, who is nothing if not thorough, has been planning her demise for more than a year, ever since he discovered that she was having an affair with Mark Halliday (Robert Cummings), an American television mystery writer. Having married Margot for her money, Tony is now afraid that she will seek a divorce, thereby depriving him of his luxurious life style.

In the first scenes, Margot, seeing Mark for the first time in a year, explains that she had stopped their correspondence after the one love letter she had saved had been stolen from her purse at Victoria Station six months before. After that she had received two extortion letters, but the money she had sent in payment had never been collected by the blackmailer. She is convinced that Tony knows nothing of their affair.

The audience soon learns that Tony not only knows about the liaison, but that he is also her extortionist. Furthermore, Margot is not the only person he is going to blackmail. Pleading a heavy workload, Tony backs out of the theater engagement he and Margot have planned with Mark. Playing the role of the congenial, unsuspecting husband, he invites Mark to join him at a banquet being held at his club the following night. After Margot and Mark leave, Tony lures Captain Lesgate (Anthony Dawson), a disreputable rogue, over to the apartment. Lesgate, whose real name is Swann, was at Cambridge at the same time as Tony, who even then recognized a soul as unscrupulous as his own. Having followed Lesgate's activities for several months, Tony has now amassed a portfolio of crimes sufficient to convince Lesgate that he must carry out Tony's well-conceived plan, or he will go to jail.

Throughout the film Hitchcock uses a ground-level camera to capture the interaction between the players. As Tony outlines the perfect murder, however, the camera shifts overhead to give the audience a godlike perspective. Lesgate is to arrive at 10:37 the following night, take the key from under the carpet of the fifth step of the stairway just outside the apartment door, enter the flat, and hide behind the draperies behind the desk. Tony will excuse himself from the dinner at 10:40 to call his boss, but first will call home. When the phone rings, Margot will get out of bed and come to the desk, where Lesgate will strangle her. He will then whistle into the phone, at which point Tony will hang up and call his boss to support his alibi. When the deed is done, Tony will pay Lesgate a thousand pounds, which he has unobtrusively been saving at the rate of twenty pounds per week.

The next night the camera is returned to the human, fallible level to watch the drama unfold. Much of Hitchcock's brilliance is revealed in the way he manipulates the audience's involvement. When Margot suddenly announces her intention to go to a movie, thereby ruining all of Tony's masterful planning, the audience roots for him as he persuades her to stay home. Ironically, his vain suggestion that she clip articles for his scrapbook results in the ultimate failure of his plan, by providing her with the weapon she needs for her own defense. Tony unobtrusively removes her latchkey from her purse and places it under the carpet in the stairway before he and Mark leave for dinner.

When Lesgate enters the apartment that night, Hitchcock uses the technique of "film time" to stretch out action which normally would take only a few seconds. The result is an increase in the level of tension as the importance of the events is emphasized. In one of the few cuts outside the apartment, the audience sees that Tony's watch is slow and that Lesgate is about to leave. To the audience's relief, the call comes through just in time, and as Margot answers the phone, Lesgate slips a knotted stocking around her neck and begins violently choking her. The dim lighting creates an ominous atmosphere which emphasizes her agony as she struggles against his superior strength. Suddenly, however, she is able to grasp the scissors on the desk and plunge them into her assailant. In the one truly gruesome shot, Lesgate falls on his back, driving the scissors in deeper.

Tony, realizing that the plan has gone awry, now comes on the line to tell Margot not to call the police until he gets home. Panic-stricken and grateful to hear his voice, Margot follows his instructions. Clever as well as diabolical, Tony quickly alters the plan to make it appear that Lesgate had been blackmailing Margot, who in turn killed him. Tony plants Mark's love letter on Lesgate, removes the latchkey from the victim's pocket and places it in Margot's purse, and hides a knotted silk stocking in the wastebasket before calling the police.

From here on the tension is derived from a cat-and-mouse game between Tony and Inspector Hubbard (John Williams), an investigator who is the epitome of the British detective. The audience now begins to identify with the inquisitive, perceptive Inspector.

The bewildered Margot is amazed to find that all the evidence is suddenly distorted against her. Tony, as her loyal husband, staunchly defends her on the surface, while subtly providing all the evidence needed to convict her of first-degree murder. He informs the Inspector that he is sure that Margot does not know Lesgate (that is, Swann), but that he had known him briefly in college; he had only seen Swann once since, and that was at Victoria Station six months before. This, together with the love letter found in Lesgate's pocket, makes the blackmail motive for murder very plausible. When the silk stocking is found in the wastebasket, it appears likely that Margot's neck bruises were self-inflicted. The most damning piece of evidence, however, is the fact that the carpet and the condition of Lesgate's shoes prove that he must have come in through the front door, and that she must have let him in.

For the trial, Hitchcock maintains a claustrophobic intensity by using an effective series of close-ups of Margot's face illuminated with colored lights against a neutral backdrop. She is convicted of first-degree murder and sentenced to death. Wiley Inspector Hubbard, however, is bothered by the fact that Lesgate carried no latchkey, so the day before the sentence is to be carried out, he devises a scheme to unearth new evidence. Hubbard goes to the apartment purportedly to question Tony about the large sums of money he has been spending lately, but during the course of the interview the Inspector manages to switch raincoats with Tony. He suggests Tony drop by the station to pick up some of Margot's possessions. After Tony goes out, Hubbard uses the key inside Tony's raincoat to enter the apartment. Upon returning, he finds that Mark has broken in hoping to find evidence to save Margot.

Inspector Hubbard then initiates step one. Margot is driven to the front door and told to go inside the apartment. The Inspector and Mark wait quietly inside the darkened flat and listen as she enters the building, walks down the hallway, and tries to open the door with the key from her purse. When she is unable to open the door, she walks back outside. Hitchcock heightens the effectiveness of this scene with the use of real tiles in the hallway which emphasize the drama as the footsteps echo and recede.

The police then rush Margot's purse back to the station where Tony soon picks it up. Inspector Hubbard explains to Mark and Margot that the key in her purse was Lesgate's own latchkey and that he has Tony's key. The Inspector has located Margot's key under the carpet on the fifth step of the stairway; she has proven that she did not know it was there; her fate now rests on proving that Tony does know. The tension mounts as Tony's footsteps are heard in the hallway. He tries the key from Margot's purse; it does not work; he starts out, then stops. Suddenly, he realizes that Lesgate must have returned the key to the step before entering the apartment. He retrieves it, unlocks the door, and turns on the light, illuminating the scene.

Though Hitchcock maintains the theatricality of the production by confining the action to one room, he uses close-ups to capture the terror on the actors' faces which would be missed on stage. Changes in lighting, from the dimly lit attack scene to the symbolic illumination of the villain at the end, add to the atmosphere. Hitchcock's use of color also helps set the mood. Margot is first dressed in lovely colors, she is wearing white when attacked, and as her plight becomes desperate she wears black.

Though most audiences saw *Dial M for Murder* in the traditional format, it was filmed in Naturalvision, Warner Bros.' version of 3-D. The 3-D format was useful in this case, not for special effects, but for giving the film additional depth and intimacy within the confining set.

Hitchcock, always noted for his inconspicuous appearances in his films, has cleverly worked himself into a reunion picture which Tony shows to Lesgate during their interview.

The performances are generally good. John Williams and Anthony Dawson reenacted their Broadway roles. Williams is well cast as the Scotland Yard-type detective who enjoys unraveling clues. Dawson has made a career out of playing snakelike villain roles. Ray Milland is convincingly pathological as the venal Tony, and Grace Kelly is good at conveying bewilderment and terror. All in all, Hitchcock's talent for creating suspense blends with Frederick Knott's well-crafted plot to provide an interesting and diverting mystery.

FOREIGN CORRESPONDENT

Released: 1940
Production: Walter Wanger for United Artists
Direction: Alfred Hitchcock
Screenplay: Charles Bennett and Joan Harrison, with dialogue by James Hilton and Robert Benchley; based on the autobiography *Personal History* by Vincent Sheean
Cinematography: Rudolph Maté
Editing: Otho Lovering
Running time: 119 minutes

> *Principal characters:*
> Johnny Jones (Huntley Haverstock) .... Joel McCrea
> Carol Fisher .... Laraine Day
> Stephen Fisher .... Herbert Marshall
> Scott Ffolliott .... George Sanders
> Van Meer .... Albert Basserman
> Stebbins .... Robert Benchley

Foreign Correspondent, released in 1940, signified a major turning point in director Alfred Hitchcock's career. Although the film was his second to be made in the United States, it constituted his first experience with a Hollywood-type production. His first American film, based on Daphne du Maurier's *Rebecca*, so retained the style and appearance of the director's English works that it is difficult to think of it as having been made in Hollywood. Interestingly, this result was not due to any stylistic intention on Hitchcock's part but was instead a reflection of the subject matter and of the production values aimed for by producer David O. Selznick.

Selznick had brought Hitchcock to Hollywood in 1940 with an $800,000 contract to make four important pictures. When the first project, *Titanic*, based upon the story of the doomed luxury liner, had to be temporarily abandoned, the director was given *Rebecca*, a property which he had earlier attempted to purchase and produce in England. Hitchcock's second chance to make this film of the Maurier novel was, of course, a major success, earning the Oscar as Best Picture of 1940, but it also proved to Hitchcock that working for Selznick would be a mixed blessing. In England, the director's creativity had been restrained by small budgets; in Hollywood, however, he could afford to explore more fully the technical tricks of movie-making and experiment with projects that were not hampered by budgetary limitations. There were, however, limitations imposed by Hollywood that Hitchcock had rarely encountered in England, where he was in almost complete artistic control of his films. In the United States during the 1940's, however, it was the producer who controlled the creative direction of the project, and his intentions and wishes always superseded those of the director. When the producer was a man like David O. Selznick, control was imperious and complete. This was the situation with *Rebecca*, even though the film seems to be a reflection of the Hitchcock style.

Foreign Correspondent, Hitchcock's second American film, provided him with more artistic freedom than had *Rebecca* and at the same time afforded the director most of the assets available at a Hollywood studio. Hitchcock had discovered that some other producers were less likely to interfere in his films than was Selznick; thus he endeavored to make additional pictures on loan to other studios. *Foreign Correspondent*, loosely based upon journalist Vincent Sheean's autobiography, *Personal History*, the first of these additional films, was made for Walter Wanger and United Artists. Its budget of one-and-one-half million dollars, which represented the most money with which Hitchcock had ever worked, was principally spent on scenery consisting of a ten-acre Amsterdam public square, a large section of London, a Dutch countryside complete with windmill, and a large transatlantic airplane. These items were planned and constructed by an army of 558 carpenters and technicians. Additionally, fourteen screenwriters worked at various times on the screenplay, and more than 240,000 feet of film were shot and edited to 120 screen minutes. The film displays some of the finest visual design and cinematography evident in any of Hitchcock's productions, indicating that the director quickly learned the manner in which to make optimum use of a generous budget.

Unlike many of Hitchcock's other famous thrillers, *Foreign Correspondent* features no superstars. Gary Cooper, for example, refused the role of reporter Johnny Jones, and although Joel McCrea was eventually placed in the role and did a solid job, he simply lacked the box-office appeal of a major star such as Cary Grant or James Stewart. The problem was that the "thriller" was held in rather low esteem by 1940 Hollywood, and Hitchcock, who had not yet established himself as the master of suspense, was not able to recruit the big-name actors he desired.

Foreign Correspondent establishes a pattern of suspense and intrigue that would become a hallmark of many of Hitchcock's American thrillers. Johnny Jones (Joel McCrea) is a tough, hard-headed crime reporter who is reassigned by his editor to investigate the prospects of an outbreak of hostilities in Europe just prior to the beginning of World War II. He thus becomes a foreign correspondent, and temporarily changes his name to Huntley Haverstock. Arriving in Amsterdam, Jones meets Van Meer (Albert Basserman), a Dutch diplomat who has memorized a secret clause in an Allied treaty for his country. Traveling with the diplomat is the head of a pacifist group, Stephen Fisher (Herbert Marshall), and his daughter Carol (Laraine Day). Van Meer is to make a speech to the pacifist organization on the opportunities of averting war.

In one of the most memorable scenes of any Hitchcock film, Van Meer appears to be assassinated as he arrives to address the pacifists; the scene occurs in the Amsterdam public square filled with people carrying umbrellas in a pouring rain, and the murderer escapes in a chase beneath the umbrellas, the scene being presented through some excellent camerawork from above. An elaborate drainage system constructed beneath the set carried off the rainwater to maintain some degree of traction for McCrea and the other actors involved in the scene. The murderer is pursued by Johnny Jones into the Dutch countryside. At a windmill, the reporter discovers the real Van Meer, kidnaped by Nazis who have staged the assassination by murdering a double. The Nazis disappear with their captive while Jones is trying to convince the Dutch police that the diplomat is a prisoner inside the windmill.

Jones searches for Van Meer both in Holland and England with the aid of Carol Fisher, who is slowly falling in love with him. They discover that Carol's father, who has been masquerading as a pacifist, is in reality an agent for the Nazis and has been instrumental in kidnaping Van Meer and in trying to extract his secret information. Jones and Herbert Ffolliott (George Sanders), an English reporter, rescue the Dutch diplomat, but Fisher escapes with his daughter, who is now confused and disillusioned in her romance with Jones. As war is declared, the Fishers take a plane from England to America only to find that Jones and Ffolliott are also onboard, and as the reporters confront Fisher, the plane, mistaken by a German ship below for an English bomber, is shot down. The survivors attempt to stay afloat upon the wing of the plane while Fisher, realizing that he faces arrest in America, sacrifices his life to save the rest. An American ship approaches, frightening off the German one, and rescues the plane's passengers. Barred from telephoning their newspapers, Jones and Ffolliott pretend to make a personal call and then reiterate the story to the captain loud enough to be heard by Jones's editor on the other end of the line. As the film ends, Jones establishes himself as a top foreign correspondent and marries Carol.

Foreign Correspondent has achieved a well-deserved reputation as a masterpiece of suspense and intrigue, and was instrumental in upgrading the reputation of the thriller genre, being nominated for Academy Awards for Best Picture and Best Screenplay. The fact that the film won in neither category may be due to one significant fault in Hitchcock's effort: the film is overly long and drags in spots because of diversions in the story line incorporated to promote America's entry into World War II. The film attempts to merge two levels in an emotional appeal to the viewer. The first, that of the suspenseful cloak-and-dagger chase across Europe, is what Hitchcock does best; the second, however, is propaganda advocating an end to American isolation and an entry into World War II, and although Hitchcock manages a merger of these two themes more successfully than many other directors at the time, the intertwining causes the film to be less taut and more meandering than many of his later masterpieces.

The best reporter in *Foreign Correspondent* is, unquestionably, the camera. When the diplomat is assassinated, Hitchcock's camera is in the right place observing the fallen man's face; when a man is on the verge of dropping from a tower, the camera follows a hat making the plunge first; as the stricken airplane hurtles to the sea at the film's climax, the camera peers anxiously from the pilot's seat, indicating that it too has the reporter's gift of not revealing everything.

According to a number of sources, Hitchcock ordered several retakes of the wreck of the *Clipper* because it pleased him to see Joel McCrea and George Sanders floundering in the water, and when McCrea protested that the scene had ruined one of his suits, Hitchcock, who claims to dislike actors, sent him a new one the next day—made for a ten-year-old. In his role, however, McCrea proves both likable and capable. His interpretation of the reporter establishes the man as a credible citizen who, as the film ends, has the audience convinced that he will stride to one journalistic triumph after another. Laraine Day performs solidly in the role of Carol Fisher, her most ambitious part to that date, but Herbert Marshall appears somewhat miscast as the peace advocate who turns out to be a spy. Although he gives a good performance, he is too suave for his character and loses a little credibility. George Sanders, Albert Basserman, and Edward Ciannelli add much to the film, but it is Robert Benchley who carries off the acting honors in his portrayal of the broken-down American journalist Stebbins in London. He brought much of his own experience to the role and was specially chosen by Hitchcock, who enjoyed his brand of satiric humor. All of the scenes in which the humorist appeared were, at Hitchcock's request, written by Benchley himself.

In viewing the film as fundamentally a spy melodrama which places more emphasis on the pacing of the action than on where the action takes us, there are still awkward aspects. The meeting of the peace society contains prominently overdone elements; the crucial secret is, for the most part, meaningless, and the speeches are sometimes heavy-handed, particularly toward the end. Otherwise, the film moves swiftly, and although the plot is bare enough, Hitchcock, in the manner of a painter, loves details and loads his set with them without weighing down his action. He makes a character out of every extra; he likes to have a bland face or a sweet old lady personify evil, while the sinister fellow turns out to be the good guy all along. He sprinkles his scenes with people and mechanical devices which are not direct accessories to the plot so that the film conveys the realities of life, with dogs and casual passersby who are real and have nothing to do with any plot.

Above all, the film exemplifies Hitchcock's ability to use people, sound, and objects for the sole purpose of suspense. The use of objects, for example, is seen in *Foreign Correspondent* in the reversing windmill, the assassin's

camera and the disappearing car. Hitchcock knows where to set the microphone and camera to catch the effect he has planned, and with all of the
devices of this complex art completely at his fingertips, his characters never
enter a deserted building or a dark alley without the viewer wondering if they
will ever come out alive.

In short, *Foreign Correspondent* provides an example of all the techniques
that make a film move in the lightest and fastest manner possible, utilizing
all of the qualities that are available through a large budget and the art of
Alfred Hitchcock. In fact, Hitchcock's only oversight in making *Foreign Correspondent* was in forgetting his invariable signature of personally appearing
in the film. Fortunately, with a generous Hollywood budget, he had the means
to reshoot a scene in a railway station in order to get himself into the picture.

THE LADY VANISHES

Released: 1938
Production: Edward Black for Gainsborough Pictures
Direction: Alfred Hitchcock
Screenplay: Sidney Gillatt and Frank Launder; based on Alma Reville's adaptation of the novel *The Wheel Spins* by Ethel Lina White
Cinematography: Jack Cox
Editing: Alfred Roome and R. E. Dearing
Running time: 97 minutes

Principal characters:
Iris Henderson .... Margaret Lockwood
Gilbert .... Michael Redgrave
Miss Froy .... Dame May Whitty
Dr. Hartz .... Paul Lukas
Mr. Todhunter .... Cecil Parker
Caldicott .... Naunton Wayne
Charters .... Basil Radford
Margaret .... Linden Travers
Madame Kummer .... Josephine Wilson

Alfred Hitchcock's last important and most acclaimed British film, *The Lady Vanishes*, in many ways epitomizes his British films, which are simpler and less pretentious than his later American ones. Few Hitchcock films have had such an enthusiastic critical reception as *The Lady Vanishes*, which is arguably the best of his British films and certainly one of his most ingenious and entertaining. The story concerns an elderly English governess whose disappearance from a train sets off a string of mysterious incidents. The pace never slackens as Hitchcock keeps the tension mounting until the final scene. Indeed, *The Lady Vanishes* is quintessential Hitchcock, complete with a beautiful heroine, a perplexed hero, international spies, and a train journey, all set amidst much suspense.

Somewhere in a Central European country, the passengers on a transcontinental train are stranded at a small inn by an avalanche. Unprepared to accommodate such a large number of guests, the innkeeper does not have enough rooms or food for all of the passengers, two of whom are very British and unflappable cricket fans who are hurrying home to see the championship cricket matches. At dinner they are forced to share a table with an elderly British governess, Miss Froy (Dame May Whitty), who is returning home after having spent six years in an unnamed Central European country and who offers to share her cheese with them since the inn's food had run out some time before. Also staying at the inn is an English heiress, Iris Henderson (Margaret Lockwood), who is having a final vacation before returning to England to be married. Upset by the noise in the room above hers, she has its occupant, Gilbert (Michael Redgrave), a music scholar recording the vanishing folk dances of Central Europe, thrown out. When he responds by threatening to occupy her own room, she hurriedly calls the manager to have him restored to his room.

The next morning the railroad track is cleared and the train's passengers prepare to continue their journey. As Iris is waiting to board the train, however, she is struck on the head by a flower pot; and her momentary unconsciousness and dizziness are conveyed on film by multiple images of her friends and the train wheels. Miss Froy kindly assists Iris into a compartment on the train and later takes her to the dining car for tea. As they pass a compartment with an English couple in it, the man quickly pulls down the blind for privacy.

In the dining car Miss Froy asks the waiter to brew her a special packet of herb tea which she takes from her handbag, and later requests the sugar bowl from the two cricket fans who are demonstrating a cricket play with sugar cubes. While they drink their tea she tries to introduce herself to Iris, but her voice is drowned out by the train's whistle, so she writes her name in the steam on the windowpane. Having introduced the principal characters in the confined setting where most of the action will take place, and having established the principal clues, Hitchcock has carefully prepared the film for the next part of the story.

After Miss Froy and Iris return to their compartment, Iris tries to sleep while Miss Froy begins to do a crossword puzzle. Iris drifts off to sleep and later, as she slowly awakens, looks sleepily around the compartment and realizes that Miss Froy is not there. When she asks the other occupants of the compartment where she is, a forbidding gray-haired Baroness assures her that there has not been any English lady besides Iris herself in the compartment and suggests that the blow on her head has made her forgetful.

Iris begins a search through the train for Miss Froy; when she reaches the dining car, the waiter who has served them insists that Iris took tea by herself, producing a bill to prove it. Unconvinced, Iris continues her search, blundering into the third-class compartment where she encounters Gilbert once again. Although their relationship is more antagonistic than romantic at this point, Gilbert sees that she is seriously upset and offers to help her since he speaks the language. In the corridor they meet Dr. Hartz (Paul Lukas), an eminent European brain surgeon who is picking up a patient at the next station. When Iris asks for his help, he suggests that she is having hallucinations caused by the blow to her head.

Not so easily persuaded, however, Iris continues her search, questioning the other English passengers who have seen Miss Froy, but all have personal reasons for not wanting to admit that they have seen her; Todhunter (Cecil Parker), the Englishman who wanted privacy, is traveling with his mistress, Margaret (Linden Travers), and does not want to be involved in any scandal, knowing that it would harm his career. The two cricket fans, Caldicott (Naunton Wayne) and Charters (Basil Radford), are afraid the affair will delay the train, causing them to miss the cricket matches.

At the next stop both Gilbert and Iris keep careful watch for Miss Froy, but she does not leave the train, and the only person boarding the train is Dr. Hartz's patient, who is wheeled aboard on a stretcher completely bandaged and accompanied by a nun.

Iris' story receives some support, however, when Margaret, hoping to force Todhunter into marrying her after she divorces her husband, admits that she has seen Miss Froy. Jubilantly, Iris tells Dr. Hartz that someone else has seen Miss Froy, but when she returns to her compartment a woman dressed in Miss Froy's clothes is occupying Miss Froy's seat. The woman announces that she is Madame Kummer (Josephine Wilson) and has been in the compartment throughout the journey. Her story is corroborated by the other occupants, and Iris, dazed and confused, appears to be convinced after Dr. Hartz explains to her that her subconscious has substituted Miss Froy's face for that of Madame Kummer.

Still beset by doubt, however, Iris asks Gilbert to take her to the dining car for some tea; there, she sees Miss Froy's name still visible on the steamy window. Her discovery is underscored by a startling blast from the train whistle just before the train hurtles through a tunnel, obliterating the name. Hysterically, Iris appeals to the other passengers to stop the train and search it for Miss Froy, but they stare unresponsively at her. Desperate, Iris wrenches free from Gilbert and Dr. Hartz and pulls the emergency cord, stopping the train just before she faints. When she regains consciousness, Dr. Hartz is trying to calm her, but she obstinately holds to her belief that Miss Froy is aboard the train. Just as Gilbert is becoming more skeptical of her story, the cook throws some kitchen garbage out of the train window. For a brief moment, isolated in a close-up, a label from a packet of herbal tea sticks to the window and is seen by Gilbert.

Now fully persuaded of the truth of Iris' story, Gilbert helps her search the train and finds, in the baggage car, Miss Froy's spectacles in the paraphernalia of a magician.

Suddenly the magician appears and tries to take back the spectacles. He and Gilbert struggle until Iris hits the magician over the head with a bottle, knocking him unconscious. Quickly, they bundle the man into a trunk, but just as quickly open it again since the magician still holds the spectacles. However, they find that he has disappeared through the false bottom of the trunk, taking with him the only evidence of Miss Froy's presence on the train.

A fantastic idea now occurs to Gilbert: what if the bandaged patient is really Miss Froy? Iris then recalls noticing that the nun was wearing high heels, and they return to Dr. Hartz's compartment to verify their wild premise. Before they can unwrap the bandages, however, Hartz appears, and Iris tells him of their suspicions. He persuades them to meet him for a drink in the dining car where they can discuss the matter more fully. After they have had their drinks he takes them back to his compartment, informing them that he has had the nun drug their drinks. He then reveals that the "patient" is indeed Miss Froy and that she will soon be removed at the next stop where he will operate on her, unsuccessfully.

Iris and Gilbert feign sleepiness to get Hartz to leave them; then, in a race against time, Gilbert climbs out the window of the locked compartment to reach the next one, where the nun is guarding Miss Froy. After telling Gilbert that she has not drugged their drinks because she could not tolerate the murder of a fellow Englishwoman, the nun helps him unwrap Miss Froy's bandages. Just as they finish, Madame Kummer enters, so they overpower her and substitute her for Miss Froy.

When Hartz discovers the deception after the "patient" has been taken off the train but before it leaves the station, he arranges to have their train car uncoupled and diverted to a branch line. Finally, realizing what has happened, Gilbert and Iris go to the dining car and tell the other English passengers of their discovery. They are not, however, believed until the train stops and an armed officer approaches and offers to escort all of them to the British Embassy. Gilbert hits the officer over the head, takes his gun, and then makes his way to the engine to get the train moving again. Meanwhile, the cricket fans, proving to be unexpectedly competent with firearms, hold off a group of armed soldiers led by Dr. Hartz. Todhunter, a pacifist, wants to surrender, but when he leaves the train waving a white flag, he is shot.

Miss Froy, who up to now has refused to reveal what is happening, confides to Gilbert and Iris that she is a British spy. Before escaping from the besieged train, she imparts the secret information she is carrying—the vital clauses of a secret treaty between two European nations—to Gilbert so that the information will have two chances of reaching the British Foreign Office. The information is coded in the form of a tune which Gilbert memorizes.

Unable to tell whether Miss Froy has escaped safely or not, Gilbert manages to get the train started just as Hartz and the soldiers prepare to board it, and they all escape across the border. Gilbert and Iris reach London safely, but when they arrive at the foreign office Gilbert finds that he has forgotten the tune. Suddenly they hear it being played on a piano in the next room and discover Miss Froy, alive and well. Needless to say, the course of events has caused Iris to forget her fiancé, and she now plans to marry Gilbert.

The tension and the chilling, undefined menace of international intrigue are masterfully maintained by Hitchock and delightfully counterpointed by the film's wit and humor. Indeed, much of the charm of *The Lady Vanishes* is due to its witty script and amusing characters. The humor is principally centered in the characters of the two British cricket fans, although Gilbert also has some funny exchanges with Iris. Perfect caricatures of the unflappable and insular Englishman, the cricket fans are disdainful of the "third-rate country" in which they find themselves temporarily stranded, and of Iris and her friends, whom they suspect of being rich Americans because of the manager's obsequious treatment of them. Their sense of decorum is offended when they are relegated to the maid's room at the inn, but even in this predicament, they insist on changing into evening clothes for dinner. They are then forced, because of the overcrowded conditions, to share a table and even cheese with Miss Froy, whom they characterize as a "queer old bird" after politely informing her that they "never judge any country by its politics." Their overriding concern throughout the film is to return to England in time to see the championship cricket matches. Reduced to reading an American newspaper, the only newspaper available, they murmur disgustedly that "Americans have no sense of proportion" since the sports section "has nothing but baseball and not a word about cricket." Later, in the midst of the gunfight, their main concern is whether they will get to the cricket matches on time; however, true to their unflappable British tradition, they remain cool and imperturbable during the crisis. Having both survived the gun battle and helped Gilbert get the train started so that they can all escape, they are dismayed to find when they arrive in London that the cricket matches have been cancelled because of floods. Indeed, the news of the cancellation is the only time they show very much emotion during the entire film. The roles, perfectly played by Naunton Wayne and Basil Radford, proved to be so popular that these actors frequently played similar roles in later films.

Margaret Lockwood as Iris and Michael Redgrave as Gilbert are particularly good in providing the romantic comedy aspect of the film with their antagonism for each other turning to love; they are equally adept at conveying the bewilderment of ordinary people caught up in extraordinary circumstances. Dame May Whitty is convincing as the little old lady spy, Miss Froy.

As usual in an Alfred Hitchcock film, *The Lady Vanishes* has tension and a good sense of pace as well as several ingenious touches. Particularly noteworthy is the manner in which the film starts out rather ordinarily with the characters having nothing more serious to worry about than finding a room in a crowded hotel. Although the opening section does not reveal the main plot of the film, it does introduce the characters to one another and to the audience without wasting one scene. Also clever is the manner in which Hitchcock manipulates the evidence of Miss Froy's disappearance. Each time Iris thinks she has definite proof, it seems to vanish; and likewise, each time she gets so discouraged that she begins to doubt her own memory, new evidence appears. To this carefully controlled confusion, Hitchcock adds the further dimension that Iris can never be quite sure who is with her and who is against her. For example, she keeps telling Dr. Hartz what she discovers only to find out, nearly too late, that he is one of the conspirators who have caused the disappearance of Miss Froy. *The Lady Vanishes* is vintage Hitchcock, with the imprint of this master filmmaker evident from the overall conception of plot to the slightest detail of filming.

LIFEBOAT

Released: 1944
Production: Kenneth Macgowan for Twentieth Century-Fox
Direction: Alfred Hitchcock
Screenplay: Jo Swerling; based on a story by John Steinbeck
Cinematography: Glen MacWilliams
Editing: Dorothy Spencer
Running time: 96 minutes

Principal characters:
Constance Porter .... Tallulah Bankhead
Gus .... William Bendix
Willy, the German .... Walter Slezak
Alice MacKenzie .... Mary Anderson
John Kovac .... John Hodiak
Charles "Ritt" Rittenhouse .... Henry Hull
Mrs. Higgins ...,........................... Heather Angel
Stanley Garrett .... Hume Cronyn
George "Joe" Spencer .... Canada Lee

Lifeboat, Alfred Hitchcock's seventh American film, marked a considerable departure from the kind of suspense thriller on which his reputation is based. This nine-character story is remarkable in that it takes place entirely in only one setting, a lifeboat—about as small and claustrophobic a space as ever challenged a film director facing a full-length production. The physical and dramatic limitations of the script present obvious difficulties but it is as if Hitchcock deliberately created this restrictive project to prove that he could overcome its inherent problems.

Hitchcock has always taken chances with his films, and *Lifeboat* is one of his most challenging undertakings. For the most part, it is a successful one. The story developed from an idea Hitchcock himself conceived and for which he enlisted the literary help of John Steinbeck to develop dramatically. Steinbeck came up with the overall plot and character development in a twenty-page screen treatment, after which Hitchcock hired MacKinlay Kantor (later author of *The Best Years of Our Lives*) to flesh out a final screenplay. Hitchcock did not like Kantor's treatment, however, and turned the project over to Hollywood veteran Jo Swerling (*A Man's Castle*, 1933; *The Westerner*, 1940; *Blood and Sand*, 1942), who collaborated with both Hitchcock and Steinbeck on the final draft.

The result is a tense drama of characterizations and allegory of the world at war in 1943. Many contemporary critics defined the film by its obvious moral message: "Judge not." However, years later, Hitchcock, who has always been loathe to define the meanings of his films, explained to French director/

critic François Truffaut, what indeed, to him, was *Lifeboat*'s theme:

> "We wanted to show that at that moment there were two world forces confronting each other, the democracies and the Nazis, and while the democracies were completely disorganized, all of the Germans were clearly headed in the same direction. So here was a statement telling the democracies to put their difference aside temporarily and to gather their forces to concentrate on the common enemy, whose strength was precisely derived from a spirit of unity and of determination."

Lifeboat's nine characters represent a microcosm of the world during World War II: Constance Porter (Tallulah Bankhead), a parasitic, luxury-laden journalist; John Kovac (John Hodiak), a crewman from a Marxist freighter; Willy (Walter Slezak), a surgeon and Nazi submarine captain; Gus (William Bendix), the seaman; Stanley Garrett (Hume Cronyn), a naval radio officer; Alice MacKenzie (Mary Anderson), an army nurse; Charles Rittenhouse (Henry Hull), a business tycoon and quintessential capitalist; Mrs. Higgins (Heather Angel), an Englishwoman who is carrying her dead baby; and George "Joe" Spencer (Canada Lee), the ship's steward.

The opening credits move across the screen in front of a sinking ship—a freighter which has been torpedoed by a German submarine—and as the camera moves across floating debris, we see eight survivors climb aboard a lifeboat. The ninth survivor to come aboard is Willy, the only survivor of the U-boat which has sunk the freighter. As his hand comes over the side of the lifeboat, the other passengers help him aboard, to which he responds, "*Danke schön.*" As the Allied passengers realize this man is their enemy, the dramatic tension of the picture is set into force. Willy, the Nazi, is the catalyst for all of the film's action.

It is soon apparent that Willy is the only one aboard who has any knowledge of seamanship; when the lifeboat almost capsizes, he is the only one to act. After several days, the survivors reluctantly concede to his taking charge. Kovac, the Communist from South Chicago, is most adamantly against Willy, but group survival overrules his objections. As the film progresses, we see that Kovac's political prejudices are as singleminded as those of Willy. Furthermore, tycoon Rittenhouse is a determined Fascist.

The interaction of these diverse characters creates what dramatic intensity there is in *Lifeboat*, and Hitchcock's orchestration of their actions and reactions prevents them from being merely stock stereotypes. Joe Spencer is presented as a Christian man rather than the usual clichéd black, and Willy, while cunning and singleminded, is not without charm and courage.

The day-by-day ordeal of surviving on the lifeboat with little food and water and fighting the elements causes the survivors to strike out against one another; yet the experience demands that they pull together to keep alive. Willy is the only passenger who remains calm throughout. Unbeknownst to his fellow passengers he has extra water and a compass. They discover that instead of heading for Bermuda as they had thought, Willy is steering them toward the safety of a German supply ship. Proving Hitchcock's thesis that they must, but will not, forget their differences and pull together, the eight passengers accept their fate in the hands of the Nazi, as if to admit that survival in a concentration camp would be better than death at sea.

Despite the single setting, the somewhat stereotypical characters, and the absence of a musical score (Hitchcock used only the sounds of the sea in the film), the realities with which the passengers are forced to deal prevent cinematic stasis. The passengers comfort Mrs. Higgins by wrapping her in Connie's fur coat, and when she is asleep they throw the dead child into the sea. Later, out of despair over her loss, Mrs. Higgins commits suicide by jumping into the sea still wearing Connie's prized possession.

Gus, the Brooklyn seaman whose leg has been seriously injured when the freighter was torpedoed, is diagnosed by Willy as having gangrene. Again the passengers are unable to pull together and amputate Gus's leg, and Willy is left to perform the primitive and gruesome operation. In one of the screen's most terrifying scenes, we see Willy give Gus some whiskey, the only thing aboard approaching medicine, and sterilize the jackknife to perform the necessary surgery.

Following the operation, with the passengers asleep and Willy at the helm, Gus, in his postoperative hallucinations, sees Willy drink from his hidden canteen; Willy, now forced to maintain his cover if any of them are to survive, pushes Gus overboard. When the truth is discovered, the American passengers turn on Willy, in Hitchcock's words, "like a pack of dogs" and beat him to death. Only Joe refuses to participate in the brutal murder.

The passengers are saved through no plan of their own when an Allied ship destroys the approaching German supply ship and rescues them, but not before a young injured German swims to the lifeboat for safety. When he pulls a pistol on the lifeboat occupants, they disarm him and then, ironically, pull him aboard. Once again Hitchcock's message is driven home. In order to overpower and destroy the enemy, people must forget their personal differences and join forces.

While Willy, the German, is the catalyst for the action in *Lifeboat*, it is the superb, offbeat casting of Tallulah Bankhead as Constance Porter that makes the film memorable. Bankhead's unique brand of theatrical acting was never used better on the screen. In the microcosm of Hitchcock's allegory, Connie represents the cynical, materialistic American. As we see her stripped of her possessions—her camera, her typewriter, her fur coat, and finally her prized diamond bracelet, which is used unsuccessfully as bait to catch a fish, she is revealed as a woman of substance and humanity. The script also incorporates the sensual attraction between Connie and Kovac. While drawn to him physically, she reviles his coarseness and his tattooed body by saying, "I never could understand the necessity of making a billboard out of the torso." Later, she mellows and tattooes her initials on his chest with her lipstick.

Bankhead's character also provides the only levity among the characters. At the end when they are about to be rescued, she exclaims, "Twenty minutes! Good heavens! My nails, my hair, my face. I'm a mess." Then seeing Kovac's dismay, she adds, "Yes, darling, one of my best friends is in the navy!" Although this was Bankhead's finest screen performance, the Motion Picture Academy overlooked her entirely for a Best Actress nomination. The New York Film Critics, however, did name her Best Actress of 1944.

Lifeboat provided Hitchcock with the problem of how to make his own brief appearance in the film (his well-known "trademark"), since the script called for only one closely integrated set. His solution, his favorite, he says, was to use "before" and "after" photos of himself advertising a diet drug called *Reduco*. The ad is seen on the back of a newspaper which William Bendix holds at one point in the film, and Hitchcock said he received hundreds of letters asking where to buy the wonder diet drug. He also appears quite briefly as a dead body floating face down in the water at the beginning of the film.

MARNIE

Released: 1964
Production: Alfred Hitchcock for Universal
Direction: Alfred Hitchcock
Screenplay: Jay Presson Allen; based on the novel of the same name by
  Winston Graham
Cinematography: Robert Burks
Editing: George Tomasini
Running time: 130 minutes

  Principal characters:
    Marnie Edgar .... Tippi Hedren
    Mark Rutland .... Sean Connery
    Bernice Edgar .... Louise Latham
    Lil Mainwaring .... Diane Baker
    Sailor .... Bruce Dern

Marnie continues Alfred Hitchcock's fascination with obsessive love and
aberrant psychology begun in films such as *The Paradine Case* (1947) and
Vertigo (1958). In both earlier films Hitchcock concentrates on the hero's
obsession with a "phantom woman," a phantom in *The Paradine Case* because
the hero has surrounded the real woman with an aura of mystery which he
chooses not to penetrate, and in *Vertigo* because the woman the hero loves
is the clever creation of two conspirators in murder. Very little attention is
paid to the psyche of the woman, for in a figurative sense she does not exist.
She is but an object on which he and/or others project a personality. The
film's subjectification is all from the hero's point of view.

Marnie, however, as the title suggests, breaks from this pattern. The "object" becomes a "subject," a subject equal in standing to the hero. Here, for
the first time, Hitchcock delves behind the mask of the cool, detached "ice-
princesses" he so favored. His heroine (played so exquisitely by Hitchcock's
discovery, Tippi Hedren) throws off her cloak of mystery, and is exposed as
ruthlessly as her male counterparts.

Marnie is a kleptomaniacal young woman who moves from job to job,
changing identities and embezzling money as she goes. With her ill-gotten
gains she supports her two overriding obsessions, her horses and her mother.
Her confusion of identity is visually underlined in the very first scenes of the
film in which she coolly and methodically dyes her hair, exchanges ID's,
switches clothes, and emerges with a different mask, one of many. The first
real clue to the origin of this woman's strange behavior is given during her
visit to her mother Bernice Edgar (Louise Latham).

Marnie's mother is a bitter, critical woman who shows no appreciation and
little affection for her doting daughter. Marnie tries to act out the role of little

girl for her mother, laying her head on her lap, reverting to childish babble, only to be rejected and replaced in her mother's affections by a neighbor's child. The fact that her mother's house is the key to Marnie's psyche, the locus where reality and illusion first became confused, is emphasized by the establishing exterior shot of the house obviously on a studio street before a painted backdrop of a port with a liner moored there. The traditional sexual symbolism associated with ships, ports, and the sea are noteworthy, especially as the understanding of Marnie's problems is rendered more and more in strict Freudian terms as the film progresses.

Marnie's deviations go undetected for an unspecified period of time until, in applying for a job in her newest guise, she is recognized by her employer, Mark Rutland (Sean Connery), as the woman who had embezzled funds from a friend. But instead of reporting Marnie, Mark decides to hire her and study her as an unusual specimen. Mark becomes fascinated by this cold, aloof woman who seems to be hiding so much behind her masks. She is a challenge, something "wild" that he has caught and must tame. In taming her he probes her mind. Holding her to him through blackmail, he questions her incessantly, trying to reconstruct the jigsaw puzzle of her past. Before long his study has turned to obsession and he forces her to marry him. On their wedding night aboard ship (again filled with the symbolism of boats and the sea), he encounters another complication in this infinitely complex woman, another facet hidden behind the masks: Marnie is frigid to the extent that she refuses to let him touch her. A few nights later, in his frustration, he rapes her.

With this impulsive act Marnie now gains the upper hand, using his violation of her as her trump card; she makes him agree never to touch her again. Mark consents, guiltily. With this shift of power Mark becomes Marnie's vassal. He showers her with gifts, including a favorite horse, protects her from his prying relatives, and honors her most difficult prerequisite. It is as if Marnie has become even more desirable in her frigidity, in her increasingly complex mystery. The affair, if it can be called that, develops into a onesided *amour fou* with Mark directing all his energy towards her and getting little response in return. Again the heroes of *The Paradine Case* and *Vertigo*, with their demented compulsiveness, come to mind.

Almost all of Marnie's problems in the film are reduced, with true Freudian prestidigitation, to the sexual level and expounded upon visually with appropriate symbols. The red flashes Marnie sees at traumatic moments are the most obvious indicators of this. The scene in Mark's office when he embraces her and a bolt of lightning thrusts a phallic limb through the window, makes up in direct visual shock what it lacks in subtlety. Her unrestrained affection for horses is also a simplistic Freudian cipher for sexual sublimation.

The unraveling of the mystery of Marnie occurs in the final scene at her mother's home. She returns there with Mark to try to piece together the sounds and images which haunt her: the red flashes, the tapping at the window, her cries for her mother, the vague memories of violence. At the house, she relives the traumatic childhood scene in which she murders a sailor (Bruce Dern) who is threatening her mother. In textbook fashion Marnie reexperiences the traumatic incident in order to purge it, and the film ends with her revelation.

Marnie is Hitchcock's most romantic film, for in it he deemphasizes almost all the elements of suspense in favor of the story's sexual-romantic overtones. There is the mystery surrounding Marnie's trauma and a few classic Hitchcockian suspense-builders, such as the robbery in which a cleaning lady appears on the scene as Marnie drops a shoe, only to find that the woman is deaf; and Mark's discovery of Marnie during a second robbery. However, the images which leave the most lasting impressions are of Marnie and Mark embracing in the thunderstorm; of Marnie's nightgown falling about her feet as Mark tears it on their ill-fated honeymoon; and a tilted, unsettling shot of Mark in a stable, lost in his mad reverie adoring the unresponsive Marnie. The ending of *Marnie* also makes it a much more positive film than its predecessors. For unlike Scottie in *Vertigo*, tottering on the edge of the abyss into which his love has fallen, or Keane in *The Paradine Case* sitting pale and drained after realizing that he has been deceived by the woman he loved, Mark is able to walk away with Marnie into a possibly brighter future.

PSYCHO

Released: 1960
Production: Alfred Hitchcock for Paramount
Direction: Alfred Hitchcock
Screenplay: Joseph Stefano; based on the novel of the same name by Robert Bloch
Cinematography: John L. Russell
Editing: George Tomasini
Art direction: Joseph Hurley and Robert Clatworthy; set decoration, George Milo
Music: Bernard Herrmann
Title design: Saul Bass
Running time: 109 minutes

Principal characters:
Norman Bates .... Anthony Perkins
Marion Crane .... Janet Leigh
Lila Crane .... Vera Miles
Sam Loomis .... John Gavin
Milton Arbogast .... Martin Balsam
George Lowery .... Vaughn Taylor

Psycho is undoubtedly Alfred Hitchcock's *chef d'oeuvre* in terror, and for many it is the quintessential horror film of our time; it is also one of the few financially successful motion pictures which can truly be termed an art film. Produced for an economical $800,000, it has grossed twenty million dollars to date.

Psycho's extraordinary appeal can be attributed to its modern universality. While its story concerns a psychopathic murderer, its technique reveals the dark side of all mankind—the inner secrets, deceits, and guilts of all human beings; and, as is so often true of even the most ordinary situations in life, nothing is as it really seems. Additionally, *Psycho* superbly plays with the viewing audience's emotions. Hitchcock makes unabashed voyeurs out of his audience more deliberately and with more subtlety and deftness than in any of his other films. Hitchcock draws the viewer into the film, into the sordid depths of a twisted world. He forces the audience to psychoanalyze themselves as they identify—for varying lengths of time and with varying degrees of intensity—with each of the film's main characters. However, Hitchcock's purpose in this film is not to build multifaceted characters; the characters are really little more than prototypes. Rather, the film is about a split personality, and the main characters in a sense are simply different sides of one collective character—the audience itself. This is Hitchcock's little joke and the reason he has described *Psycho* as a "fun picture."

In *Psycho*, Hitchcock attempts to make the "horror" of the film take place in the minds of the audience. While there are only two actual violent occurrences—the deaths of Marion Crane and the insurance investigator—the real terror is in the minds of the viewer; suspense arises from wondering what is going to happen next and who else is going to be murdered. Manipulative as these devices are, Hitchcock carries them out with such finesse that the ambience of horror which he achieves is memorable even after many viewings.

Psycho is based on the novel by Robert Bloch which fictitiously dealt with a real incident in Wisconsin. Hitchcock's locale is Phoenix, and the very ordinariness of the opening sequences of the film and the characters themselves belie the terror that follows. However, the clever title designs by Saul Bass have already prepared us for an excursion in psychological terror: the credit names appear on the screen split apart and then disappear, all to the accompaniment of Bernard Herrmann's vibrant music score.

Marion Crane (Janet Leigh) is a secretary whom we first meet in a motel room where she is having a lunch-hour tryst with her lover, Sam Loomis (John Gavin). Their romance is frustrated by the fact that Marion lives with her sister Lila (Vera Miles), and she and Sam are unable to marry because Sam is financially burdened by his dead father's debts and the alimony he must pay to his ex-wife. Following this frustrated scene of secret lovemaking— a scene which throws our sympathies towards Marion—Marion returns to her office where she listens to a coworker's complaints about *her* mother. Also, Marion's boss, Mr. Lowery (Vaughn Taylor), introduces Marion to a client who turns over $40,000 to her to be placed in a safety deposit box.

We next see Marion in her bedroom with the money, packing a suitcase. It is obvious that she plans to flee with the money, but the sympathy of the audience remains with this seemingly put-upon, almost mousey woman. The audience has already been drawn into Hitchcock's voyeuristic manipulation. We have seen Marion in partial undress in a motel room with her lover and have seen her changing her clothes in her bedroom. Throughout these few scenes, we have seen reflections of Marion in mirrors and through windows, all intimating the split personality aspect of the plot.

Marion drives away from Phoenix until she becomes tired and pulls the car over to the side of the road; there she sleeps until morning, when a policeman approaches the car and awakens her. Marion drives away to a used car lot where she exchanges her car for one which will not be identified. As night approaches again, we see Marion approach a seedy motel, next to which is a gothic-style California house. As Marion steps out of her car, she sees an old woman sitting in the second story window of the house. The motel, which is run by Norman Bates (Anthony Perkins), a timid taxidermist, contains numerous samples of stuffed birds, all Norman's handiwork, as well as many photographs of birds.

Marion registers as Marie Samuels (after her lover Sam), and Norman shyly shows her to her room and offers to bring her a bite to eat. While he is away getting the food, Marion overhears a shrill conversational exchange between Norman and the old woman upstairs, who is his mother. When he brings her tray of food, which he suggests she eat in his office because it is more comfortable, he comments, "Mother—what is the phrase? isn't quite herself today."

Back in her motel room, we see Marion make the decision to return the stolen money and prepare to take a shower before retiring. The famous shower sequence—which runs only a minute—took a week to film. It was extremely daring for its time because it appeared to show Marion nude, but in fact it never really does. As the shadowy figure enters and repeatedly knifes Marion to shrieking musical phrases, the audience, caught completely off guard, is terrified. Why this inexplicable, unpremeditated, and horrible death? These bizarre happenings, which occupy only the first third of the film, are among the most memorable in the horror film genre. The audience is left without its focus of sympathy. Hitchcock shrewdly switches our attention to all-American Norman Bates, whom we see enter Marion's cabin, aghast at what he finds, then dispose of her body and belongings by sinking her car into a nearby swamp.

When Milton Arbogast (Martin Balsam), an insurance investigator, arrives at the motel, he questions Norman, who at first denies he had any recent guests but finally admits that a woman did stop for the night. The investigator senses something amiss and attempts to search the Bates home where he is brutally and repeatedly stabbed on the ornate staircase as Marion had been in the shower.

Subsequently, when Arbogast fails to report in, Sam and Lila set out on their own. Hitchcock's Freudian denouement unfolds with no abatement of suspense and an atmosphere of impending doom. Sam and Lila learn there is no Mother Bates. Norman had found his mother and her lover dead together in bed years earlier. It is Lila who discovers the corpse of Mrs. Bates in the cellar of the house, where she is attacked by a hideously laughing old woman: it is Norman, a true split personality, in his mother's clothes. The obligatory scene in which the psychologist explains Norman's schizophrenia is indeed anticlimactic, but it nonetheless serves to release the audience from the sense of desolation and futility with which Hitchcock has gripped and held them for almost two hours.

Janet Leigh as Marion has a winning screen presence to which the audience is naturally attracted despite her role as a thief. Anthony Perkins as Norman to many represents aspects of the all-American boy, shy and harmless; Vera Miles, John Gavin, and Martin Balsam are also perfectly cast.

Psycho is Hitchcock's film all the way, a directorial *tour de force*, but an essential ingredient to the film's success is the splendid music by Bernard Herrmann. It is impossible to think of watching this film without the accompaniment of Herrmann's psychologically terrifying and yet very human music.

REBECCA

Released: 1940
Production: David O. Selznick for Selznick International and United Artists
  (AA)
Direction: Alfred Hitchcock
Screenplay: Robert E. Sherwood and Joan Harrison; based on the novel of
  the same name by Daphne du Maurier
Cinematography: George Barnes (AA)
Editing: Hal C. Kern
Running time: 130 minutes

Principal characters:
Mrs. de Winter	Joan Fontaine
Maxim de Winter	Laurence Olivier
Jack Favell	George Sanders
Mrs. Danvers	Judith Anderson
Mrs. Van Hopper	Florence Bates
Major Giles Lacy	Nigel Bruce
Beatrice Lacy	Gladys Cooper
Colonel Julyan	C. Aubrey Smith
Man outside phone booth	Alfred Hitchcock

When David O. Selznick brought Alfred Hitchcock to the United States from England in 1939, Hitchcock's films had been popular as well as influential in this country since *The Man Who Knew Too Much* (1934) and *The 39 Steps* (1935). *Rebecca*, his first American film, remains a distinctly British work: a gothic mystery by a British author, set mostly in England, with a predominantly British cast. It is an expensively mounted film, typical of Selznick's production values, and the only Hitchcock film ever to win the Academy Award for Best Picture. George Barnes also won a well-deserved Oscar for his black-and-white cinematography. Hitchcock had already made a film of a novel by Daphne du Maurier the preceding year, just before he moved to America—his unexceptional *Jamaica Inn*. Nonetheless, du Maurier's *Rebecca*, published in 1938, provided Hitchcock with an especially comfortable source, a stagy, atmospheric story of intrigue and deception readily adaptable to the kind of studio-bound production familiar to him in England.

Rebecca begins with a voice-over recollection—"Last night I dreamt I went to Manderley again"—and a shot through thick, dank foliage of the burned-out shell of a once grand English country house. It is the story of the narrator, an unnamed young girl (Joan Fontaine) who marries a haunted, aristocratic British widower, Maxim de Winter (Laurence Olivier), and gradually learns the truth about his first wife, Rebecca, and the circumstances of her death.

This gauche, timid girl, the traveling companion of a wealthy bourgeois

American matron, Mrs. Van Hopper (Florence Bates), meets de Winter in Monte Carlo. After a strange courtship during which he treats her both brusquely and superciliously, they marry and return to England to his family estate, Manderley. There the new Mrs. de Winter immediately encounters the enmity of the housekeeper, Mrs. Danvers (Judith Anderson), a sinister woman pathologically devoted to the memory of Rebecca. Rebecca's presence fills the house, creating a stolid distance between de Winter and his bride. By chance, the boat in which Rebecca had presumably drowned turns up one night, with holes smashed in its bottom and her remains inside. Mrs. de Winter fears that this will revive old memories and widen the breach between her and her husband. For the first time de Winter talks to his wife about Rebecca and how she died. At the inquest Jack Favell (George Sanders), a "cousin" of Rebecca, had attempted blackmail with a letter that threw suspicion on de Winter. But he was cleared when an interview with Rebecca's doctor proved that she was dying from inoperable cancer. When de Winter returned to Manderley he found that Mrs. Danvers has set it afire, remaining inside with the memories of her beloved Rebecca. The final frames show the fire spreading across Rebecca's monogrammed pillow case.

The film embraces such notable Hitchcockian concerns as intimations of pervasive, faintly concealed evil, inescapable guilt, and the power that the dead can exercise over the living. Still, it remains a woman's picture, the story of a wife's nightmarish sojourn in the shadow of her predecessor, while its Brontëlike atmosphere conveys the feeling of a costume drama.

Rebecca details the progressive victimization of a young woman whose sense of identity depends upon her pleasing others. At first she is dominated by Mrs. Van Hopper, then by de Winter, and finally by Mrs. Danvers. She serves Mrs. Van Hopper dutifully, although not enthusiastically, recognizing the absurdity of her mistress' attempts to be accepted by fashionable Continental society. After her marriage to de Winter, he continues to act condescendingly toward her; moreover, he actually shuts her out. She fights for her husband against a rival both strong and invisible, under the misapprehension that the dead woman was devoted and gracious, as much renowned for her character as for her beauty. That picture of Rebecca is reinforced by de Winter's unwitting brother-in-law (Nigel Bruce) and sister (Gladys Cooper), the Lacys, and, to be sure, by the reverent admiration of Mrs. Danvers. The new Mrs. de Winter understandably mistakes the guilty surliness and moodiness of her husband for sorrow. Mrs. Danvers first makes her feel unwelcome, like an intruder at a shrine; then she openly seeks to destroy her. An especially embarrassing and humiliating incident occurs at a large costume ball at Manderley, when, through Mrs. Danvers' design, the new wife unknowingly appears in a dress identical to one worn by Rebecca at an earlier ball. Afterwards, Mrs. Danvers encourages her to jump from the window onto the rocks below, leaving de Winter alone with "her."

The secret of Rebecca's life, as well as of her death, underlies the young woman's relationship with both her husband and Mrs. Danvers, directing it in ways that she, an outsider, cannot recognize. Mrs. Danvers obsessively protects her dead mistress, yet finally announces to the new Mrs. de Winter, with great pride, how clever and how manipulative Rebecca had been, how she had laughed at men because love was merely "a game" with her. But her death becomes a murder mystery that is never completely solved.

The high point of the film is de Winter's eight-minute monologue in the old boat house on the night that her boat reappears, the camera following his reconstruction of the events. Beginning with "Rebecca has won," he explains to his wife that he had come to hate the conniving, promiscuous Rebecca shortly after their marriage. One night in the boat house she was killed during one of their quarrels; and after putting her body in her boat, he sank it in the sea. It remains unclear whether he purposely killed her in his rage at her goading, thus making him guilty of murder and Rebecca, morally at least, guilty of suicide, or whether, regardless of his ultimate intentions, he in fact accidentally killed her in the tussle.

One of the strongest features of the film is its atmosphere. The bright, sharply lit scenes in Monte Carlo find enhancement in Mrs. Van Hopper, magnificently played by Florence Bates in her screen debut and best-remembered performance. Her antics fool no one. Despite her wealth she remains a petulant, chocolate-gorging vulgarian who puts out her cigarette in a jar of cold cream. A prefiguration of Mrs. Danvers, she proves even more demanding, although certainly less baleful. For the scenes at Manderley, especially, Hitchcock concentrates on subdued tones, sometimes shadows, to underline the mystery of Rebecca and the helplessness of the new wife. Judith Anderson's Mrs. Danvers expertly blends the macabre in this world with that of the next. Attired in black, she seems neither to come nor to go but simply to be an omnipresent extension of the darkness at Manderley.

The opportunistic Jack Favell introduces himself from the shadows outside the window, then enters and subsequently exits by climbing through it. As Favell, George Sanders projects a frank indecency that in its smoothness and complexity never offends and becomes almost attractive; he continually upstages Olivier's monochromatic de Winter. He is at the center of the best scenes in the film, in particular the one where he tries blackmail with a letter Rebecca had written to him on the day of her death, purportedly showing that she was hardly suicidal and, by implication, that de Winter had killed her. After inviting himself to lunch with de Winter and his wife in their car, he helps himself to a drumstick and then blandly inquires of de Winter what one does with "old bones." In defeat he ungraciously but legitimately complains that class privilege shields de Winter from further investigation, the chief constable, Colonel Julyan (C. Aubrey Smith), being an old friend of de Winter.

Not entirely to the story's credit, peripheral factors have dimensions that outweigh the central relationships. Despite the sensitive portrayal by Joan Fontaine, the young wife commands little sympathy. Her ingenuousness and sincerity cannot match the air of patiently suffering masochism that surrounds her devotion to de Winter. She is a ninny, and her husband a boor, too preoccupied with his fear and guilt to recognize her loneliness or the indignity she suffers at the hands of Mrs. Danvers. Neither Hitchcock nor Olivier seem to know what to do with de Winter's character; and Olivier gives a bloodless, at times careless performance, leaving the wife's unflinching love nearly incredible. De Winter's love-hatred for Rebecca makes for a theme more worthy of development than his dispassionate second marriage, as does also the malevolent presence of Rebecca in her ally Mrs. Danvers that summons him to psychological destruction.

The film combines, not always successfully, melodrama with mystery, atmospheric effects, and the supernatural. It reflects the nostalgic romanticism of earlier Selznick products, notably *Gone with the Wind* (1939), and belongs to that group of moody, darkly executed films about the palpable influence of women either dead or thought to be dead, including William Wyler's *Wuthering Heights* (1939), Otto Preminger's *Laura* (1944), and George Cukor's *Gaslight* (1944). *Rebecca* has all the necessary carpentry for suspense: the old mansion presided over by a strange, tormented figure, the frightened girl innocent of the past, and the housekeeper in league with the world of spirits. The fire set by Mrs. Danvers presumably consumes the past, the horror and the guilt embedded in Manderley, thus releasing de Winter and his young wife to begin anew. As both domestic melodrama and Cinderella story, *Rebecca* has considerable appeal; but its best qualities derive from the traditions of the murder mystery and ghost story which give the film its particular flavor.

SHADOW OF A DOUBT

Released: 1943
Production: Jack H. Skirball for Universal
Direction: Alfred Hitchcock
Screenplay: Thornton Wilder, Alma Reville, and Sally Benson; based on a screen story by Gordon McDonell
Cinematography: Joseph A. Valentine
Editing: Milton Carruth
Running time: 108 minutes

Principal characters:
Charlie Oakley .... Joseph Cotten
Young Charlie .... Teresa Wright
Jack Graham .... Macdonald Carey
Emma Newton .... Patricia Collinge
Joseph Newton .... Henry Travers
Herbie Hawkins .... Hume Cronyn

Regarded by many critics as Alfred Hitchcock's best American film, *Shadow of a Doubt* certainly displays the master of suspense thrillers in top form. Mixing doubt and fear with ordinary small-town life, Hitchcock keeps his audience off balance throughout the film. The story is set in the town of Santa Rosa, California, and the film was largely shot there. Such use of location shooting was not a usual practice in the 1940's, but in *Shadow of a Doubt* the contrast between the placid, conventional life in the town and the twisted mind of Uncle Charlie Oakley (Joseph Cotten) is definitely aided by the real setting.

The film portrays throughout the theme of the affinity between Uncle Charlie and his niece Charlie (Teresa Wright), who is named after him. The niece feels that the presence of her uncle is what the family needs to get it out of its rut, and she decides to telegraph him, only to find that he has just telegraphed the family himself. Young Charlie is delighted with this example of what she sees as telepathy and keeps stressing to her uncle that they are closer than uncle and niece. As the plot progresses, however, she begins to fear their closeness. At first she gleefully tells him that he cannot hide anything from her, but by the middle of the film she wishes he could. Instead of being kindred spirits, the two Charlies turn out to be opposites—the good and evil parts of the same personality.

There is, of course, suspense and mystery in *Shadow of a Doubt*. The mystery is not, however, who committed the crime but rather what crime was committed. As the first half of the film progresses, we grow more and more certain that Uncle Charlie is a criminal, but we have no idea what his crime is. It is not until a suspenseful scene in which the niece rushes to the library to find a newspaper article that she learns that her uncle is the so-called Merry Widow murderer, a man who has been murdering rich widows for their money. Before this is discovered, however, we have reason to become increasingly suspicious of him. The first time he appears he is in a furnished room with a great deal of money lying about, and when his landlady tells him two men want to see him, he decides to escape from them by visiting his sister and her family in Santa Rosa.

In Santa Rosa, Uncle Charlie at first seems to be a personable, successful individual, but he becomes unreasonably upset when he thinks people are trying to find out about him. After the library scene, the mystery and suspense change. Now the questions center on what Uncle Charlie will do (he has already met a rich widow in Santa Rosa), whether the detectives will find him out, and what young Charlie will do with her information. Young Charlie does not feel she can turn in her own uncle, especially since she believes that it would kill her mother to find out that her younger brother is a murderer. Once Uncle Charlie realizes that she knows of his guilt and even has a ring which connects him with the murders, young Charlie's life is in danger.

When the detectives drop the case because they think another man is the murderer, the danger to young Charlie increases, since she is now the only threat to her uncle. After surviving two "accidents" which are clearly murder attempts by Uncle Charlie, she finally persuades him to leave town by threatening to turn her evidence over to the police. When she boards the train to see him off, he again tries to kill her; they struggle, and finally he falls into the path of a speeding train. The film ends with Uncle Charlie's funeral. He is eulogized, and only young Charlie and Detective Jack Graham (Macdonald Carey), with whom she has fallen in love, know the true story.

Hitchcock makes a point of contrasting the large city with the small town. Before we see Uncle Charlie, we see establishing shots of the city in which he lives; then, as we hear him say "Santa Rosa" on the telephone, we see establishing shots of that quiet town. Indeed, Hitchcock chose Thornton Wilder as the principal screenwriter for the film because of his splendid evocation of small-town life in his play *Our Town*. It is ironic, then, that in finding something to lift the family out of its rut, young Charlie gets more than she bargains for. It is almost as if the film is suggesting that to have excitement you have to have danger or decadence also. In fact, Uncle Charlie himself, though he is part of the problem, decries cities and modern life.

Under the opening credits we see couples in old-fashioned dress waltzing to "The Merry Widow." This scene is inserted or superimposed several times during the film, but it is not until we see it immediately after young Charlie finds the article about the Merry Widow murderer that we realize its significance. In a sense, the music has a dual meaning which reflects the distorted mind of Uncle Charlie. He frequently says that the modern world is corrupt, a "foul city" he calls it, and contrasts it with his romanticized idea of the past.

Thus the "Merry Widow" dancers represent both the idealized past and the grotesque situation of the present.

The film is filled with other deft Hitchcock touches besides the motif of the dancers. The affinity of the uncle and niece is brought out by the fact that each is first shown in profile lying on a bed. The scene in which Uncle Charlie tries to kill young Charlie by shutting her in a garage where a car's motor is running is ironically set up by a previous scene in which Graham proposes to young Charlie in the same garage. The pace of the film is also carefully controlled, with some scenes being deliberately slowed down. After the telegraph office calls the family about Uncle Charlie's message, for example, it takes them an inordinately long time to find out what the message is. When young Charlie decides to go to the library, however, the pace accelerates and the tension increases; she has only a few minutes to reach the library before closing time, and we see shots of her rushing through the streets heedless of the traffic; of the town clock showing the time; and of the library lights being turned out just as she arrives. After she manages to get in—despite the protestations of a stereotyped old-maid librarian—and finds the damning information, the camera pulls back for a long shot from above which dissolves into the shot of the "Merry Widow" dancers. After the quick and exciting editing of the scene on the train in which uncle and niece struggle until the uncle falls in front of a speeding locomotive, Hitchcock slows down the pace for the ironic ending at the funeral. Graham and young Charlie, who are the only ones who know the truth, listen to the service as Uncle Charlie is eulogized. The last words in the film are "the sweetness of their characters live on forever."

Joseph Cotten and Teresa Wright as the uncle and niece contribute excellent performances which give vitality to the conception of their like but opposite personalities. Cotten is able to convey the surface charm which almost covers the menace within, and Wright convincingly shows us a naïve young woman who finds herself in a situation she could not imagine, much less suspect. The others in the cast are adequate, including Henry Travers and Hume Cronyn as Charlie's father and his friend, who both read pulp mystery stories and continually talk about murder while they are unaware that a real murderer is right under their noses.

Shadow of a Doubt is vintage Hitchcock. From the overall conception to the smallest detail, the imprint of this master filmmaker is evident.

SPELLBOUND

Released: 1945
Production: David O. Selznick for Selznick International; released by United
 Artists
Direction: Alfred Hitchcock
Screenplay: Ben Hecht; based on Angus MacPhail's adaptation of the novel
 The House of Dr. Edwardes by Francis Beeding (Hilary St. George Saun-
 ders and John Palmer)
Cinematography: George Barnes
Editing: William Ziegler and Hal C. Kern
Music: Miklos Rozsa (AA)
Running time: 111 minutes

Principal characters:
Dr. Constance Peterson	Ingrid Bergman
John Ballantine (J. B.)	Gregory Peck
Dr. Murchison	Leo G. Carroll
Dr. Edwardes	Edward Fielding
Garmes	Norman Lloyd
Mary Carmichael	Rhonda Fleming
Dr. Alex Brulor	Michael Chekhov

Alfred Hitchcock is one of the best-loved and most widely respected directors in American and British cinema. His films are financial, critical, and
popular successes that continue to be named among the "ten best films of all
time." The enormous satisfaction people find in his greatest works is a function
of his admirable union of visual and narrative expression, and of the meta-
phors he uses for the emotional malaise with which twentieth century audiences can readily identify.

Hitchcock's characters suffer from dislocation and isolation which is expressed in terms of identity confusion (*North by Northwest*, 1959; *Psycho*,
1960; *Marnie*, 1964; *The Birds*, 1963; *Spellbound*); dislocation in which a
character finds himself or herself on the wrong side of the law (*Young and
Innocent*, 1937; *Spellbound, Strangers on a Train*, 1951; *The Man Who Knew
Too Much*, 1955; *The Wrong Man*, 1957); isolation from land itself (*Lifeboat*,
1944); political dislocation (*Torn Curtain*, 1966; *Topaz*, 1969; *Sabateur*, 1952;
Sabotage, 1936); or dislocation from their own sexuality and their very souls
(*Marnie, Vertigo*, 1958). The unity of all forms of isolation is the genius of
Hitchcock's vision: the inner, psychological forms lead to the external, legal,
or physical forms and are accurate maps of the characters' souls. For Hitchcock, the rectifying of any of these states of isolation is part of and a metaphor
for emotional integration. Even in his thrillers and whodunits, the crime or
mystery in which the hero is embroiled is an indication of his or her emotional

integration, and only through reaching out emotionally (usually in the form of sexual love) do these characters break through their isolation. Or, if they are unable to break through they are lost (*Psycho*, *Vertigo*).

In Hitchcock's early films, the external dislocation (usually legal) was the focus of the narrative, and the accompanying emotional health achieved by the characters was almost a side benefit. In his later films, however, and in all of his great 1950's and 1960's masterpieces, the emotional (usually sexual) integration of the characters is the real subject (*Marnie*, *The Birds*, *Vertigo*, *Rear Window*, 1954; *Notorious*, 1946; *Psycho*, *North by Northwest*).

With *Spellbound*, Hitchcock wanted to "turn out the first picture on psychoanalysis." It is not, of course, the first, but it remains one of the best of the "madmen take over the asylum" genre films. An amnesia victim, John Ballantine (Gregory Peck), thinks he has murdered his friend, Dr. Edwardes (Edward Fielding), a psychiatrist due to take over the head position at a mental hospital. Ballantine masquerades as the murdered man, joins the hospital staff as their leader, and falls in love with Dr. Constance Peterson (Ingrid Bergman). Ballantine behaves strangely when he sees parallel lines, and Constance discovers he has amnesia and believes himself to be a murderer. She takes him to her old teacher and psychoanalyst, and together they analyze his dreams (surreal sequences created by Salvador Dali) to find the source of his trauma. The dream imagery reveals the source of his problem to be his guilt over his role in the accidental death of his younger brother. This was transferred when he saw the murder of Dr. Edwardes by the man Edwardes was to replace at the hospital, Dr. Murchison (Leo G. Carroll). Murchison kills himself in a spectacular burst of red (a subjective shot, with the audience in Murchison's place as he pulls the trigger), and the lovers are free to begin their life together.

The joining of the crime (or at least its essential clue) to a psychological neurosis is the essence of Hitchcock's vision. Ballantine's legal dislocation is bound up in his mental loss of identity, and the solution to both is primarily love and secondarily analysis. The dream interpretation of Ballantine's symptoms (aversion to parallel lines) are too simplistic, but the essential unity of all forms of isolation is as clear here as it was to be in Hitchcock's later, greatest films.

John Ballantine is not the only dislocated character in the film. Hitchcock's films are insistent that the seemingly "normal" characters are implicated as well, and Dr. Peterson is characterized as a psychiatrist who is unfeminine, cold, and emotionally crippled, and who is perhaps unable to give her patients the understanding they require because she is so shut off from the world and the range of human emotion. In the first scene she is accused by a fellow doctor (who would like to initiate her into the world of romance) and then by a woman patient (who appears to be a nymphomanic, making the contrast clear) of having only a textbook knowledge of life. Her pulled-back hair and glasses further lock her into a stereotyped image of a frigid woman.

This aspect of the film is rather grating; it is never implied that the male doctors are hiding from their real selves in their work. Constance's professor (Michael Chekhov) is the perfect father and the perfect psychiatrist, complete with Austrian accent. Constance's oppressively narrow character development is a flaw of the kind which does not occur in Hitchcock's later films (such as *Marnie* and *The Birds*), where women's sexual neuroses are fully as complex as men's and proceed from more than their choice of a traditionally male profession.

In *Spellbound*, it is John who will awaken Constance from her frigidity. Their meeting, in a scene that is rather irritating because of its conventional romance cues, is accompanied by an upsurge of music. The climactic opening of doors, while questionable as a cinematic device, certainly makes clear Hitchcock's feelings of what is wrong with Constance: she has been isolated from the world of feeling, and in a graphic depiction of her reaction to Ballantine, superimposed doors actually open in her psyche. The job of the film is for both characters to rediscover themselves, to break through their own isolated situations into emotional commitment, and they do this through each other's love. This is not easily accomplished, and the fact that surrealism is used in the film is perhaps a key to understanding a cinematic device of Hitchcock's which is widely misunderstood. The effect of his artificial backgrounds and rear-screen projection is to cut his characters off from their physical surroundings and thus to put them into closer contact with their inner environment.

This cutting off seems the point of the surrealism in *Spellbound*: through a total warping of the objects of reality and their environment, the inner conflicts of the character whose surrealism we are seeing are better brought into focus. The effect is the same in the skiing sequence: the obviousness of the rear-screen projection may annoy people seeking unobtrusive, technical realism, but it seems that what Hitchcock is forcing us to do is to see that artificial background as a metaphor for the character's inner state. By isolating him from his environment totally, he has achieved a condition of unreality that is responsive to the demands of the characters' emotional torments and release: we see what they are feeling, not what they are seeing, and their emotions which are reflected in their surroundings are the impressions to which we respond.

Hitchcock carries out his theme of isolation in visual nuances as well. When John and Constance are at her old teacher's house, joined in two-shot and talking intimately, the wall behind her is a totally different tone from the one behind him, thus separating them emotionally even though they are together in the shot. Sometimes John's head is perfectly framed by the frame of a picture behind him, cutting him off from the rest of the composition and presenting him in a metaphoric cage. This meticulous attention to technical detail as well as to narrative is characteristic of Hitchcock, and makes his films textbooks for the creation of an idea through both formal and narrative means.

Spellbound was both a commercial success and a critical success, and it earned a place on the *New York Times* "Ten Best Films of 1945" list. Ingrid Bergman was the New York Film Critics Circle Award's choice for Best Actress of 1945. Although the 1945 film does not achieve the total artistic success of Hitchcock's later films, it points to them in its themes and formal expression, and is one of his finest pre-1950 productions. *Spellbound* was parodied, along with other Hitchcock films (notably *Vertigo*), in Mel Brooks's 1978 tribute to the master, *High Anxiety*.

SUSPICION

Released: 1941
Production: RKO/Radio
Direction: Alfred Hitchcock
Screenplay: Samson Raphaelson, Joan Harrison, and Alma Reville; based
  on the novel *Before the Fact* by Francis Iles
Cinematography: Harry Stradling
Editing: William Hamilton
Score: Frank Waxman
Running time: 99 minutes

> *Principal characters:*
> Johnnie Aysgarth .... Cary Grant
> Lina McLaidlaw .... Joan Fontaine (AA)
> General McLaidlaw .... Sir Cedric Hardwicke
> Beaky .... Nigel Bruce
> Mrs. McLaidlaw .... Dame May Whitty

When Francis Iles wrote the novel *Before the Fact*, from which *Suspicion* was drawn, it had a fascinating ending. While the film was in production, Hitchcock must have been aiming toward that same ending since the shooting title of the film remained *Before the Fact*. The picture was then previewed with several conclusions before one was decided to be best for film audiences, and the film was released as *Suspicion*, because that is what the story line is about. Originally, the heroine, becoming convinced that her husband, whom she adores, is going to murder her, drinks the poisoned milk he offers her; for even though love has betrayed her, she will not betray that love. Thus, she becomes an accessory before the fact to her own murder.

Such an ending, of course, would be unsatisfactory for the average filmgoer, especially since the star of the film is Cary Grant, who was, by the time he filmed *Suspicion*, one of the greatest film idols of the time. To portray him as the murderer of his own wife, especially when that wife was played by Joan Fontaine, would have been to invite audience displeasure. Changing the ending, however, meant that the whole theme of the story would have to change. Without the twist of making the husband appear guilty only circum-stantially, the theme becomes one in which the obligation of mutual trust in any love affair is mandatory: a wife must not suspect her husband of the worst when she loves him because her love is then not complete. The ending switch involves so many moral turns that it puzzled many a film writer; one critic reported that a large percentage of trade reviewers must still be sitting in the projection room after the previous day's showing, waiting for the story to end.

Suspicion is an intriguing film and one of Hitchcock's best; it is beautifully made and perfectly played, Joan Fontaine as the loving heroine Lina Mc-Laidlaw, a wife forced to doubt her husband, won her an Academy Award as Best Actress. It was a well-remembered year, especially since she was in competition with her own sister, Olivia de Havilland, who was nominated for *Hold Back the Dawn*. Fontaine had been one of the nominees the previous year for *Rebecca*, her first big role, but she had lost the Oscar to Ginger Rogers for *Kitty Foyle*. Some maintained that she won for *Suspicion* the following year because she should have won the year before; but Fontaine handles her role in *Suspicion* with remarkable sensitivity and assurance. Her victory was an honest one in an Oscar race for Best Actress that was even closer than before, for her competition involved not only her sister, but also Bette Davis, Greer Garson, and Barbara Stanwyck.

The role of Lina McLaidlaw is not unlike that of the nameless heroine of *Rebecca* (1940). Lina is a shy, self-effacing, repressed English girl, the daughter of a retired general (Cedric Hardwicke) and his respectable wife (Dame May Whitty). Nothing exciting or adventurous has ever happened to her, and she is almost resigned to ending her days as an unwanted spinster with a sheltered existence. Then she encounters Johnnie Aysgarth (Cary Grant), a lovable scoundrel, and is swept head over heels into romance. She cannot believe that Johnnie returns her love, but when he woos her boldly and asks her to marry him, she blindly consents, knowing little about him and turning a deaf ear to her parents' disapproval of him.

In order to prove his love, Johnnie takes a job when he learns that his wife's monthly income is not sufficient to support them both, but he bets on the races with his earnings and is soon driven to stealing from his employer to pay his gambling debts. Gradually, the evidence against him builds. He is exposed as a liar and a thief, charming but completely irresponsible, and little by little Lina begins to suspect him of the worst.

Johnny has a drinking buddy, a jovial, well-meaning friend named Beaky (Nigel Bruce). One night, as Lina plays anagrams with them, her thoughts are clouded by her gathering suspicions about Johnnie. As her thoughts drift from the men's conversation, she rearranges the letters on the blocks before her, and they spell out the word "murder." Immediately she leaps to the conclusion that Johnnie intends to kill Beaky. Soon after, Beaky is found dead, and, in Lina's mind, circumstances point to Johnnie as the killer. The suspense and sense of dread builds slowly but inevitably.

When Lina learns that her husband could benefit by her death, and when she is driven ill to her bed and he waits on her, she is more certain than ever that he intends to kill her. He brings her the fateful glass of milk to aid her in sleeping, and the suspense Hitchcock achieves during this sequence is maddening. Will she remain silent and drink the milk? Does she subconsciously desire to be the willing victim of her husband's villainy? Will she plan an accident and upset the glass, at least postponing the moment of death?

Or is the whole pattern of suspicion a false one, a web that she herself has spun in her mind? Could it be that Johnnie is utterly innocent, a victim of circumstances?

In the film's last reel, Hitchcock proves himself to be the ultimate master of suspense. He builds on every clue, every plot turn. In the final confession scene, he is dependent upon Cary Grant's skill as an actor, just as he was dependent on Laurence Olivier's in the confession he made to Joan Fontaine in *Rebecca*.

Hitchcock has been accused of making the same picture over and over again, and, in effect, this may be true. However, it must be remembered that there are only so many elements to be used in building a suspense story pictorially. The central character must either run away from damaging evidence, or he must blindly run toward it. He is either in danger himself, or he is creating danger for another. Ultimately, it is Hitchcock's penchant for minor detailing in the development of each film that persuades the audience that this time the situation is truly different, and there is always that certain Hitchcock twist which could make it seem so.

Actually, it is only when one examines the full Hitchcock catalogue that one realizes how very different each Hitchcock film is from the others. The best ones are those which fall, in part, into the gothic romance class: *Rebecca*, *Suspicion*, *Notorious* (1946), *Shadow of a Doubt* (1943), *Strangers on a Train* (1951), *Vertigo* (1958), and *Psycho* (1960). Yet, all have only one characteristic in common: the suspense is gained by honest cinematography, with the camera used as a reflection of the mind of the audience. Hitchcock knows his use of the camera well, and he always tells his tale with it. This is true even when he presents his most un-Hitchcocklike story: *The Wrong Man* (1957), based upon a true story of a miscarriage of justice, in which the wrong man has been accused circumstantially of a crime, and is found guilty. In all his films, Hitchcock's sense of humor always takes an impudent turn; drollery, audacity, and mockery are integral parts of his method. In addition, no one knows better than he how to achieve the most from a stunning moment of shock, or even horror.

Since he favored such stunning blondes as Madeleine Carroll and Grace Kelly as heroines, Hitchcock has been accused of prejudice in favor of the stylish but icy blonde. Yet in some of his best accomplishments, nonblond heroines such as Joan Fontaine and Ingrid Bergman have been warm, compassionate, and moving. Cary Grant is considered the definitive Hitchcock hero; he effectively plays against adventure and melodrama with a becoming tongue-in-cheek disbelief of what is happening to him in such films as *Notorious*, *North by Northwest* (1959), and *To Catch a Thief* (1955), in addition to *Suspicion*. But Hitchcock has been as compatible with other actors quite unlike Cary Grant. James Stewart, for example, responded to the Hitchcock spell in such films as *Rear Window* (1954), the remake of *The Man Who Knew*

Too Much (1955), and *Vertigo*, a rare masterpiece for both Hitchcock and Stewart.

Suspicion, however, was the real challenge, and early proving ground for Hitchcock. Selznick had brought him to Hollywood from England, and his first picture in Hollywood, *Rebecca*, was an overwhelming success. His next two films, *Foreign Correspondent* (1940) and the unlikely *Mr. and Mrs. Smith* (1941), had almost been enough to brand him as a one-time success in this country. But *Suspicion* proved his talent anew, and from this film forward he has seldom erred; no other director has been so consistently successful. He has been admired and imitated, but he remains uniquely Hitchcock, "master of suspense." He has made films his primary interest in life, and *Suspicion* is an important title in any list of his work.

THE 39 STEPS

Released: 1935
Production: Michael Balcon and Ivor Montagu for Gaumont-British
Direction: Alfred Hitchcock
Screenplay: Charles Bennett, Alma Reville, and Ian Hay; based on the novel
    of the same name by John Buchan
Cinematography: Bernard Knowles
Editing: D. N. Twist
Running time: 81 minutes

    Principal characters:
        Pamela .... Madeleine Carroll
        Richard Hannay .... Robert Donat
        Annabella Smith .... Lucie Mannheim
        Professor Jordan .... Godfrey Tearle
        Margaret .... Peggy Ashcroft
        John .... John Laurie
        Mrs. Jordan .... Helen Haye

    The 39 Steps is vintage British Hitchcock at its best, and, similar to *The Lady Vanishes* (1938), it manages to blend comedy and suspense to just the right degree. Yet the reason for much of the appeal of *The 39 Steps* lies not in its direction or in the fairly obvious studio-bound production, but in the script. Full credit for this must go to Charles Bennett, who took the original novel by John Buchan and completely rewrote it for the screen, adding not only a romantic interest but also a new story, leaving in essence nothing of Buchan's original but the basic idea. Charles Bennett's contribution to the success of Hitchcock's British films should never be underestimated; he was involved with the director's most famous films of that era: *Blackmail* (1929), *The Man Who Knew Too Much* (1934), *The 39 Steps*, *The Secret Agent* (1936), *Sabotage* (1936), and *Young and Innocent* (1937).

    The 39 Steps features Robert Donat, fresh from his success in *The Count of Monte Cristo* (1934), and Madeleine Carroll, who might be described as the first in a long line of classic and cool Hitchcock blondes, a line which was later to include Grace Kelly and Tippi Hedren. The two have the distinction of being starred in a film which Alfred Hitchcock has described as one of his favorites and one of his first major successes in the United States.

    Richard Hannay (Robert Donat), a Canadian living in London, is first seen at a London music hall, where an act named "Mr. Memory" is onstage. In the act, Mr. Memory identifies Hannay as a Canadian, and that is about all the audience ever learns of him. Outside the music hall, Hannay meets Annabella (Lucie Mannheim), who has fired some shots in the auditorium; she explains to him that she was forced to do so in order to create a diversion and thus escape from two men who were trying to kill her. She tells Hannay, "I'd like to come home with you," to which he replies, prophetically as it transpires, "It's your funeral." At Hannay's apartment, Annabella tells him of a plot to take military secrets out of England and that her destination is Scotland. Hannay is somewhat unbelieving, again prophetically telling her that the episode sounds like a spy story; but Hannay is rapidly made aware of the reality of the situation when he is literally awakened in the middle of the night by Annabella's staggering into his room and falling dead across his bed, a knife in her back.

Hannay finds himself trapped in his apartment, and is only able to escape by changing places with the milkman. He heads for Annabella's destination, Scotland, with no further clues and pursued not only by her killers, but also by the police, who suspect him of being Annabella's murderer. On the train, there is a brief comic interlude with two traveling salesmen, surely forerunners to Naunton Wayne and Basil Radford in *The Lady Vanishes*; this is one of a series of comedy moments which enliven what has now become little more than a chase film. Another great comedy sequence has Hannay forced, for his own protection, to pretend to be a political candidate addressing a meeting; the speech is so full of double-talk and sounds so much like a genuine political tirade that it warrants a round of applause from the audience in the Assembly Hall.

Back on the train, Hannay is forced to fake a friendship with a woman named Pamela (Madeleine Carroll) to evade the police; however, she identifies him to the law, and Hannay jumps from the train as it crosses the Forth Bridge. Fleeing across the Scottish moors, Hannay takes shelter with a stern, middle-aged Calvanistic crofter named John, magnificently played by character actor John Laurie, and with the crofter's young wife Margaret (Peggy Ashcroft). The wife seems romantically inclined towards Hannay and helps him; but later she suffers a beating from her husband for her interest in him. The crofter directs Hannay to the house of a professor (Godfrey Tearle) who seems to be the most pleasant of the characters in *The 39 Steps*. He is a genial family man, the only character who welcomes Hannay with friendship, but he is also the leader of the spies. Annabella, before she died, had warned Hannay to beware of a man with part of his finger missing, and Hannay recognizes that man as the professor.

Hannay escapes from the professor, locates and again turns to Pamela for assistance, this time during the political speechmaking at the Assembly Hall. He is again turned in by her, this time to the spies who are forced to take Pamela with them; she and Hannay are handcuffed together. Because of the obtrusion of a flock of sheep, Pamela and Hannay are separated from the spies, and, handcuffed together, wander across the moors. The handcuffs obviously have sexual overtones, not only as a form of fetish—symbols of a love-hate relationship—but because they force the couple to spend the night very much together. While Hannay sleeps, however, Pamela manages to slip off the handcuffs since they are a man's and she has a small feminine wrist. She is about to desert Hannay, when she overhears the professor talking of "thirty-nine steps" and arranging a meeting with his fellow conspirators at the London Palladium.

At the Palladium, Mr. Memory's act is again on the bill and all the elements of the plot merge. As the police arrive to arrest Hannay, he shouts out the question to Mr. Memory, "What are the thirty-nine steps?" Mr. Memory, who has been taught all his life to respond with the truth even if that truth means his death, replies before he is shot by the professor, "The thirty-nine steps is a political organization of spies collecting information on behalf of the foreign office of. . . ." We never do discover which foreign government was involved. Unlike John Buchan's novel in which the thirty-nine steps are a place, in the film the designation refers to a group of people. *The 39 Steps* was remade in 1960 and 1978, in versions starring Kenneth More and Robert Powell respectively; both the later versions are dull, tedious affairs, perhaps because they are closer to John Buchan's novel than they are to Charles Bennett's script, and both were only moderately successful, with the 1978 remake not even being released in the United States until 1980.

TO CATCH A THIEF

Released: 1955
Production: Alfred Hitchcock for Paramount
Direction: Alfred Hitchcock
Screenplay: John Michael Hayes; based on the novel of the same name by
  David Dodge
Cinematography: Robert Burks (AA)
Editing: George Tomasini
Running time: 97 minutes

Principal characters:
John Robie	Cary Grant
Frances Stevens	Grace Kelly
Jessie Stevens	Jessie Royce Landis
Bertani	Charles Vanel
Danielle	Brigitte Auber
H. H. Hughson	John Williams

By 1955, when he made *To Catch a Thief*, Alfred Hitchcock had long since established his reputation as a master of suspense. From *The Man Who Knew Too Much* (1934) and *The 39 Steps* (1935) to *Dial M for Murder* (1954) and *Rear Window* (1954), Hitchcock's admirers reveled in the tension for which his films were justly famous. Some of these admirers were, therefore, taken aback somewhat by *To Catch a Thief*, a lush comedy. Not that the film is entirely devoid of suspense—there is a mystery to be solved, after all. But *To Catch a Thief* finds Hitchcock in a playful mood, and the film never generates any real tension. However, a relaxed Hitchcock is still Hitchcock, and *To Catch a Thief* is a richly rewarding cinematic experience.

The film's title is derived from the old proverb "Set a thief to catch a thief," and Hitchcock populates the film with thieves and manipulators of all sorts. Some of them are reformed thieves; at least one of them is an active jewel thief; some of them are merely expense account padders; and some are manipulative lovers. As the film opens, they have at least one thing in common—none knows which of the other characters fits into which category. Indeed, one of the director's themes (although he never presses his case to the point of didacticism) is that the moral implications of theft are, if not entirely subjective, frequently dependent upon the perspective of the observer.

The film opens with a typical Hitchcock shock, this time laced with humor. The credits roll as the camera first focuses on the window of a travel agency and then pans to a sign that reads "If you love life, you'll love France." As the camera pulls in on the sign, Hitchcock suddenly cuts to a close-up of a woman screaming, "My jewels! I've been robbed." In one fell swoop, Hitchcock has established both the film's location and its subject—jewelry theft. The scene continues with a montage of similar screams, intercut with shots of a black cat running across a series of tiled roofs; the obvious association is that of a cat burglar.

Hitchcock introduces us to a real cat burglar (albeit a retired one) in the next scene. John Robie (Cary Grant) strides into Bertani's Restaurant on the French Riviera with a grim look on his face, a look which the restaurant's staff reciprocates. He walks back to the glassed-in kitchen, where he stands for a long moment peering through the transparent door. As the camera moves in for a close-up of Robie's face, Hitchcock delivers his second visual shock of the film—a raw egg splatters against the glass in front of Robie's face.

An explanation is soon forthcoming. Robie is an American who had fought alongside Bertani (Charles Vanel) and most of his kitchen help in the French Resistance during World War II. After the war, he remained in France and became a famous, and for a time successful, jewel thief, growing rich at the expense of those who could afford the losses he inflicted ("I never stole from anyone who would go hungry," he remarks at one point). Long since retired from the burglary business, Robie nevertheless finds himself under suspicion, both from the police and from his former Resistance comrades, for the latest string of thefts, all of which seem to bear his mark. Robie's assertions of innocence are met with skepticism by all concerned; some are angry, a few are amused, and Danielle (Brigitte Auber), the young daughter of the wine steward, is obviously smitten with Robie.

Robie realizes that the only way he will be able to prove that he is telling the truth is to apprehend the new cat burglar himself. To do so, he must set a trap for the "Cat," and he asks Bertani's help to do so. The pair are interrupted by the police, however, who are hot on Robie's trail. Danielle helps him to escape. Eventually Bertani puts Robie in touch with a man named H. H. Hughson (John Williams), an insurance adjuster from Lloyd's of London. Robie again protests his innocence and outlines his plan to Hughson. In return for a list of Lloyd's of London's most prominent insurees, who will, therefore, likely be the thief's next victims, Robie will undertake to apprehend the new Cat. The two men engage in some intense verbal sparring. Hughson, a proper Briton, is puzzled by Robie's cheerful, guiltless acknowledgment of his past crimes. Robie responds by forcing Hughson to admit that he occasionally pads his expense account and takes towels from hotels as souvenirs; thus, the boundaries of morality are blurred a bit. "You're a thief," asserts Robie. Hughson gives in and provides the American with a detailed list of his clients and their jewels.

Most prominent on the list are Jessie Stevens (Jessie Royce Landis), a rich American widow, and her beautiful blonde daughter, Frances (Grace Kelly). Robie contrives to meet them, and, as "Mr. Burns," ingratiates himself quickly. Mrs. Stevens is a blunt, humorous woman who is open and outgoing; Frances is almost the exact opposite. Cool and virginal, she hardly says a word all night. Thus it comes as a surprise, both to the audience and to Robie, when she kisses him passionately at the end of the evening.

With the introduction of Jessie and Frances Stevens, Hitchcock's cast is virtually complete. He then sets about complicating their lives, much to the audience's delight. Hitchcock presses the theme of the hunter hunted, as the depredations of the new Cat continue, and Robie, who is pursuing the Cat, is himself pressed by both the police and his former friends in the Resistance, who vow to kill him for discrediting them. Meanwhile, Danielle and Frances quarrel bitchily over which of them has the right to pursue the bemused and befuddled Robie, who wants as little as possible to do with either of the young women.

Two long scenes between Robie and Frances demonstrate the playful mood that Hitchcock was in while making *To Catch a Thief*. He even relaxes enough to permit his characters some witty double entendres (both verbal and visual)—a rarity for the moralistic director. The first of these scenes involves a high-speed car chase in which a calm Frances helps a nervous Robie elude the police once again. She is driving, and Hitchcock shows their contrasting moods by focusing on their hands. Hers rest lightly on the steering wheel, even as she careens around curves; his hands clench and unclench helplessly as he wonders whether capture by the police might not be preferable to death in an automobile accident on a remote French road. Having successfully eluded the police, the two banter a bit. When Robie calls her "a rich, headstrong young girl," she replies challengingly, "the man I want doesn't have a price." "That eliminates me," Robie chuckles. Then Frances reveals that she knows that "Mr. Burns" is actually John Robie, the jewel thief. Far from being shocked or offended, she is thrilled; it makes him all the more attractive to her. She pulls off the road to a secluded picnic area and offers him some fried chicken: "Do you want a leg or a breast?" she inquires meaningfully. When she announces that she plans to join him on his "crime spree," he groans in dismay. "Don't say it," he pleads, but she does anyway: "The Cat has a new kitten."

The second of Hitchcock's playful scenes occurs back at the hotel. Frances decides to force Robie into admitting his passion; but whether for her or for the glittering jewels she is wearing, Hitchcock leaves an open question. The director intercuts some marvelously photographed shots of exploding roman candles with the sexual fireworks provided by Frances and Robie. The double entendres fly, as Frances seduces Robie by extolling the beauty of either (or both) her diamonds or her breasts. The evening proves eventful; Frances loses her virginity and her mother loses her jewels. Frances tearfully accuses Robie of being the thief. Mrs. Stevens believes Robie's denials—like her daughter, she finds his former career more than a little intriguing—but Frances calls the police, and Robie is on the run again.

Hitchcock has one more shock scene up his sleeve. Robie is once more on the track of the Cat. Quite suddenly, he is jumped from behind. The figures grapple in the darkness on a cliff near the water's edge, and one man—we do not know who at this point—plummets over the side. For a moment, we fear that Robie has been killed, but the dead man turns out to be Danielle's father, the wine steward. The wine steward is immediately branded as the jewel thief, but Robie knows otherwise; the old man lacked sufficient agility to prowl the rooftops like the Cat. The mysterious sequence does tip the real thief's identity to him, however, and he begins to set his trap.

Robie springs the trap at a delightful costume ball on the Côte d'Azur. With the help of Jessie and Frances Stevens, who play along, and Hughson, who surreptitiously slips into Robie's nubian slave costume and holds the attention of the police by dancing the night away with Frances, Robie is free to track his Cat. He stations himself on the roof of the villa, where he awaits his victim. As the party is breaking up, the thief emerges, and a rooftop chase is on. Dodging bullets from the police below, Robie unmasks the Cat—who turns out to be Danielle. She breaks Robie's grip, but trips as she turns to run. Robie grabs her hand to keep her from falling off the roof, but threatens to drop her unless she confesses, and loudly enough for the police to hear. Trapped, she admits her guilt, and implicates Bertani, the restaurateur, as well.

Hitchcock ends the film on what he humorously calls "a pretty grim note." Back at Robie's villa, Frances and Robie stop sparring long enough to realize that they love each other. They kiss, and Frances remarks "So this is where you live. Oh, mother will love it up here!" A brief look of undisguised dismay crosses Robie's face as Hitchcock brings the film to a close.

Neither Cary Grant nor Grace Kelly were strangers to Alfred Hitchcock by 1955, Grant having appeared in *Notorious* (1946) and *Suspicion* (1941), and Kelly in *Dial M for Murder* and *Rear Window*. Hitchcock melded their talents expertly. It is difficult to imagine anyone other than Grant as John Robie; his sophisticated charm and his genius for light comedy make him perfect for the role. Kelly, too, is superb; she brings talent as well as beauty to the role of Frances Stevens, and she works exceptionally well with Grant. Jessie Royce Landis also deserves special mention for her supporting role as Frances' mother; her irreverent, wisecracking portrayal of Jessie Stevens stands out, even in the company of Grant and Kelly.

The direction, of course, is up to the usual high standards of Hitchcock. The film is expertly paced, with just enough jolts interspersed with the comedy to remind the audience that it is, after all, viewing an Alfred Hitchcock film. As Hitchcock himself has admitted, *To Catch a Thief* is a "lightweight story," at least compared to such thrillers as *Strangers on a Train* (1951), *Rear Window*, or *Psycho* (1960), to name a few of the film's approximate contemporaries. But a lightweight story in the hands of Alfred Hitchcock does not necessarily make for an inconsequential film. *To Catch a Thief* is an outstanding comedy, highlighted by the acting of Grant, Kelly, and Landis, and the Academy Award-winning cinematography of Robert Burks, all guided by the incomparable hand of the master, Alfred Hitchcock.

THE TROUBLE WITH HARRY

Released: 1955
Production: Alfred Hitchcock for Alfred Hitchcock Productions; released by Paramount
Direction: Alfred Hitchcock
Screenplay: John Michael Hayes; based on the novel of the same name by Jack Trevor Story
Cinematography: Robert Burks
Editing: Alma Macrorie
Music: Bernard Herrmann
Running time: 99 minutes

Principal characters:

Captain Albert Wiles	Edmund Gwenn
Sam Marlowe	John Forsythe
Jennifer Rogers	Shirley MacLaine
Miss Gravely	Mildred Natwick
Mrs. Wiggs	Mildred Dunnock
Calvin Wiggs	Royal Dano
Arnie Rogers	Jerry Mathers

For Alfred Hitchcock, *The Trouble with Harry* is an eccentric film. Although it relies little on the particular techniques of suspense usually associated with his work, it does have a subtle tension of its own. It is an uncharacteristically mellow film in which Hitchcock makes considerable use of his very droll English sense of humor, while at the same time demonstrating his gift for using real locations as counterpoint to his fanciful ideas. The exteriors of *The Trouble with Harry* were made in Vermont during the autumn, and the camera captures beautifully the reds, oranges, and yellows of the changing leaves and the tranquility of a peaceful countryside.

In the midst of this beauty, a corpse is discovered; three people believe themselves responsible. Captain Wiles (Edmund Gwenn), a kindly retired seaman, believes he has accidentally shot the man while hunting. Miss Gravely (Mildred Natwick), a prim spinster who believed the man meant to attack her, has struck him on the head with her hiking shoe. The man's estranged wife, Jennifer Rogers (Shirley MacLaine), has hit him with a bottle, which has resulted in his staggering away into the woods in a stupor. A fourth person, Sam Marlowe (John Forsythe), conspires with the three guilty parties to hide the corpse. For the entire length of the story, these four people find themselves burdened with the dead man as a result of their indecisiveness about what to do with him. Finally, they hit upon the idea of having Jennifer's son, Arnie (Jerry Mathers), whose understanding of time is totally confusing, rediscover the dead man at his original resting place.

This is admittedly a slim premise for a film, but for Hitchcock it is only a premise and not the substance of the realized work. The director troubles the audience by making death amusing and by showing no sentiment for Harry, who is unlamented even by his wife and son. More perversely, he uses Harry's death to bring together two couples, Sam and Jennifer and the Captain and Miss Gravely. The film clearly shows that death may be beneficial to the living, since these characters do not know one another before Harry's death, and develop deep mutual affection through their common cause. All four characters refute the mistaken view that Hitchcock is only able to take an interest in mentally unhealthy relationships and psychopathic murderers. Each member of this group may be a bit eccentric in some way, but each has an attitude toward life that is essentially healthy and positive.

The character of Sam is unique in the fact that he is the only major character in a Hitchcock film who is an artist. He is a young man whose talent is unrecognized; all of his paintings are unsold, although his fortunes change at the end. John Forsythe is ideally cast as Sam, who alone does not share in the imagined guilt of his companions, but who assumes the role of leader in all of their schemes by virtue of his quick mind. Forsythe conveys the charm and intelligence necessary to make Sam's manipulation of the others credible.

The other characters are equally well realized. Shirley MacLaine, in her first film, makes an uncommon Hitchcock heroine, and there is no question that she was chosen for the qualities which set her apart from other actresses. Rather than the pathos associated with MacLaine's most celebrated roles (*Some Came Running*, 1958; *The Apartment*, 1960), Hitchcock brings out her comic flair and ability to project sexiness in an amusing way, qualities also evident in her next film, *Artists and Models* (1955). Edmund Gwenn and Mildred Natwick, both endearing character players, make an unusual romantic couple. They take full advantage of the film's rich possibilities for humor, and are unexpectedly touching in the courtship scenes, evoking the combination of shyness and bravado more commonly associated with romance between adolescents.

The Trouble with Harry was made in Hitchcock's richest period. Robert Burks, a constant collaborator for over a decade, had already photographed a number of Hitchcock films, and his work in VistaVision and Technicolor is entrancing, especially in the attractive scenes of New England which are visually unlike those in any other film. Bernard Herrmann, another valuable collaborator in this period, composed his first Hitchcock score for *The Trouble with Harry* and expressed regret in later years that he had not been able to score more comedies. His music for the film is alternately wistful and whimsical. John Michael Hayes was scenarist for four consecutive Hitchcock films; these four screenplays abound in verbal wit and are easily Hayes's best work. Hayes deserves special praise for the dialogue in the first meeting between

Sam and Jennifer, in which they sit on the porch drinking lemonade as Jennifer talks matter-of-factly about her marriage to the ill-fated Harry. This sequence is one of the most outrageous boy-meets-girl episodes on film and would by itself be enough to justify Hitchcock's high opinion of *The Trouble with Harry*, which he always cites as a personal favorite.

THE WRONG MAN

Released: 1957
Production: Alfred Hitchcock for Warner Bros.
Direction: Alfred Hitchcock
Screenplay: Maxwell Anderson and Angus McPhail; based on a screen story
    by Maxwell Anderson and an actual criminal case
Cinematography: Robert Burks
Editing: George Tomasini
Sound: Earl Crain, Sr.
Music: Bernard Herrmann
Running time: 105 minutes

    Principal characters:

Christopher Emmanuel (Manny) Balestrero	Henry Fonda
Rose Balestrero	Vera Miles
Frank O'Connor	Anthony Quayle
Lieutenant Bowers	Harold J. Stone
Detective Matthews	Charles Cooper

Christopher Emmanuel Balestrero (Henry Fonda), a New York bass player, works nights at the Stork Club and comes home to his wife Rose (Vera Miles) and their children in the early morning. Although he likes to chart the horses while riding the subway, perhaps because his family is never financially ahead, he seldom bets on his selections. He and Rose lead what might be described as a life of quiet desperation; soon, however, they find out what true desperation is. "Manny," as Balestrero is nicknamed, goes to borrow money on his wife's insurance policy and in the process is misidentified as a holdup man by one of the cashiers, whose fellow employees join in the error. Returning home, Manny is picked up by two detectives who take him in for questioning. In the course of interrogating him, they ask him to write the words of a note which had been used by the holdup man. The anxious Manny accidentally misspells a word and soon finds himself charged with robbery and spending the night in a Queens jail.

In the morning, he is freed on the bail raised by his family and proceeds to engage a lawyer, Frank O'Connor (Anthony Quayle), who believes in his innocence. O'Connor explains to Manny and Rose the importance of establishing an alibi, but the people he might have used as witnesses either have died or cannot be found. Rose begins to despair and finally has a nervous breakdown. After she is placed in a mental hospital, the saddened Manny stands trial, but a mistrial is declared and he must face the entire process once again. He prays; and at that very moment, the holdup man walks into a store to rob again but is subdued by the owners. One of the detectives who arrested Manny notices the resemblance between the two, and Manny is finally cleared of the charges and released. He goes to the mental hospital to tell Rose that the nightmare is over, but for her, it is not. "That's fine for you," she tells him, staring blankly into space.

Although this story sounds similar to the sort of nightmarish fabrication which might be expected from Alfred Hitchcock, the premise is not his own. *The Wrong Man* is singular among his works in that the story is a true one, a fact that he emphasizes in a personal appearance at the beginning of the film. It is sometimes said that Hitchcock needs very fanciful plots in order to make the kind of film associated with him, but it is impossible to believe this after seeing *The Wrong Man*, which is one of his most hypnotic and compelling films.

In *The Wrong Man*, we find both the themes and techniques closely associated with Hitchcock. He engages freely in the subjective shots for which he is celebrated, building up in the audience the same fear and claustrophobia which Manny feels when he is arrested and locked up. These sequences have a quiet intensity and concentration which reflect the director's masterful control over what may be his own anxiety; Hitchcock has stated many times that he has a dread of jails and the police as a result of a traumatic childhood experience. The mistaken identity theme is one which Hitchcock has favored often, but as a rule, it has appeared in films with considerably less sobriety of tone than *The Wrong Man*. *Saboteur* (1942) and *North by Northwest* (1959) are more appropriate works to display Hitchcock's rich sense of humor than the story of a man and his wife who actually suffered the tragedy described by the film. Regarding the theme of the transfer of guilt, one of Hitchcock's most striking and individual motifs, nowhere in the director's work is there a more dramatic example than that of the wife who goes mad by assuming the guilt she perceives to be part of the fabric of her life and her husband's even though he is completely innocent.

The exteriors and certain interiors of the film were shot on location in New York, and Robert Burks resourcefully varies the black and white tonality of the film without ever departing from the prevailing visual mood, delicately poised between realism and expressionism. Although Hitchcock and Burks had become enthusiasts of the expressive use of color long before this black-and-white film was made, they are no less inspired here in the use of the drab settings and downbeat images which dominate the story. Their imaginative re-creation of the cheerless environment into a visualization of an emotional nightmare is one of the finest aspects of the film. Hitchcock creates tension in the opening sequence as Manny leaves the nightclub simply by introducing the figures of two policemen who stroll along behind the musician for a few moments.

After Manny is arrested, the scene of his interrogation is handled with a restraint and matter-of-factness which generally characterizes the style of the film, but at a key moment, the suppleness of Hitchcock's technique enhances the presentation of the scene. Manny has been attempting to remain calm and cooperative, but when he is finally overcome by feelings of helplessness and frustration, the camera withdraws to a high angle, making him appear even more vulnerable than before despite the fact that he has become vocally assertive. Similar touches enhance other scenes, such as the one in the jail cell, in which Manny is overcome by a feeling of claustrophobia and the camera begins to move in a little circle around him, the movement becoming increasingly rapid so that the still man eventually seems to whirl helplessly in the space of the frame. The severity of Hitchcock's formal control results in the film's most ostentatious and stirring moment, which occurs late in the film. In the scene there is a slow dissolve from the face of the praying Manny to the face of the actual holdup man, a dissolve in which the faces of the men merge as if Manny's prayer is mysteriously being answered.

The filming of Rose's breakdown is characterized by a thoughtfulness and visual tension which make this sequence perhaps the most outstanding in the film. Most of it is directed with visual restraint, as Rose, initially calm but becoming increasingly disturbed, expresses her feeling of helplessness over their situation. When he perceives that she is becoming hysterical, Manny moves to touch her and she picks up a hairbrush and hits him on the head with it. Hitchcock breaks up this brief action within the long sequence into a series of short shots—close-ups of Rose and Manny, the raising of the brush, the smashing of the brush into a mirror after Manny has been hit, and Manny's face distorted by its reflection in the broken mirror. The sequence ends with Rose retreating into a trance and oppressively dominating the compostion as she stares blankly and virtually whispers that she is ill.

Although it is important to realize that each shot in a Hitchcock film is carefully prepared so that it will relate both visually and psychologically to the overall conception in Hitchcock's mind, it is also important to note that Hitchcock's interpreters play an essential part in this conception. It is possible that the very fact of having to follow direction so closely in terms of movement and gesture has a liberating effect on actors and actresses in a Hitchcock film. Whatever the reason, no director elicits better performances than Hitchcock, and Henry Fonda and Vera Miles are among the finest examples of this. Miles's restrained dialogue and her subtle changes of expression which culminate in the empty gaze she finally assumes for the remainder of the film produce one of the most credible and brilliantly realized nervous breakdown sequences in cinema. Similarly, Fonda expresses his subdued character remarkably, mostly through the ways in which Manny looks at the world around him.

The calmness of the film, a result of Hitchcock's understanding of the characters and his attitute toward the story, makes it more dramatic than if it were overwrought, and every aspect of the film contributes to this sense

of calmness. The music of Bernard Herrmann, which appropriately emphasizes the bass, is discreetly somber, and the complex soundtrack is also subtle
and restrained. The screenplay is admirably straightforward, and the relatively prosaic quality of the dialogue not only encourages identification with
the characters, but also sets off the more poetic quality of Hitchcock's cinematic realization.

Although it is relentlessly bleak, *The Wrong Man* betrays no cynicism and
makes no recourse to a facile pessimism. This apparent destruction of a man
by a merciless stroke of fate, which becomes the actual destruction of his
more fragile wife, describes a cruel and uncaring universe with great spiritual
resonance. Perhaps this is because the characters are whole human beings,
not choosing to suffer in the manner of crippled characters found in more
neurotic films, but suffering nonetheless against their will, their limitations
used against them by the caprices of circumstance. The gentle Manny journeys
through hell with a childlike awe, but this same innocence prevents him from
ever knowing of the inner hell of his wife, burning quietly until it blazes out
of control to provide this masterpiece of the desolation of human existence
with its final tragic irony.

There is something strangely consoling in Hitchcock's presentation. His
subjective techniques are used to encourage identification with Manny, but
we are not encouraged to the same extent of identification with Rose, at least
not by the camera. With Manny, we find at last that we are overwhelmed
with sadness for her assumption of his nonexistent guilt. Hitchcock's choices
when determining the visual and psychological nature of each shot result in
the possibility of feeling compassion, a consoling emotion. He makes *The
Wrong Man* appear to be a detached and restrained film, even while reaching
profound fears within the consciousness of the spectator, until the final meeting in the mental hospital between the heartbroken Manny and the insane
Rose, which brings forth the feeling of catharsis which he has held in suspense.

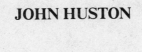

JOHN HUSTON

THE AFRICAN QUEEN

Released: 1951
Production: S. P. Eagle (Sam Spiegel) for Horizon Romulus Productions; released by United Artists
Direction: John Huston
Screenplay: James Agee and John Huston; based on the novel of the same name by C. S. Forester
Cinematography: Jack Cardiff
Editing: Ralph Kemplen
Costume design: Katharine Hepburn's costumes by Doris Langley Moore
Running time: 103 minutes

> *Principal characters:*
> Rose Sayer .... Katharine Hepburn
> Charlie Allnut .... Humphrey Bogart (AA)
> Reverend Samuel Sayer .... Robert Morley

The African Queen is a tale of adventure and of an implausible love affair that develops in spite of the disparate personalities of the two main characters, Charlie Allnut and Rose Sayer. While the adventure element had already been seen in director John Huston's previous films, the technicolor and the almost continuous low humor that accompanied the development of the relationship between Charlie and Rose was new. Huston has written that the humor was not apparent in the original C. S. Forester novel, nor was it written into the screenplay, but that it evolved naturally as the stars, Humphrey Bogart and Katharine Hepburn, reacted to each other. Hepburn has stated that nothing was happening at all until Huston suggested that she play Rose like Eleanor Roosevelt.

Most of the scenes were filmed on location in what was then the Belgian Congo and the British protectorate of Uganda. Huston felt that if the actors were living under hardships on location that it would translate into their performances. Even on an English soundstage, where the swamp scenes and the early mission scenes with Robert Morley were shot, he insisted on reality. When Bogart emerges from the river covered with what look like leeches, they are real leeches.

Huston uses few cinematic devices to tell his tale. The cinematography is straightforward and beautifully done, but the camera never lingers too long on the steamy lushness of Africa. The setting and the adventure are important elements in the movie, but they are secondary to the development of the characters.

The story takes place on a partially uncharted river in Africa in 1914. Charlie Allnut, the uncouth, gin-swizzling captain of an equally disreputable mailboat, the *African Queen*, arrives to deliver mail and news to the English missionaries, Reverend Samuel Sayer and his sister Rose. The differences in personality and social station between Charlie and the missionaries are de-lineated as a grubby Charlie observes the high-collared, fervent twosome trying to lead a group of atonal natives in hymn singing. Charlie smiles at the din and absently tosses away his cigar. The noise reaches a crescendo as a group of natives pounce on the discarded stogie and add their yells to the singing. Samuel glares humorlessly as Charlie slyly enjoys the distraction he has caused. Their differences are further underscored when the missionaries stiffly ignore Charlie's uncontrollable stomach rumblings while at tea. Charlie proceeds to make things worse by trying to apologize. They stonily ignore him and continue their polite conversation.

Charlie leaves after giving the missionaries the alarming news of a state of war between England and Germany; World War I has begun. Rose and Samuel's fear about being aliens in German East Africa is soon realized as the Germans arrive and destroy the mission. Samuel tries to stop the de-struction, but he is hit on the head, has a breakdown, and dies. Charlie returns a day later and offers to take Rose into hiding with him, as the Germans will surely return in search of the *African Queen* and her cargo: oxygen and hydrogen cylinders and blasting gelatin. Escape is impossible since the Germans are all along the river, and even the lake at the end of the river is patrolled by a German gunboat, the *Louisa*.

The adversary relationship, which is the source of much of the film's humor, begins as Rose's English patriotism is stirred by the words "explosives" and "*Louisa*." She develops a plan from which she never wavers: to go to the lake and torpedo the *Louisa*. She goads Charlie into continuing the voyage and makes him promise to sink the *Louisa*.

Later, his courage buoyed by much gin, Charlie reneges on his promise because they would have to get past a German fort in full daylight; and after the fort there are rapids, and then unknown territory. Rose archly calls him a liar and a coward. Charlie fights back by mimicking her speech, whimpering as he recalls his poor old mother, and calling Rose a "crazy, psalm-singing, skinny old maid." Rose retaliates by pouring his liquor overboard and by unnerving the sociable Charlie with the silent treatment. For all his bravado, Charlie is no match for Rose, and he gives in. The stars supply most of the humor here, but Huston also gives us a touch of his own: one of Charlie's outraged outbursts causes the entire jungle to erupt in animal roars, bellows, and screeches.

As they prepare for and stand together through the dangers of getting past the fort and shooting the rapids, their relationship evolves into one of mutual admiration and love. During the flight past the German fort, Rose witnesses Charlie's courage. As they are fired upon, the steam hose on the *African Queen* disconnects and the boat loses power in front of the sharpshooters, making them easy targets. To repair it, Charlie must expose himself and risk being shot. Huston maintains a fast, exciting pace as the *African Queen* begins its journey past the fort and through the rapids; and the pace is set with sharp editing rather than with tricks. The action jumps from long shots of the *African Queen* as seen from the fort, to close-ups of Rose and Charlie, to groups of riflemen, and finally to a single sharpshooter and Charlie as seen through the German's gunscope. Charlie is saved when the sun blinds the shooter.

At first triumphant at having made it safely past the fort, Rose's joy gives way to fear again as they rush directly into the rapids. They both struggle with the rudder to keep the boat from hitting the rocks, and miraculously, they make it. Wildly exuberant at having accomplished two seemingly impossible feats, they forget themselves completely and embrace and kiss. It is the beginning of one of the most memorable love scenes on film. At first awkward and embarrassed, they slowly succumb to each other's charms. The humor remains even here when, after their first night together, Rose asks Charlie, "Mr. Allnut—dear—what is your first name?"

The film next takes a serious turn as the *African Queen* enters the uncharted portion of the river, and Charlie and Rose are beset by bugs, leeches, and the increasingly swampy condition of the river. Here, the camera as much as the acting creates the oppressive atmosphere when it closes in on Bogart's exhausted and tense face as he pulls his boat through the muck. Finally, unable to continue, they face the fact that they are beaten and will probably die. Having done the impossible has given the feverish Charlie some pride, and he gently tells Rose that it was all worth it. As they fall asleep the camera retreats from the *African Queen* and we see that they are only yards away from their goal, the lake.

During the night, a rainstorm raises the level of the river, and the *African Queen* is freed from her swampy grave. Charlie and Rose awaken and joyfully view the lake—and the *Louisa*. With their humor and spirits restored, Charlie makes the torpedoes, and they head for the gunboat under cover of night. However, a storm arises, and Charlie and Rose are separated as the *African Queen* sinks in the choppy water. Morning finds the two on board the *Louisa* and undergoing trial as spies. When Charlie is sentenced to death, Rose decides to die with him and tells the Germans of their plans to sink the *Louisa*. She looks on with pride as Charlie tells how he made the torpedoes. The exasperated Germans hurry them on deck for the hanging. As a last request Charlie asks the captain to marry him and Rose. The captain assents, and then immediately orders the executions to proceed. Interspliced between the action of the trial, marriage, and execution preparations are scenes of the *African Queen* slowly rising from the lake until the torpedoes are above the waterline and aimed directly at the oncoming *Louisa*.

Just before the nooses are tightened an explosion erupts, and the Allnuts make their escape as the *Louisa* sinks. As they swim toward shore they find a piece of the *African Queen* floating in the water and realize that they have accomplished their goal.

While reviews were generally excellent, critics pointed out the weaknesses of a story that was too pat: the Reverend is too conveniently eliminated; the love affair is too predictable; and the ending is too melodramatic and contrived. To the audiences that flocked to see the film, however, these factors were inconsequential in comparison to the stellar acting of Bogart and Hepburn, the cinematography, and the adventure.

The film earned Academy Award nominations for Huston and Agee for Best Screenplay, Huston for Best Direction, Hepburn for Best Actress, and Bogart for Best Actor. Bogart was the only one to win, and it was to be his only Oscar in a career studded with memorable performances.

Indeed, it is the acting and charisma of Bogart and Hepburn which have given the film its lasting appeal. Hepburn's primly determined Rose is the perfect foil for Bogart's belligerent Charlie. Her very primness makes her thawing and capitulation to Charlie all the more enjoyable. Bogart's Charlie is a masterpiece of comic characterization, and even after Charlie has gained some dignity, the old Charlie, however sober, is still evident. As Rose and Charlie's relationship evolves from polite tolerance of each other to adversaries to lovers, they make the audience believe that a pious, teetotaling, iron-willed spinster really could fall for a boozy, seedy boatman.

KEY LARGO

Released: 1948
Production: Jerry Wald for Warner Bros.
Direction: John Huston
Screenplay: John Huston and Richard Brooks; based on the play of the same
  name by Maxwell Anderson
Cinematography: Karl Freund
Editing: Rudi Fehr
Running time: 101 minutes

> *Principal characters:*
> Frank McCloud .... Humphrey Bogart
> Johnny Rocco .... Edward G. Robinson
> Nora Temple .... Lauren Bacall
> James Temple .... Lionel Barrymore
> Gaye .... Claire Trevor (AA)
> Ziggy .... Marc Lawrence
> Ben Wade .... Monte Blue
> Clyde Sawyer .... John Rodney

After winning two Oscars in 1947 for Best Director and Best Screenplay in *The Treasure of the Sierra Madre*, John Huston was asked by Bogart: "So what do we do for an encore, kid?" Huston encored with *Key Largo*, a project that had no problems, merely lots of hard work and laughs with Bogart. Playwright Maxwell Anderson's plays were produced for stage and screen for almost thirty years, yet today, few perform his plays and many critics consider him overrated. Wedding social commentary to blank verse, he wrote in a style which, although popular at the time, is now found burdensome. He is remembered more for the films which were made from his plays than for the actual plays themselves. Anderson wrote *Key Largo*, a formal pre-World War II drama, in 1939, four years after *Winterset*, his most famous play; but it was not one of his better efforts. The story deals with a Spanish Civil War deserter who tries to rationalize himself into performing a duty that might cost him his life.

John Huston and Richard Brooks completely rewrote Anderson's material making many improvements; their script tones down the pompous verse and adds outdoor action as well as an original ending. Confined mostly to a single, handsome set, the story moves along at a steady pace, and if the script has a problem it is limited to the dialogue. (For example, Bogart sounds unnatural speaking blank-verse lines such as "You don't like it, Rocco, the storm?") *Key Largo* is a director's film, and Huston is in full control of the story and actors. Huston's directing adds a vitality, insight, and continuity within each scene that is inventive and imaginative. His characters, atmosphere, emotions, and ideas evolve exactly as they should. His direction improved upon the script, which was overly preachy. The dialogue about courage and good *versus* evil seems somewhat stilted and dated today, and even in 1945, the gangster theme was becoming obsolete.

Huston was impressed by the problems facing the returning soldiers after World War II. He saw the collision of postwar realities with the expectations of men trying to find themselves again. In *Key Largo* he wanted to touch upon this theme and to say that a man cannot dispel his problems by avoiding them, nor can he find personal freedom without taking a stand. Anderson's original protagonist, a deserter from the Spanish Civil War, was transformed into a disillusioned GI who has difficulties adjusting to postwar life.

The atmosphere is established firmly at the beginning of the film. A bus is seen moving across the bridge leading to the Florida Keys. A sheriff's car overtakes it and brings it to a stop; the sheriff is looking for two Indians who have escaped from jail. This scene introduces the main character of the film, Frank McCloud (Humphrey Bogart), who is one of the passengers. His destination is the Florida Keys. It is the dead of summer when tourists avoid the heat and humidity that settles over the Key Largo Hotel, which is closed for the season. Ex-army major McCloud has come to the island to see James Temple (Lionel Barrrymore) and his daughter-in-law Nora (Lauren Bacall), the father and widow of a wartime buddy.

McCloud finds Key Largo a place where he can establish roots in the home of a dead friend's family and reaffirm who he is and what he believes in. He has been fighting for his country, but the realities of death on the battlefield have changed him. He claims that he will only fight again for himself and what is his, but he has never had to make that distinction before. He had a commitment to World War II, and although he makes passing reference to cowardice, we learn that such references are only a part of his disillusionment with all war.

McCloud finds the hotel inhabited by strange guests: a "Mr. Brown" (Edward G. Robinson), his alcoholic girl friend Gaye (Claire Trevor), and his henchmen. The first shot of Brown is a famous one which shows him sitting in a bathtub, mouthing his cigar in typical Edward G. Robinson style. McCloud recognizes Brown as Johnny Rocco, a notorious racketeer who had been deported from the United States. At Key Largo, Rocco is making an attempt to regain his former power after a long absence from this country. He decides to hold McCloud and the others at the hotel prisoners while he awaits the arrival of another gangster to buy a fortune in counterfeit money. A battle of wits ensues between McCloud and Rocco—a battle that results in death, but at the same time resurrects McCloud's moral commitment.

Temple and Rocco become foils not only for each other but also for McCloud. Here Huston attempts to establish his perception of postwar America. McCloud returns to the States only to find the same delusions despite the war's end. Temple, as a flag-waving patriot, believes in the absolute truth of noble ideals. The limitations of his views are handled well by Huston. Temple is a cripple confined to a wheelchair (as was the case with Barrymore himself); therefore he is incapable of fighting for what he believes in, and must have a champion to do it for him. Rocco, too, has a strict code of ideals, although they differ from those of Temple. Both men have witnessed the passing of an earlier era, a time when there was no conflict between a man's heart and his head. They both live in the past, while McCloud struggles to cope with the present.

Huston utilizes aspects of the gangster film genre to heighten his theme. With a collection of stars who made many of the original gangster films, such as Edward G. Robinson and Bogart, the allusions are all the more evident. In fact, this film becomes a parody of its type, especially as it develops Rocco's character. He is like many of his cinematic predecessors, small and tough, yet he is also a pathetic figure as he tries to regain his former stature. He foresees the return of the glorious days of prohibition, beginning with his venture of running counterfeit money. When McCloud has a chance to kill Rocco, however, he passes up the opportunity because he is too concerned with saving his own life, and because his disillusionment makes him reluctant to fight again for any cause. When the island is swept by a storm, Rocco loses control and refuses to let Temple admit a group of Indians requesting shelter in the hotel. Seeing this injustice renews McCloud's strength.

Just before another gangster, Ziggy (Marc Lawrence), arrives Rocco humiliates Gaye, the star turned alcoholic, by forcing her through a painful attempt to sing her old theme song. The scene ironically parallels that of a nightclub with an audience sitting around and the singer at the center. She has no stage, no spotlight highlighting her painted face, however; instead empty tables and chairs piled on them surround her, and no piano accompanies her almost hysterical voice. Gaye fails miserably, and when Rocco cruelly refuses her a promised drink, McCloud pours it for her, receiving a slap from Rocco for his trouble.

After the storm ends, Rocco receives a visit from Ziggy, who has come to buy a shipment of counterfeit money. Rocco's meeting with Ziggy underscores the pathos of his position. He calls for Gaye when Ziggy appears and treats her as a plaything in order to show her off in much the way that women were used in earlier gangster films. Ziggy is immediately impressed, and before he has a chance to see what a shell she has become, Rocco dismisses her. The two gangsters' meeting seems like a college reunion where they laugh about old times far too loud and too long. They make their deal, but it does not matter, for Prohibition and its accompanying gangsterism is not coming back, because people like McCloud will not let it.

When Ziggy departs, Sheriff Ben Wade (Monte Blue) comes looking for his deputy, Clyde Sawyer (John Rodney), who was after the two Indians who escaped from jail. When Wade finds the body of Sawyer, whom Rocco has killed, Rocco implies that the fugitives are guilty. Wade finds the Indians and, when they try to get away, he kills them both. Sickened by all of this, McCloud realizes finally that there can be no compromise with Rocco, who destroys innocent people. McCloud thus agrees to pilot a boat for Rocco, who is going to Cuba. Before leaving, Rocco tells Gaye that he is leaving her behind, so she takes a gun from his pocket and passes it unseen to McCloud. With the smuggled gun, McCloud plans to get rid of the mob once out at sea.

A cat-and-mouse chase on the small cruiser ensues, with McCloud picking off the henchmen one by one. Finally, when Rocco is the only one left, he bargains with McCloud, while hiding below deck, offering him all the money obtained from Ziggy. McCloud waits patiently for Rocco to show himself, then kills him when he does. Turning the boat around, McCloud heads back to Key Largo and the waiting Nora, who had been attracted to McCloud. The film falters somewhat in this rather melodramatic ending which sends the victorious McCloud cruising back to Nora through a blanket of sunlight; this sentimental conclusion detracts somewhat from the strength in the rest of the film. Beyond this flaw, however, the film reflects Huston's ability to find within another work elements relevant to his own ideas and to transform that work into a unique creation of his own.

Humphrey Bogart, playing more of a human being than many of his previous characterizations, gives a strong performance which lacks overdone heroics; instead, he moves the audience by his subtlety. Edward G. Robinson returns to the familiar role of the gangster who struts, leers, snarls, and gestures. Rocco is a different type of gangster, however; he is deeper, an almost bizarre deviation from the usual "tough guy." Claire Trevor gives a performance that makes one wonder why she was so rarely used to best advantage in films. Her part as a drunk and a moll is superlative, as she captures the pathos of her character, especially in the sequence in which she tries to recapture the days of her singing career. This particular scene has been credited as the reason why she won an Oscar for Best Supporting Actress.

Because most of the action takes place within the confines of the resort, Huston shot much of the picture at Warners' sound stages. He did travel to Florida for some location cinematography, however, and his cameraman, Karl Freund, gave the film its compact, moody sheen.

THE MALTESE FALCON

Released: 1941
Production: Hal B. Wallis for Warner Bros.
Direction: John Huston
Screenplay: John Huston; based on the novel of the same name by Dashiell Hammett
Cinematography: Arthur Edeson
Editing: Thomas Richards
Running time: 100 minutes

Principal characters:

Sam Spade	Humphrey Bogart
Brigid O'Shaughnessy	Mary Astor
Miles Archer	Jerome Cowan
Iva Archer	Gladys George
Kasper Gutman	Sydney Greenstreet
Joel Cairo	Peter Lorre
Wilmer Cook	Elisha Cook, Jr.
Effie Perine	Lee Patrick
Detective Lieutenant Dundy	Barton MacLane
Detective Tom Polhaus	Ward Bond
Captain Jacobi	Walter Huston

John Huston's film version of Dashiell Hammett's *The Maltese Falcon* was the third that Warner Bros. produced in a decade. The first version, directed by Roy del Ruth in 1931 (the year after the novel appeared), cast Ricardo Cortez as an overly charming Sam Spade and Bebe Daniels as Brigid; the second, a silly piece of bravura called *Satan Met a Lady*, directed by William Dieterle in 1936, featured Warren William and Bette Davis as Spade and Brigid. *The Maltese Falcon* was Huston's first directorial assignment, and although he has equaled his work in this film, he arguably has never surpassed it. Prior to directing, Huston had collaborated on screenplays for the earnest, socially conscious films typical of Warners' during the 1930's and early 1940's, such as Dieterle's *Juarez* (1939), Raoul Walsh's *High Sierra* (1941), and Howard Hawks's *Sergeant York* (1941). But Hammett's novel furnished a cynical realism combined with a restrained moral sensitivity that proved even more suited to Huston's talents. As screenwriter-director he understood the advantages of adhering closely to Hammett's plot and preserving his unsentimental depiction of Spade. The film received good notices and was nominated for the Best Picture Academy Award, but the 1941 award went to John Ford's *How Green Was My Valley*.

The Maltese Falcon has exercised an impressive influence on cinema. If it did not initiate the *film noir*, then certainly it presaged the cycle. In turn, it redefined the strategies of the private-detective film or "thriller," previously the account of a puzzle unraveled by an eccentric or debonair sleuth (realized most notably by William Powell as Philo Vance and Nick Charles) in which evil becomes simply an aberration, an annoyance that can provide an entertaining challenge. With *The Maltese Falcon*, Huston adds to the genre not only an emphasis on motivation and characterization—Spade, while tainted, evidences a strong moral awareness—but a preoccupation with the evil in human nature and the way it corrupts everything it touches.

Compared with most subsequent private-detective films, *The Maltese Falcon* appears markedly subdued, even muted. Yet the difference only in part results from increasingly relaxed censorship standards. The strength of the story rests in the web of interactions among the characters: the posturings and deceptions, along with a pervasive greed, that finally lead to collective collapse. In the beginning, Brigid O'Shaughnessy (Mary Astor) comes to Sam Spade (Humphrey Bogart) and Miles Archer (Jerome Cowan) in their office ostensibly for help in finding her sister, whereas she actually is looking for a means of ridding herself of her partner, Thursby (who never appears in the film). Soon, both Archer and Thursby are murdered, and Spade allies himself with Brigid, Joel Cairo (Peter Lorre), and Kasper Gutman (Sydney Greenstreet) and his companion Wilmer Cook (Elisha Cook, Jr.) in search of a black statuette.

In his second interview with the mysterious fat man Gutman, Spade at last learns the origin and value of the statuette: a golden, jewel-encrusted falcon sent by the Knights of Rhodes to Emperor Charles V of Spain in 1539 in appreciation for his granting them the island of Malta. Brigid continues to tell Spade conflicting accounts of her actual involvement in the affair, while Gutman and the others leave him drugged and unconscious in a hotel room when they believe him no longer necessary to their plans. Spade, however, gets the statuette first. He makes a bargain with Gutman for the statuette, but it turns out to be a fake, a piece of lead. The real Maltese Falcon presumably remains in Istanbul. When Gutman, Cairo, and Wilmer depart, Spade reports them to the police; and then Brigid, through Spade's insistence, admits to him that she in fact murdered his partner Archer.

Thus, the major characters, with the exception of Spade, are bound together by a determined quest for riches. Brigid, Cairo, Gutman, and Wilmer prove themselves murderers, or conspirators in murder, because of the falcon. Brigid kills Archer in order to incriminate Thursby; and Wilmer kills both Thursby and Captain Jacobi (Walter Huston), who brings the falcon to Spade's office only to die clutching it in his arms. For Gutman, moreover, under whose orders Wilmer has acted, the quest translates into obsession. Mesmerized by the dream of possessing the Maltese Falcon, he has devoted seventeen years to the search for this thing that is in part grail, in part will-o'-the-wisp. In the end he decides to spend yet another year on the quest by going to Istanbul, "an additional expenditure in time," he remarks philosophically, "of only five and fifteen-seventeenth percent."

For Spade the quest becomes twofold. He views the Maltese Falcon with a certain detachment. Though he knows the value in human lives the others put on it, he seems never fully to believe Gutman's reassurances about great profits for all. In his bargain with Gutman he settles for ten thousand dollars. On the other hand, Spade quietly demonstrates throughout the action, then articulates plainly at the end, a professional integrity with broad social responsibilities: Archer's killer must be brought to justice. "When a man's partner is killed," he tells Brigid resolutely, "he's supposed to do something about it." He defines the issue as a question of professional ethics, of that code by which he must abide in spite of his own feelings. It would be "bad for every detective everywhere" were he to let Brigid go unpunished for Archer's murder, even though he loves her and had little regard for his ex-partner.

By turning Gutman, Wilmer, and Cairo over to the police Spade fulfills an equally important part of his code—his commitment to protect society by cleansing it of the elements that pollute it. Spade moves beyond the immediate issues of the Maltese Falcon and Archer's murderer to an idealistic search for justice. From the beginning, Spade's quest has entailed a metaphorical journey through darkness, a descent into the nether world of crime and decadence. Spade moves easily within this world, undistinguishable in manner and appearance from the criminals he deals with there. The police, knowing of his affair with Archer's wife (Gladys George), suspect him of having killed Archer. Brigid, Cairo, and Gutman (who frankly admires Spade) trust him enough to hire him, or trust their own intuitions about his readiness to be involved in illegal activities that could include murder, provided the money is right. His secretary (Lee Patrick) alone understands that Spade is a man of convictions, dedicated to uncovering the truth and restoring order.

Throughout, Spade remains outside the evil of his antagonists and their environment, implicitly identifying himself with the values of the normal world. He slaps Cairo around with the disgust of one determinedly antihomosexual; several times he humiliates Wilmer in front of others, reducing him to a hollow adolescent trying hard not to be absurd in the adult world, although he realizes that Wilmer could well kill him; he hands the thousand dollars Gutman had given him over to the police for evidence and then lies by telling them it was a bribe, when he had in fact legitimately earned it, regardless of its source. And too late Brigid learns that Spade is not as crooked as people suppose—that sort of talk, he reminds her, is simply "good for business." He shows her almost the same disdain he now has for Archer's widow. He can love Brigid and still distrust her, for how does he know that she would not someday kill him? He plays the sucker for no one.

Huston surrounds the characters with cluttered, harshly lighted interiors, restricting the physical action mainly to Spade's sardonic triumphs over Cairo and Wilmer. He uses low-angle shots to emphasize Gutman's menacing bulk, as well as to project the sneering viciousness of which Spade is capable. He indirectly makes clear Spade's affairs with Archer's wife and with Brigid, as well as the homosexual relationships within Gutman's entourage. Huston lets the audience examine his characters thoroughly, in a sense microscopically. The characterizations themselves are a triumph in casting. Bogart's Spade confronts greed and human weakness with a tarnished yet lively sense of moral responsiveness. Astor as Brigid sustains a fluttery, transparently bogus innocence (Huston had her run around the set several times before a take to ensure her off-balance, quick-breathing delivery). Greenstreet's Gutman is a prissy, waistcoated pansy whose cultured background and affected banter only momentarily conceal his disregard for anything that keeps him from the Maltese Falcon. Lorre's effeminate, gardenia-scented Cairo combines whining and sulking with outbursts of hysteria, while Cook's Wilmer is a ludicrous psychopath, a caricature of the strutting, baby-faced killers who populate gangster films of the 1930's.

The closing sequences of the film consist largely of portraits of defeat and frustration. Gutman, Cairo, and Wilmer are reported to be in jail; Detective Lieutenant Dundy (Barton MacLane) is openly disappointed that Spade did not kill Archer. Spade has turned Brigid over to the police after snidely reassuring her that he will be waiting when she gets out or, if they hang her, that he will always remember her. He watches as the steel gate and the opaque glass door of the elevator close on her motionless, tear-stained face, as her shadow disappears down the shaft. Spade is part romantic figure and part fragmented man, suspicious and perhaps a trifle paranoid. But he upholds his code, not to his own advantage, then affirms some belief in human aspirations. The worthless Maltese Falcon, he tells his friend Detective Sergeant Polhaus (Ward Bond), is "the stuff that dreams are made of." Presumably not all dreams are bad.

THE MAN WHO WOULD BE KING

Released: 1975
Production: John Foreman for Allied Artists; released by Columbia
Direction: John Huston
Screenplay: John Huston and Gladys Hill; based on the short story of the
    same name by Rudyard Kipling
Cinematography: Oswald Morris
Editing: Russell Lloyd
Art direction: Alexander Trauner
Costume design: Edith Head
Music: Maurice Jarre
Running time: 132 minutes

    Principal characters:
        Daniel Dravot .... Sean Connery
        Peachy Carnehan .... Michael Caine
        Rudyard Kipling .... Christopher Plummer
        Billy Fish .... Saeed Jaffrey
        Kafu-Selim .... Karroum Ben Bouih
        District Commissioner ....Jack May
        Roxanne .... Shakira Caine

    This rousing, old-fashioned adventure tale that director John Huston had wanted to make for almost twenty years was finally filmed in 1975 and greeted with almost unanimous critical acclaim. In 1956, Huston first envisioned filming Rudyard Kipling's yarn of two British former army sergeants who decide to travel from India to remote and primitive Kafiristan in search of wealth and power. Huston wanted Humphrey Bogart, an actor he thought would be richly suited for the role of Peachy Carnehan, to play the more down-to-earth and realistic of the two ingenious heroes. The team of Huston and Bogart had enjoyed great success in previous films such as *The Maltese Falcon* (1941), *The African Queen* (1951), and *Key Largo* (1948). With the added attraction of Clark Gable in the role of the daring, courageous Daniel Dravot, Huston thought he had a hit that could not miss, either financially or critically.

    These early plans were foiled when Humphrey Bogart was stricken with cancer and died in January, 1957. Huston continued working on other projects but never gave up the idea of filming what would eventually become one of his pet projects and one of the few critical successes of his twilight years.

    In the early 1960's, Richard Burton and Marlon Brando were mentioned as costars for a reactivated *The Man Who Would Be King*. Work on the film was postponed until 1967 to await Burton's availability. However, this attempt also fell through and was only revitalized when Huston showed the script to producer John Foreman, who thought it might make a good starring vehicle for Paul Newman. Newman read the script, admired it, but decided it was not for him. Finally, producer Foreman sent the script to Sean Connery and Michael Caine. At last, Kipling's likable rough rogues had their cinematic counterparts.

The final version of the script by Huston and his longtime associate Gladys Hill admirably transfers the spirit of Kipling's yarn to the screen and amplifies some of his literary devices. In the 1880's, Kipling (Christopher Plummer), a young newspaper editor working in Lahore, India, encounters Daniel Dravot (Sean Connery) and Peachy Carnehan (Michael Caine), two rascally and footloose soldiers of fortune. Soon realizing that all are fellow Masons, Daniel and Peachy confide in the somewhat straitlaced young journalist. They tell of their plans to journey through Afghanistan to a primitive, remote country called Kafiristan where they plan to set themselves up as kings. Having been soldiers in India, Daniel and Peachy feel that by gaining the confidence of one of the country's many warring tribes and training its members to vanquish their rival tribes, they can soon take over Kafiristan and avail themselves of the country's fabled wealth. Kipling listens in total disbelief and tries to discourage the pair of plucky opportunists by reminding them of the incredible harshness of the journey; they will in all probability never even reach Kafiristan. Not to be dissuaded, the two pore over maps in Kipling's office, make a contract not to touch liquor or women until the adventure is over, and soon set out on their way with appropriate disguises, twenty rifles, and a Masonic fob given to Daniel by Kipling.

Ambushes and harsh elements produce many adventures on the journey until Daniel and Peachy come to the point of no return. High in the Himalayas, they come to a gorge that they cannot cross. The likable humor of the men comes across as they sit waiting to freeze to death, all the while reminiscing in a jovial spirit of camaraderie. Amazingly, their raucous laughter causes an avalanche that fills in the once unpassable gorge; after this stroke of luck, the men quickly reach the villages of Kafiristan where, with the help of a former Gurkha soldier whom they name Billy Fish (Saeed Jaffrey), they begin to work on their dream. Many battles follow as the newly trained natives conquer rival tribe after rival tribe. Finally, another stroke of luck proves to the priests and people that Daniel is worthy to be their king. An arrow that strikes Daniel hits a bandolier beneath his shirt, and all who see the incident believe that Daniel must be a god to be so wounded and not suffer. More good luck befalls the heroes when the people of Kafiristan see the Masonic medal worn by Daniel. A similar medal was worn by the first Western conqueror of Kafiristan, Alexander the Great, and it has now become a powerful religious symbol.

Thus far in the story, the rowdy protagonists have met with only good luck, and they seem to be nearing the fulfillment of their ambitions. However, the last half of the story dramatically portrays Kipling's and Huston's shared theme of the tragic results of man's pride and avarice.

Daniel, now confirmed as King and God of Kafiristan (Peachy being his assistant), has absolute control over the priceless treasure of jewels and gold left by Alexander the Great. A combination of the unbelievability of such riches and the heady egotism of total power begins to work on Daniel until he comes to believe himself a god and a direct descendant of Alexander. Full of pride, Daniel does not fear breaking the no-liquor and no-women contract he and Peachy had made at the adventure's inception, so, to perpetuate his royal line, he decides to take a local girl as wife and queen. The girl Roxanne (Shakira Caine) has the same name as Alexander's wife. Peachy, meanwhile, sees the danger in Daniel's delusions and would like to grab some of the riches that had been the original goal and leave Kafiristan while they are still able to do so.

Not blinded by pride as is Daniel, Peachy realizes that their secure position rests on the people's belief in Daniel's invincibility. He tries to warn Daniel of the dire consequences if the priests and subjects ever found out the truth, but Daniel will not heed his loyal friend's warning or take seriously the rumblings of the people who do not think their god should marry in such a fashion. Then at the wedding ceremony, the frightened bride bites her new husband on the cheek and draws his blood. The horrified crowd of onlookers no longer see an invincible god, but an ordinary mortal. What earlier were murmurings of doubt from the crowd now swell into hostile, murderous shouts. Daniel, knowing the grand adventure is over, exhorts Peachy and Billy Fish to save themselves and leave him to his fate. But the ever-loyal Carnehan and Billy Fish remain to fight the lost battle. Even as he prepares to do battle, Peachy, the ever-worldly opportunist, unsuccessfully tries to carry away some of the fabulous treasure. Billy Fish, in the spirit of Gunga Din, is killed while bravely trying to stave off the onrushing crowd of attackers. Daniel is chased onto a bridge by his former subjects. Whereas the filling up of the gorge by the laughter-induced avalanche had been an early sign of hope and good luck, the gorge under this bridge turns out to be Daniel's last stand. His luck has run out, destroyed by his greed and lust. As Peachy watches and later recounts to Kipling, Daniel plummets from the bridge, "turning round and round and round . . . for he took half an hour to fall till he struck the water, and I could see his body caught on a rock with the gold crown close beside."

Although Peachy is captured by the berserk natives of Kafiristan, he survives their tortures and, penniless, makes his way back to India where he visits an astounded Kipling; it is Kipling to whom an incredibly aged and crippled Peachy recounts the rise and fall of Daniel and Peachy. Having struggled through and endured an arduous journey back, Peachy is prepared to die. The only task remaining is to tell Kipling the tale and to show the horrified editor (and viewers) the dried head of Daniel Dravot still wearing its golden crown.

The appeal in this tale of two scoundrels is complex and yet simple. First, there is that spirit of adventure, of longing for the unknown, and of conquering new worlds that remains in most of us even after we outgrow our childhood dreams. Peachy and the dreamer Daniel were not after treasure alone; they also needed the thrill of the conquest to test themselves as men. Connery and Caine, especially early in the film, display a charm and easiness in their roles that is truly infectious. Peachy and Daniel, by virtue of their Masonic connections and their many shared adventures, are as close as any brothers. The portrayal of their loyalty and friendship is one of the film's strengths. Throughout their triumphs and disasters, they maintain this moving relationship. Another excellent performance that lends much to the film is that of Christopher Plummer as Kipling; his restraint balances the two exuberant performances of Connery and Caine.

Thematically, Huston continues his ironic treatment of man's avarice. Critics pointed out the similarities between Peachy's sack of treasures sliding down a mountain top and the blown away gold dust in *The Treasure of the Sierra Madre* (1948) as well as the lost paper money in *The Asphalt Jungle* (1950). Those who loot and plunder without any respect for the people and the land will always pay the price in Huston's world.

Oswald Morris, Huston's favorite cinematographer, shot the film in earthy subdued tones of rust and brown mostly on location in Morocco. The photography is done in a very straightforward manner. Humor, dialogue, and characterization are stressed, rather than the vastness or grandeur of the romance.

This film that Huston waited so long to make shows the love of the director for his material. The screenplay by Huston and Gladys Hill was honored with an Academy Award nomination; other nominations went to Alexander Trauner for Art Direction and Russell Lloyd for Editing. In the sly but warm humor of its protagonists and the exciting, romantic aspects of the tale itself, Huston and his coworkers have created a rousing yet moral tale of adventure and ambition.

THE MISFITS

Released: 1961
Production: Frank E. Taylor for Seven Arts Productions; released by United
 Artists
Direction: John Huston
Screenplay: Arthur Miller; based on his novelette of the same name
Cinematography: Russell Metty
Editing: George Tomasini
Running time: 124 minutes

> *Principal characters:*
> Gay Langland .... Clark Gable
> Roslyn Taber .... Marilyn Monroe
> Perce Howland .... Montgomery Clift
> Isabelle Steers .... Thelma Ritter
> Guido .... Eli Wallach

The story line for *The Misfits* has its basis in fact. When playwright Arthur
Miller was staying in Nevada, where he was divorcing his first wife, he met
a group of contemporary cowboys who captured wild horses to be used for
dog food. Intrigued by these throwbacks to another era, Miller wrote a
novelette entitled *The Misfits* which appeared in *Esquire* magazine in 1957.
By the time *The Misfits* came to the screen in 1961, Miller's screenplay, his
first, included a role written for Marilyn Monroe—Miller's wife at the time
of the filming.

The Misfits has the distinction of bringing together three legendary performers—Clark Gable, Marilyn Monroe, and Montgomery Clift—under the
direction of the equally colorful John Huston. Filming was marked by a string
of well-publicized problems, including persistent rumors of a shaky Monroe-
Miller marriage. Monroe's frequent inability to remember her lines, as well
as her habitual tardiness to the set, caused inconveniences. The film's Nevada
locations, where temperatures sometimes climbed to 110 degrees, also
brought discomfort. Once completed, *The Misfits* continued to generate publicity, for mostly sad reasons. Shortly after filming, Gable died of a heart
attack; the picture is also the last completed work of both Monroe and Thelma
Ritter. Also, after filming, Clift became ill with cataracts while working on
Huston's *Freud* (1962).

The Misfits is a thought-provoking film in terms of its thematic content,
which explores rugged individuality against the changing scope of the West.
Loneliness and the inability to communicate underline this contemporary
Western's study of shifting relationships. The film opens in Reno, Nevada,
famed at the time for tourism and divorce. Roslyn Taber (Marilyn Monroe),
who has just divorced her husband, is befriended by her landlady, Isabelle

Steers (Thelma Ritter), whose rentals cater to women heading for divorce court. Through Isabelle, Roslyn meets Guido (Eli Wallach), an ex-mechanic. When Guido introduces Roslyn to his mustanger buddy, Gay Langland (Clark Gable), the chemistry between Roslyn and Gay is immediate.

The four leave the city for a night of partying at Guido's half-finished house in the desert. Only Isabelle and Guido return to Reno, Roslyn and Gay having decided to remain in the desert sharing the house. Each is wary of a long-term emotional commitment. Roslyn, fresh from her divorce, is afraid to love again so soon, and Gay shirks responsibility. Still, the love they feel for each other grows, and as it does, the desert house begins to take on a look of completion.

When Gay, Guido, and rodeo rider Perce (Montgomery Clift) team to round-up some "misfits" (horses that are too small to ride), Roslyn comes along. The film has its climax after Roslyn learns the captured horses are to be slaughtered and used for dog food. The mustanging sequence, which comprises the final third of the film, gives *The Misfits* its strongest, most stirring moments; but the scenes that precede it are important in understanding the film's introspective relationships.

It is Isabelle, whose character is abandoned as the story unfolds, who earlier had tabbed cowboys "the last real men." Actually, the three cowboys in *The Misfits* are anachronisms; they are misfits, the last romantics, who are out of place in their time. The three cowboys are also adrift in their personal lives; each is alienated from his family. Gay's first failed marriage and his children are never explained; his love for his children is exposed, however, when he misses a meeting with them and runs into the street drunk, crying and calling their names. His breakdown is brief, however; Gay is a leader, proud and assertive, who refuses to be ashamed for his actions.

Guido's marriage also remains cloudy. We know he is a widower who has been aimless since his wife died in childbirth. A wanderer, he is haunted by his memories of the war, in which he was a pilot, and he avoids returning home to the half-finished house he was building for his wife. Perce, also a drifter, defies death by riding the rodeo circuit. After one injury, he puts in a call to his mother, who he feels betrayed him by marrying his stepfather. Angered after the phone call, he sets out for another dangerous ride.

By their own decision, the three cowboys are outside of society's mainstream; but after meeting Roslyn, their lives have renewed meaning. They are captivated by her spontaneity and her almost childlike fascination with life. Each of them also wants her. It is if as Guido and Perce are waiting Gay out, and Roslyn, in the meantime, returns the affections of Guido and Perce with motherly love. While Roslyn has an earth-mother quality, she is also strongly sensual, as demonstrated in the scene in which she dances in the bar, much to the delight of the cowboys. In another scene she displays her paddle-ball talents while her body sways, keeping rhythm to the springing ball.

Roslyn is not callous or unable to feel; she is humanistic and emotional and has not yet given up on life.

The film's tenuous relationships are probably best underlined by Isabelle. At one point, she recognizes her former husband with his new wife. Unaffected, she invites them to drop by for a visit. Unlike the cowboys, who cannot come to grips with their failed family associations, Isabelle is a weather-beaten survivor.

Often rhetorical in tone, *The Misfits* speaks for the independent, assertive spirit which helped to carve its niche in the West. "I don't want nobody makin' up my mind for me—that's all," insists Gay. It is that strong will which comes up against Roslyn's gentle spirit during the rousing, breathtakingly photographed mustanging sequence. Guido herds the horses into sight with his plane; then, with Roslyn at his side, he mans the truck while Gay and Perce lasso the animals—a stallion, four mares, and a colt—all thundering across the hot, endless salt flats.

Horrified by what she sees, Roslyn jumps from the cab. Running at the cowboys, she screams, "Freedom! You and your God's country . . . ," but the cowboys continue battling the horses, which rear up, fight, and even drag the men. When Perce is finally broken down by Roslyn's pleas, he defies Gay and sets the captured horses free. Angered that his domination has been broken, Gay singlehandedly pursues the lead stallion, finally capturing and subduing it after a long, weary battle. Once Gay has made his point, he sets the animal free.

Through the mustanging sequence, each character comes away with a better understanding of himself. Guido and Perce go their separate ways, but Gay and Roslyn and their unborn child will try to make a go of it together. As the two head for home, Roslyn wonders, "How do you find the way in the dark?" Gay's answer is, "Head for the big star up ahead." His response emphasizes a new hope and a willingness to try, and his optimism is in contrast to Guido's earlier observation that by the time light from a star reaches earth, the star may no longer be there.

With a budget of $4,000,000, *The Misfits*, which was filmed in continuity, garnered the reputation at the time of its release of being the most expensive film ever made in black-and-white. Huston was in the midst of a prolific period; he had just completed *The Unforgiven* (1960) and would next make *Freud* (1962) with Clift in the starring role. *The Misfits* marked the first time in eight years that Huston had filmed in the United States. Though the film generated box-office interest, especially in the light of Gable's last performance, it was met with mixed reviews and reactions at the time of its release.

As Gay, Clark Gable at fifty-nine strikes a rugged stance in a role that seems streamlined to suit his size and legend. Marilyn Monroe is also effective in this, her twenty-eighth film, which gave her the only role written especially for her (there were many parallels between Roslyn's character and Monroe).

The film allowed her to reach into new dramatic pockets, and also reunited her with Huston, with whom she had worked eleven years earlier, in a minor role, in *The Asphalt Jungle* (1950). Although by 1961 she was at the wane of her career, she radiates a compelling beauty throughout *The Misfits*. Working with a more thinly etched character, Montgomery Clift is nonetheless in control, as are Thelma Ritter and Eli Wallach. An Alex North score served to further enhance the film.

With its focus on people who are unable to communicate and relationships that founder, *The Misfits* has an aura of being perhaps a decade ahead of its time. Although the film did not earn any Academy Award nominations, it nonetheless remains an intense study of loneliness, friendship, and love. The coming-together of three screen giants, the presence of the commanding Huston, and the backdrop of the changing West continue to distinguish *The Misfits*.

MOULIN ROUGE

Released: 1952
Production: Romulus Productions for United Artists
Direction: John Huston
Screenplay: Anthony Veiller and John Huston; based on the novel of the same name by Pierre La Mure
Cinematography: Oswald Morris
Editing: Ralph Kemplin
Art direction: Paul Sheriff (AA)
Set decoration: Marcel Vertes (AA)
Costume design: Marcel Vertes (AA)
Running time: 118 minutes

Principal characters:

Toulouse-Lautrec/Comte de Toulouse-Lautrec	José Ferrer
Marie Charlet	Colette Marchand
Myriamme	Suzanne Flon
Jane Avril	Zsa Zsa Gabor
La Goulue	Katherine Kath
Countess de Toulouse-Lautrec	Claude Nollier
Patou	Georges Lannes

"José Ferrer electrifies the screen . . . ," raved *Motion Picture Daily* in a review of Ferrer's portrayal of Count Henri de Toulouse-Lautrec in John Huston's *Moulin Rouge*. The film received seven Academy Award nominations in 1953, for Best Picture, Best Actor (José Ferrer), Best Supporting Actress (Colette Marchand), Cinematography (Oswald Morris), Editing (Ralph Kemplin), Costumes, and Art Direction, with Marcel Vertes receiving the award for Costumes and Paul Sheriff for Art Direction. Lautrec's unconventional, intense, and dramatic life made ideal subject matter for John Huston and Anthony Veiller's screenplay, which they based on Pierre La Mure's fictionalized biography of the same name. Both Ferrer and Huston had been great admirers of Lautrec, and they familiarized themselves intimately with the details of the artist's tragic life. Ferrer had obtained an option on the novel, intending to produce, direct, and cowrite a biographical play about the dwarfish painter. Ferrer originally had no intention of playing Lautrec in his own production, but he ultimately went on to receive the highest praise for his performance in Huston's film. He had won the Academy Award for Best Actor for his portrayal of Cyrano de Bergerac in Richard Brooks's film of the same name in 1950, and many critics saw his performance as Toulouse-Lautrec as even more powerful. John Chapman of the *New York*

News called Ferrer the ". . . ablest actor in America" and found his instinctual interpretation of Lautrec "unerring."

Extensive research was undertaken during the film's preparatory period. The film employed both authentic Parisian settings as well as an Academy Award-winning "Moulin Rouge" set, designed by art director Paul Sheriff, which was the largest of its kind ever erected in a European studio. Ferrer played the dual role of Henri de Toulouse-Lautrec and Lautrec's father. Lautrec was born in 1864 to one of the best of French families. Afflicted early with a disease that causes brittle bones, Lautrec fell down the stairs as a child, and his broken legs never mended properly, remaining childlike as the rest of his body grew into fully developed manhood and giving him the appearance of a dwarf. As a result, the life of an aristocratic gentleman was denied him; he died at the age of thirty-seven in 1901 of unhappiness and absinthe. Lautrec lived a feverish life trying to forget his pain and deformity in liquor, which, combined with his periods of deep depression and hot temper, caused him to spend time in a madhouse; he embraced a bohemian way of life, frequenting the lower depths of Paris. His most precious avenue of escape, however, was his artistic talent, which eventually afforded him the honor of being the first artist to have a show in the Louvre during his lifetime. Proving that in art the ugly can be beautiful, he left a vivid record of his own unique Paris—characterizations of the misfits, the harlots, the disfigured, the defeated and forgotton. His most famous paintings were of his favorite cafe— The Moulin Rouge—and its inhabitants.

José Ferrer achieved a startling physical likeness to Lautrec; with bulbous nose, thickened lips, bushy beard, and bowler hat, Ferrer became a near double of the homely, aristocratic dwarf. The only real difficulty was reducing Ferrer's five-foot, eleven-inch, height to Lautrec's four-foot, seven-inch, stature. To create the illusion of smallness, Ferrer relaxed his leg muscles and bent his knees for the medium shots and close-ups, which is how most of the picture is filmed. For several sequences, however, his legs were painfully strapped behind his knees, in the manner of Lon Chaney, and Ferrer walked on his knees, standing in little boots, for the close-ups; an actual dwarf was used for long shots.

Ferrer and Huston came up with a radically different concept of Lautrec's character than that of the novel, which only tended to show the artist in the romantic atmosphere of sin and poverty. Ferrer saw the Lautrec character as a ". . . gentleman who was bright, witty, and charming—more capable of beguiling women than many of the more handsome and physically perfect men of his day." Ferrer does not capitalize on Lautrec's infirmity; he uses it only as an incident in the character's life rather than as his complete motivation. Lautrec is portrayed as masterful, sensitive, witty, and dignified, and Ferrer retains this dignity even when projecting the dark moods, sarcasm, periods of self-pity, and unhappiness of the character. Historically, Lautrec was personally remembered in France as being witty, friendly, and gregarious. He was never a starving artist, and he enjoyed spending his money as star boarder in many Parisian brothels. Capitalizing on his deformity and his love of travesty, he frequently appeared at gala affairs as a diminutive, self-effacing aesthetic or a Japanese dignitary, and he reveled at carnival time, appearing in outlandish costumes and riding through the streets of Paris on a float. He loved being photographed and painted in women's clothes, as a clown, or whatever suited his fancy at the moment; these more Rabelaisian aspects of Lautrec's life and personality are unfortunately absent from Ferrer's characterization.

The outstanding feature of this film is the evocation of the historic period by means of costumes and cinematography. Utilizing *Life* photographer Eliot Elisofon as special color consultant, Oswald Morris rendered the most imaginative use of color cinematography seen in years. Huston attempted to capture much of the quality of Lautrec's own work, and he succeeded with the help of filters and blue-green backgrounds splashed with burnt orange, yellow, and pink. Huston felt that Technicolor appeared too sharp in its contrasts, so he remedied this situation by sometimes using a rainbow of spotlights in the manner of paint on an artist's palette to tint each shadow and highlight. As the audience watches Can-Can dancers in their swirl of black silk stockings and white petticoats and sees the other colorful entertainers of the Moulin Rouge shot with this photographic technique, it receives the impression that a Lautrec painting has come to life. Huston's idea was to make the film "look as though Lautrec directed it himself."

Huston's final choices for the other leading roles were Colette Marchand, the talented French ballerina, playing Marie Charlet, the prostitute who almost drove Lautrec to suicide; Suzanne Flon, a French actress, as Myriamme, the perceptive, understanding model whom Lautrec loved; Zsa Zsa Gabor as Jane Avril, the beautiful singer, one of Lautrec's favorite subjects from the Moulin Rouge who frankly credited her success to the posters Lautrec drew of her (which were not always flattering); Katherine Kath as La Goulue, the tigerish, red-headed dancer; and Claude Nollier as Lautrec's gentle mother.

Set against the background of Paris in the 1880's, the film opens in the fabulous Moulin Rouge with Lautrec sitting at a table sketching the Can-Can dancers. The audience is introduced to several of the main characters as he greets his friends of the colorful café: La Goulue, the most famous of the dancers, the bartender, the proprietor, and Jane Avril, the beautiful singer whose infatuation with romance and physical beauty leads her into a succession of meaningless affairs. The evening comes to an end, and Lautrec wanders off down the cobblestone streets. He recalls the days before the accident when he was a healthy, normal child, adored by his mother the Countess and held in high expectation by his father (José Ferrer), a nobleman who was required only to practice the pleasures of his social class. Lautrec spent much time sketching and satirizing situations around him, but after his tragic fall, he laid motionless in bed with only his mother to console him. He bitterly recalls his childhood sweetheart who turned from him in disgust when they were grown and he proposed marriage.

The sound of running heels jars Lautrec back to the present as a girl runs up to him and begs him to say that he is her companion. Lautrec protects the streetwalker, Marie Charlet (Colette Marchand), from the plainclothesman Patou (Georges Lannes) and consents to let her spend the night when they arrive at his home. Inside the studio, Marie quickly takes over, reveling in the luxury of her first bath in a real bathtub and asking him matter-of-factly about his legs. From this introduction, there evolves a tempestuous love affair between them. Marie is fond of debasing Lautrec at every opportunity: she makes him pay her to pose for him even though he supports her and buys her everything she wants. As he becomes more infatuated with her, it becomes easier for her to hurt and torment him. His hours without her Lautrec spends drinking. One night he takes her to an elegant restaurant where she behaves abominably and leaves him. He tries to forget her but eventually goes looking for her, only to find her unkempt and in a drunken stupor at the Bon Vivant, a sleazy café. Lautrec begs her to come back but, in front of everyone, she reveals the humiliating truth that she has lived with Lautrec to support her lover, a pimp who appears at the table and tries to smooth over her shrewish confessions. With her raucous laugh still ringing in his ears, Lautrec returns home, closes the windows, turns on the gas jets, and begins to paint feverishly; but then, becoming very enthralled in his work and beginning to be annoyed by the feeling of perspiration and faintness, he opens the windows and continues to paint.

Rejected by Marie, he now turns to the one place where he feels the happiest, the Moulin Rouge where Jane Avril sings. She is more beautiful than ever and equally insincere, but so stunning that Lautrec paints her. Then he begins making posters for the Moulin Rouge in collaboration with the noted lithographer Pere Cotelle. Lautrec's poster of La Goulue, another entertainer of the café, advertising the rowdy night club in Montmartre, jolted Paris to attention and made Lautrec and the Moulin Rouge famous overnight. Patou comes to ask him to paint a portrait of his daughter, and Lautrec agrees in return for one favor from the policeman—that he may buy a pushcart license for Marie Charlet.

Lautrec's father violently disapproves of his son's ambitions as an artist as well as his life style, but Lautrec, reinforced by success, resists his father's will, thus creating a final breach between them. Lautrec, however, no longer cares; he has found himself artistically, and is now the hero of the Moulin Rouge, which is filled to capacity each night because of Lautrec's fame. With a bottle always at his side, Lautrec paints with feverish intensity, trying to exclude any other emotional needs, until he meets Myriamme (Suzanne Flon), a model who truly comes to love Lautrec. Lautrec, however, is careful never to let himself be hurt again, and keeps their arrangement cool and impersonal, believing that she cannot possibly really love him. As he becomes more nervous, jealous, and suspicious, he begins to lose control and inflicts such verbal abuse on her that Myriamme finally makes the decision to marry a handsome and wealthy man who has long been her admirer. She sends the news to Lautrec in a letter. When he reads it, he considers that his life is over. He no longer finds satisfaction in his work, and his drinking begins to claim his health. At the bar where he drinks absinthe every night, he completely loses control, and Patou arrives to take him home. Once home and planning to call Lautrec's mother, Patou is interrupted by a scream as Lautrec, swaying unsteadily at the top of his staircase, accidentally plunges headfirst down the steps.

At the Lautrec's chateau, a robed Priest stands beside the dying Henri de Toulouse-Lautrec. His father is also present, begging his son's forgiveness and humbly telling him the wonderful news that he has become the first artist to be honored with a collection in the Louvre while still alive. Lautrec indicates his recognition of the statement with a smile and turns his head towards the door where an imaginary closing sequence begins. In dances Chocolat, La Goulue, Valentine Dessossee, her partner Aicha, and the beautiful Jane Avril, who speaks for all his cherished friends from the Moulin Rouge as she bids adieu to "the wonderful little monster." A blare of music is heard and Can-Can girls—their jeweled garters glittering amongst their lace petticoats and black mesh stockings—flash onto the screen, the familiar scene radiating through Henri de Toulouse-Lautrec's fading memory.

Moulin Rouge is an exuberant, distinguished, and visually striking re-creation of an artist and an era. Huston's story and direction suggest that everybody is a cripple in the sense that everyone is influenced by the consciousness of some defect in themselves.

THE TREASURE OF THE SIERRA MADRE

Released: 1948
Production: Henry Blanke for Warner Bros.
Direction: John Huston (AA)
Screenplay: John Huston (AA); based on the novel of the same name by B. Traven
Cinematography: Ted McCord
Editing: Owen Marks
Art direction: John Hughes
Sound: Robert B. Lee
Music direction: Leo F. Forbstein
Music: Max Steiner
Running time: 126 minutes

Principal characters:
Fred C. Dobbs .... Humphrey Bogart
Howard .... Walter Huston
Curtin .... Tim Holt
Cody .... Bruce Bennett
McCormick .... Barton MacLane
Gold Hat .... Alfonso Bedoya

The Treasure of the Sierra Madre is a powerful film, which, although it can take its place unblushingly among the best that Hollywood has made, is nevertheless a difficult movie to classify. At the time of its release in 1948, some critics labeled it a masculine adventure and some a Western, while a number of trade publications reported that in more than a few instances audiences had responded to it as a comedy. John Huston, who wrote the screenplay and directed the film, adapted it from a novel by the mysterious author B. Traven. As a written piece, it was a sardonic and intensely realistic fable masquerading under the guise of an adventure story. Huston's screen adaptation transformed it into a bitingly cynical character study dealing with the corrosive effect of greed on a trio of down-and-out prospecting bums.

During the writing of the script for *The Treasure of the Sierra Madre*, Huston was in constant correspondence with its illusive and mysterious author. Novelist Traven had an enormous following in Europe, but little was known of him except that he had lived invisibly somewhere in Mexico for many years. Traven made numerous suggestions for the film treatment that were so intelligent and knowledgeable that Huston was fascinated and wanted to meet him. One day in the Hotel Reforma in Mexico City, Huston was confronted by a thin little man who presented his card. He was Hal Croves, a translator who claimed to be Traven's old friend and to know the author better than Traven himself did. Huston hired him at $150 a week as technical adviser for the film. By the time Croves had done his job and disappeared, the director was almost certain that the uneasy little man was indeed Traven himself.

Set in Mexico in 1920, the riveting story concerns three dirty, unshaven, penniless Americans: Fred C. Dobbs (Humphrey Bogart), the most fanatic and avaricious of the trio; Curtin (Tim Holt), who is relatively stable and decent; and Howard (Walter Huston), the philosophical old-timer who is the most experienced of the group. After Dobbs wins some money in a lottery, the three pool their limited resources, leave their Tampico flophouse, and head toward the Sierra Madre Mountains in search of gold. Despite old Howard's warnings of what the lust for gold can do to a man's soul, Dobbs and Curtin dismiss the notion of any possible dangerous consequences. In the midst of the hostile environment of the mountainous jungles, however, the surface friendship of the three men begins slowly to crumble. When they do uncover a gold field and strike it rich in the Mexican wilderness, distrust and suspicion erupt; rather than setting up a common treasury, each character hides his own share of the gold in greedy self-preservation. In the tension of the dark and lonely nights, emotions become more and more strained; Dobbs begins to accuse the others of trying to steal his share of gold.

Following an attack by bandits led by the malevolent Gold Hat (Alfonso Bedoya), the three decide that they have enough gold. Approached by a group of friendly Indians who ask Howard's aid for a dying child, the old-timer goes off and saves the small boy. Meanwhile, the other two partners move onward. Because of their exhaustion and the tension caused by distrust, a quarrel ensues, whereupon Dobbs shoots and wounds Curtin and steals his share of the gold. Howard finds and saves Curtin, but Gold Hat's Mexican bandits ambush Dobbs, rob him, and slay him.

With the men's feverish greed the film's tone becomes cynical, violent, and macabre. The heart of the story is its simple revelation of three types of human character altering in the presence of the sinister catalyst, gold. The tale is told with humor, wisdom, and suspense. It is by turns exceedingly funny and completely terrifying. In the film's final shot, the gold is mistaken for sand and tossed away; as the gold dust is scattered by the whirlwind, the bitter but wise Howard cries out to Curtin, "Laugh, Boy, it's a joke played on us by the Lord or Fate or whatever. . . . The gold's gone right back where we got it."

The performances are uniformly excellent. Humphrey Bogart cannot completely eliminate the existence of his own screen *persona* as established by such films as *Casablanca* (1942) or *To Have and Have Not* (1944), but he makes a noble effort here to alter that image and the result is arguably the best work of his career. As the unkempt, unsavory Dobbs, he creates a well-developed character. At the peak of his popularity in 1948, he could afford to eschew more romantic roles to play an unscrupulous character.

Yet it is the character of Dobbs as written or interpreted that constitutes the only fundamental weakness in the film. Although the story is about gold and its effects on those who seek it, it is also a fable about all human life and about the essence of good and evil. A number of the possibilities inherent in this idea are treated but some of the most telling implications are missed. Because the Dobbs character is so undisciplined and troublesome from the beginning, it is impossible to demonstrate or even hint at the ultimate depth of the problem; instead, his character dominates much of the film. Since a bit of Dobbs is realistically a part of every human being, it would have made a much more dramatic tragicomedy if the character had been more restrained. In that way the demonstration of the effect of gold upon men could have been more neatly rendered as the fanatical side of Dobbs's character slowly and believably emerges and establishes its universal implications.

At the other extreme is the character of Curtin, the youngest member of the trio. Tim Holt is perhaps less an actor than a presence, but he is a powerful presence. Not nearly as base as Dobbs, the essentially moral Curtin, who plans to use his money to settle on a farm, is sympathetically portrayed by Holt in a role originally intended for John Garfield. The most memorable performance of the film, however, is that of veteran character actor Walter Huston. As the grizzled and toothless old prospector who learns true wisdom from the peaceful life of the Indians, Huston is both charming and eccentric. He totally submerges himself in the role to the extent that he appears short and stocky, even though he appeared tall and lanky when he played Abraham Lincoln in an earlier film. Although the character is extremely well-conceived and competently written, it is still the actor who lends the character its charm and wisdom. In spite of the significant amount of other talent involved in the picture, Huston carries the entire film as deftly and easily as he handles his comedy lines.

Like John Huston's other films, *The Treasure of the Sierra Madre* deals with a harsh, masculine environment and is concerned with men under pressure. Often presented in a romantic context, the films involve violence and danger in exotic locales: Mexico in this case, Revolutionary Cuba in the 1930's in *We Were Strangers* (1949), and India in *The Man Who Would Be King* (1975). Huston has little patience with theories of aesthetics or matters of style; his sharp, crisp directing is intuitive. He has a coldly intelligent aptitude for how much to leave free within the frame and the true artist's passion for the possibilities inherent in his medium. He has been quoted as saying that in any given scene, "I have an idea of what should happen but I don't tell the actors." Instead, he lets them go ahead and do it and sometimes they do it better. "Sometimes they do something accidentally which is effective and true. I jump on the accident."

Huston's most remarkable single achievement is that he focuses all of the symbolic elements as finely as light rays through a magnifying glass. All that is evident to the viewer is a story told so masterfully and realistically that the picture's most ideal, and, in fact, most knowledgeable audience is one made up of the kind of man the film is about. Yet this single accomplishment is the result of many components. The film is one of the most masculine in style ever made and displays a strikingly true cinematic understanding of character and of men. The bums depicted in the film seem real, and their lives and circumstances are as a bum's would be. Also, the city is presented as a bum would see it; it is not glamourized.

The film is, on several levels, a cruel presentation of an almost absolute desolateness in nature and its effect on men. The hardship, labor, and exhaustion of the gold-seeker's existence is skillfully sketched and also enhanced by the introduction and expert handling of amateur and semiprofessional character actors; significantly, Alfonso Bedoya in the role of Gold Hat gives the film a frightening realism. Huston's starkly depicted scenes of violence or those that build toward it combine with his treatment of location and scenery to unfold gradually the film's perspectives on human nature.

The perfect blend of actors and scenery is sustained throughout by the superb camerawork of Ted McCord. There is not one superfluous, arty, or self-conscious shot in the film. The camera is always in its proper position and never exploits or dwells too long upon its subject. Instead, there is a sense of leanness and vigor in every scene without any sacrifice of sensitivity. There is, for example, a shot of Gold Hat reflected in muddy water which is so subtly photographed that, although the film is shot in black-and-white, his hat seems to shed a golden light. McCord's style is so delicate as to be almost invisible and yet he effectively conveys the symbolism of the scene. The film's studio exteriors offer a jarring and unfortunate contrast to the location shots, however, and detract from the overall effect of the film. The score by Max Steiner is also, at times, intrusive, and perhaps unnecessary.

The Treasure of the Sierra Madre marked the first time in Academy Award history that a father and son both won an Oscar for the same film in the same year. Walter Huston won an Oscar for Best Supporting Actor, and his son John (who has a bit part in the film as the American in the white suit) won Oscars for Best Screenplay and Best Direction. The film is indeed an outstanding motion picture and a true representation of Huston's fine work, as well as that of Humphrey Bogart and Walter Huston.

ROUBEN MAMOULIAN

DR. JEKYLL AND MR. HYDE

Released: 1932
Production: Rouben Mamoulian for Paramount
Direction: Rouben Mamoulian
Screenplay: Samuel Hoffenstein and Percy Heath; based on the novel of the same name by Robert Louis Stevenson
Cinematography: Karl Struss
Editing: William Shea
Running time: 90 minutes

Principal characters:

Dr. Henry Jekyll/Mr. Hyde .... Fredric March (AA)
Ivy Pearson .... Miriam Hopkins
Muriel Carew .... Rose Hobart
Brigadier General Carew .... Halliwell Hobbes
Dr. Lanyan .... Holmes Herbert
Poole .... Edgar Norton

Very few characters have struck the chord of man's imagination with more resonance than Robert Louis Stevenson's Dr. Jekyll, for in his duality he represents the struggle of good and evil within the individual. It is a struggle that has always intrigued, puzzled, and preoccupied men. As early as 1908, Hollywood's fledgling filmmakers recognized the potential box-office appeal of Stevenson's spine-chilling classic. It was a story that possessed all the winning ingredients: horror, suspense, romance, and morality. Only three of the Jekyll and Hyde films have done justice to Stevenson's literary master-piece—the inspired performance given by John Barrymore in 1920, the 1932 version starring Fredric March as the infamous doctor, and the Victor Fleming 1941 production starring Spencer Tracy. The 1932 film was produced and directed by Rouben Mamoulian, who was acknowledged and esteemed as one of the most inspired and innovative Broadway directors during the 1930's. Although *Dr. Jekyll and Mr. Hyde* was only Mamoulian's third film, he infused this stunning melodrama with a theatrical virtuosity which perfectly expressed the brooding, bizarre quality of Stevenson's character.

Dr. Jekyll (Fredric March), is a man unshackled by the taboos of conven-tion. As Karl Struss's camera pans a filled-to-capacity auditorium of students and distinguished medical men, Dr. Jekyll leans on his dais and elaborates on his theory of the dualistic nature of the human psyche. "I have found," he explains, "that certain agents, certain chemicals have the power to disturb the trembling immateriality of the seemingly solid body in which we walk." The reaction to this heretical proclamation is immediate and sharply divided, some believing the doctor to be a savior, others convinced that he is in league with the devil.

In addition to his research and lectures, Jekyll unselfishly devotes long hours of his time to a free medical clinic, causing him, on this particular evening, to arrive late at a dinner party held at the home of Brigadier General Carew (Halliwell Hobbes), Jekyll's future father-in-law. However, Muriel Carew (Rose Hobart), Jekyll's fiancée, forgives the good doctor for his tardiness, and as they stroll in the garden, they discuss their impending marriage on which the general has imposed an eight-month waiting period. Jekyll leaves the Carew home in the company of his good friend, Dr. Lanyan (Holmes Herbert). Suddenly their reverie is broken by a noisy scuffle between a man and a woman in the dimly lit street ahead. Rushing forward, Jekyll drives off the assailant and helps the manhandled young woman upstairs to her rooms. Encouraged by his solicitous ministrations, the cockney woman, Ivy Pearson (Miriam Hopkins), becomes coquettish and attempts to seduce him. However, she fails, and with the scene rather abruptly ended, the audience realizes that Ivy will reappear later in the film.

Following this is a scene which takes place in Jekyll's laboratory where, after three days of unflagging experimentation, Jekyll has produced a bubbling elixir which awaits its final test. The doctor hesitates for one long moment, then raises the flask and drinks the foaming potion. Suddenly, a spasm convulses his body, and he writhes in pain, his face horribly contorted. This scene portraying the initial transformation from Dr. Jekyll to Mr. Hyde is a cinemagraphic masterpiece since it was done without the usual series of dissolves to accommodate makeup changes. The use of a number of colored gelatin filters caused March's makeup to appear to change and, as Struss's camera relentlessly focuses on Jekyll's face, the audience watches in horror as the evil in his soul permeates and contorts his features into a dark and loathsome mask of wickedness and malice before their very eyes. Moving with an animal's quick grace, Hyde grins savagely in the mirror and then, throwing a cape around his shoulders, leaves the lab by the back door.

In a later scene, the doctor restlessly paces his lab, his life in limbo. General Carew, concerned over Jekyll's refusal to give up his research, has taken his daughter to Bath on an extended holiday. A telegram from Bath informing the doctor that Muriel will not be returning for at least another month incites Jekyll to action. Downing a draft of the potion, he changes quickly to Hyde and slinks off into the foggy London streets. After making inquiries at Ivy Pearson's boarding house about her whereabouts, Hyde proceeds to the Blue Boar dance hall where, amidst the bacchanalian revelry, he observes Ivy flitting about with debauched abandon. Hyde snatches up a broken glass and with a savage, threatening gesture, chases away Ivy's escort. Then, with a wolfish, terrifying intensity, he turns to Ivy and says, "You'll come with me, eh?"

From this point on, the pace of the movie quickens dramatically; time lapses are effected through a series of dissolves and slow fades as Jekyll catapults, through the character of Mr. Hyde, toward an abyss from which there is no escape. The sound effects, including the use of quickening heartbeats, builds suspense throughout the ensuing scenes to a raw, nerve-jangling level of intensity. Having been informed of the recent return to London of General Carew and his daughter, Jekyll is deeply disturbed and full of remorse over his recent indulgences. Deciding to end his double life, he sends his butler, Poole (Edgar Norton), with a fifty-pound note and a message to be delivered to Ivy. In addition, he gives his butler the key to the rear door of his lab, stating that he will no longer have need of it.

Later, Ivy arrives at the doctor's home to return his money and beg his assistance in freeing herself from Hyde's sadistic attentions. Jekyll, remorseful over the anguish which he has caused her, promises that she will never see Hyde again. However, Jekyll has unleashed the licentious Mr. Hyde once too often. The fragile chain of conscious control has been irrevocably broken and the beast lurks ever-present, unshackled, and ready to claw its way into the upper consciousness of Jekyll's mind. Totally unaware of this irreversible change that has occurred within himself, Jekyll strolls happily through the park on his way to the Carew home. Following their return from Bath, the General has undergone a change of heart and agreed to an early marriage between Dr. Jekyll and his daughter, and this is the night the formal wedding announcement is to be made. Suddenly, with dynamic primitive force, Hyde takes over Jekyll's body and walks towards Ivy's flat. Here, he informs the terrified Ivy that he is the wonderful Dr. Jekyll in which she has believed; then, with a pagan enjoyment, he wantonly takes her life. Smashing his way through the curious onlookers who have heard Ivy's screams and gathered on the stairs, Hyde escapes into the safety of the darkness.

Unable to return to his laboratory and no longer being in possession of the rear door key, Hyde sends a message by porter to his friend Lanyan, instructing him to retrieve certain chemicals from his lab and give them to a messenger whom Jekyll will send to Lanyan's home at midnight. Lanyan, however, refuses to release the package to the suspicious-looking Mr. Hyde. Having no choice, Hyde mixes and drinks the potion, reverting to Dr. Jekyll before the disbelieving, horrified eyes of his friend. Jekyll swears Lanyan to secrecy, promising that in return for his trust, he will give up Muriel and never again take the potion.

With a heavy heart, Jekyll arrives at the Carew home and informs Muriel that he is releasing her from her marriage commitment. However, as he leaves the house, Hyde again takes possession of Jekyll's mind and body. Reentering the house, he pursues Muriel, who screams at the sight of this horrifying stranger. General Carew comes to his daughter's rescue, but Hyde savagely beats the old man with his cane and escapes into the night. Two constables, alerted by the General's cries for help, take up the chase, tracking their suspect to the home of Dr. Jekyll. Frantically Hyde mixes his potion with the constables pounding on the door. At the last second, as the door finally succumbs to their persistent barrage, Hyde changes back to Jekyll and convinces the officers who have burst into the room that the murderer, Hyde, has been there but has escaped by the back door. At this moment, Lanyan appears and reveals to the constables that Jekyll himself is the ruthless, cold-blooded killer whom they seek. Shock and anger at Lanyan's betrayal brings the ever-present Hyde back to the surface. He attacks Lanyan and then the police until his frenzy of unbridled hatred is finally halted by a bullet; and, as the formless evil power slowly dissipates, Jekyll emerges to claim his dying and desecrated body.

Mamoulian's finely etched, visual interpretation of *Dr. Jekyll and Mr. Hyde* possesses the timeless elegance of the Stevenson classic. Each scene is a hand-carved cameo, perfect in lighting and composition. The characters of Jekyll and Hyde allowed Mamoulian to draw upon the full range of his theatrical genius, to portray the elemental struggle of man's emotions against a background of rich symbolic imagery. In one scene, violence is juxtaposed against a lyric view of romantic statuary, and in another, a bubbling cauldron flickers in the flames of a fireplace, providing a fleeting symbolic glimpse of the hell lurking in man's soul. March is stunning in his portrayal of Jekyll and Hyde, a role which earned him an Academy Award for Best Actor. His interpretation of Hyde's unsheathed wickedness pares Jekyll's civilized veneer in one clean, devastating stroke, stupefying audiences with its raw and savage intensity, and making the Mamoulian production of *Dr. Jekyll and Mr. Hyde* a classic of the horror film genre.

GOLDEN BOY

Released: 1939
Production: William Perlberg for Columbia
Direction: Rouben Mamoulian
Screenplay: Lewis Meltzer, Daniel Taradash, Sarah Y. Mason, and Victor Herman; based on the play of the same name by Clifford Odets
Cinematography: Nicholas Musuraca and Karl Freund
Editing: Otto Meyer
Music: Victor Young
Running time: 98 minutes

Principal characters:
Lorna Moon .... Barbara Stanwyck
Tom Moody .... Adolphe Menjou
Joe Bonaparte .... William Holden
Eddie Fuseli .... Joseph Calleia
Mr. Bonaparte .... Lee J. Cobb
Siggie .... Sam Levene

When Columbia first announced its purchase of Clifford Odets' Group Theatre play *Golden Boy*, it seemed a strange choice, because that studio had never favored dramas of strong social significance. Odets was not hired to adapt his own play for film; instead, four top writers carefully deleted the play's social comment from the screenplay that was being prepared. Some of the controversial characters were completely eliminated; the romance was built up; and the hero's conflict was simplified. A happy ending was devised as a substitute for the play's conclusion. All things considered, the screenwriters did a good job, for *Golden Boy* as a movie proved to be much stronger entertainment than the play. Today the play is dated, but the movie is still as pertinent as it was at the time of its initial release.

When the production was first announced in the trade magazines, it featured an appealing painting of Jean Arthur, who was announced as its star. Producer Harry Cohn was biding his time, hoping to borrow John Garfield from Warner Bros. for the title role, but Jack Warner and Harry Cohn were feuding, so Garfield could not be secured for the part. Things began to fall into place, though, when Rouben Mamoulian was signed as director. Mamoulian was a versatile man who could never be typed in any one kind of film. Whatever the background of the story he was directing, its cinematic mood was always beautifully sustained. He was faced with two strong dramatic story lines to resolve: the romance between an unworldly youth and a sophisticated girl; and the internal struggle of the boy who had to choose between fulfilling himself artistically through his music, and the opportunity to achieve quick success as a boxer. Mamoulian had one advantage in telling the story on the screen that could never be realized in the theater: he could show the prizefight sequences realistically. In the theater these scenes had to take place offstage; in the film they are superbly done, and convey an electric charge of quick ringside excitement and suspense.

Mamoulian demonstrated superb taste in casting his picture. He was fortunate in being able to get Barbara Stanwyck for the heroine, Lorna Moon, the girl friend of the fight manager Tom Moody, who is perfectly played by Adolphe Menjou. Stanwyck had just finished her last scenes as the heroine in De Mille's *Union Pacific* (1939), and she came over to Columbia with almost no break from her Paramount duties. Lee J. Cobb had been in the original stage play in a minor part, but was cast by Mamoulian in the more important role of Mr. Bonaparte, the boy's father, who dreams of his son's becoming a great violinist and who strongly opposes his son's boxing career because of the threat it holds of injuring the boy's hands. Joseph Calleia was exactly right for the mobster, Eddie Fuseli, and Sam Levene, as the taxi driver Siggie, provided the humor the story needed.

The most difficult role to fill was that of the young hero, the golden boy himself, Joe Bonaparte. Sixty-five youthful actors were tested for the part, and Mamoulian, a perfectionist, found fault with all of them. He finally tested an unknown, a youth of twenty-one, who was under contract to Paramount but had done virtually nothing on the screen except a few appearances in such routine pictures as *Prison Farm* (1938) and *Million Dollar Legs* (1932). His name was William Holden, and Mamoulian detected something in his screen test that was just what he wanted to portray in the character of Joe Bonaparte. Harry Cohn opposed the casting, but Mamoulian went to bat for young Holden; so did Barbara Stanwyck. Grudgingly, Cohn agreed to Holden's playing the part, but when he made the deal to borrow the boy from Paramount, he insisted on buying half of his contract. Because Holden was only under stock contract at that time and Paramount was paying him fifty dollars a week, it meant that Columbia was getting him for a weekly twenty-five dollars.

Holden's performance is workmanlike, believable, often brilliant, and deserving of the stardom he subsequently gained. Joe Napoleon is a sensitive youth whose father has sacrificed much to make him an accomplished musician. The boy is dual-natured, for he has mastered the difficult violin and is on the threshold of a career as a virtuoso. Yet, in exercising at the gym, he has gained a reputation as an amateur boxer, and when an impecunious manager, Tom Moody, sees him fight in the ring, he envisions a winner and signs the boy to a contract, promising him a quick rise to fame and fortune. Moody, also aware of the boy's innocence concerning women, instructs his own mistress, Lorna Moon, to lure the boy and entice him to stay in the fight world rather than pursue his music. Lorna does as Moody wishes, but she falls in love with Joe, even as she is urging him to stay with his fighting career.

Joe introduces Lorna to his family. When she understands what Joe's life has been and comprehends his genuine love of music, she switches her loyalties to persuade him to give up his fighting career. A gangster, however takes over the boy's contract for betting purposes, causing Lorna to be so disillusioned and disgusted that she agrees to marry Moody.

In the big fight, Joe's opponent is a young black prizefighter. Joe knocks him out with such a punch that he breaks his own hand and kills the black boy. Joe, overwhelmed by this tragedy, throws away his gloves and all thoughts of a career in the ring. In a well-played scene, he goes to the black fighter's father, who is mourning his dead son. The father tells him tearfully that he does not blame Joe for his boy's death. He had never wanted his son to fight, and he is sorry that it had to be a boy of Joe's caliber who killed him.

Lorna breaks with Moody and his way of life and comes to Joe. They are reunited, with his father's blessing. This ending was generally applauded by film critics. Even the few who were disappointed did admit that the double suicide of the boy and the girl in the play had been meaningless and that the movie reconciliation was done with taste and tenderness and did not signify a "tacked-on" happy ending.

Golden Boy was one of Columbia's all-time best films, and the fact that it gained only one Academy Award nomination—to Victor Young for Original Score—should not be held against it. It was released in 1939, frequently cited as the greatest year for the talking film, and was in competition with *Gone with the Wind*; *The Wizard of Oz*; *Wuthering Heights*; *Mr. Smith Goes to Washington*; *Goodbye, Mr. Chips*, and other films that are still favorites among both moviegoers and moviemakers. *Golden Boy* remains well-liked, however, and gains new admirers whenever it is revived, for it is one of Mamoulian's finest contributions to the cinema.

LOVE ME TONIGHT

Released: 1932
Production: Rouben Mamoulian for Paramount
Direction: Rouben Mamoulian
Screenplay: Samuel Hoffenstein, Waldemar Young, and George Marion, Jr.
Cinematography: Victor Milner
Editing: Merrill White
Music: Richard Rodgers and Lorenz Hart
Running time: 89 minutes

> *Principal characters:*
> Maurice Courtelin .... Maurice Chevalier
> Princess Jeanette .... Jeanette MacDonald
> Viscount de Varese .... Charles Ruggles
> Duke .... C. Aubrey Smith
> Count .... Charles Butterworth
> Countess .... Myrna Loy
> Emile .... Bert Roach

For many years, critics and historians tended to see *Love Me Tonight* as an unsuccessful imitation of the great director Ernst Lubitsch. In recent years, however, this extraordinarily stylish musical has come into prominence and has been recognized as a key film in the liberation of the screen from the limitations of early sound recording. If it does not quite reach the height of sly wit which was the hallmark of "the Lubitsch touch," it has an audaciousness and a fresh taste for experimentation which give it unique status among screen musicals.

Director Rouben Mamoulian had directed opera in Rochester, New York, and had done distinguished work on the Broadway stage after having been brought to this country in the 1920's by the Kodak magnate George Eastman. He was ripe for being summoned to Hollywood in 1928 when the film studios were in a panic over how to produce the sound films which the public increasingly demanded. Dealing with words had been the one commodity which Hollywood had treated with disdain during its silent era; suddenly, however, it was being forced to mine the seeming center of dialogue expertise—the legitimate stage. Mamoulian was one of a horde of Broadway types who trekked West, but he was virtually alone in his artistic belief that directing for films required an entirely new technique from that of the stage. In the direction of his first film, *Applause* (1929), he stubbornly insisted on experimenting with techniques which the all-powerful sound engineers pronounced impossible. He was allowed to have his own way by the front office, presumably on the assumption that he would fall on his face and return East. *Applause* was a sensation, however, and directors all over town began copying Mamoulian's techniques.

Not content to repeat himself, this gifted man went on to direct many different kinds of films, including the gangster film *City Streets* (1931) and the first talking version of *Dr. Jekyll and Mr. Hyde* (1932). *Love Me Tonight* was the director's first musical. He later went on to direct the stage originals of such landmark musical works as *Porgy and Bess*, *Oklahoma!*, and *Lost in the Stars*.

Love Me Tonight concerns Maurice Courtelin (Maurice Chevalier), a Parisian tailor who, in order to collect unpaid bills for himself and his fellow shopkeepers, visits the debtor, the Viscount de Varese (Charles Ruggles), at the chateau of his uncle the Duke (C. Aubrey Smith). Maurice allows himself to be mistaken as the Baron Courtelin upon the urging of the Viscount. His ulterior motive is to get to know the Princess Jeanette (Jeanette MacDonald), whom he had met by accident on his way to the chateau. Although the Princess is seemingly unimpressed by Maurice, during the course of a hunt and the Ball following, the two fall in love. The following morning, Maurice is revealed as merely a tailor. The Princess, although initially shocked by the revelation, reconsiders her feelings, and in a dramatic horseback chase of Maurice's departing train, effects a happy ending.

Such a bald recitation of the plot cannot begin to suggest the charm and spirit of the film, but a closer look at the film's extraordinary opening sequences might convey a sense of its real worth. In a fifteen-minute sequence, consisting of two extended songs and a minimum of dialogue delivered both in rhyming couplets and in blank verse, an entire universe of characters and their relationships is created in a dazzling display of virtuosity which would be extraordinary in any filmmaking era. In the early days of sound, however, when experimentation was discouraged and stage-bound conventions were the rule, it was absolutely unique.

A shot of Paris rooftops and the Eiffel Tower in the distance establishes the locale as Paris. Deserted streets in the first glow of morning are just beginning to come alive with people. A road crew begins paving operations; shoemakers set up their benches, and the sounds of their hammers hitting nails acts as counterpoint to the paving sounds; some derelicts' snores add a different rhythm; a housewife shakes out the bed linen; cars and taxis begin to rattle, honk, and cough their way through the streets. A young woman throws open her window and starts a phonograph record and the camera moves through the open window of a young tailor named Maurice, who is dressing for the day. Hanging from a crack in the wall is the characteristic straw hat which tells us even before he appears on film that the young man is Maurice Chevalier.

Meanwhile, the street noises have coalesced into a symphony of cacophony which proves too much for Maurice, who closes his window to sing "The Song of Paree." He continues the song, and it becomes a running recitative as he proceeds from his house along the street to his tailor shop. This sequence introduces various neighborhood types along the way and defines Maurice's character entirely through song. After Maurice opens his shop, Emile (Bert Roach) arrives to pick up the tuxedo in which he will be married. As he is trying it on, a marathon race passes the shop, and one of the entrants, who is wearing his underwear instead of track shorts and carrying a sign from a fruit stand, runs into the shop. He is the Viscount de Varese who had earlier ordered fifteen suits from the struggling Maurice. Explaining that he has just escaped from a jealous husband, the Viscount takes a suit and borrows money from Maurice, promising to return soon with "bags of gold." Maurice then sings to Emile of his good fortune and his optimistic view of life in "Isn't It Romantic?" As Emile leaves the shop he begins humming the catchy tune as he walks, and then turns down the offer of a ride in a taxi. A musician rushing for the train station jumps into the cab, and he and the driver pick up the tune as they drive along. Although the scenes change rapidly from one locale to another, they are all bridged by the same song.

On the train, the musician decides to add words to the tune. He is surrounded by soldiers who pick up the song and sing it in military fashion both on the train and then on maneuvers in the countryside. A strolling gypsy violinist hears the tune and plays it in his camp, gypsy-style. The song wafts through the forest to the balcony of a magnificent chateau where, as destiny would have it, it is ended in operettic fashion by Princess Jeanette (Jeanette MacDonald). Before she finishes singing the song, an elaborate series of vignettes introduces the other denizens of the chateau. They include a milquetoast Count (Charles Butterworth); the stuffy Duke; the Viscount; his cousin, the nymphomaniac Countess (Myrna Loy); and three maiden aunts who invariably appear together, share dialogue, and do imitations of the witches in *Macbeth*.

The sequence is a masterpiece of writing, acting, musical and lyric composition, editing, and sound recording. In an imaginative and totally cinematic manner, all the major characters are introduced and their relationships with one another are established; and all is accomplished with wit, grace, and movement.

Aside from the charm and audacity of the direction, *Love Me Tonight* boasts a landmark score by Richard Rodgers and Lorenz Hart. Although they had earlier written a score for a musical called *The Hot Heiress*, Rodgers considers this his finest film score—and with good reason. In addition to "The Song of Paree" and "Isn't It Romantic?," the score includes the waltz "Lover" and a classic recitative of subtle eroticism in which a doctor says to the ailing Princess: "You're not wasting away, you're just wasted." At the Ball, Maurice sings "I'm an Apache" and the title love song "Love Me Tonight." As he is unmasked, the entire household sings the patter song, "The Son-of-a-Gun Is Nothing But a Tailor!"

More than any other film score, the music in *Love Me Tonight* acts to propel the plot along; it predates, in this regard, Rodgers' score for *Oklahoma!* The script is very witty, particularly in dealing with Myrna Loy as the sex-starved Countess. In one memorable scene when the Princess has fainted, the Viscount says to the Countess, "Can you go for a doctor?" Straightening her hair, she responds, "Certainly, bring him right in." *Love Me Tonight* is so full of good humor that it is the only known film in which C. Aubrey Smith, the very symbol of the British Empire, actually sings a song. In fact, he is so flabbergasted by his own rendition of "Isn't It Romantic?" that he puts his arm in the wrong sleeve of his robe. The gaffe was left in the film.

The supporting cast is first-rate, including Myrna Loy, Charles Ruggles, Charles Butterworth, Elizabeth Patterson, and Ethel Griffies. The physical production is stunning, re-creating Paris streets, bucolic chateaus, and the French countryside on the Paramount backlot. In viewing the film closely, one can observe three zoom shots which are puzzling when one thinks of the zoom lens as an invention of the 1950's. Mamoulian was once asked about this. Frank Capra was standing alongside him at the time, and when asked why, if the zoom was available in 1932, it was not used extensively until thirty years later, Capra said, "We had taste then."

THE MARK OF ZORRO

Released: 1940
Production: Darryl F. Zanuck for Twentieth Century-Fox
Direction: Rouben Mamoulian
Screenplay: John Taintor Foote; based on Garrett Fort's and Bess Meredyth's adaptation of the story "The Curse of Capistrano" by Johnston McCulley
Cinematography: Arthur Miller
Editing: Robert Bischoff
Costume design: Travis Banton
Music: Alfred Newman
Running time: 93 minutes

Principal characters:
Don Diego Vega	Tyrone Power
Lolita Quintero	Linda Darnell
Captain Esteban Pasquale	Basil Rathbone
Inez Quintero	Gale Sondergaard
Fray Felipe	Eugene Pallette
Don Luis Quintero	J. Edward Bromberg
Don Alejandro Vega	Montagu Love
Senora Isabella Vega	Janet Beecher
Rodrigo	Robert Lowery
Don Miguel	Pedro de Cordoba
Turnkey	Chris-Pin Martin
Sergeant Gonzales	George Regas

In 1920, Douglas Fairbanks, Sr., virtually invented the swashbuckling film with *The Mark of Zorro*. There were period and costume films before that, and some of them included a perfunctory duel, but they were merely reverent, stiff, and usually very short adaptations of literary classics. None of them had any flair, panache, humor, or acrobatics. Though *The Mark of Zorro* was Fairbanks' thirtieth film, all his previous movies had been contemporary comedies. *The Mark of Zorro* is far from being a literary classic; it derives from Johnston McCulley's pulp adventure "The Curse of Capistrano," which appeared in the August 9, 1919, issue of *All-Story Weekly*. Directed at a brisk pace by Fred Niblo, who later directed the silent *Ben-Hur*, with Marguerite de la Motte as the heroine and Noah Beery, Sr., as the heavy, it is an immensely entertaining blend of comedy and adventure, with Fairbanks duelling all over the place and bounding about like a trapeze artist. It is perhaps his best film, yet he was so uncertain of it that he followed it with another contemporary comedy, *The Nut*. *The Mark of Zorro*, however, was such a huge hit that it changed the course of Fairbanks' career. For the next ten years, he made nothing but costume swashbucklers, such as *The Three Musketeers* (1921), *Robin Hood* (1922), and *The Iron Mask* (1929). In 1925, he played both Zorro and his son in *Don Q, Son of Zorro*. Elaborately produced, these were among the most popular films of the decade. Suddenly, most romantic stars were making swashbucklers—John Barrymore, Ramon Navarro, Rudolph Valentino, John Gilbert, Joseph Schildkraut, and even Conrad Nagel.

With *The Mark of Zorro*, Fairbanks set the model for the swashbuckling hero. Zorro, however, fell into a decline when the character was borrowed for two Republic serials—*Zorro Rides Again* (1937) and *Zorro's Fighting Legion* (1939). In these low-budget programmers, the story degenerated into a series of routine Western adventures, with Zorro as a California version, not of d'Artagnan, but of the Lone Ranger—just one more masked man. Instead of period elegance, wit, and dazzling swordplay, there are merely routine stagecoach holdups, bandits, and head-'em-off-at-the-gulch heroics. One would have expected this sort of treatment to have weakened the image of Zorro except with children cheering at Saturday matinees, but surprisingly, Twentieth Century-Fox resurrected Zorro in a major production of 1940, with the studio's biggest star, Tyrone Power.

Power had his first major role in a period film, *Lloyds of London*, in 1936; and since then he had cut a handsome figure in other costume films such as *In Old Chicago* (1938), *Suez* (1938), and *Marie Antoinette* (1938). *The Mark of Zorro*, however, was his first cape and sword swashbuckler. It became one of his most popular films and perhaps the one for which he is best remembered. Though he was careful to vary them with other roles, Power made a number of superior swashbucklers—*The Black Swan* (1942), *Captain from Castile* (1947), *Prince of Foxes* (1949), and others. Since his chief rival, Errol Flynn, made no cape and sword films between *The Sea Hawk* (1940) and *The Adventures of Don Juan* (1949), Power was the preeminent swashbuckler of the 1940's.

The Mark of Zorro was not only Power's first swashbuckler, but in some ways it is also his best. The story opens at the beginning of the nineteenth century in Spain. There Don Diego Vega is the most dashing and skilled student of the Madrid military academy. Known as the "California cockerel," he is the best horseman and swordsman in his class. He has so many duels on his hands that he cannot remember them all. "Santa Maria, it slipped my mind," he says in chagrin when reminded of an appointment on the field of honor. Unfortunately, he cannot keep this engagement, for his father summons him back to California. As a farewell gesture, he hurls his sword into the ceiling of the *salle des armes*, to hang there as a memento.

Landing in San Pedro, Diego finds the servants sullen and unresponsive until he says that he is the son of the *alcalde*, whereupon they respond with a cringing alacrity. During the reunion with his parents, Diego learns that his father has been deposed by a corrupt tyrant, Don Luis Quintero (J. Edward Bromberg), who has taken away the power of the old *hidalgos* and suppressed them with a military force headed by the sneering Captain Esteban Pasquale (Basil Rathbone). Together, they are bleeding the peasants with exorbitant taxes. Apprised of the situation, Diego instantly forms a plan. To his father's amazed disgust, he languidly disclaims any interest in politics, as a wearisome subject. Like the Scarlet Pimpernel, Diego has decided to disguise his real actions by posing as an effeminate fop. The finest swordsman and horseman of Madrid secretly transforms himself into Zorro the fox, a masked Robin Hood who gallops about the countryside on his horse Tornado robbing the tax collectors and giving the money to Fray Felipe, the only person to whom he has confided, who returns it to the poor. Whenever he strikes a blow against tyranny, Zorro slashes a "Z" on the furniture, the walls, or the uniforms of Don Luis' guardsmen, both as a calling card and as a warning.

When he calls upon Don Luis as himself, Diego is a frilly, scented popinjay who minces about with a lace handkerchief, a lorgnette, and a snuff box. He pretends to be terrified at the daring deeds of Zorro by declaring, "My blood chills at the very thought." Thus he disarms any possible suspicion that he himself might be the masked marauder. Captain Pasquale, who is perpetually brandishing a sword and making passes in the air at imaginary opponents, feels nothing but scorn for this effete dandy. Don Luis' wife, Inez (Gale Sondergaard), however, finds him fascinating, certainly more handsome, gallant, and sophisticated than her rotund husband. She flirts with Diego seductively, and he pretends to respond in kind.

The Mark of Zorro is superior to most swashbucklers in that it invokes a great deal of humor as Diego alternates between swishing and swashing. The audience relishes being in on a secret that everyone else fails to perceive. Tyrone Power proved himself a skilled hand at drawing-room comedy as well as being a dashing adventurer. Even the love scenes maintain a comic touch. When Don Luis' beautiful and innocent niece Lolita (Linda Darnell) goes to the chapel and begs the Virgin Mary to "Send one to take me from this place. Let him be kind and handsome and brave," Zorro appears disguised as a monk to hide from the soldiers. She finds him sympathetic, and he forgets all about escaping and tells her, in distinctly unclerical tones, that she is "more radiant, more lovely than a morning in June." She tries to see who is hidden beneath the cowl, but he keeps retreating into the shadows. When she detects a rapier beneath his robe, she realizes that she has been conversing with Zorro, who makes a spectacular escape when the soldiers come for him.

To Lolita's dismay, she is betrothed by her uncle to Don Diego. At first, the handsome young man makes a good impression; for when they dance together, he forgets his foppishness and performs with passion. But he instantly relapses into his languid pose. Arriving late at the betrothal dinner, he apologizes that his bath water had been drawn too soon and had become tepid and that there was a further delay over adding the proper scented salts. Captain Pasquale smirks to Inez that he fears Lolita's married life will be as tepid as the bath water. The Captain resents Diego's flirtation with Inez because he has designs on her himself. However, Don Alejandro Vega (Montagu Love) is furious at his son's declaration that he plans to marry the niece of the hated tyrant. When his mother begs him to follow his father's advice, he responds superciliously, "I had no say in my father's marriage, so why should he in mine?"

This comic masquerade draws to an end when Captain Pasquale discovers that Father Felipe is Zorro's accomplice, disarms him in a brisk bit of swordplay, and imprisons him. Pursued by soldiers, Zorro enters the *alcalde*'s hacienda by a secret passageway and transforms himself back into the foppish Diego. By now, Captain Pasquale has had enough of this butterfly, taunts him with cowardice, and dares him to a duel. To his amazement, Diego accepts. As they prepare to fight, Pasquale slashes through a candle with his rapier, slicing off the top and leaving the bottom intact. Diego makes a pass at another candle and appears to miss. "Hah!" sneers Pasquale. "Hah, hah!" responds Diego, as he lifts off the top of the candle, which he has severed without seeming to touch it. (Rathbone later parodied this scene in *The Court Jester* with Danny Kaye in 1956.) The duel that follows is one of the finest on film, done authentically without the suicidal leaping about on furniture, fireplaces, and chandeliers by which too many movie heroes leave themselves off balance and off guard. At the climax, Diego runs Pasquale through; the captain falls, knocking down a picture, behind which a Z is carved on the wall. Don Luis, who has witnessed the fight, is terrified; "You handle a sword like a devil from hell," he says. Diego's plan, in fact, has been to frighten the *alcalde* into resigning and returning to Spain. Doña Inez is his ally in this scheme, for she believes Diego will return with them and become her lover. Just as the plot is about to succeed, soldiers enter through the secret passageway, and Diego is revealed as Zorro.

Part of his foppish masquerade consisted of showing off insipid parlor tricks with cards and handkerchiefs. Now in prison he dupes the jailor into thinking he can transmute a copper coin into gold. Instead, he seizes the man and takes his keys and pistol. At this point, his father and the other *hidalgos* enter under guard; the *alcalde* has rounded them up for imprisonment and gloats that he has captured Zorro. Don Alejandro scoffs that it is merely his foolish son. "Have you seen this trick, father," simpers Diego in his last performance, and whips out the pistol from beneath his handkerchief. Overpowering the guards, the *hidalgos* begin an attack from within the prison, as a horde of peasants try to storm the outside gates. Performing spectacular feats of swordplay, Diego fights his way over the rooftops, leaps upon the guards at the gate, and opens it for the peasants. At the end, justice is served. His fighting days over, Diego announces that he will marry Lolita, who now loves him, raise fat children, and settle down in California. He hurls his sword into the ceiling, this time to hang for good.

The Mark of Zorro was one of the hits of 1940 and remains one of the half dozen most durable and satisfying of all swashbucklers. Children frustrated their parents by slashing "Z's" in the family furniture. Though Bosley Crowther and a few other critics preferred Douglas Fairbanks, who performed more acrobatic stunts than Power, Power was younger (twenty-six to Fairbanks' thirty-seven), handsomer, more plausible, a better swordsman, and a skilled light comedian. Fairbanks' version leaned more heavily upon slapstick humor; the 1940 film is more sophisticated. Crowther objected to "a note of seriousness, as though Mamoulian or some one were sincerely concerned about the poor oppressed peons," but such an objection is supercilious. Even in a romance, there must be some awareness of man's inhumanity to man or the conflict has no foundation, and some genuine sympathy for the downtrodden peasants was by no means amiss in a year when *The Grapes of Wrath* was filmed.

Rouben Mamoulian, the distinguished director of such films as *Applause* (1929) and *Golden Boy* (1939), directed with a fine flair for action, comedy, and visual effects. Together with the eminent cinematographer Arthur Miller, he reconstructed the look of Spanish California. Alfred Newman contributed one of his most stirring scores. The cast was first-rate, with Basil Rathbone, Eugene Pallette, Montagu Love (all three borrowed from *The Adventures of Robin Hood*, 1938), Gale Sondergaard, and J. Edward Bromberg lending Power able support. In her second year of filmmaking, nineteen-year-old Linda Darnell played the third of her four romantic roles opposite Power. She was decorative and showed the touch of the comic skill which she contributed to her best roles in the late 1940's.

After the 1940 *The Mark of Zorro*, the story again declined into two more Republic serials, *Zorro's Black Whip* (1944) and *The Ghost of Zorro* (1949, starring Clayton Moore, who later became successful as The Lone Ranger on television). In the 1950's, Walt Disney ran a *Zorro* series on television starring Guy Williams, and later released an edited version as a feature film. Other Zorro films include *The Sign of Zorro* (1962, with Errol Flynn's son Sean), Frank Latimore in *Shadow of Zorro* (1962), the Italian *Zorro the Avenger* (1963), Pierre Brice in *Zorro versus Maciste* (1963), George Ardisson in *Zorro at the Court of Spain* (1963), Gordon Scott in *Zorro and the Three Musketeers* (1963), a pornographic *The Erotic Adventures of Zorro* (1972), and Alain Delon in *Zorro* (1974). Most of these were cheap potboilers that took considerable liberties with the story. A fairly authentic remake was done for television in 1974 on ABC's "Movie of the Week," with Frank Langella as Don Diego and Ricardo Montalban as Captain Pasquale. This version borrowed Alfred Newman's score from the 1940 film and followed that script closely, though with some condensation. Langella was fine as the fop but not very dashing as the masked adventurer. The two memorable versions remain those of 1920 and 1940. At any rate, Zorro has entered modern mythology; his name has become symbolic of the dashing swordsman *par excellence*.

QUEEN CHRISTINA

Released: 1933
Production: Walter Wanger for Metro-Goldwyn-Mayer
Direction: Rouben Mamoulian
Screenplay: H. M. Harwood and Salka Viertel, with additional dialogue by
   S. N. Behrman; based on a screen story by Salka Viertel and Margaret P.
   Levino
Cinematography: William Daniels
Editing: Blanche Sewell
Costume design: Adrian
Running time: 103 minutes

Principal characters:
Queen Christina	Greta Garbo
Don Antonio de la Prada	John Gilbert
Lord Treasurer Count Magnus	Ian Keith
Lord Chancellor Axel Oxenstierna	Lewis Stone
Countess Ebba	Elizabeth Young
Aage	C. Aubrey Smith
Prince Charles Gustavus	Reginald Owen
Pedro	Akim Tamiroff
Christina (younger)	Cora Sue Collins

When *Queen Christina* opened at the end of 1933, Greta Garbo had not
appeared in a film for eighteen months, and rumors were circulating that she
was ready to give up the screen—something which was to happen later after
her unsuccessful *Two-Faced Woman* (1941). Made as an artistic rewrite of
history, *Queen Christina* has been called Garbo's most memorable film.
Garbo's favorite cinematographer, William Daniels; art director, Alexander
Toluboff; music director, Herbert Stothart; and costume designer, Adrian, all
contributed to the overall excellence of the film. Garbo also insisted on John
Gilbert, with whom she was having a passionate affair, as her leading man
instead of Laurence Olivier, in the hopes that the role of Antonio would
restore Gilbert's prestige. Although his role is definitely secondary, Gilbert
makes a vivid impression; in spite of the legend that the advent of sound to
motion pictures ruined the famous silent screen star's career because of his
voice, his diction here is certainly acceptable. In any case, following *Queen
Christina*, Gilbert made only one other film, *The Captain Hates the Sea* (1934),
before his death in 1936.

In *Queen Christina*, director Rouben Mamoulian uses loving close-ups of
Garbo, together with his customary long shots, to create the lush image of
a queen who renounces her throne for love. The writers of the story and
screenplay forsook historical accuracy in favor of a more entertaining mixture

of love, sacrifice, and duty. The actual Queen Christina of Sweden (1626-1689) had a love of the arts and a disdain for most people which is not apparent in the screenplay; and her abdication was not over a love affair but because of a desire to pursue her artistic interests and to convert to Catholicism. (In a later version of the story of the queen, Christina, played by Liv Ullmann, falls in love with the cardinal, played by Peter Finch, who must test her sincerity on behalf of the Church; she is also at odds with her chancellor, Oxenstierna. By contrast, Garbo's Christina tells her chancellor—played in both movies by Lewis Stone—that he is the one person she trusts above all others.)

The film opens with a foreword that tells of the death of King Gustavus Adolphus of Sweden on the battlefield in 1632 during the Thirty Years' War. His Lord Chancellor, Axel Oxenstierna, announces to the court that after fourteen years of war, a new ruler will reign: Gustavus' six-year-old daughter Christina (Cora Sue Collins), who has been reared as a boy. Mounting the throne by herself, she promises "to be a good and just king." Years later, Christina enjoys dressing as a man and riding at breakneck speed with her faithful servant Aage (C. Aubrey Smith). She declines Oxenstierna's advice that she wed her heroic cousin, Prince Charles Gustavus (Reginald Owen), and also puts off amorous Count Magnus (Ian Keith), her Lord Treasurer and partner in a secret affair which no longer stirs her.

Christina is next seen in bed, reading early in the morning to satisfy her constant thirst for knowledge. She likes Molière and dislikes Magnus, she tells Aage. Dealing with affairs of state, she speaks to Ambassador Chanoux (George Renavent), who wants her to sign a treaty with France. She tells Oxenstierna that she sees nothing eye to eye with Charles and is tired of duty; however, she says she will not die an old maid, but a bachelor. Magnus feels Charles would be an ideal husband, since he spends his time reviewing the troops, which prompts Christina to wonder if she ever really cared for Magnus. Later, on the stairs, Christina eavesdrops on Ebba and her sweetheart count Jacob (Edward Norris), who is insisting that they wed. Ebba's remark that Christina is too stubborn to give her consent angers the queen. After bowing to peasants who shout for her to wed Charles, Christina angrily decides to get away from everything.

As Christina, dressed as a man, and Aage ride through the snow, they see a coach fall into a rut. Christina's laughter annoys the coach's passenger, Don Antonio de la Prada, a Spanish ambassador on his way to see her on behalf of his King. Christina has Aage help the coachman and then tells Antonio the way to an inn. Not recognizing her, Antonio has his servant Pedro (Akim Tamiroff) give her a coin with her own likeness engraved upon it.

When Christina arrives at the inn and takes the last available room, the innkeeper (Ferdinand Munier), thinking she is a man, offers her a companion for the night; Antonio recognizes her from the road and also believes she is a man. (In these sections of the film in which Christina successfully carries out the male masquerade, Garbo takes a delightful tongue-in-cheek approach, and when the scene calls for a hearty laugh from the supposedly stoic star, Garbo rises to the occasion.) Although she has never been to Spain, Christina tells the Spanish ambassador that his homeland is close to her heart. When Antonio brings up the topic of love, Christina defines love as something simple and elemental. She then stops a fight between two drunks who argue that the queen has had either six or nine lovers in the past year. The correct number, she announces, is twelve. The innkeeper then asks the two gentlemen to share the room, and she agrees after Antonio is insulted by her offering it to him completely. Elsa, a saucy maid (Barbara Barondess), tries to entice Christina, who defers. When Christina removes her coat, it is obvious to Antonio that she is a woman. Because of the snows, they spend several days together, and Christina promises to see Antonio in Stockholm.

Donning a gown for the first time in the film, Christina forgives Ebba and again scorns Magnus, who notices how beautiful she looks. In court, Antonio is shocked into silence at the first sight of the queen. Magnus gives him a "friendly warning" before Christina grants Antonio a private audience. While he appreciates a royal jest, Antonio feels unlucky being her thirteenth lover. She laughs at the portrait of King Philip of Spain, who seeks a marriage, and tells Antonio she loves him.

Magnus uses agents to stir resentment against Antonio; he also gets Charles's attention. When a mob storms the castle, Christina confronts them alone and tells them that she is doing her job by right of inheritance and that they should do the same. Later, Magnus takes Antonio away for the latter's "safety" and confronts Christina with his treachery. She signs an order for Antonio to sail home, but secretly intends to go with him. Late at night, Christina tells Oxenstierna that she is tired of being a symbol; he counters with, "Greatness demands all." After nominating Charles to succeed her, Christina abdicates and rides to the ship, where she finds Antonio mortally wounded in a duel with Magnus. Promising never to leave him, Christina watches Antonio die; then she prepares to sail for his homeland and his house on a cliff.

SILK STOCKINGS

Released: 1957
Production: Arthur Freed for Metro-Goldwyn-Mayer
Direction: Rouben Mamoulian
Screenplay: Leonard Gershe and Leonard Spigelgass; based on the play of
   the same name by George S. Kaufman, Leueen McGrath, and Abe Bur-
   rows, adapted from the film *Ninotchka*
Cinematography: Robert Bronner
Editing: Harold F. Kress
Choreography: Hermes Pan and Eugene Loring
Music: Cole Porter
Running time: 117 minutes

> *Principal characters:*
> Steve Canfield .... Fred Astaire
> Ninotchka .... Cyd Charisse
>   (sung by Carol Richards)
> Peggy Dayton ....Janis Paige
> Vassili Markovitch .... George Tobias
> Brankov .... Peter Lorre
> Bibinski .... Jules Munshin
> Ivanov ....Joseph Buloff
> Peter Ilyitch Boroff .... Wim Sonneveld

   A Cold War commentary on Soviet-American relations, Rouben Mamoulian's *Silk Stockings* also develops the theme of an individual's emotional
awakening and lightly satirizes the popular entertainment of the 1950's. Based
on the film *Ninotchka* (1939) by way of the 1955 stage play *Silk Stockings*,
the film not only serves as a showcase for the dancing of Fred Astaire and
Cyd Charisse, but also reflects the political, social, and cultural values of
the times. Politically, the film captures the stereotypes of Communist and
capitalist ideologies that pervaded much of American culture. Socially, *Silk
Stockings* celebrates an American view of warm femininity contrasted with
the cold, brusque manner attributed to Russian women. Culturally, it reacts
to the trend in motion pictures toward extravaganza and to a new musical
form, rock and roll. Throughout, the musical numbers choreographed by
Hermes Pan and Eugene Loring effectively provide continuity in plot, underscore the film's thematic import, and graphically portray the awakening
experience.
   Although the film mirrors American values, the setting is elegant Paris,
whose luxuriant decadence provides an antithesis to bleak Soviet life. During
a concert tour in the French city, acclaimed Soviet composer-pianist Peter
Ilyitch Boroff (Wim Sonneveld) is persuaded by American film producer
Steve Canfield (Fred Astaire) to write the music for his new film, supposedly

a version of *War and Peace*. This production will inaugurate the serious film career of Peggy Dayton (Janis Paige), already well-known to moviegoers as "America's swimming sweetheart." The Soviet government, upset by Boroff's impending defection, sends Brankov (Peter Lorre), Bibinski (Jules Munshin), and Ivanov (Joseph Buloff) to effect his return to Moscow. But Canfield introduces the three to the pleasures of wine, women, and song in capitalistic Paris, and they forget their mission. Meanwhile, back in Moscow, Vassili Markovitch (George Tobias) has become Minister of Culture in one of the characteristically abrupt changes in regime said to define Soviet politics. Reflecting the hypocrisy of the Communist system, the minister's businesslike exterior is belied by his less than businesslike interest in one of the ballerinas under his charge. But now he faces the task of sending someone to retrieve the wayward Boroff and the three errant emissaries. The assignment falls to Ninotchka (Cyd Charisse), who appears before him in the drab garb of Soviet officialdom named Yoshenko, spouting Communist and antiindividualist rhetoric and exhibiting an impressive portfolio of credentials.

After Yoshenko arrives in Paris, Canfield tries to convince her by means of a falsified affidavit that Boroff's father was a French traveling salesman, thus making Boroff a French citizen. A day's tour of Paris with Canfield makes no dent in the comrade's severity. Although Canfield emphasizes the romantic beauty of Paris, she is interested only in mills and factories. However, later that evening in his hotel room, Canfield introduces Comrade Yoshenko to emotional warmth. Though she asserts that love is merely a chemical reaction, Canfield proves her wrong with the concrete illustrations of dance, kiss, and the song "All of You." Under his spell, Comrade Yoshenko begins to awaken and to doff Soviet impersonality and conformity for Western individuality. She becomes Ninotchka.

The activities of the couple are interrupted by the intrusion of Peggy Dayton, who reveals Canfield's plan to have Boroff compose music for his film. Her Soviet dignity and pride offended, Ninotchka leaves. Canfield then convinces Peggy to use her considerable charms to enlist Boroff himself in their cause; that is, to allow his music to be converted into tunes appropriate for the hit parade. For Canfield's plan is not to produce a version of *War and Peace* at all, but a spicy account of the life of Josephine in "glorious technicolor, breathtaking CinemaScope, and stereophonic sound"—features of the Hollywood spectacular which earlier provided a rousing, satiric musical number for Canfield and Peggy.

The next morning, Ninotchka is so starry-eyed from Canfield's dancing, singing, and kissing that she cannot seriously deal with the matter which has brought her to Paris. As her three colleagues discuss Boroff with her, she dreamily picks at the typewriter. Her hair, softened into waves which contrast with the austere style of the previous day, signals the feminizing process inherent in her awakening experience.

In the meantime, Peggy has lured Boroff to her fashion designer's, where she seduces him by modeling the latest undergarments. Her song, "Satin and Silk," expounds the power of such feminine clothing to make a woman feel alluring and attractive. Peggy's song and its effect on Boroff testify to the power of feminine wiles.

This scene is effectively juxtaposed with one in Ninotchka's room. Having called off a meeting with Boroff, she draws the curtains, turns Lenin's photograph face down, and exchanges her dark stockings for ones made from Parisian silk—garments she had sneered at upon her arrival in Paris. In a sensuous dance, she casts off her uniform for the Western accouterments she has secreted around her suite: delicate underwear, a bracelet, earrings, perfume, high-heeled slippers, and an evening gown. Her metamorphosis complete; she is ready for a night on the town with Canfield. She now represents the 1950's feminine concept, in contrast to her dowdy and severe appearance upon arriving in Paris. Returning at two o'clock in the morning after drinking much champagne, Ninotchka is even more starry-eyed. When she slips into a tipsy sleep, Canfield chastely lays her on a couch and leaves.

The next day at the movie studio where they have gone to watch the filming of Canfield's movie, Steve proposes marriage to Ninotchka, singing that they are "Fated to Be Mated." Although she yearns to accept, she fears the repressive Soviet government will prevent it. On the set itself the expected serious treatment of *War and Peace* turns out to be a travesty. Peggy, playing a sultry Josephine, performs Boroff's "Ode to a Tractor" in the style of American popular music. The Soviets, Ninotchka included, view this as an affront to their culture and return to Moscow.

In one of the film's few technical lapses, we find ourselves without transition in Russia about a year later. The Soviets meet for a reunion in Ninotchka's portion of a somber flat shared with several others. Soviet life is depicted as void of luxury, privacy, pleasure, and beauty. Ninotchka receives a letter from Canfield, completely censored except for the salutation and closing. Boroff reveals that he has adopted a new musical style and performs "The Red Blues." The other occupants of Ninotchka's flat join the singing and dancing to express their dissatisfaction with Soviet life.

When Brankov, Bibinski, and Ivanov are sent to Paris again, an anonymous letter informs the Minister of Culture that they have again been taken in by the city's decadence. Ninotchka must go once more to bring them home to Russia. When she arrives at the hotel in Paris, she is struck by the Soviet motif in the decor. Her three comrades, dressed in Western clothing, insist that she see the show at the cafe. The production features Steve Canfield dancing and singing "The Ritz Roll and Rock," a piece written especially for the film by Cole Porter to comment on a brash new musical genre. In their office afterwards, the three Russians tell Ninotchka that they have bought the cafe and do not intend to return to Moscow. She also learns that the anonymous letter was sent by Canfield, who had finally decided it was the only way that he could get her out of Russia. He announces his intention to marry her, and the film ends with "Too Bad," the same song with which it began.

Silk Stockings was the last show which Cole Porter wrote for the stage, the last film directed by Rouben Mamoulian, and the last musical film in which Fred Astaire appeared as leading man. Contemporary critical response varied from the opinion that the story line was too ponderous for musical comedy treatment to rhapsodies over the dancing of Astaire and Charisse. The dancing is, indeed, the film's strongest point. Whether it be an expression of the sexual chemistry between the two principals, a manifestation of the frivolity of gay Paris, or merely a showcase for the talented cast, the dancing in *Silk Stockings* makes the film a worthwhile experience even in an age when the values of the 1950's seem peculiarly foreign.

GEORGE STEVENS

ALICE ADAMS

Released: 1935
Production: Pandro S. Berman for RKO/Radio
Direction: George Stevens
Screenplay: Dorothy Yost and Mortimer Offner; based on Jane Murfin's
adaptation of the novel of the same name by Booth Tarkington
Cinematography: Robert de Grasse
Editing: Jane Loring
Running time: 99 minutes

Principal characters:

Alice Adams	Katharine Hepburn
Arthur Russell	Fred MacMurray
Mr. Adams	Fred Stone
Mrs. Adams	Ann Shoemaker
Walter Adams	Frank Albertson
J. A. Lamb	Charley Grapewin
Malena	Hattie McDaniel
Mildred Palmer	Evelyn Venable
Frank Dowling	Grady Sutton

Alice Adams is a poignant story of a young woman's social ambitions and romantic dreams which are almost thwarted by her family's lack of money. The film is both a romance with a fairy-tale ending and a commentary on middle-class mores in a small Midwestern town in the first quarter of the twentieth century. Katharine Hepburn vividly depicts both the affectations and the vulnerability of a young woman who sees a respectable marriage as the only means to fulfillment and happiness.

The small-town milieu is quickly and indelibly established in the opening scenes, beginning with the camera moving from a sign reading "South Renford, Ind. The town with a future," past storefront signs, until it tilts down to reveal Alice Adams emerging from a department store. She stops at a florist shop to order a corsage for the dance that evening but nothing seems to satisfy her. We realize that she cannot really afford a corsage when the next scene shows her picking violets in a park to make her own. The sequence conveys perfectly Alice's poverty, affectation, and aspirations.

Alice's father (Fred Stone), who is recovering from a long illness, is content with his clerical job with the wholesale drug firm of J. A. Lamb (Charley Grapewin), but her mother (Ann Shoemaker) is not. Bitterly, she tells her husband that they have been left behind in the race for money and social position and that his refusal to start his own business has endangered Alice's chance to marry well.

Alice's brother, Walter (Frank Albertson), is not interested in society or social position and has to be cajoled by his mother into taking Alice to the dance given by Mildred Palmer (Evelyn Venable), a member of a socially prominent family. Walter does not like what he calls those "frozen-faced" society people and is rude to Alice and his mother, saying that Alice should be able to get somebody to take her since she tries so hard. Underneath his reluctance and brusque exterior, however, he does feel sorry for Alice and finally allows himself to be persuaded.

One of the most memorable sequences in the film, the Palmers' dance interweaves the romantic fairy-tale element with sharp commentary on Alice's pretensions and those of the rich and socially prominent people around her. Alice makes Walter park their old car on the street so she can pretend to the butler that their car has broken down. Once inside, she puts on her best society manners, simpering and giggling and talking breathlessly to Walter on inane topics when anyone can overhear their conversation. Walter is embarrassed by her play-acting but agrees to dance the first dance with her. Walter is an excellent dancer, but he mortifies Alice by greeting the black orchestra leader as an old friend.

Abandoned by Walter, who goes off to shoot dice with the cloakroom attendants, Alice, alone and uneasy, pretends desperately that she is having a good time. She is ignored by several men obviously searching for partners, and several of the women comment on her outmoded gown. She is finally rescued by fat Frank Dowling (Grady Sutton), an undesirable partner, who humiliates her by his awkwardness on the dance floor and bores her with his lack of conversation. Finally, even Frank is taken away by his mother, and Alice is alone, pretending she is waiting for a partner. Furtively, she pushes her now bedraggled homemade corsage under her chair and watches as Mildred Palmer greets a tall handsome stranger at the door. When Mildred and the stranger walk by, Alice goes into her act, posing, laughing to herself, and pretending she is having the most amusing thoughts as she waits for her partner.

We sympathize with Alice through this period of suffering because, despite her outward pretentiousness, snobbery, and silliness, her vulnerability—the eager, expectant look in her eyes—shines through. We realize that her pride demands this show of bravado, which reveals how she thinks a society girl enjoying herself at a party would act. At last, giving up all hope of a partner, Alice is going to sit with the old chaperones when she is rescued by the tall dark stranger, whom Mildred introduces to her as Arthur Russell (Fred MacMurray). Here is Prince Charming, but Alice, thinking Mildred has asked him to dance with her out of pity, is for once silent and natural. After the dance, she asks Russell to find Walter for her so she can go home.

The next day Alice meets Russell again just as she has worked up enough nerve to enter a business college to seek a secretarial job. Having rescued her from a horrible fate—one that would have put any chance of social advancement entirely out of her reach—Russell proceeds to tell her he has been thinking about her and wants to see more of her. Alice immediately assumes her airs and mannerisms, talking incessantly, giving little trills of laughter, fabricating a social background similar to those of the other girls of his acquaintance, and guarding herself against gossip by telling him she is not very popular with men because she shows them she is bored by them.

Russell is anxious to visit and further his acquaintance, but Alice, who is ashamed of her family's shabby house, refuses to let him come inside. Indeed, their entire courtship is conducted on the front porch of the house or at restaurants. Finally, Mrs. Adams practically forces Alice to invite Russell to dinner. Up to this point Alice's strategy has been masterly. She has already warned him against listening to gossip about herself or her family and has used her father's illness as an excuse for always entertaining him outside and not going to dinners and dances to which, unknown to Russell, she has not been invited. As she tells him, with more truth than he knows, she would not dare to be merely herself with him.

Meanwhile, her mother's constant nagging has worn her father down, and despite many misgivings, he has mortgaged the house to start his own glue factory. Virgil Adams feels it is like stealing to take a glue formula developed on company time to start his own business. He likes and trusts his paternalistic employer, J. A. Lamb (for whom he has worked for twenty-five years), and does not want to anger him. But under his wife's relentless hammering he makes the break and rents an old warehouse for his factory. On the evening of the ill-fated dinner he is worried because there has been no response to this action from Lamb, who is not a man to let someone else get the best of him.

In order to do the dinner in style, her mother hires a black maid and cook, Malena (Hattie McDaniel), for the evening. Although it is a hot, humid night, the meal is heavy and elaborate, beginning with caviar sandwiches and hot soup. The slow-moving, gum-chewing Malena, with her maid's cap askew, inelegantly removes plates and thrusts serving trays under people's noses. Everything that can go wrong, does. Virgil Adams' shirtfront keeps popping open, and when he wants more water, he cannot remember the maid's name. The smell of Brussels sprouts pervades the little house, and Russell is obviously ill-at-east as he mops his sweaty neck. Alice chatters brightly, trying to retrieve what she knows is a disaster, but Russell is politely unresponsive. When she offers a penny for his thoughts, he replies uncomfortably that he hasn't any. She takes him outside, "where we belong," and indicates her understanding of his feelings by telling him she knows it is over, that he will not be coming to see her again. After all, when "everything's spoiled you can't do anything but run away," she tells him.

If Alice's romance has reached a crisis point on this hot, humid evening, so have the affairs of her father. Walter tells him he has embezzled one hundred and fifty dollars from Lamb's firm and could be sent to jail. Lamb himself pays a visit and informs Adams he is starting a glue factory of his own, which will mean ruin for Adams. Though Alice's hopes may have been destroyed, she is determined to save her father's dreams if she can. In an emotional scene she persuades Lamb that it is the fault of her and her mother that her father defected. After her plea Lamb agrees to work something out to save both her father and her brother.

The film continues in this fairy-tale manner as Alice goes back out onto the porch to find Russell still there. She will keep her Prince Charming and have a happy ending. When Russell tells her he loves her, her response is the most natural and unaffected thing she says in the whole film—"Gee Whiz!"

Although *Alice Adams* makes some trenchant comments on middle-class society, particularly in the dance and dinner scenes, and although the arguments between Mr. and Mrs. Adams are sharply realized and almost painful to watch, the film is not wholly successful as social commentary, primarily because of the unrealistic happy ending which was tacked on by the script-writers. In the Booth Tarkington novel on which the film was based, Russell leaves and does not return, and Alice actually does climb the stairs to the business college to get a job. It is doubtful, however, that the moviegoing public of the 1930's would have accepted such a downbeat ending (or so the studio believed). Even Tarkington thought the novel's ending would have to be changed before it could be filmed.

Aside from the ending, the film is a perfectly realized portrait of an intelligent, socially ambitious young woman, struggling to find a foothold in a society that has left her and her family behind. At a time when a woman's only socially acceptable career was marriage, Alice looked upon a job as the last resort, and as one which would spell the end of her social aspirations.

The role is sensitively played by a luminous, tremulous Katharine Hepburn. Although Alice's mannerisms and snobbishness are tiresome, we nevertheless become emotionally involved with her and sympathize with her. This is due in no small measure to Hepburn's skill at letting the essential loneliness and vulnerability of the heroine shine through her artificial society manners. It is one of Hepburn's most memorable performances of the 1930's. The rest of the cast lends excellent support, particularly Fred Stone and Ann Shoemaker as Alice's parents, and Hattie McDaniel in a bit part as the hapless Malena. Fred MacMurray is not required to do much except look handsome and romantic, but he is certainly credible as the Prince Charming of a young woman's dreams. All in all, the film is a touching, sometimes realistic, sometimes romantic portrait of small-town life.

GIANT

Released: 1956
Production: George Stevens and Henry Ginsberg for Warner Bros.
Direction: George Stevens (AA)
Screenplay: Fred Guiol and Ivan Moffat; based on the novel of the same name by Edna Ferber
Cinematography: William C. Mellor
Editing: William Hornbeck, Philip W. Anderson, and Fred Bohanen
Music: Dmitri Tiomkin
Running time: 198 minutes

Principal characters:
Leslie Lynnton Benedict .... Elizabeth Taylor
Bick Benedict .... Rock Hudson
Jett Rink .... James Dean
Luz Benedict (the older) .... Mercedes McCambridge
Vashti Snythe .... Jane Withers
Uncle Bawley Benedict .... Chill Wills
Luz Benedict (the younger) .... Carroll Baker
Jordan Benedict III .... Dennis Hopper
Juana Benedict .... Elsa Cardenas
Judy Benedict .... Fran Bennett

Giant belongs to the Hollywood era that saw the release of films such as *The Ten Commandments*, *Around the World in 80 Days*, *War and Peace*, and *The King and I* all in the same year. Emphasis was on spectacle, grandeur, extravagance, and length. Producer/director George Stevens, in keeping with the trend, ambitiously attempted to film a great American epic from Edna Ferber's sprawling best seller about a colorful, land-rich Texas family. The film's mixed critical reviews did not prevent its commercial success and kudos for individual performances and Stevens' overall work in the film. Some skeptical critics attributed the film's success to the last performance of James Dean, who became an object of adulation after his death in a fiery car crash. Dean portrayed Jett Rink, one of the three central characters in this saga that covers approximately twenty-five years of American, and especially Texan history.

Before Jett Rink is introduced, the two other central characters meet, fall in love, and set the stage for their future conflicts. The film opens with Texas cattle baron Bick Benedict, played with authority by Rock Hudson, being out of his element in Maryland, in the elegant, cultured society of the prominent Maryland surgeon, Dr. Horace Lynnton, whose prize stallion Bick has come to purchase. While visiting the Lynntons, he meets their lovely daughter Leslie (Elizabeth Taylor). Although Bick and Leslie sense an immediate attraction to each other, their totally dissimilar natures and backgrounds spark some spirited and lively scenes. Leslie Lynnton is the despair of her social-climbing mother because she has a sharp mind and a tongue to match. Mrs. Lynnton fears that Leslie, although she is engaged, may never marry the "right" husband. Bick is attracted to Leslie but is totally immersed in his ranch and completely convinced of the greatness of the Texas way of life. When Leslie tries to discuss certain controversial points of Texas history, such as how the large landowners obtained their vast holdings, Bick's response is hardly polite. Key areas of conflict are identified early in the film, even during this courtship stage, and foreshadow the power struggles and troubles to come.

These opening Maryland scenes are photographed in bright colors amid lush surroundings. There are shots of the green, rolling, fox-hunting country of Maryland, detailed close-ups of the lavish life style of the Lynntons, and lingering close-ups of the attractive Bick and Leslie as they fall in love. Stevens is painstaking in portraying small, sensitive details.

The scene now changes. Mr. and Mrs. Bick Benedict and the prize stallion, War Winds, are off to Texas to Bick's massive ranch, Reata, and to a bout of culture shock for the former Leslie Lynnton. Again, differences between Bick and Leslie are shown in Leslie's gracious greeting of a Mexican youth who has come to meet them at the train station. Bick tells her that she should not make such a fuss over a Mexican boy. They have their first quarrel as man and wife, but are reconciled on the drive to their home, which is a memorable visual experience. In contrast to the green, lush countryside of Leslie's Maryland home, Texas is introduced desolately as the speeding car kicks up the brown-gray dust for mile after mile of the vast, treeless ranch until the stark Gothic outline of the Big House emerges above the horizon.

Leslie is the outsider now. She must grapple with a new set of customs, beliefs, and people. First, there is Luz (Mercedes McCambridge), Bick's spinster older sister who finds it impossible to relinquish her tightly held rein on the Big House and on her younger brother. Luz is cordial to Leslie but treats her as a guest rather than as the new mistress of Reata. Other people whom Leslie meets are friends and neighboring ranchers. Leslie, who has spent her mature life engaging in adult conversations with men such as her father and other cultivated society folk, now is part of a completely different society. In Texas, the men talk only to other men about substantive matters. The women spend idle lives filled with shopping, endless coffee-klatching, and frivolous gossip. The prime example is Vashti (Jane Withers), the bulky awkward daughter of the neighboring ranch owner, who had hoped to land the dashing Bick and who marries one of her father's ranch hands out of spite.

Leslie's liberal instincts are stimulated by the plight of the Mexicans on the ranch and in the surrounding community. Her attempts to aid them only arouse Bick's anger, and this prejudice shown early in the film eventually will build to a climax in which Bick must come to terms with his own weaknesses and complacency.

The presence of the swaggering wrangler, Jett Rink (James Dean), adds a dimension of menace to the plot. The Benedicts of Reata are the "haves"; the insecure, upwardly striving, threatening Jett is a "have not." In his early scenes as a sullen ranch hand, he conveys an adulterous lust for Leslie, an arrogant hostility towards his employer Bick, and the hint of an unhealthy relationship with Luz. Jett's interference in Benedict affairs causes Luz, who is feeling spurned by her brother, to ride out in a fury on the stallion, War Winds. She suffers a fatal fall, and in a rage Bick runs Jett off the ranch. Luz, however, has willed Jett a seemingly worthless bit of land on the ranch and Jett will be heard from again. James Dean's performance, straight method acting, is photographed almost entirely in shadows. Together, Stevens and Dean have captured a sense of dramatic unity.

After Luz's death, a pattern of living emerges for Bick and Leslie. The slow pace is one method Stevens uses to reinforce his vision of reality. He wants to convey the feeling of twenty-five years slowly passing, of the adjustments and responses to change that his characters must make. Bick and Leslie become the parents of a son, Jordy (Dennis Hopper), and two daughters, Judy (Fran Bennett) and Luz (Carroll Baker), after her aunt. Now a new generation of Benedicts must deal with the conflicting values of their parents: Bick, who lives for the ranch and his traditions, and Leslie, still the liberal, fighting for causes and trying to impose some elegance and taste on the bleak Texas atmosphere.

Young Jordy, the pride and hope of his father, shows a marked distaste for the life of a rancher. In temperament, he takes after his mother, and, as he grows up, he longs to be a doctor. Jordy's twin sister Judy is a disappointment first to her mother for her tomboy ways, and, later, to her father for her growing attachment to an experimental farmer named Bob Dietz (Earl Holliman), whom she eventually marries. More arguments occur between Leslie and Bick as their preconceived expectations for the children do not take into account that they are individuals with individual needs and desires. Even Leslie becomes narrow-minded as she insists on molding her daughters into unsuitable, unwanted roles.

Part of the pattern of Texas living is the old cattle aristocracy making way for the new oil rich. In some of the most carefully crafted scenes in the film, Stevens shows Jett Rink's financial rise. Jett's character develops as Stevens portrays his enthusiasm in working his own piece of land. Jett at last has something that belongs to him, and he feverishly works his "worthless" land for oil harder than he ever worked for the Benedicts. At last, his gusher comes in, and a rapturous Jett is drenched by the black gold. His tie to the Benedicts, part resentment, part envy, and part desire to show off to Leslie, prompts him to race over to the Big House where the Benedicts are entertaining. Smirking over his success, he becomes a bit too familiar with Leslie, which causes Bick to strike him. Jett recovers quickly, delivers a sharp blow in return, and then furiously rides off.

Jett's increasing wealth and power in the state are often discussed by the other characters. Years later, still crude and insecure in spite of his wealth, he is back on the scene trying to woo young Luz. He has planned a huge party to celebrate the grand opening of one of his hotels. All Texas society, new and old, feels obliged to attend, including the Benedicts, despite their aversion to Jett. Dr. Jordan Benedict III and his Mexican wife Juana (Elsa Cardenas) make the trip, as well as graying Bick and Leslie. The Bob Dietzes and their young child are the only family members who do not attend the great affair. Juana has made an appointment with the hotel's beauty parlor under the name Mrs. Jordan Benedict. When she arrives, she is told that Mexicans are not served. She calls Jordy, who demolishes the beauty parlor in a rage and proceeds to the big banquet hall for a confrontation with Jett. Jett is surrounded by bodyguards who hold Jordy down for Jett's attack in front of a crowd of people which includes the other Benedicts. Bick, in spite of his conflicting emotions, rises to defend his son, and he too is felled by Jett.

Drunk and despondent over his failed attempt to impress Texas society, Jett has a touching scene in which he makes a pathetic speech to the deserted banquet hall. The speech is overheard by Luz, who earlier had defended Jett in defiance of her parents. Now at last she realizes that in Jett's eyes she is no more than a substitute for her mother.

After the disastrous banquet, Bick and Leslie drive Juana and her young son back to the ranch. They stop at a roadside restaurant where once again Juana is refused service. All the years of Bick's prejudice and conservatism now intermingle with his sense of family pride and Leslie's liberal influence. He engages in a wild brawl with the restaurant owner, amid the strains of the film's popular ballad "The Yellow Rose of Texas." The film ends back at Reata where Bick and Leslie compromise their old positions and look to their two grandchildren, one half Mexican, the other a blond toddler, to bring about needed changes and social justice.

A major criticism of *Giant* is that the film, like the Edna Ferber novel, has no focus, that it has combined melodramatic themes of family conflict, the alien outsider, and racial prejudice, without any true resolution. Another criticism is that the disdain for the crass, bigoted, materialistic society on the move is not balanced by a sensitive understanding of the individual motivations of the people in that society. These points may be valid, or only partially so; but such deficiencies are redeemed by the strengths of George Stevens' work. He is able to elicit more than competent performances from Rock Hudson and Elizabeth Taylor, especially before they are required to age. James Dean ended his career with a stunning characterization that received almost universal praise. Dean, Rock Hudson, and Mercedes McCambridge received Best Actor and Best Supporting Actress nominations, respectively. Other nominees from the film were Dmitri Tiomkin for the scoring; William Hornbeck, Philip W. Anderson, and Fred Bohanen for film editing; Ralph S. Hurst for art and set decoration; Moss Mabry and Marjorie Best for costume design; and Fred Guiol and Ivan Moffat for the screenplay.

Despite its faulty plot, George Stevens is able to bring to this film a visual sweep, careful attention to sound, and many striking small touches. Examples of Stevens' sensitive direction include the shot of the drunken Jett walking to the dais at his banquet, the beautifully framed long shot of the horse that has just thrown Luz on her return to Reata, and the warm pillow-talk conversations between Bick and Leslie. For his efforts in delineating a sensitive landscape of the human condition, Stevens the producer received an Academy Award nomination for Best Picture and won the Best Director Award for 1956.

THE MORE THE MERRIER

Released: 1943
Production: George Stevens for Columbia
Direction: George Stevens
Screenplay: Robert Russell, Frank Ross, Richard Flournoy, and Lewis R. Foster
Cinematography: Ted Tetzlaff
Editing: Otto Meyer
Running time: 104 minutes

> *Principal characters:*
> Connie Milligan .... Jean Arthur
> Joe Carter .... Joel McCrea
> Benjamin Dingle .... Charles Coburn (AA)
> Charles J. Pendergast .... Richard Gaines
> Evans .... Bruce Bennett
> Pike .... Frank Sully

World War II brought a dramatic change to the life-styles of many Americans who were still recovering from the ravages of the Great Depression. Most found the intrusion of war into their daily lives a considerable hardship to face; nevertheless, the American people persevered and set to work winning the war, just as they had conquered the Depression and returned to prosperity. As American life on the home front changed, one manifestation of Hollywood's reaction was a curious subgenre of film—pictures dealing with conditions in wartime Washington. In some cases, filmmakers concentrated on melodrama, such as Fox's 1942 production of *Careful—Soft Shoulders*, in which a Washington debutante, bored with society life, took up spying. In others, the issue of housing problems set the stage; RKO contributed *Government Girl* (1943) with Olivia de Havilland; Paramount's *Standing Room Only* (1944) had stars Paulette Goddard and Fred MacMurray taking jobs as servants in order to have places to live; and even Universal, turning out dozens of "B" pictures, managed to squeeze the housing problem into a tuneful little gem like *Get Going* (1943).

The best of the films taking place in wartime Washington, however, was Columbia's *The More the Merrier* directed by comedy ace George Stevens and starring Jean Arthur, Joel McCrea, and Charles Coburn. Four writers—Richard Flournoy, Lewis Foster, Robert Russell, and Frank Ross—were credited with the original screenplay, leading one to believe that perhaps the best elements of two or three treatments were probably combined for the finished product. Stevens gave the film an "A" production, and Jean Arthur, as one of Columbia's top stars, lent valuable audience appeal to the property. Viewed historically from afar, of course, the concept dates poorly; housing shortages related to wartime seem a thing of the past, and many younger Americans of the postatomic age have difficulty comprehending the climate of past times. Nonetheless, *The More the Merrier* holds up quite well in a comic sense, and is arguably Stevens' finest comedy.

Working girl Connie Milligan (Jean Arthur) lives in Washington and, against her better judgment, makes her sacrifice to the war effort by renting half of her apartment to distinguished, elderly Benjamin Dingle (Charles Coburn)—who bills himself as a "retired, well-to-do millionaire" in Washington on business. Dingle, obviously unaccustomed to the fast pace Connie is forced to keep, is experiencing a great deal of difficulty in keeping up with her schedules, designed to keep the two people out of each other's way. In one memorable sequence, the befuddled Dingle tries to remove his bathrobe while holding a hot coffee pot, managing to spill most of the coffee into the bath water. Later, still hurried, he makes his bed with his pants inside.

As if matters are not complicated enough, Dingle rents half of his half of the apartment to Army sergeant Joe Carter (Joel McCrea), who is in town on special duty. This infuriates Connie, who is finding it difficult enough to share the apartment with one man. Dingle, however, sees in Joe an ideal man for Connie, who is already engaged to Charles J. Pendergast (Richard Gaines), a rather pompous and bland government official. He convinces Connie to try the situation, and she agrees to let Joe stay for a one-week trial period. All appears to go smoothly for a short time, but then Connie discovers Mr. Dingle reading her diary; terribly upset at her lack of privacy, she asks him to leave, and to take Joe with him. The next morning Dingle leaves, but Joe remains behind, convincing Connie to let him stay. Joe, previously having professed to have little interest in women, is becoming very fond of Connie.

Although Mr. Dingle no longer lives in the apartment, he still manages to play Cupid by engineering an evening in which he manages to get Connie away from Pendergast and alone with Joe. In one sequence, she reminds the soldier that she is engaged to Pendergast since he becomes somewhat amorous, kissing her neck; Connie continues to speak fondly of Pendergast, but it is apparent that her emotions are weakening toward Joe. Inside the apartment later on, they admit that they love each other but Joe is scheduled to leave Washington the next day.

At this point the fates seem to take the upper hand as the FBI shows up to take Joe into custody. Apparently, in a rash moment, Joe has scared away a pestering neighborhood boy by claiming that he was a Japanese spy, and the boy has reported him to the authorities.

Joe's denials avail him little, and he finds himself and Connie at the police station trying in vain to explain the situation. In the ensuing confusion, both Dingle and Pendergast turn up, with the latter horrified to see his betrothed in custody. As he hears the story, however, he becomes less interested in the claims that Joe is a spy, and more interested in the revelation that he has been sharing Connie's apartment. It is a development that he can scarcely tolerate. Simultaneously, one of the newspapermen, knowing that Pendergast is a government official, sees the making of a great story as Pendergast sees the making of a great scandal; his future would certainly be ruined by being linked to such a scandalous woman. Pendergast therefore steadfastly maintains that the only solution to this sticky situation is for Connie to marry Joe quickly and then get an immediate annulment. This is a side of Pendergast that Connie has not seen before, and she finds it distasteful. She agrees reluctantly to his idea, however, and she and Joe, cleared of the charges that he is a foreign agent, return to the apartment, where they regretfully agree to play out Pendergast's scheme. Mr. Dingle, however, convinces them to get married but not have an annulment, leading them at the film's finale in a chorus of his favorite saying: "Damn the torpedoes! Full steam ahead!"

The role of Connie was one of Jean Arthur's best; her winsome charm suited the working-girl character perfectly, and a more glamorous star in the same role might have robbed it of credibility. McCrea, another successful "Everyman" type of character, is likewise effective as Joe. Most, however, agreed that the film was stolen by Charles Coburn, who won the Academy Award for Best Supporting Actor for his rich comic performance. The film's other nominations included Jean Arthur for Best Actress, Stevens for Best Director, Ross and Russell for Best Original Screenplay, and the film for Best Picture. The basic plot of *The More the Merrier* was updated and remade as *Walk Don't Run* (1966), starring Cary Grant in the Coburn role, with the romantic leads Samantha Eggar and Jim Hutton. Capitalizing on the housing shortage in Tokyo during the 1964 Olympics, the remake was a pale shadow of the original, lacking the innate charm given it by the stylish direction of George Stevens.

A PLACE IN THE SUN

Released: 1951
Production: George Stevens for Paramount
Direction: George Stevens (AA)
Screenplay: Harry Brown and Michael Wilson (AA); based on the novel *An American Tragedy* by Theodore Dreiser
Cinematography: William C. Mellor (AA)
Editing: William Hornbeck (AA)
Costume design: Edith Head (AA)
Music: Franz Waxman (AA)
Running time: 122 minutes

Principal characters:

George Eastman	Montgomery Clift
Angela Vickers	Elizabeth Taylor
Alice Tripp	Shelley Winters
Hannah Eastman	Anne Revere
Anthony Vickers	Shepperd Strudwick
Mrs. Vickers	Frieda Inescort
Earl Eastman	Keefe Brasselle
Bellows	Fred Clark
Frank Marlowe	Raymond Burr

From its opening shot, in which George Eastman (Montgomery Clift) is drawn by twin images of luxury—a billboard beauty reclining in her bathing suit and Angela Vickers (Elizabeth Taylor) driving past in her convertible—*A Place in the Sun* identifies George as a man virtually without a will of his own. His life is made up of women and the demands they make on him. His mother wants him to be a good God-fearing boy, and his girl friend, Alice Tripp (Shelley Winters), wants him to marry her so that their child will not be illegitimate. Angela, too, wants to be his wife and to ease him into her life of privilege and security.

It is easy to understand George's predicament. A poor boy of no innate gifts who takes a job in his uncle's factory and who makes his way along the management chain while simultaneously ascending the social ladder, he is an apt victim of twentieth century venality, a prime candidate for the way of life offered by his milieu. But George has already made his first mistake when the opportunity of marrying Angela is presented. He has become involved with Alice and gotten her pregnant, not only in contravention of society's laws, but of the plant's "no fraternization" rule as well.

From then on the dual images are those of Alice, spilling out of her clothes, pig-eyed and frightened, and of Angela, voluptuous, rich, and gorgeous. The choice is made before George knows that he has made it. Here director

George Stevens is very subtle. In George's room there is a picture, a sort of Maxfield Parrish representation of Ophelia drowning. A shot which was cut from the release print shows George looking speculatively at the picture. As the film stands, it is in the background, a morbid decoration for George's cheerless room. The idea is that the print inspires George to commit murder, but the George Eastman that Stevens gives us is without conscious volition, a man as incapable of killing as he is of taking charge of his own life.

George is not, however, without blame. Stevens' film does not specifically indict American mercantilism and the work ethic to censure George, but these themes are in the background. They are the forces which have molded him and from which he is powerless to escape. The film was made in 1951, making George Eastman a member of the mid-century "silent generation" that elected Eisenhower and allowed Joe McCarthy to run rampant. Insofar as he is without a will of his own, George is part of that group; inasmuch as he is a fictional creation of Michael Wilson and Harry Brown, not to mention Theodore Dreiser, he is "Everyman," rootless and drifting until he is taken in tow by Angela and his uncle and made into something he could not have become without them.

In fact, George is colorless and uninteresting. If he were not played by Montgomery Clift at the height of his good looks and talent, he would be a bore. The circumstances surrounding the filming of *A Place in the Sun* are germane to what is visible on the screen. Clift coached Elizabeth Taylor into giving an extraordinary performance. She had previously starred in *Father of the Bride* (1950), the first film in which her breathtaking beauty was in full bloom; but her great performance in Stevens' film resulted as much from Clifts's efforts as from Stevens' direction.

Stevens used a number of innovative techniques in making this picture. He would compel Taylor and Clift, or Clift and Winters, to rehearse their scenes without dialogue, communicating their thoughts and feelings through gestures and facial expressions. He played "mood music" on the set, principally Franz Waxman's haunting love theme from the film's score. When it came time to shoot the climactic love scene between Clift and Taylor, he moved in with a six-inch lens and shot everything in enormous close-ups, seeming to roll the camera back and forth between the actors' faces until at times one is momentarily lost, unsure whether it is Clift or Taylor who is in view. The effect is that of incredible heat, of exploding passion, of the sensation that these two beautiful people are caught up in something over which they have no control. The scene is sensuous and inflaming, yet reticent and hesitant. It takes places on a terrace, almost in public, and both Angela and George seem to be on guard. Their reserve makes the scene more sensual than if they had been wanton.

Stylistically, *A Place in the Sun* is a *film noir*. It is dark enough for a gothic horror film and mannered enough for Orson Welles. Scene after scene dissolves in slow motion, and the eerie cries of a loon are used as overlapping sounds throughout. Stevens is not afraid to use close-ups in sequences other than love scenes. There is nothing natural about the movie, and that is the secret of its success, as Stevens' painstaking methodology grips his audience's emotions. Because the audience's complicity in the resolution is part of Stevens' aim, he at once involves the viewer in George's fate. It is an extraordinary achievement and one that did not go unrewarded. Stevens, his cinematographer William C. Mellor, his editor William Hornbeck, his writers Harry Brown and Michael Wilson, and his costumer Edith Head, all won Academy Awards. Only Montgomery Clift, nominated for the second time for Best Actor, failed to win. Charles Chaplin stated unequivocally that "This is the best film ever to come out of Hollywood."

Today, however, *A Place in the Sun* is a period piece. Society has done a complete about-face; the Angela Vickerses of society scarcely exist, and where they do no one pays any attention to them. Abortion is regarded as a woman's right, not her shame; poor boys like George Eastman are well up the ladder in multinational corporations by the time they are his age, having bypassed the stock room on the way toward the board room.

It is as an influence that *A Place in the Sun* is perhaps most advantageously seen today. It certainly made acceptable the extreme stylization of films such as *Bonnie and Clyde* (1967) and *Johnny Guitar* (1954). It prepared audiences for the notion that style is substance, that the medium is the message, and that if you do not get the message, you can at least understand the medium.

Three years before *A Place in the Sun* was made, the studio system had been eroded by the antitrust decision divorcing the studios from their theaters; while approximately three years after its release, television's enormous inroads would be felt in the industry. It was to become increasingly difficult for directors and studios to make films that bore the imprint of one man. The Fred Zinnemanns, William Wylers, George Stevenses, and the like, would go on making their movies. The *auteur* theory would eventually be propounded, but things would never be quite the same again. *A Place in the Sun* stands as a glorious monument to that era when it was possible for a movie to stand both as one man's work and as the product of an efficient studio organization.

SHANE

Released: 1953
Production: George Stevens for Paramount
Direction: George Stevens
Screenplay: A. B. Guthrie, Jr., with additional dialogue by Jack Sher; based on the novel of the same name by Jack Schaefer
Cinematography: Loyal Griggs (AA)
Editing: William Hornbeck and Tom McAdoo
Running time: 118 minutes

Principal characters:
Shane .... Alan Ladd
Marian Starrett .... Jean Arthur
Joe Starrett .... Van Heflin
Joey Starrett .... Brandon De Wilde
Wilson .... Jack Palance

Of the countless Westerns produced in Hollywood, *Shane* is among the most familiar and highly regarded. Its significance can be measured in terms of Hollywood's Western past, since *Shane* is a film that reflects upon the Westerns preceding it. It draws on the residue of this most enduring of film genres and abstracts its standard conventions, transforming them into myth. Given that many of the film's narrative events are seen through the eyes of a small boy, *Shane* further underscores the mythic status of the genre, suggesting its function as an outlet for the dreams and fantasies of youngsters.

The film's plot is deceptively simple. Shane (Alan Ladd), a mysterious, buckskin-clad loner, rides into a Wyoming valley during the late 1860's. He soon becomes a hired hand on the fledgling homestead of the Starrett family: Joe (Van Heflin), Marian (Jean Arthur), and young Joey (Brandon De Wilde). Shane is in fact a gunfighter who wants to change his ways; he hopes to settle down and start his own homestead. But Ryker, a cattle baron, intends to drive Starrett and the other homesteaders out of the valley, and Shane finds that he is being gradually drawn back into his past way of life. Because of Starrett's determined leadership, Ryker is unable to harass the homesteaders into leaving, so he hires Wilson (Jack Palance), a cold-blooded hired gun, to scare them out. After Wilson taunts, then easily kills one of the homesteaders in a one-sided gunfight, Starrett decides to put on his guns and stand up to Wilson and the Ryker bunch. Shane, however, knows that Starrett does not stand a chance against these seasoned killers, so he straps on his gun again. When Starrett insists on going, he and Shane wage a furious fistfight; Shane emerges victorious and rides off to meet the killers. In the town saloon, Shane outdraws and kills Wilson, as well as the Rykers. Though wounded, Shane rides out of the valley after indicating to Joey that he will never return.

Crucial to an understanding of *Shane* is its depiction of a mythic genre figure who tries to adapt to changing times by divesting himself of his heroic stature. The difficulty in making this transformation is first suggested when Shane trades in his buckskins for an outfit of drab workclothes. In these clothes, Shane enters a saloon, where he orders not the traditional shot of whiskey, but a bottle of soda pop. In the garb of a homesteader, Shane is taunted by one of the Ryker bunch. Since Shane wants to avoid trouble, he backs down from a fight, which leads the homesteaders to think him a coward. Wearing the same outfit, Shane eventually returns to the saloon, and with Starrett's help, bests the Rykers in a fistfight. The change of clothes allows Shane to initially "become" like a homesteader, but unlike them, Shane ultimately cannot back down from a fight.

Shane's relationship to the Starretts also points to him as one outside the locus of family/community/progress which they embody. While Joe likes Shane, and Joey worships him, Shane is nevertheless positioned as an outsider to the family unit. This is underscored by the unspoken love that he shares with Marian. Marian represents the nonheroic life style Shane can never attain, and their relationship is an idealized one. She is an insider while Shane is an outsider. The inside/outside duality is pointed up during a scene in which Shane stands outside in the rain while Marian is inside the Starrett house. The cross-cutting between the two emphasizes the inside/outside relationship, just as the gentle rendition of "Beautiful Dreamer" on the soundtrack at this point emphasizes the impossibility of Shane's transformation. When Shane finally goes to his quarters—which are, appropriately enough, away from the main house—Marian implies her love for Shane to Joey, telling him, "He'll be moving along one day and you'll be upset if you get to liking him too much." She then blows out a candle, causing the room to go dark. This suggests that her own attraction to Shane is as unattainable as his desire for her.

While Shane can never be a part of this family, he performs a heroic deed so that they—and the other homesteaders—can thrive in the valley. Before Shane rides off to meet Wilson, Marian asks, "Are you doing this just for me?" Shane replies, "For you—and Joe—and little Joey." As Shane rides off to the gunfight, he is again clad in his buckskins and, of course, is wearing a gun. Once again, his outsider status in relation to the family unit is suggested by editing: the Starretts are seen together in a single frame, while Shane rides off alone. Moreover, the ensuing long shots of Shane framed against the sky and mountains reaffirm his status as mythic figure.

Shane's relationship with Joey points to the Western genre as a source of preadolescent wish-fulfillment. This relationship is delineated in a number of ways. The lengthy fight in the saloon contains several cut-ins of Joey watching in fascination, as does the final gunfight. During the gunfight, Joey gets to realize his wish of participating in Shane's heroic actions, since he warns Shane that one of the Rykers is about to ambush him from upstairs, enabling Shane to kill the man. Prior to the climax, Joey gets to "be like" Shane be means of cutting on sound. During the saloon fight, after Shane lands a punch on the jaw of a Ryker henchman, a cut to Joey shows him biting hard on a candy stick. Here, the snapping sound of the bite replaces the sound of the punch.

Also crucial to an understanding of the film is the structuring opposition of civilization *versus* savagery that is a vital part of the generic structure of the Western. The valley town is not a thriving community but a few spread-out buildings and some tents. We see a disparate group of settlers (including an immigrant family and a family headed by a man who fought for the Confederacy), and the film posits that this cross-section holds the promise for a future—the transformation of a wilderness into a garden. The settlers are shown as nonviolent, and they are further ennobled by their harmonious relationship with the earth. During the scene in which they ride into town as a group, they are framed against the majestic mountains, the morning mist, and a sparkling brook. Moreover, the settlers clearly represent progress. This is suggested when Joe looks at a store catalogue from the East, and from his point of view we see the pages, full of appliances, dress suits, and so forth. The settlers, however, lack the ability to bring law to the savage land; they are ill-equipped to stop Ryker from transgressing nature. One homesteader notes that there is not a marshal within a hundred miles. The law, then, belongs to whomever has the fastest gun.

Within this opposition, Ryker and Shane, both of whom represent savagery, have no place in the advent of civilization. While Ryker is a villain, there are shades of gray to his character. He is the man who tamed the valley with his own sweat and blood. As he tells Starrett at one point, "We made this country. We found it and we made it." But Ryker's frontier dream has been perverted by his capitalistic greed, and Starrett's reply to his remark, "That ain't the way the government sees it," suggests the homesteaders are sanctioned by culture and law. The film closely equates Starrett with democratic populism. This is especially suggested during the Independence Day celebration—the day honoring the establishment of the United States is also the anniversary date of the Starretts. During the celebration, the American flag is featured prominently.

While *Shane* clearly champions the populism represented by Starrett and the settlers, it also sadly concludes that there is no place for the rugged individualist within this new system. Finally, the film demonstrates that Ryker's kind of capitalist individualism violates law and community, while Shane's individualism enforces the principals of collective life. When Shane tells the cattle baron, "Your kind of days are over," Ryker replies, "My days? What about yours, gunfighter?" But Shane's next line, "The difference is I know it," stresses his own awareness of what he is. Shane, then, is the noble outlaw/savage who cannot be accommodated by civilization. It is he alone who is equipped to take effective action when words have proved to be inadequate.

In recent years, many revisionist critics have sought to devalue *Shane* because of its rigorous classicism. These critics argue that the "real" Hollywood Westerns have been made by once-slighted directors such as John Ford, Howard Hawks, Anthony Mann, and Budd Boetticher. While the great contribution made to the genre by these directors is incontestable, George Stevens' brief foray into a genre in which he had never worked (and never again worked) can be equated with the writers who came from the East to write about the frontier. Stevens takes the most familiar conventions of the West and stylizes them considerably. For him, the generic material becomes a means of glamorizing this most durable of Hollywood forms. This material also becomes a means of self-expression, and *Shane*'s greatness is due in no small measure to Stevens' pictorial style and personal vision. Stevens himself has been devalued by revisionist critics, but he represents the best of the classical Hollywood cinema. Few directors used the close-up as effectively as Stevens, and the editing patterns linking close-ups of Shane, Marian, and Joey serve to make the film genuinely touching and dramatically potent. This kind of editing recalls Stevens' great love stories, including *Swing Time* (1936), *Woman of the Year* (1942), *The More the Merrier* (1943), and *A Place in the Sun* (1951). After *Shane*, Stevens was weighted down by several elephantine spectacles which contain only flashes of his early brilliance. *Shane* is perhaps his last fully realized work. It is like those Stevens films in which a social misfit/outcast helps to make life better for someone who has a position within the social order, but who has certain problems which only the misfit/outsider can resolve. Notable among these films are *Vigil in the Night* (1940) and *The Talk of the Town* (1942). Other Stevens films detail the trials and tribulations of the social misfit/outcast in general, especially *Alice Adams* (1935), *A Damsel in Distress* (1937), *A Place in the Sun*, and *The Diary of Anne Frank* (1959).

Shane was made during the peak of Stevens' career, when the release of any film from him was considered an event (in this sense, Stevens was like Capra, Wilder, and Hitchcock). At the time of its release, *Shane* earned as much acclaim as any film of the 1950's. It was nominated for Academy Awards for Best Picture, Best Director, and Best Writing (screenplay). De Wilde's poignant performance was nominated for Best Supporting Actor, as was Palance's menacing Wilson. Loyal Griggs received an Oscar for his breathtaking color cinematography. Stevens won the National Board of Review's Best Director award, and was also honored by the Director's Guild for quarterly directorial achievement. *Shane* was included on the ten best films of the year lists of the National Board of Review, *Time* magazine, and the *New York Times*. The film's box-office gross of eight million dollars made it the third biggest moneymaker of 1953, and even today, it is one of the most financially successful Westerns of all time.

THE TALK OF THE TOWN

Released: 1942
Production: George Stevens for Columbia
Direction: George Stevens
Screenplay: Irwin Shaw and Sidney Buchman; based on a screen story by Sidney Harmon
Cinematography: Ted Tetzlaff
Editing: Otto Meyer
Running time: 118 minutes

> *Principal characters:*
> Leopold Dilg .... Cary Grant
> Nora Shelley .... Jean Arthur
> Michael Lightcap .... Ronald Colman
> Sam Yates .... Edgar Buchanan

The romantic comedy is a staple of the Hollywood film. In this type of film a woman usually chooses between two men, and she virtually always chooses the more romantic and unconventional of the two after getting to know him through some unusual circumstance. This is the basic outline for many films which are merely mindless fluff, but it is also the outline for such fine films as *It Happened One Night* (1934) and *Holiday* (1938) (though the latter finds a man choosing between two women). An outstanding example of what can be done in this genre is *The Talk of the Town.* Not only does it have a schoolteacher having to choose between a law school dean and an escapee from jail but also all three are fully developed, interesting characters and a serious theme is explored—the value of the intellectual life as opposed to the practical. *The Talk of the Town* is both thought-provoking and highly entertaining.

The film is built around an ideological opposition which also becomes a romantic triangle: Leopold Dilg (Cary Grant) represents the unintellectual, even antiintellectual, position; Michael Lightcap (Ronald Colman) the purely intellectual one; and Nora Shelley (Jean Arthur) a middle ground between them. The three come together one night in the house owned by Nora which she is preparing for Lightcap, a law school dean who is renting the house for the summer and is scheduled to move in the next day. First Dilg, a local political activist who has escaped jail just before his trial for murder, comes to the house to hide. Though she knows him somewhat and does not seem to think he is dangerous, Nora does not welcome him, but she does consent to his staying the night in the attic. Minutes later, Lightcap arrives one day early. The next day when Dilg's lawyer, Sam Yates (Edgar Buchanan), tells Nora to keep Dilg there and take care of him, Nora, to make the best of the situation, gets the job of cook and secretary to Lightcap, and Dilg comes out of hiding to pretend to be the gardener. Three quite different people are now forced to spend quite a great deal of time together. Romance develops, but more important is the effect they have on one another's ideas.

At the beginning Lightcap thinks that law is a theoretical matter and that he cannot concern himself with individual cases. Dilg, being an individual case himself, takes the opposite position that the law has no soul, that it needs human qualities.

Dilg is accused of starting a fire in which a man was killed. He knows he is innocent, but he is unwilling to risk standing trial because a very powerful man in the town, Andrew Holmes, does not like him or his ideas and has enough influence to ensure that the trial will go the way he wants. Yates, Nora, and Dilg begin a campaign to convince Lightcap of Dilg's innocence and the impossibility of his getting a fair trial. Lightcap, who has taken the house for the summer so he can write a book, at first resents this intrusion of the real world on the time he was planning to spend on scholarship, but he is gradually convinced as Nora uses such tactics as taking him to a baseball game where they "happen" to sit near the judge who would try the case and Lightcap hears how biased the man is.

Events begin moving quickly as Lightcap discovers that the gardener is actually Dilg, and Nora and Lightcap discover that no one was killed in the fire—the supposedly dead man, Clyde Bracken, is merely hiding out. Lightcap gets so involved in the intrigues that when he finds out that Bracken has a girl friend in town, he takes her dancing merely to get information from her. He finds that Bracken is in Boston getting his mail at the general delivery window and takes Nora and Dilg to Boston to capture him though he has to lie to the police to get them to release Nora and also has to knock out Dilg in order to get him to come along on the trip. Thus Lightcap, having begun the film as the standard ivory-tower intellectual, is so changed by his experiences that by the end he has lied to the police, refused to turn in a wanted person, and used force to achieve his goals—all things he would not have countenanced before, but all things done in the interest of true justice.

Even though Lightcap is told the first day he is in town that he is to be appointed to the Supreme Court and should keep his name out of the newspapers, once he gets involved in the case he insists on seeing it through. The culmination of the change in his thinking comes when he uses a gun to capture Bracken and take him to the courtroom, which is being stormed by an angry mob threatening to lynch Dilg. He gives an impassioned speech in which he says that the law must be "engraved in our hearts," and that both those who want to ignore the law completely and those who think of it as a set of abstract principles are wrong. Even though this speech might sound platitudinous in another context, the fact that it comes out of Lightcap's experience makes it effective and moving. As Dilg says after Lightcap is appointed to the Supreme Court, he is a better Justice for his experience.

These changes in Lightcap's ideas are not the only changes that occur. A suggestion of a romance begins to develop between Nora and each of the men. Neither openly admits his own feelings, but instead each talks to Nora about the other man. Dilg, for example, tells Nora that Lightcap is in love with her and adds, "I know just how he feels." Each man seems inhibited by his respect for the other as well as his uncertainty about the choice she will make.

In romantic comedies a woman usually has to choose between two men or a man between two women, and the choice is nearly always quite predictable. For example, though the film *It Happened One Night* is quite good, there is little doubt that in the end Claudette Colbert will prefer Clark Gable over Jameson Thomas. In *The Talk of the Town*, however, both men are played by actors who were frequently romantic leading men. When Nora has to choose between the two, it is a difficult choice that cannot be so easily predicted, especially since Lightcap has changed so much during the film. In fact, the choice between the two men is so close that the filmmakers shot two endings and made the choice themselves only after previewing the film.

The decisive moment comes on the day Lightcap takes his place on the bench of the Supreme Court. Nora goes to see him in his chambers where he suggests that she choose her "reckless friend." A few minutes later she sees Dilg, who recommends Lightcap because of his "position, dignity, and place in life" and tries to walk away, but Nora, saying she is tired of people trying to make up her mind, kisses him. He then leaves but immediately comes back to take her with him as the film ends.

Although *The Talk of the Town* is a film which deals with ideas, its characters are not always engaged in heavily philosophical discussions. The film's humor runs from the near-slapstick as Nora attempts to keep Lightcap from seeing Dilg at the beginning to such little touches as Dilg seeing his picture on a wanted poster and remarking, "No one would recognize me from that—doesn't catch the spirit." Indeed, it is a comic scene in which the discussions between Dilg and Lightcap begin. The morning after Lightcap's arrival he is dictating to Nora, but she has trouble concentrating on the work because she can see Dilg sneaking into the kitchen to get something to eat. As Dilg is getting food out of the refrigerator, he hears Lightcap describe law as "an instrument of pure logic" and casually walks out to argue with him, much to the consternation of Nora. She quickly explains, however, that Dilg is the gardener and they are able to keep his true identity secret for a little longer.

The screenplay by Irwin Shaw and Sidney Buchman is excellent, but the actors deserve a good portion of the credit for creating such interesting characters. Michael Lightcap seems at first to be merely an intelligent but emotionless man who thinks of everything outside of his work as merely a distraction, but as the film progresses, we learn more about his background, and we see him discover more about himself and about the rest of the world.

He tells Nora that he first grew his beard because he was one of the youngest ever to graduate from Harvard Law School and wanted to look older and more professional. He admits, however, that he began to hide behind that reserved appearance; it became his fortress. The beard, therefore, is emblematic of his detached outlook both for him and for others; it is more significant than it might seem when he shaves it off. Colman, with his usual cultured voice and demeanor as well as his considerable acting ability, perfectly brings to life this complex character. Leopold Dilg and Nora Shelley may be somewhat less complex than Lightcap but are no less interesting, and certainly the performances of Grant and Arthur are equal to Colman's; they are amusing without letting the comedy overshadow the serious side of their characters. Edgar Buchanan also does a fine job in the important supporting role of Sam Yates, Dilg's lawyer who sometimes comments on the action and sometimes keeps it going.

George Stevens ably directs with a lighter touch and quicker pace than in some of his other films, and the efforts of all involved were rewarded. *The Talk of the Town* was a critical and commercial success.

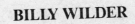

BILLY WILDER

THE APARTMENT

Released: 1960
Production: Billy Wilder for the Mirisch Company; released by United Artists (AA)
Direction: Billy Wilder (AA)
Screenplay: I. A. L. Diamond and Billy Wilder (AA)
Cinematography: Joseph LaShelle
Editing: Daniel Mandell (AA)
Art direction: Alexander Trauner (AA); set decoration, Edward G. Boyle (AA)
Running time: 125 minutes

Principal characters:
C. C. (Bud) Baxter ....Jack Lemmon
Fran Kubelik ....Shirley MacLaine
J. D. Sheldrake ....Fred MacMurray
Dr. Dreyfuss ....Jack Kruschen
Miss Olsen ....Edie Adams

Originally branded "a dirty fairy tale," Billy Wilder's *The Apartment* combines irony, burlesque, soap opera, and truth into a morality play whose message is "be a *mensch*," a Yiddish term for a human being. Filmed in black-and-white, Wilder's story expresses the moral ambiguities facing a hero and heroine who are neither innocent nor evil, just human. By dealing with pandering, adultery, and suicide in an often poignant, yet entertaining way, Wilder created one of the most sophisticated Hollywood movies of its time. The innovativeness of *The Apartment*, however, is due not so much to the types of activities it portrays, but rather to the fact that Wilder allows his principal characters to sin, suffer the consequences, and yet be redeemed for a happy ending.

Wilder's sharp wit and satiric sword begin by slicing into the heart of Manhattan society's immorality and callousness as seen through the corporate world. The protagonist, C. C. (Bud) Baxter (Jack Lemmon), is a basically decent young executive with an undeveloped code of morality who finds himself reacting to, rather than shaping, the events around him. Bud begins as a night school graduate relegated to Section W, desk number 861 of the Ordinary Policy Department in the home office of Consolidated Life, an insurance company in New York. His is but one of hundreds of steel gray desks lined up row upon row in a huge office filled by people with equally gray, expressionless faces. Art director Alexander Trauner and set director Edward G. Boyle exhibited their Academy Award-winning techniques in the early office scenes by enhancing the effect of a vast sea of faces with the use of tiny desks with dwarfs in the rear of the set, followed by even tinier desks with cut-out figures operated by wires.

Bud has learned that in an organization with more than 31,000 employees, a person has to have something more to offer than training, industry, and dedication. Bud stumbled onto his key to success—his apartment. Though small and rather dreary, the apartment has quickly become the favorite love nest shared by four of Bud's bosses. In exchange for providing a bed and catering service, Bud has been rewarded with glowing performance evaluations which will lead to promotions and one of the coveted glass-enclosed cubicles along the office's sidewall. Though less than enthusiastic about this arrangement, Bud is pliable whenever the fruits of society, measured in money, status, and sex, are dangled in front of him.

Throughout the first half of the movie, Bud's objections to the services he is providing are based on personal inconvenience rather than moral conviction. Lonely Bud, instead of spending his evenings eating TV dinners, watching old movies, and reading the men's fashion section of *Playboy*, often ends up spending the night in the cold, damp park, while one of his bosses shares his bed with the latest office ingenue. Wilder and Lemmon skillfully milk the laughs out of Bud's predicament as he catches an awful cold one night and then sniffles his way around the office the next day, alternating his attention between a handkerchief, nasal spray, and a thermometer.

It is on this day that Bud comes to the attention of Mr. Sheldrake (Fred MacMurray), the Director of Personnel, who, after delivering a sermon on morality, offers to trade two tickets to *The Music Man* and a future promotion for exclusive rights to Bud's apartment. As Bud's reluctance turns to elation, he finds the courage to invite the girl of his dreams, Fran Kubelik (Shirley MacLaine), an elevator operator in the building, to join him at the theater. She hesitatingly agrees to meet him at 8:30 in the lobby. That night, while Bud waits for her at the theater, Mr. Sheldrake is busy convincing Fran that if she will resume their affair, he will divorce his wife. Sheldrake prevails and Bud gets stood-up.

Throughout the next month, on Mondays and Thursdays the apartment is reserved for Mr. Sheldrake, and true to his word, he promotes Bud to one of the glass-enclosed cubicles. It is now December 24, and the wild office Christmas party serves as a dividing point in the movie. Wilder helped to capture the true spirit of office parties, where everyone forgets his inhibitions in a swirl of booze, music, and laughter, by actually shooting the scene on December 23. Until now the movie has concentrated on Bud's culpability and ambitiousness, and on his bosses' lechery. At this point, however, the human consequences begin.

During the Christmas party both Fran and Bud have their illusions shattered. First a drunken Miss Olsen (Edie Adams), Mr. Sheldrake's secretary, taunts Fran about the number of conquests, herself included, which Mr.

Sheldrake has scattered throughout the building. Then, when Bud asks her opinion of his new derby, Fran lets him look at himself in her compact's cracked mirror. Startled, Bud recognizes it as the compact he had found in his apartment and returned to Mr. Sheldrake a few weeks before.

While the disillusioned Bud drowns his sorrows in martinis at the local bar, Fran confronts Sheldrake at the apartment. Realizing that he regards her only as a mistress and not as his future wife, the despondent Fran happens to find a bottle of sleeping pills in the bathroom. Wilder uses the mirrors in the bathroom and her compact to symbolize the identity crisis with which she is suffering. Unable to cope with the reflection she sees in the glass, Fran takes the pills.

When Bud returns home, he finds Fran unconscious with the bottle of pills in her hand. He quickly summons his neighbor, Dr. Dreyfuss (Jack Kruschen), who pumps out her stomach, and, believing Bud to be responsible for her suicide attempt, delivers a lecture on being a *mensch*. Dr. Dreyfuss, an honest, straightforward human being, presents Bud with an alternative role model to the corporate connivers he has been trying to emulate. It has become clear that in the world presented in *The Apartment*, corporate success and integrity cannot coexist, and Bud will soon be forced to make a choice. Wilder, however, manages to keep the suicide attempt and the moral dilemma from becoming too bleak through the use of plenty of deft comedy.

Fran and Bud spend the next two days swapping hard luck stories and playing gin rummy while she recovers enough strength to go home. Here Wilder mixes sentimentality and light-hearted buffoonery in a classic scene where Bud dexterously uses his tennis racquet to drain their spaghetti dinner.

In the meantime, Sheldrake fires Miss Olsen, who in turn informs Mrs. Sheldrake of his philandering habits. Sheldrake, who has been more concerned with preventing a scandal than in caring for Fran, rewards Bud with a promotion to Assistant Personnel Director and the key to the executive washroom. Though still willing to accept the rewards, Bud is no longer willing to play the game. He has fallen in love with Fran and is dismayed to hear that Sheldrake, who was thrown out by his wife, now intends to marry her— eventually, but not just yet.

On New Year's Eve day, when Sheldrake asks for the apartment key, Bud symbolically renounces corporate success and becomes a *mensch* by giving Sheldrake the key to the executive washroom instead. That night at dinner Sheldrake recounts Bud's inexplicable action to Fran, who realizes that Bud really loves her. Leaving Sheldrake sitting in the restaurant, she rushes off to Bud's apartment, where they welcome in the New Year with a game of gin rummy.

The happy ending was met with surprise by some critics who did not feel that protagonists who transgressed sexually deserved to find happiness. But Wilder has created human beings, not stereotypes, and they are capable of developing some self-recognition and capacity for growth. The question the movie does not successfully answer is why five supposedly well-paid executives are so totally dependent upon using Bud's rather dingy little flat.

The performances are universally good. Jack Lemmon and Shirley MacLaine make an appealing couple, capable of evoking both tenderness and humor. Ultimately, however, it is Lemmon's performance which gives the film the vitality to remain entertaining in the face of some pessimistic assessments of the human character.

The Apartment won the Academy Award for Best Picture in 1960 and is one of the best achievements in Wilder's illustrious career.

DOUBLE INDEMNITY

Released: 1944
Production: Joseph Sistrom for Paramount
Direction: Billy Wilder
Screenplay: Billy Wilder and Raymond Chandler; based on the novel *Three of a Kind* by James M. Cain
Cinematography: John F. Seitz
Editing: Doane Harrison
Costume design: Edith Head
Music: Miklos Rozsa
Running time: 107 minutes

Principal characters:
Walter Neff .... Fred MacMurray
Phyllis Dietrichson .... Barbara Stanwyck
Barton Keyes .... Edward G. Robinson
Mr. Jackson .... Porter Hall
Lola Dietrichson .... Jean Heather

It is difficult to believe that such a brilliant film as *Double Indemnity* was only Billy Wilder's second directorial assignment. An immensely talented and volatile Austrian who left Europe in the 1930's to escape from Hitler, Wilder had a long and successful career as a screenwriter, both in Europe and the United States, but often made studio producers uneasy because of his ability to expose human weakness on the screen. Wilder has a sardonic wit and the ability to turn bad taste into good box office, as demonstrated in his first film directed in the United States—*The Major and the Minor* (1942), a pre-Lolita comedy in which Ray Milland is attracted to Ginger Rogers disguised as a twelve-year-old child.

In spite of the fact that *Double Indemnity* is now firmly established as a classic, it was a difficult project for Wilder. Paramount producer Joe Sistrom discovered James M. Cain's novella "Double Indemnity," which had appeared as a serial in Liberty magazine in 1936. The plot appealed immediately to Wilder but Charles Brackett, his long-time collaborator, hated the story so much that he refused either to work on the screenplay or to produce the film. This refusal terminated a working relationship that had lasted for seven years, and another writer had to be found. James M. Cain was the obvious choice to help adapt the story, but he was at that time working at Twentieth Century-Fox on *Western Union* (1941). Sistrom then suggested Raymond Chandler, since he thought that his writing style was rather similar to Cain's—a comparison that never failed to annoy Chandler.

Sistrom was partly right: although Chandler was a better writer than Cain, both men were particularly responsive to the ambience of California. Chandler's style was quite unique, however; and after reading a copy of *The Big Sleep* at one sitting, Wilder realized that its author was an ideal partner for this film. Unfortunately, Chandler had a severe drinking problem and no experience at writing screenplays (it was his first assignment); he did not seem much interested in moviemaking, had never collaborated with another writer, and hated Wilder on sight (the feeling was mutual). Chandler had hoped to finish the screenplay quickly, and he produced his version in five weeks. Wilder was not satisfied, and they worked together on the script for six months; Chandler was also forced to stay around the studio during filming.

Then came the problem of casting, although in retrospect it seems strange that any problems arose at all. The screenplay was touted around Hollywood, and not one of the leading actors of the day wanted to play the part of Walter Neff; *Double Indemnity* was considered to be a distasteful and immoral film. Wilder wanted Fred MacMurray to play the role—a strange choice, since the role of Neff required him to play a likable insurance agent who commits a brutal murder. The murder was not a crime of passion which the audience could understand, nor an accidental murder, but a calculated crime for lust and gain. Until then, MacMurray's career had been in light comedy, but Wilder finally persuaded him to accept the part; MacMurray thought it would end his career, but instead it was the best role he ever had in films.

Double Indemnity has an unusual plot in that the killer is identified in the opening scenes, a technique used repeatedly since then but uncommon at the time. Walter Neff (Fred MacMurray) is dictating an office memo to his boss. Neff is clearly dying from gunshot wounds but has returned late at night to the offices of the large insurance company for which he works. The dictation allows Neff's voice to change subtly from that of confessor to narrator and leads us into the flashback. This device is almost always effective but works exceptionally well in this case for it allows Chandler's descriptive linking passages to be spoken by a narrator, using language which would have been too literary as spoken dialogue.

The events related in the flashback begin as Walter Neff makes a seemingly routine call on a customer about auto insurance. The house he visits is a Spanish-style and slightly run down house in Glendale, California; the customer is out but Neff asks to see the man's wife instead. It would be difficult to forget Barbara Stanwyck's first appearance as Phyllis Dietrichson: she has been taking a sunbath and appears at the top of the staircase wearing only a bathtowel and a look of cool appraisal. Stanwyck is a gifted and intelligent actress, not strictly beautiful in the Hollywood style of Lana Turner or Heddy Lamarr, and her career has been that of an actress rather than a sex symbol. In this role, however, she conveys superbly a kind of sluttish sexuality. It is clear that there is a mutual attraction between Neff and Phyllis. His is a purely physical one, but she has a strangely calculating look. Neff is invited back to the house, Dietrichson is again out, and this time the maid is significantly absent as well.

Phyllis is wearing a dress this time, sexy but not blatantly so, and as she descends the staircase, the camera tracks along focusing on her chain anklet. She is, of course, unhappily married to an older man (his second wife), and is desperate to escape the boredom of life with a husband she hates, a resentful stepdaughter, and an allowance that does not begin to buy all the things she wants. She married for a kind of security and now finds herself a prisoner; but she does not intend to walk out empty-handed. She is obviously an experienced predator, and after conveying her interest in Neff, she warily outlines her plan to take out a large insurance policy on her husband's life. She wishes to have the policy signed as though it were for auto insurance, and she wishes her husband to know nothing about the arrangement. The conversation is like a chess game. Neff is responsive to her, but too astute to be fooled by an insurance deal which is obviously a prologue to murder. He rejects the whole idea and leaves, but the attraction is too strong; they meet again and he is drawn into her plan. Perhaps he also feels that as an insurance agent he is in an ideal position to plan and execute a fool-proof insurance fraud.

Like all murders planned so that two people can be together, the planning and aftermath of the crime inevitably mean that from the beginning, the parties concerned cannot meet without arousing suspicion. Most of their meetings take place in the very mundane atmosphere of a supermarket (Chandler used Jerry's Market on Melrose Avenue in Los Angeles for the locale), and these scenes are stunningly effective. Phyllis methodically selects groceries and at the same time coolly outlines the murder plan. It is in these scenes particularly that Stanwyck's acting is so strong, as she convinces us not only that Phyllis is capable of getting rid of her husband, but also that she is capable of persuading her lover not only to be an accomplice but also actually to commit the crime. The murder is carried out, while the camera rests on Phyllis Dietrichson's face as she remains virtually unmoved by the brutal killing taking place beside her. After the body has been carefully placed near the railway tracks (the policy now includes a double indemnity clause to include a rail accident), they must now wait for the insurance company to pay. The authorities seem to accept a verdict of accidental death, but the insurance company is more suspicious and throws out the claim.

Neff's boss at the insurance company is Burton Keyes (Edward G. Robinson), and he and Neff are friends as well as colleagues. Keyes loves the insurance business and seemingly has no private life at all. It is significant that at one time he was engaged, but this was abruptly terminated after he had the insurance company investigate his prospective wife. Keyes looks upon the insurance company business not as a collection of files and claims but as an endlessly fascinating series of case histories, constantly challenging him. When Keyes gets a phony claim, his dyspepsia gives him no peace; and the

Dietrichson claim gives his digestion a very hard time indeed.

The role of Burton Keyes could have been a rather colorless one had it not been for the magnetic presence of Edward G. Robinson. In one scene he reels off a long list of insurance company statistics on different types of death, with subdivisions for each section, to illustrate the improbability of the Dietrichson claim. Very few actors could have brought that kind of dialogue to life, but Robinson succeeds.

As the story draws to a close, the lovers continue to meet only in the supermarket, but now Neff is very nervous and wants to get out. Phyllis takes off her dark glasses, and, over a display of canned goods, informs him with chilling calm that people who commit murders cannot get off the trolley car when they choose but must stay together "all the way down the line." Neff finally kills Phyllis, and the film ends as he painfully makes his way to Keyes's office and, while dying of gunshot wounds himself, confesses his crime to his boss. The ending of *Double Indemnity* was changed after filming the original ending showing Neff in the gas chamber at Folsom. Wilder, against all advice, insisted on scrapping the footage and writing and filming a different ending. His decision was a fortunate one: the final scene between Keyes and Neff is beautifully done and manages to convince the audience that Walter Neff, although a murderer, does deserve some sympathy.

THE LOST WEEKEND

Released: 1945
Production: Charles Brackett for Paramount (AA)
Direction: Billy Wilder (AA)
Screenplay: Billy Wilder and Charles Brackett (AA); based on the novel of the same name by Charles R. Jackson
Cinematography: John F. Seitz
Editing: Doane Harrison
Running time: 101 minutes

Principal characters:

Don Birnam	Ray Milland (AA)
Helen St. James	Jane Wyman
Wick Birnam	Philip Terry
Nat	Howard da Silva
Gloria	Doris Dowling

The Lost Weekend is a painful account of one man's battle against alcoholism. The film was revolutionary for Hollywood in its uncompromising treatment of the subject, and its success was quite a surprise. Both financially and critically, *The Lost Weekend* swept the industry, receiving four Oscars in 1945 including one for Best Picture. Paramount was relieved after warily producing and releasing *The Lost Weekend* with its controversial topic and its casting of Ray Milland in a role unlike the romantic leading man he usually played. Milland's inspired performance earned him the Oscar for Best Actor. Billy Wilder received two Oscars, one for Best Direction and another with Charles Brackett for Best Screenplay, which was adapted from Charles R. Jackson's novel.

The story deals with one weekend in the life of an alcoholic would-be writer named Don Birnam (Ray Milland). It is a Friday afternoon as Don and his brother Wick (Philip Terry) are about to leave for a weekend in the country. While attempting to stall for enough time to smuggle liquor along for the trip, Don gets drunk and misses the train. Wick goes alone and leaves Don to begin his drunken weekend. This particular weekend, no doubt like his other "binges," drives Don to lie and steal in his desperation to get liquor. His only other concern is avoiding his well-meaning lover, Helen St. James (Jane Wyman), who persistently stands between him and his bottle.

The story line is certainly simple, but it comes to life with the power of the dialogue and the inventive structure of the screenplay. The intelligent and at times poetic dialogue helps create in Don a character who speaks with style and education. He has the power to make people feel with his words, but in the context of the film, he only uses that power to get drinks. His metaphoric speeches as he sinks into drunkenness are a fascinating insight into his ability to write.

The structure of the screenplay and Wilder's direction essentially create and maintain a feeling of enclosure. Don is enclosed in his world of alcoholism. His struggle is internal; his self-doubts and hopelessness are his prison. Many structural devices are used to stress this feeling of enclosure. A circle motif, symbolizing enclosure, is apparent in both literal images and references to circular concepts. Literally, circles appear in the form of glass rings on the bar counter as one ring after another indicates the number of drinks Don is having. When Nat (Howard da Silva), the bartender, starts to wipe them away, Don stops him with, "Let me have my vicious circle."

The marking of time is also essential to the feeling of enclosure. The title, *The Lost Weekend*, creates a perimeter around the story, defining a fixed period of time during which Don, as the protagonist, must go through a great amount of change. As time runs out, his futility becomes more devastating. Days are marked off by the collection of newspapers and milk bottles outside the Birnam door which remind the audience how much time has passed and, consequently, how much time remains.

Wilder creates a cinematic circle as part of the circle motif utilizing flashbacks and carefully planned visual techniques. Flashbacks could potentially be ways of escaping from the enclosure of story time and therefore offer some relief, but Wilder's handling of them works only to increase the feeling of enclosure. The cinematic circle, in terms of leaving from one place in the story and returning to that same place is achieved through flashbacks. Noteworthy is the visual technique used to get the audience in and out of the flashbacks. A dissolving pan going from screen left to screen right allows the flashbacks to enter. To exit the flashbacks and return to present time, the move is repeated in the same direction. By this movement, the flashbacks are structured as full circles and work perfectly with their content to show a younger and healthier Don who is already in the grips of alcoholism. Don narrates the flashbacks in the third person as though describing an imaginary character; in them, he cannot even remember a time when alcohol did not run his life. Both the content of the flashbacks and the technique in presenting them work to cement Don to his world of no escape.

The slow pacing of the film greatly enhances the dramatic effect as each episode is laboriously presented. Lengthy shots from one camera position while Don has drink after drink hold the audience for an uncomfortably long time. Other shots painfully invade Don's life with his bottle. A seemingly endless trek around New York as he desperately searches for an open pawn shop is a particularly exhausting segment.

It is crucial that the audience never completely lose faith in Don's worth, and the credibility of the story balances on this premise. The secondary characters that surround Don help confirm his value. A devoted brother and a sophisticated girl friend such as Helen continue year after year to devote time and energy to helping him. Even Nat the bartender, who sees Don at his lowest alcoholic ebb, sides with him to the point of regaining his pawned typewriter for him.

The inherent positive qualities of Don Birnam, however, are mostly believable because of Ray Milland's outstanding performance. Milland skillfully runs the gamut of emotions that make up both Don the drunk and Don the author. Within the confines of the weekend, as well as the flashback excursions, he goes from an appealing and intelligent gentleman to a ruthless, broken alcoholic with no more vision or purpose than locating his next drink.

As both screen time and story time (it is Sunday) near an end, Don's crucial moment for decision arrives. He experiences a psychic death caused by his first case of delirium tremens, an attempted suicide, and watching Helen beg him to drink rather than see him die. The climactic moment offers him the options of shooting himself, getting drunk once again, or letting Helen help him find the strength to change. The turning point of Don's character occurs when Nat arrives with his pawned typewriter—an action which serves as the final impetus Don needs to dry out and start his novel. The importance of the typewriter's arrival, however, seems exaggerated in proportion to the emotional impact of the moment; it is rather too speedy and simple a solution. Don's rebirth comes in the form of a commitment to his novel and an active attempt to stop drinking.

The optimistic ending is the one major difference between the screenplay and Jackson's novel. In the novel Don does not escape his world of alcoholism. For a film of the 1940's it is not surprising that the decision was made to change the original story. The social implications of a film which delved into the psyche of an alcoholic were great, since treating an alcoholic as a sick person requiring help was a recent approach in 1945. Thus, *The Lost Weekend* succeeded in being artistic entertainment while at the same time increasing social awareness of alcoholism as an illness.

LOVE IN THE AFTERNOON

Released: 1957
Production: Billy Wilder for Allied Artists
Direction: Billy Wilder
Screenplay: I. A. L. Diamond and Billy Wilder; based on the novel *Ariane* by Claude Anet
Cinematography: William C. Mellor
Editing: Leonid Azar
Running time: 125 minutes

> Principal characters:
> Frank Flannagan .... Gary Cooper
> Ariane Chavasse .... Audrey Hepburn
> Claude Chavasse .... Maurice Chevalier
> Michel .... Van Doude
> Monsieur X .... John McGiver

Love in the Afternoon is perhaps writer-director Billy Wilder's most unusual film. It is certainly one of his least appreciated. That this film has never received the attention it deserves is unjust, for while Wilder eschewed his customary cynicism for a mellower perspective, the film nevertheless expressed many of his fundamental concerns. In addition to embodying Wilder's concern with deception, which in effect pervades all of his work, *Love in the Afternoon* also concerns a romantic, free-spirited female who draws a misanthropic male out an of an absorption with himself, a motif that is apparent in much of Wilder's serious work, notably *The Major and the Minor* (1942) and *Sabrina* (1954). *Love in the Afternoon* also briefly examines the opposition between European culture and American culture, a theme Wilder developed more fully in *One, Two, Three* (1961).

In *Love in the Afternoon*, the traditional tension between male and female opposites amplifies a portrayal of a relationship between age and youth which is illustrative of a 1950's casting trend, that of pairing a contemporary female star and an aging male superstar—in this case, Audrey Hepburn and Gary Cooper. Wilder had earlier teamed Hepburn with a craggy Humphrey Bogart in *Sabrina*, and during the same year as *Love in the Afternoon*, Hepburn had shared romance with an aging but still agile Fred Astaire in *Funny Face* (1957). The May-September romances in light comedies or musicals such as *The Band Wagon* (1953; Fred Astaire and Cyd Charisse), *Daddy Long Legs* (1955; Astaire and Leslie Caron), and *But Not For Me* (1959; Clark Gable and Carroll Baker) point to the Hollywood star system in transition. These pairings served to join the romantic masculinity of these Hollywood greats with contemporary figures in movie stardom embodied by the female leads. It should also be added that the May-September format occasionally utilized aging female superstars and young males, as seen in the melodramatic pairing of Joan Crawford and Cliff Robertson in *Autumn Leaves* (1956). In all of these films, the superstar's age becomes an issue within the story. But more crucially, the films are of considerable historical value insofar as they provide a point of reference for the changing of the guard in Hollywood. Stars of the magnitude of Cooper, Astaire, Bogart, Gable, and Crawford have not shone since. These films show them at the twilight of their careers, resourcefully adapting their personalities to new trends.

What distinguishes *Love in the Afternoon* from other films of its type is its nostalgic re-creation of the kind of film comedy practiced by the great Ernst Lubitsch, a re-creation accomplished by Wilder's use of the traditional meeting between a classic star and his contemporary leading lady. Wilder has no interest in "going modern"; rather, he sought to re-create an out-of-fashion tone and style represented by classical Hollywood filmmaking. It is no coincidence that Wilder chose Lubitsch as a source of inspiration. Wilder had coscripted two of Lubitsch's films, *Bluebeard's Eighth Wife* (1938) and *Ninotchka* (1939). Similar to *Love in the Afternoon*, these films are set in Paris, stressing the old world charms of the "City of Light," and depicting the difficulty involved when two unyielding opposites fall in love. Cooper's presence is yet another reminder of "The Lubitsch Touch"—he starred in *Design for Living* (1933) and *Bluebeard's Eighth Wife*.

Wilder uses his traditional context to tell a story of Paris in the spring. We are first introduced to Ariane (Audrey Hepburn), the incurably romantic daughter of Claude Chavasse (Maurice Chevalier), a private detective specializing in marital cases. Ariane indulges her romantic curiosity by reading her father's case files, and consequently becomes fascinated with the exploits of one Frank Flannagan (Gary Cooper), whose name appears frequently. The files make it clear that Flannagan, a high-living executive for the Pepsi-Cola company, has refined romantic entanglements with married women to a high art. When Ariane learns that one of her father's clients plans to catch Flannagan with his wife and shoot him, she rushes to Flannagan's hotel. Without revealing her name or purpose, Ariane replaces the wife in question just as the husband makes his entrance. The husband is confounded, and so is Flannagan, who wants to know more about the mysterious girl. He arranges to meet Ariane again, and the pair meet during the afternoons over the next several months. Their relationship develops into love, which both of them try to deny. For Flannagan, love means commitment, something he has always avoided by dallying with married women. Eventually, however, he decides to renounce his roguish life style and marry Ariane, but he has one obstacle to overcome: Ariane has never told him her name or where she is from. To learn the identity of the girl who has captivated him, Flannagan hires none other than Claude Chavasse to investigate her background.

Ariane clearly embodies Wilder's concern with deception. She feigns an aura of sophistication and continually creates fictions to convince Flannagan that she is a worldly woman. She effects this ruse because she assumes that Flannagan can only be attracted to a certain kind of woman. Ironically, the world-weary Flannagan sees through her false appearance, and is actually attracted to her youthful innocence and freshness. The film's ultimate merging of these diametrically opposite lovers results in one of the screen's most romantically charged climaxes: Flannagan sweeps the surprised Ariane off her feet and onto a train while his personal quartet of gypsy musicians play their violins on the station platform.

Overall, *Love in the Afternoon* is more than a mere homage to Lubitsch. Wilder's personality is dominant throughout, as indicated not only by the presence of some of his primary concerns, but also by his frequent swipes at the kind of American capitalism represented by Flannagan. Wilder has always been a perceptive critic of American business ethics, as evidenced by *The Emperor Waltz* (1948), *The Apartment* (1960), *One, Two, Three* (1961), and *Avanti!* (1972). Wilder's stylistic imprint is also visible, especially with regard to William C. Mellor's somber cinematography, which creates ominous shadows and silhouettes. This style is unconventional in romantic comedy, and is more in line with Wilder melodramas such as *Double Indemnity* (1943) and *The Lost Weekend* (1945). Yet the cinematography provides the perfect complement to the deception central to the film, as well as a counterpoint to the Wilder wit, which in this film is less caustic than usual.

The film's charm owes much to its three leads. Clearly, no one could possibly extol the virtues of Paris with more authenticity than Chevalier. But Chevalier portrays Chavasse as more than merely a continental charmer. It is his realization that his "little girl" has blossomed into a woman that leads him, against his better judgment, to bring Ariane and Flannagan together at the end of the film. While Chevalier is a pleasing presence, the film centers on the relationship between Flannagan and Ariane. Here, the chemistry between Cooper and Hepburn is crucial to the believability of the relationship. No doubt Wilder was attempting to duplicate the chemistry that existed between Hepburn and Bogart in *Sabrina*.

The Hepburn-Cooper pairing in many ways surpasses that of *Sabrina*. As always, Hepburn is wistful and engaging, and the film demonstrates why America was captivated by her "kookiness" and unique blend of waifishness and sophistication. Yet, it is Cooper's aging visage that imparts to the relationship genuine poignancy and tenderness. Throughout his career, Cooper displayed an amazing ability to underplay scenes. His manner of expressing himself with gestures and barely perceptible facial expressions is the essence of classical film acting, and Wilder is obviously fascinated with Cooper's forceful presence. *Love in the Afternoon* contains several references to Cooper's star status. For example, Flannagan at one point confesses to Ariane, "I'm not much of a talker," a comment on his terse portrayals in previous films. And Flannagan's last gesture in the film—hoisting Hepburn aboard the train—is typical of the kind of masculine gallantry Cooper displayed in earlier roles.

Indeed, Cooper's enduring popularity enabled *Love in the Afternoon* to be produced in the first place. From 1950 to 1957, Cooper maintained his position among the Top Ten most popular box-office performers, just as he had done throughout the 1940's. *Love in the Afternoon* was produced during an era when studio productions declined in number. The new trend was toward independent productions financed on the basis of proven box-office names and on-location filming. When Cooper committed himself to the project, Allied Artists made one of its few forays into prestige production.

Yet, Wilder deemphasized the on-location trend in his attempt to recapture the studio artifice of Lubitsch's work. While the film was made in Paris, everything except exterior establishing shots were done in a studio. Enhancing the studio settings were Alexander Trauner's sumptuous set designs. Trauner, regarded as one of the greatest set designers in film history, had worked with Marcel Carne and René Clair and went on to collaborate with Wilder throughout the 1950's and 1960's. Also *Love in the Afternoon* was Wilder's first script collaboration with I. A. L. Diamond, with whom he went on to write ten more screenplays.

Unaccountably, *Love in the Afternoon* failed to improve the estimable box-office records of Wilder, Cooper, and Hepburn. Audiences rejected the film, possibly because of its length and the use of low-key cinematography in a comedy. But these are only slight debits in a film laden with charms. Not even the tune "Fascination" (which became a popular recording as sung by Jane Morgan), played continually by Flannagan's gypsy violinists, could entice the public. Some critics have argued that the film's failure was a result of the implausibility of a May-September romance; yet, other films centering on such pairings did well at the box office, including Wilder's own *Sabrina*.

In spite of its reception by the public, however, *Love in the Afternoon* enjoyed moderate critical success. Both the *New York Times* and *Time* magazine included it on their list of Ten Best films of 1957, and the Writer's Guild designated it as the Best-Written American Comedy of the year. Still, *Love in the Afternoon* remains one of Wilder's least discussed and least revived films. Hopefully, a realization of what it represents in terms of both the writer-director's overall world view and the history of the star system will bring about an appreciation of its considerable qualities.

THE MAJOR AND THE MINOR

Released: 1942
Production: Arthur Hornblow, Jr., for Paramount
Direction: Billy Wilder
Screenplay: Billy Wilder and Charles Brackett; suggested by Edward Childs
   Carpenter's stage adaptation *Connie Goes Home* of the story "Sunny Goes
   Home" by Fannie Kilbourne
Cinematography: Leo Tover
Editing: Doane Harrison
Running time: 100 minutes

Principal characters:
Susan Applegate	Ginger Rogers
Major Philip Kirby	Ray Milland
Pamela Hill	Rita Johnson
Lucy Hill	Diana Lynn
Colonel Hill	Edward Fielding

The Major and the Minor was the first film directed by Billy Wilder, and its commercial and critical success launched his distinguished directorial career. The film itself is an engaging one with many well-constructed comedic situations reminiscent of the screwball comedies of the 1930's. Though Wilder's direction is competent rather than brilliant, he is able to rely on the lively script, which he wrote with Charles Brackett, and the warmth and deft comic timing of his star, Ginger Rogers, to put across the film's improbable premise: a grown woman pretends to be a twelve-year-old child and fools an Army major and assorted other adults for several days. That the viewer can accept and be entertained by this wildly improbable notion testifies to the successful blending of acting, writing, and directing that makes the film so delightful.

After a year in New York City and twenty-five jobs, Susan Applegate (Ginger Rogers) is disillusioned and bored. Following the payment of a fee for a hair treatment course she is almost broke, and when a client makes a pass at her, it is the last straw. She walks out in disgust and decides to go back to Iowa. She has carefully saved the exact amount for her train fare, but when she reaches Grand Central Station she discovers that the fare has been raised. Desperate, she decides to pose as a twelve-year-old child so she can purchase a half-fare ticket. With her hair in pigtails, wearing ankle socks and a sailor hat and holding a balloon filched from a child, she manages to fool the ticket agent.

This impersonation plunges Susan into a number of unforeseen and ambiguous situations, the comedic possibilities of which are employed to full advantage by the script. One of the funniest situations involves Susan with two suspicious conductors on the train. When they comment on how well-developed she is, Susan replies that she comes from Swedish stock and has gland trouble. Still suspicious, they ask her to say something in Swedish. Susan responds by imitating Greta Garbo—"I vant to be alone." Later, when they see her smoking a cigarette, she has to escape by ducking into an unlocked compartment occupied by Major Philip Kirby (Ray Milland), an instructor at an Indiana Military Institute who is returning from Washington after an unsuccessful attempt to be transferred to active duty. Thinking quickly, Susan tells him that she is called Sue-Sue and persuades him to let her sleep in the lower berth.

During the night there is a thunderstorm, and, believing that Sue-Sue must be frightened, Philip puts his arm around her and tells her stories to calm her. Finding herself attracted to Philip, Susan decides to reveal her masquerade in the morning, but before she can do so she is discovered in the compartment by Philip's fiancée, Pamela Hill (Rita Johnson), and her father, Colonel Hill (Edward Fielding), Philip's commanding officer, who are angry and upset. Puzzled by their behavior and determined to clear up the matter, Philip asks Susan to accompany him to the Institute.

After their arrival at the Institute, Susan convinces Pamela, Pamela's father, and the faculty of the Institute that she is indeed an innocent child, and Philip is reinstated in everyone's good graces. But the masquerade becomes even more complicated when Susan is invited by Pamela to stay at her house for a few days. Pamela's sister, Lucy (Diana Lynn), who is a real twelve-year-old, discovers the truth but agrees not to expose her if Susan will help thwart Pamela's efforts to keep Philip out of active service.

Up to this point the film has proceeded briskly with some good comedic situations on the train and with warm, believable characterizations by Ginger Rogers and Ray Milland. Their scenes together are played with taste and warmth and with no hint of condescension towards their material.

Wilder has, however, saved his most amusing situations for the last half of the film, which is set in the Military Institute. Susan discovers that the cadets are just as worldlywise and amorous as any New York "wolf" and even more ingenious in devising ways of making passes. When Philip sees her struggling in the embrace of a young cadet, he realizes it is his responsibility to tell her the facts of life. Awkwardly and with much embarrassment, he tells a wide-eyed, straight-faced Susan that a girl is like a light bulb which attracts moths. Indeed, he confesses that he finds her strangely attractive himself and at times she seems almost grown-up to him. Demurely, Susan promises to try not to be a light bulb.

Now completely in love with Philip, Susan renews her efforts to free him from Pamela and have him transferred to the active duty he longs for. Her machinations lead to a hilarious scene with a cadet on duty at the central switchboard. Though he is at first unresponsive, she manages to lure him away from the switchboard by promising to show him some new dance steps if he will fetch his portable radio. The moment he leaves she puts through a call to Washington and impersonates Pamela to convince an influential General's wife to expedite Philip's transfer. Meanwhile, she mixes up all the other telephone calls, and the scene ends with Susan surrounded by irate, frustrated callers, including Pamela's father, as the unsuspecting cadet returns, jitterbugging and singing "a woman's a two-face" to the tune on his portable radio.

The cadets are well directed by Wilder and provide many of the funniest situations in the film, particularly one at a dance where they are scornful of the girls from a nearby girls' school, all of whom, including the teacher, wear Veronica Lake hairstyles. At the dance, though, Susan is recognized by a visitor who discloses her identity to Pamela. Pamela threatens a nasty scandal if Susan does not leave immediately without saying good-bye to Philip.

In the closing sequence we see Susan lying dreamily in a hammock on the front porch of her Iowa home watching moths as they flutter around a light bulb. When Philip telephones to say that he is on his way to the West Coast for active duty and wants to see Sue-Sue, Susan decides on a final impersonation in order to talk to him without his knowing who she is. Pretending to be Sue-Sue's mother, she listens as the unsuspecting Philip tells her that Pamela has married another man. She waits until he leaves and then hurries to the train station where she reveals her masquerade. The film ends as they both happily run to board the train.

Without Ginger Rogers and Ray Milland it is hard to believe that the sassy script would have been as effective or as funny. They receive fine support from Rita Johnson as Pamela and Diana Lynn as her little sister, Lucy. Both are given some good lines by Wilder and Brackett, and they make the most of them. After Lucy has discovered that Susan is not a child, she tells her to stop talking baby talk, that Susan cannot fool her because she is going to be a scientist, "something like Madame Curie." She then offers Susan a cigarette but says she does not smoke herself because "adolescence makes me nervous enough." Pamela has her moments also, especially when she tells Philip that she does not want a condensed wedding or a condensed husband, with "everything a bit like *Reader's Digest*."

The Major and the Minor was a box-office success largely because it combines the theme of patriotism (Philip's wish to be transferred to active duty) with light escapist comedy. Its basic idea is improbable if not incredible, but the witty, effervescent script, brisk direction, and convincing, tasteful acting of the stars make it an engaging, captivating comedy for which audiences are able to suspend disbelief.

SABRINA

Released: 1954
Production: Billy Wilder for Paramount
Direction: Billy Wilder
Screenplay: Ernest Lehman, Samuel Taylor, and Billy Wilder; based on the
  play *Sabrina Fair* by Samuel Taylor
Cinematography: Charles Lang
Editing: Doane Harrison and Arthur Schmidt
Costume design: Edith Head (AA)
Running time: 113 minutes

> *Principal characters:*
> Sabrina Fairchild .... Audrey Hepburn
> Linus Larrabee .... Humphrey Bogart
> David Larrabee .... William Holden

Comedy in any medium depends a great deal upon the mixing up of mes-
sages, the deliberate switching of a communication context, and the swapping
of labels on statements. Billy Wilder's comedies generally avoid slapstick
switches which pull the rug out from under characters. Nevertheless, his films
subtly manage to swap around the foundations of their behavior. *Sabrina* is
a good example. Audrey Hepburn played a variety of gamin girls gone elegant
in the 1950's and early 1960's, and as Sabrina she once again made her way
from simple innocent to beloved of the rich. What she learns in the process
allows Wilder to make some sharp comments on how victimized an elusive
waif, with a refined yet childlike sensuality, can be.

A large number of American movies, from war films to artists' biographies
to Andy Hardy pictures, portray the education of their male hero. He is
taught the proper values in life and weaned away from shallower ambitions
by a good woman, who patiently and lovingly helps him see the error of his
selfish hopes and assumptions. This narrative pattern is altered significantly
when the sexes are reversed: if a man is to educate a woman in the proper
set of values, a Pygmalion story is in order. In this sort of story, the woman,
unlike her male counterpart, lacks the desire for money; her aspiration to a
higher social order is a romantic one. As a rule, the relationship of teacher
and pupil begins as a nonsexual one. The man adopts a somewhat fatherly
role and only gradually drifts from benign paternalism to a more romantic
interest in a woman who changes under his guidance. That teacher and pupil
will eventually have some romantic involvement is understood by any viewer
familiar with genre convention. The innocent girl about to learn something
about life, however, is not meant to approach her education through a sexual
relationship within this convention; thus, her first love interest can be counted
on to be a mistake, and the man unsuitable. She can trust those with a

paternal, less sexual interest more than those with romantic designs.

Wilder bases much of the comedy in *Sabrina* on this distinction; in fact, he so strongly lampoons Sabrina's interest in the handsome romantic bachelor, as well as his wiser, less handsome alternative, that the whole implicit system of girlhood education proposed by convention acquires the look of the ridiculous. Wilder's subtle humor arises from some of the incongruities of the "poor girl makes good" story.

Sabrina Fairchild (Audrey Hepburn) is a chauffeur's daughter whose father works for the wealthy Larrabee family on Long Island, New York. Sabrina is dissatisfied with life in the servants' quarters. She develops a crush on the younger Larrabee son, David (William Holden); but he thinks of her as a girl, not a woman. He has been married three times and is now an unattached playboy. One night Sabrina, unseen, watches him romance a woman on the family tennis court. Her own chances for David now seem so slim that Sabrina decides life is not worth living and tries to commit suicide by locking herself in the garage with the car motors running. Fortunately the older Larrabee brother, Linus (Humphrey Bogart), who is definitely not a handsome playboy, saves her.

Sabrina is next sent to Paris by her father, who hopes that the cooking school she attends will cure her of her hopeless ambitions and romantic dreams and prepare her for servant work. Sabrina, however, cannot cook no matter how hard she tries, and she is miserable in cooking school. Then an elderly baron adopts her, and two years later, Sabrina returns to Long Island a glamorous, chic, and poised woman, thanks to the baron's tutelage. As Sabrina waits for her father to pick her up from the station, David happens to drive by, and, not recognizing Sabrina as the chauffeur's daughter, he picks her up. Not until they both arrive at her destination and David realizes that he is home does Sabrina reveal her identity; and David determines to see more of the transformed woman.

At this point Sabrina enters another important phase in her education. On the verge of beginning a romance with a womanizer, she meets a second man, older and wiser than David—his brother Linus. In terms of convention, he represents the perfect match for Sabrina: he is wise and reliable as well as romantically interested, and Sabrina is gradually won over. Wilder, however, turns the genre conventions topsy-turvy by making the older man turn out to have dishonest intentions, and making the shallow playboy show him the error of his ways. Sabrina, trying to make sense of the men who court her, follows the path the audience expects any girl in her position to follow—and her world almost collapses around her as a result.

Sabrina is at first delighted to have made a big hit with David. She accepts his invitation to a party at the Larrabee mansion, and when she arrives, she is the center of attraction and has all the men in the room interested; but David keeps his prize to himself. Linus, meanwhile, watches his brother's growing involvement with Sabrina with some trepidation. Linus, for business purposes, has already arranged for his easily amused brother to marry a sugar heiress. The marriage will improve the Larrabee fortune and make little difference to David, who can never keep his mind on anything for long anyway. In the best interest of the business, Linus decides to date Sabrina himself and wean her away from his brother. It is also, incidentally, in her own best interest, since she is still too naïve to see David for what he really is.

Linus thus wines and dines Sabrina, who soon realizes that David suffers by comparison. She begins to fall in love with the man who seems to have the better character; and, to his dismay, Linus also develops a keen interest in Sabrina. Linus, however, is determined to belong only to his business and plans to get rid of Sabrina. He tells her that he has booked passage for them aboard an ocean liner; when the ship sails, Linus is not on board, and Sabrina heads out to sea alone. When Linus shows up at the board meeting, David, who expected his brother to be honeymooning at sea, realizes what Linus has done. David gives his brother a lecture on the importance of love over business; Linus sees his error and takes a helicopter out to the ship to join Sabrina. David stays to watch over the family fortune, and so an uncertain role reversal is made complete.

With that ending *Sabrina* manages to include one more form of conventional film education, that of the singleminded businessman discovering the importance of his private life. In the combination of these various conventions, however, *Sabrina* manages to undercut them all. The viewer feels uneasy about any of the structures of romantic education proposed in the film. The happy ending does have a couple sailing for Paris, but the complications which got them there reveal a fragile set of assumptions.

THE SEVEN YEAR ITCH

Released: 1955
Production: Charles K. Feldman and Billy Wilder for Twentieth Century-Fox
Direction: Billy Wilder
Screenplay: Billy Wilder and George Axelrod; based on the play of the same
   name by George Axelrod
Cinematography: Milton Krasner
Editing: Hugh S. Fowler
Running time: 105 minutes

> *Principal characters:*
> The Girl .... Marilyn Monroe
> Richard Sherman .... Tom Ewell
> Helen Sherman .... Evelyn Keyes
> Ricky Sherman ....Butch Bernard

A delightful and witty farce, *The Seven Year Itch* combines the talents of Marilyn Monroe and Tom Ewell with hilarious results. Adapted by George Axelrod and Billy Wilder from Axelrod's Broadway play, it is essentially the extended reverie of a plain, middle-aged publisher of paperback books concerning his amorous fantasies. Ewell's deft comic timing, Wilder's brisk direction, and the radiant presence of Marilyn Monroe give luster to this sophisticated comedy.

The script sets up situations bound to have many comic possibilities, then explores most of them inventively and at a rapid pace, and quickly finishes before we tire of the gags. New Yorker Richard Sherman (Tom Ewell) sends his wife, Helen (Evelyn Keyes), and son, Ricky (Butch Bernard), to Maine for the summer so they can escape the city's heat and humidity. Although he has a vivid sexual imagination continually kept sharp through its exercise, he is determined to lead a sensible life during the summer and not be like the other men he knows who start playing around as soon as their wives leave town. The very first night he is alone, however, he finds his good resolutions severely tested by The Girl upstairs (Marilyn Monroe)—she is never given a name—a summer tenant in the building where he lives.

Having decided not to smoke, drink (following the orders of Helen and his doctor), or give in to other forms of temptation, he goes to a vegetarian restaurant for dinner. All the other diners are elderly. Even the waitress is plain and middle-aged and does not accept tips; she does, however, solicit a contribution for the nudist fund, explaining that without clothes there would be no wars: soldiers would not be able to tell enemies from friends. Depressed by this experience, Sherman returns to his comfortably cluttered apartment, stepping on one of Ricky's roller skates in the process, and then prepares to read a manuscript his firm is planning to publish.

At this point he meets the new summer tenant in the apartment above his—a shapely, wide-eyed blonde in a tight dress. The meeting triggers his always active imagination, and instead of reading the manuscript which he has brought home, he begins to fantasize. Written by a psychiatrist, the manuscript is about the repressed urges of middle-aged men. Sherman thinks it will be boring, but when he later reads it, he finds it describes a condition particularly applicable to himself—the tendency of men married for seven years to seek extramarital adventures. The psychiatrist calls it the seven-year itch. In his fantasy, Sherman tells his wife he has an "animal thing" which arouses something in the women he meets. He tells her of the attempts of his secretary, a beautiful nurse, and finally her best friend to seduce him (the scene with her best friend taking place on a deserted beach with waves crashing on the shore in a parody of the famous love scene in *From Here to Eternity*, 1953). His wife, however, refuses to take him seriously and just laughs at his stories.

Soon after he returns to reality from this fantasy, he meets The Girl again when she knocks a tomato plant off her balcony onto his—in fact, onto the chair he has just vacated. He invites her down for a drink, unlocks the drawer where he keeps his cigarettes, turns down the lights, and plumps up the pillows before he realizes what he is doing. As he turns up the lights, he begins another fantasy in which The Girl appears in a slinky strapless evening gown and black gloves, flourishing a long cigarette holder. Sherman is at the piano in an elegant dressing gown, silk scarf wound about his throat, distinguishedly gray at the temples, lighted candelabra on the piano, playing Rachmaninoff's *Second Piano Concerto*. The Girl is overwhelmed, swept away by the music. As they embrace on the piano bench (in a manner reminiscent of the famous Tabu perfume advertisement), the doorbell rings, and he awakens from his fantasy. It is only the slovenly janitor who wants to pick up the rugs for cleaning. Sherman gets rid of him just before The Girl arrives in tight slacks and matching pale pink blouse. He tells her that he is not married and has no children, explaining away the roller skate he is holding (on which he has once again slipped as he rushed to answer the door) by telling her he likes to rollerskate.

The Girl does not know what a martini is but lets him make her one while she stands in front of the air conditioner, raising her blouse to let the cool air blow on her midriff. New York is in the middle of a heat wave, and her apartment is not air conditioned. She tells Sherman she tried to sleep in a bathtub full of cold water but had to call in the plumber because her toe got stuck in the faucet. It was embarrassing, she says, because the man was a stranger and she had not polished her toenails. She also discloses that she has posed for an "artistic" picture in *U.S. Camera* and does Dazzledent toothpaste commercials for television. "More people see me than saw Sarah Bernhardt," she muses.

The Girl's artless conversation establishes her character; she is the empty-headed but beautiful and desirable blonde, the natural object of a quiet middle-aged man's fantasies. She is so amiably childlike and innocent that she cannot be considered immoral. When she accidentally discovers that Sherman is married, she is relieved because nothing can get "drastic" with married men. "No matter what happens he can't ask you to marry him," she says.

When Sherman plays a recording of the Rachmaninoff Piano Concerto, she is not swept away as he had fantasized, but exclaims that it must be classical music because there is no vocal. "I have this big thing for Eddie Fisher," she informs him, dipping her potato chip in champagne. The Girl's favorite expression of approval is "delicate," which she uses to describe drinking champagne with a married man in an air-conditioned apartment. She is trusting, too, not suspecting or looking for hidden motives in Sherman's actions. He is able very easily to trick her into kissing him by saying that he doubts the truth of the Dazzledent commercials. Like a child, she is pleased by the cool breeze that escapes from the ducts of the subway when a train whishes through, and squealing delightedly, she allows her full skirt to billow up.

The Girl is presented as more than merely an object. Although she is not sophisticated, she is kind and smart enough to realize that Sherman's self-confidence needs bolstering. In a scene that demonstrates her kindness and gives some individuality to her character, she reassures Sherman, telling him that not every girl wants a man who looks like Gregory Peck. What is really exciting, she tells him, is the nervous, shy man sitting in a corner at a party. At first he may be overlooked, but a woman can sense that he is gentle, kind, and sweet, and will be tender with her. She ends by assuring Sherman that if she were his wife she would be very jealous of him and awards him her ultimate accolade: "You're just delicate."

In the play Sherman spends one night with The Girl, but in the film he merely lets her use his air-conditioned bedroom while he sleeps on the living room couch. His conscience having become as active as his libido, he then flees to Maine to spend two weeks with his wife and son. The Girl kisses him good-bye and tells him not to wipe off the lipstick, implying that a little jealousy on Helen's part will make her more aware of his appeal to other women.

Under the direction of Billy Wilder, Marilyn Monroe and Tom Ewell give remarkable performances which are funny and entertaining while keeping the lighthearted eroticism of the film from becoming vulgar. Evelyn Keyes is good as the wife, particularly in the fantasy scene in which she discovers The Girl with her husband and shoots him, saying, "The wives of America will give me a medal." Indeed, the fantasy scenes are well handled throughout to show us the workings of Sherman's hyperactive imagination.

It is not difficult to see why *The Seven Year Itch* was the most popular film released by Twentieth Century-Fox that year, and remains one of Marilyn Monroe's most noteworthy films.

SOME LIKE IT HOT

Released: 1959
Production: Billy Wilder for the Mirisch Company; released by United Artists
Direction: Billy Wilder
Screenplay: Billy Wilder and I.A.L. Diamond; suggested by a story by R. Thoeren and M. Logan
Cinematography: Charles Lang
Editing: Arthur Schmidt
Costume design: Orry-Kelly (AA)
Running time: 120 minutes

Principal characters:
Sugar .... Marilyn Monroe
Joe/Josephine .... Tony Curtis
Jerry/Daphne ....Jack Lemmon
Spats Colombo ....George Raft
Mulligan .... Pat O'Brien
Osgood Fielding III ....Joe E. Brown

Billy Wilder's *Some Like It Hot* is an outrageous, satirical spoof of the 1920's in which Wilder deftly spends two hours milking one joke, that of two musicians on the run from Chicago mobsters, who disguise themselves as women and join an all-girl band. With its broad humor and its period costumes, *Some Like It Hot* is reminiscent of the Marx Brothers, early Woody Allen films, and Mack Sennett comedies. It is a madcap lampoon of the 1920's, encompassing speakeasies, gangsters, gambling, bootlegging, and even murder by machine gun.

Musicians Joe (Tony Curtis) and Jerry (Jack Lemmon) accidentally witness the St. Valentine's Day massacre. With an angered Spats Colombo (George Raft) and his boys on their trails, they have to flee. First, however, they need disguises, and the presence of an all-girl band is the answer to their problems—but only after they shave their legs and become members. In a clever, breezy transition, the boys discuss the possibility of shaved legs in one scene; the next scene begins with a close-up of their legs wobbling on high heels.

Disguised as Josephine (Joe) and Daphne (Jerry), the two share a train car with other members of the band, including the luscious (and a bit of a "lush") Sugar (Marilyn Monroe). Both experience uneasy moments during the train ride, Joe's (Josephine's) taking place when the train makes an unexpected stop, throwing the lovely Sugar into his arms. Jerry's (Daphne's) dilemma occurs when Sugar climbs into his berth to thank him for saving her job; when she was going to get the ax because of her drinking, Daphne stepped in to take the blame. Lonely Sugar in a seductive black nightgown proves too much for Jerry to handle, and he asks Sugar to join him in a drink, at which time a surprise—his real identity—will be revealed. In no time at all, Sugar has passed the word about the drinking party, which Jerry had wanted to be private. Thus, Jerry winds up with an eight-girl slumber party in his berth.

Some Like It Hot is highlighted by a delicious tangle of identities. Once the all-girl group arrives in Florida, for example, Jerry is coaxed by Joe into encouraging the advances of the wolfish Osgood Fielding III (Joe E. Brown), who has admired Daphne's legs, in order that Joe can assume another identity. Josephine, who, like Daphne, has become one of Sugar's best "girl friends," has talked with her about the kind of man she is looking for. Joe is determined to be it. With Jerry as Daphne flirting with Osgood, Joe can assume the identity of "Junior" (of "Vanity Fair and Shell Oil fame"). In order to appear with the accouterments to be "Junior," Joe requires the use of the preoccupied Osgood's yacht.

As Junior, Joe dons glasses, a Cary Grant accent, and yachting jacket and cap. After luring Sugar to his yacht, he tries to evoke the indifference of the upper class. He keeps a copy of the *Wall Street Journal* at hand, discusses the art of water polo (on horses), and, in pointing out the difference between the fore and aft of a ship, explains that it depends "whether you're coming or going." Junior, who maintains he gets no thrill at all from women, utilizes psychiatric jargon so that Sugar will ask for the privilege of seducing him. Although he gets no "thrill" from women, however, his glasses begin steaming when Sugar tries to help him overcome his "problem."

While Joe carries on his Junior identity, Jerry as Daphne is also undergoing an identity crises. The absurdity of the tangled identities comes into focus when Daphne, after a night of dancing the tango with Osgood, decides to marry him. "It's my only chance to marry a millionaire," insists Jerry, explaining that "security" is what he is seeking; and improbably, he winds up becoming engaged to Fielding.

The romances, however, are all cut short when the mob makes its appearance at the hotel. Both Joe and Jerry think their numbers are up, but in typical Wilder fashion, the gangsters themselves come to an untimely and comical end with Spats being machine-gunned through the vehicle of a six-foot-tall birthday cake out of which pops the assassin. The remainder of the mob then kill one another off.

Joe is now ready to reveal the truth about "Junior" to the unsuspecting Sugar, who loves both his personalities, Josephine as well as Junior. Jerry, in the meantime, sadly realizes that he must break the news of his identity to Osgood, who is looking forward to marriage. In the film's classic closing scene, Jerry, who now wants to discourage Osgood's affection, rips off his wig, revealing his true identity. Unruffled by it all and with his love apparently still intact, Osgood merely replies, "Well, nobody's perfect."

Visually and verbally, *Some Like It Hot* is a frantic, nonstop barrage of one-liners and comic invention. Tony Curtis as Joe/Josephine/"Junior" and Jack Lemmon as Jerry/Daphne deliver their lines with expert timing; and Lemmon garnered an Oscar nomination for his work. Marilyn Monroe is the wistful Sugar, the ukelele-strumming singer who joins the all-girl group because when she works for male groups, she always falls for the saxophone player. This was Monroe's second film with Wilder (the first was *The Seven Year Itch*, filmed in 1955), and although he managed to elicit a fine comic performance from her, as well as several highly entertaining musical numbers (including "Running Wild," and "I Wanna Be Loved by You"), the battles the two had on the set have become part of Hollywood lore. One sequence in *Some Like It Hot* that involved Monroe required a legendary fifty-nine takes.

In its final form, *Some Like It Hot* was a box-office bonanza, grossing more than twenty million dollars. With its fast and furious premise, as well as its constant humor, *Some Like It Hot* was the funniest film of 1959. Its humor runs the gamut from broad slapstick to sly sexual innuendo. With Lemmon and Curtis delightfully appearing in women's clothes, the film suggests transvestite jokes but never plays on them seriously. Curtis, a frequently underrated actor, delivers an especially good Cary Grant take-off; and the supporting players, including Joe E. Brown as Osgood, are slickly in control all around.

Some Like It Hot was Wilder's fifteenth film, following dramatic successes such as *Double Indemnity* (1944) and *Sunset Boulevard* (1950), as well as comedies such as *Stalag 17* (1953) and the more fanciful *Sabrina* (1954). It ranks as Wilder's funniest film, and paired him for the first time with Lemmon; the two would go on to collaborate in films such as *The Apartment* (1960), *The Fortune Cookie* (1966), *Avanti* (1972), and *The Front Page* (1974).

With the exception of Lemmon's Best Actor nomination, *Some Like It Hot* did not get any major award nominations, although Orry-Kelly's costumes did take an award. The film nevertheless remains a classic comedy whose genuinely affectionate nostalgia merges with an irreverent story line that tampers with social taboos and sensibilities. With their portrayals of Joe/Josephine and Jerry/Daphne, Tony Curtis and Jack Lemmon made their marks as a great and decidedly unsung cinema team.

SUNSET BOULEVARD

Released: 1950
Production: Charles Brackett for Paramount
Direction: Billy Wilder
Screenplay: Charles Brackett, D. M. Marshman, Jr., and Billy Wilder (AA)
Cinematography: John F. Seitz
Editing: Doane Harrison and Arthur Schmidt
Art direction: Hans Dreier and John Meehan (AA)
Set decoration: Sam Comer and Ray Moyer (AA)
Music: Franz Waxman (AA)
Running time: 111 minutes

Principal characters:
Norma Desmond	Gloria Swanson
Joe Gillis	William Holden
Max Von Mayerling	Erich Von Stroheim
Betty Schaefer	Nancy Olson
Artie Green	Jack Webb
Cecil B. De Mille	Himself

In *Sunset Boulevard*, writer-director Billy Wilder provides us with a "behind the scenes" investigation into Hollywood. While Wilder's caustic wit is apparent throughout, the investigation is a serious one. As such, *Sunset Boulevard* can be seen as an influence on many subsequent films about Hollywood. With the notable exception of *A Star Is Born* (1937), films about Hollywood prior to *Sunset Boulevard* had tended to be light comedies and musicals. These films served to demonstrate that Hollywood people had plenty of heart and were basically "just plain folks." But *Sunset Boulevard* was made during a period in which Hollywood was reevaluating itself, and audiences were reevaluating the Hollywood product they had been accustomed to. Hollywood was steadily losing its audience, partially as a result of television, but more crucially, as a result of government antitrust action and a Supreme Court decision which forced a restructuring of studio distribution and exhibition policies. *Sunset Boulevard* was also made during a period when audiences were being exposed to films from Europe which were more realistic in approach, as well as independently produced American films which strived for social relevance.

Sunset Boulevard responded to these shifts in the film industry by demystifying star mythology and exposing the more cold-blooded aspects of the studio system. In doing so, it purports to be "realistic," but because the film is a commercial Hollywood product, it ultimately equates star mythology with transcendent and larger-than-life qualities, and reveals that decency does exist beneath the corruption induced by working in the studio system. It is this opposition between exposing Hollywood's "dirty laundry" and reaffirming the value of Hollywood itself that influenced later films such as *The Bad and the Beautiful* (1952), *A Star Is Born* (1954), and *The Barefoot Contessa* (1954). Like *Sunset Boulevard*, these films show movie people who are creative but also obsessed, ruthless, or deeply troubled as a result of making movies. Once having detailed these various personal problems, however, the films stress that movies and what the stars do *in front* of the camera—and the public—are what really matters in the final analysis. The simple message is, "The show must go on."

What makes *Sunset Boulevard* truly unique among these films is its blend of fact and fiction. For the role of Norma Desmond, the legendary star of the silent screen who has deluded herself into attempting a comeback, Wilder cast Gloria Swanson. Absent from the screen for nine years, Swanson was attempting a comeback of her own. While she had made several sound films (including 1934's *Music in the Air*, coscripted by Wilder), her career had never attained the heights she had reached during the silent era, when her name was synonymous with Hollywood glamour. As Norma's faithful butler as well as former director and husband, Wilder cast Erich Von Stroheim, who in 1943 had appeared in Wilder's *Five Graves to Cairo*. As a director, Von Stroheim was among the truly great innovators of the silent screen, and in 1928 he had directed Swanson in *Queen Kelly*, a film that was never released. At one point in *Sunset Boulevard*, Norma shows a scene from *Queen Kelly*. Norma also dresses up in a "Bathing Beauty" outfit, another reminder of Swanson's career since she made her first screen appearances as one of Mack Sennett's "Bathing Beauties." To complete his casting, Wilder used several Hollywood figures as themselves. Cecil B. De Mille appears as one of Norma's directors from the silent days; De Mille had directed Swanson in such films as *Male and Female* (1919) and *Don't Change Your Husband* (1919). Columnist Hedda Hopper also appears, as do Buster Keaton, Ann Q. Nilsson, and H. B. Warner, all of whom were silent era stars who did not make a successful transition to sound, Wilder furthers the sense of verisimilitude by setting many scenes at Paramount Studios.

These legends from Hollywood's pioneering days are clearly opposed to the new Hollywood, represented by a down-on-his-luck young screenwriter named Joe Gillis (William Holden). When Joe pulls into a driveway in an exclusive residential section off of Sunset Boulevard to elude two men who intend to repossess his car, his luck takes a fateful turn; the driveway leads to Norma's decaying mansion. Norma first mistakes Joe for an animal undertaker, but when she learns his occupation, she tells him of her plans to return to the screen in a version of "Salome," which she has scripted herself. Joe finds the script unbearable, but he sees an opportunity to make the money he so desperately needs. He tells Norma that the script has potential, but needs the kind of contemporary slant that he can provide. Norma hires him and soon moves him into the mansion, making him her "kept man." Joe lets Norma pick up the bills while he fuels her delusions of a comeback and makes love to her.

It is significant that Norma mistakes Joe for an undertaker, for his presence at the mansion will eventually lead to his death by her hand. The mansion itself intensifies the foreshadowing of doom. Its gothic ambience is established by rats in the empty swimming pool, the midnight burial of Norma's chimpanzee, and the eerie organ music that punctuates the musty night air.

Joe's death is a result of his romantic involvement with Betty Schaefer (Nancy Olson), a Paramount script girl. The relationship induces Joe to reach beneath his cynical veneer and draw upon his innate decency. Joe's admission to Norma that he has been lying to her and his attempt to make her face reality only serve to make her mind snap. Ever the prisoner of inescapable self-delusion, Norma shoots Joe, and he falls into the now-filled swimming pool, a symbol of filmland status providing Joe with a watery grave.

Wilder continually points out that both Joe and Norma are victims of Hollywood. We are told that Joe has talent, but the studio doors are closed to him because he refuses to turn out hack work. A Paramount producer and Joe's agent, representatives of Hollywood business practices, are both callous individuals. The power structure is presented as unfeeling, while those who toil in the ranks, such as Betty Schaefer and Joe's friend Artie Green (Jack Webb), are depicted in positive terms. Norma's victimization results from her refusing to leave the Hollywood past behind. She believes that her legion of fans are still anxiously waiting her return, but we later discover that the fan letters she has received over the years have been forged by Max (Erich Von Stroheim), her butler. A call from Paramount convinces Norma that her comeback is assured.

The call leads Norma to visit Paramount, and this constitutes the most poignant scene in the film. When Norma enters a soundstage to visit her mentor Cecil B. De Mille (played by himself), she is mobbed in adoration by the technicians and extras who worked with her during the old days. But even here her victimization is suggested, as the mike boom on the set continually casts a shadow over her. It finally swings down to her, and she pushes it away as if it were a pesky insect. Yet Norma cannot get rid of what the mike boom represents—the progress made by Hollywood. Certainly, Norma is one of the inevitable victims that progress must leave in its wake. After Norma leaves, we learn that Paramount had called her to request the use of her vintage automobile in a film. De Mille demonstrates the decency of the Hollywood pioneer when he orders that Norma is never to be told the reason for the call.

Norma leaves the studio convinced of the imminent production of *Salome* and prepares for her triumphant return. Even when she finally lapses into madness, she holds onto her conviction. After Joe's murder and the arrival

of the police and reporters, she believes that the newsreel cameras are there
to film her comeback. She then descends the stairway for her final close-up.
But this close-up is not directed at the filmers of the newsreel, but rather at
the audience, as Norma walks past the newsreel cameras and directly toward
the offscreen camera filming the scene. The texture of the image then blurs,
giving her a transcendent and illusory appearance. It is supremely fitting that
Norma, who has been unable to distinguish illusion from reality, should take
on such an appearance. Her walking past the fictional characters and toward
the audience finally establishes her as a mythic figure.

Like *Double Indemnity* (1944), the events of *Sunset Boulevard* are related
through a flashback structure narrated by the male protagonist. But in this
instance Wilder adds a gimmick to the structure—the narrator is Joe, who
is seen floating in the pool at the beginning. In other words, it is a tale told
by a dead man. This gimmick was not an original idea in itself, as evidenced
by Charles Chaplin's *Monsieur Verdoux* (1947), which begins with Verdoux's
voice-over as a shot of his headstone is seen. But unlike *Sunset Boulevard*,
Monsieur Verdoux is not bracketed by this narrative device, nor does it contain
continual voice-over narration. Actually, Wilder had originally filmed a different dead narrator device, in which Joe sits upright in a morgue and tells
his story to the other corpses; but the director scrapped this footage when
audiences laughed during a sneak preview.

As it is, the device is audacious enough. What makes it work is Holden's
deft reading of Wilder's crisp, cynical dialogue. Despite the publicity surrounding Swanson's return to the screen and her undeniably powerful presence, it is Holden who provides the film with its central source of tension.
The look of revulsion on his face when he gets ready to make love to Norma
is chilling, and it is one of the many expressive resources Holden draws on
to make his dilemma touching. Holden plays Joe as more than a callow
manipulator. Indeed, his fleshing in of the character earned him recognition
as a serious actor and enabled him to move away from the bland leading roles
he was known for prior to *Sunset Boulevard*. Under Wilder's direction in
Stalag 17, Holden won an Academy Award as Best Actor of 1953, and the
actor would later appear in two subsequent Wilder films, *Sabrina* (1954) and
Fedora (1979). Without Holden, *Sunset Boulevard* might have been a merely
a unique collection of old Hollywood relics; with him, the film becomes
poignant in its delineation of the past against the present.

Wilder has often been quoted as saying that many Hollywood moguls
reacted adversely to the film, but the 1950 Academy Award nominations
show that *Sunset Boulevard* was highly regarded within the film industry. The
film won Oscars for Best Writing (story and screenplay), Best Score of a
Dramatic or Comedy Picture, and Best Art Direction/Set Direction (black-
and-white). It was also nominated in several major categories: Best Motion
Picture, Best Director, Best Actress, Best Supporting Actress (Olson), and

Best Cinematography (black-and-white). (Ironically, the film honored as Best Motion Picture, Joseph L. Mankiewicz's *All About Eve*, was another exposé of show business with a unique flashback structure in which the narrative is connected by the "unconscious" thoughts of three of its principals.)

In addition to these industry accolades, *Sunset Boulevard* earned far-reaching critical acclaim. The Hollywood press awarded "Golden Globe" Awards to the film as Best Drama, Best Director, Best Actress in a Drama, and Best Score. The National Board of Review honored the film as Best American Film and Swanson as Best Actress, and also included it on its ten best films list, as did the *New York Times* and *Time* magazine. While the film was only moderately successful at the box office, its popularity with audiences—as well as its stature—has increased over the years. In a 1977 survey conducted by the American Film Institute, *Sunset Boulevard* was listed forty-fourth on the list of the fifty most popular films of all time. The film's reputation is richly deserved, for it provides us with a look at an introspective Hollywood and an insight into the mind of its genius creator.

WITNESS FOR THE PROSECUTION

Released: 1957
Production: Arthur Hornblow, Jr., for Theme Pictures; released by United
   Artists
Direction: Billy Wilder
Screenplay: Billy Wilder and Harry Kurnitz; based on Larry Marcus' adapt-
   ation of the story and the play of the same name by Agatha Christie
Cinematography: Russell Harlan
Editing: Daniel Mandell
Running time: 114 minutes

>   *Principal characters:*
>   Leonard Vole .... Tyrone Power
>   Christine Vole .... Marlene Dietrich
>   Sir Wilfrid Robarts .... Charles Laughton
>   Miss Plimsoll .... Elsa Lanchester
>   Brogan-Moore .... John Williams
>   Mayhew .... Henry Daniell
>   Janet McKenzie .... Una O'Connor
>   Mrs. French .... Norma Varden
>   Mr. Myers .... Torin Thatcher
>   Diana .... Ruta Lee

The witness for the prosecution, a surprise witness, is Christine Vole (Marlene Dietrich), presumably the wife of the man on trial for murder, Leonard
Vole (Tyrone Power), a ne'er-do-well gadget peddler. She claims that she
is not legally Leonard's wife, then refutes his alibi. The next day, however,
Leonard's counsel, Sir Wilfrid Robarts (Charles Laughton), destroys Christine's testimony with a small bundle of letters that she had written to her
"Beloved Max" in Germany, and consequently wins Leonard's acquittal. The
trial over, Christine tells Sir Wilfrid that she knew Leonard to be guilty all
along, that she, disguised, had tricked Sir Wilfrid into taking the phony letters
the night before, perjuring herself in order for Leonard to be freed. When
Leonard appears with a young, pretty blonde (Ruta Lee) and announces that
he plans to go away with her, Christine, enraged, stabs Leonard there in the
courtroom, using the knife presented in evidence as the murder weapon. Sir
Wilfrid then makes plans to defend Christine against the charge of murder.

The multifaceted trick ending of Agatha Christie's original play made it
highly popular in London's West End and on Broadway, where it ran for
almost two years. Although the play was done as a straight mystery, Billy
Wilder and Harry Kurnitz in their screenplay insert a good deal of humor
and emphasis on character, their main addition being Miss Plimsoll (Elsa
Lanchester), Sir Wilfrid's private nurse, the source of some of the finest
comedy in the film. At the time of this film Wilder had earned considerable

fame for a group of excellent *films noirs* that began with *Double Indemnity* in 1944; and in the 1950's and early 1960's he was highly regarded also for his dark comedies such as *Stalag 17* (1953) and misanthropic farces such as *The Apartment* (1960) and *Kiss Me, Stupid* (1964). *Witness for the Prosecution* combines the usual Wilder touches—masquerade, verbal wit, intimations of a corrupt environment—but emerges one of his lightest, least trenchant works, without denying in the end the reality of human baseness.

The film's effect depends upon misleading appearances, things turning out to be not what they originally seemed. The climax follows smoothly from the deceptions, not all of them malicious, that run throughout the various relationships within the story.

The humor in the film derives largely from the attempts of Sir Wilfrid, recovering from a coronary, to outwit Nurse Plimsoll, his "jailer" (he calls her) and the surrogate for his doctor, who has forbidden him a number of amenities, including participation in murder trials. Sir Wilfrid plays the naughty school boy to Miss Plimsoll's matron. He evades her naps, shots, pills, and, especially, injunctions against cigars and brandy. His antics extend to outright rebellion the night he receives the phone call from the mysterious cockney woman about the letters, as he rushes off to Euston Station after grabbing Miss Plimsoll's poised hypodermic and sticking it in the end of his cigar. Her browbeating and smothering attention, however, give way finally to pride and admiration at Leonard's trial: "Wilfrid the fox—that's what they call him" she proclaims to everyone in the balcony when Sir Wilfrid confronts Christine with the letters. She is also the one who orders the return of the luggage from the boat train, decisively announcing that Sir Wilfrid will appear for the defense of Christine. He has never really fooled her, anyway, as she makes clear when she reminds him that he has forgotten his brandy (his thermos of "hot cocoa"). Their growing camaraderie furnishes a healthy, innocent contrast to the treachery, both real and feigned, that marks the Voles's relationship.

Christine's deceptions underlie the major part of the film's climax. She bears out Sir Wilfrid's initial suspicion of her when she appears for the prosecutor Mr. Myers (Torin Thatcher), claiming that she was already married to a man named Helm when she went through a ceremony with Leonard in Hamburg while he was serving with the British occupation forces after World War II. Her testimony proves in fact no deception at all—Leonard did return home late on the night in question with blood on his clothes, admitting that he had murdered Mrs. French (Norma Varden)—although at the time it seems to be outright betrayal. She sounds convincing enough, particularly after Myers admonishes her in her own language about perjury, *Meineid*. In spite of Leonard's artless rebuttal, the jury members, as Brogan-Moore (John Williams) points out later, did not like Christine but believed her, whereas they liked Leonard but did not believe him.

Christine's *tour de force* of deception and disguise is her impersonation of a cockney trollop at Euston Station. She readily convinces both Sir Wilfrid and Mayhew (Henry Daniell) that they are interviewing a woman wronged by Christine Vole, who stole her lover and caused him to disfigure her right cheek. "Wanna kiss me, Ducky?" she asks Sir Wilfrid, pulling back her hair to show him her scar. In court the next day she continues her deception as Sir Wilfrid, with one of the bogus letters in hand, meticulously exposes her commitment to Max and her plan to give false testimony against Leonard. She follows through until after Leonard has been acquitted, even though some of the spectators physically abuse her as she tries to reach Leonard and Sir Wilfrid.

Leonard's masquerade is equally as expert as Christine's. Like his wife, he must hoodwink Sir Wilfrid at close quarters. In the initial conference Leonard wins Sir Wilfrid over, presenting himself as a sincere, talented young inventor, the victim of unfortunate circumstances. Sir Wilfrid decides to rescue him when Brogan-Moore as well as Christine show hesitation about his innocence. Already Leonard had convinced Mrs. French, a wealthy, middle-aged, lonely widow, that he would marry her, or convinced her of something that caused her to change her will and leave him eighty thousand pounds. Christine apparently knew little enough about the details of that relationship, and certainly nothing at all about his involvement with Diana, his blonde girl friend.

To give the story pace and to lead up to the action of the trial, Wilder uses flashbacks that fill in Leonard's relationship with the murdered woman and with his wife. Since the two episodes are narrated by Leonard, they lend credibility to his story. He tells how he happened to see Mrs. French from outside a milliner's shop, where he volunteered advice on a new hat, then in a cinema, and of their ensuing friendship and the encouragement she gave him for his inventions. He also tells of his first meeting with Christine, in the midst of a brawl, at the Hamburg cabaret where she performed. The fight had broken out when, after she sang a song, some of the patrons began to quarrel over her (presumably the sequence was thus staged in order to give the audience a glimpse of the famous Dietrich legs).

Wilder never lets the story become introspective: he mutes the tension between devotion and perfidy by keeping the audience entertained with various gimmicks. *Witness for the Prosecution* has an intelligent balance of courtroom drama, suspense, multilevel humor, and consummate acting. Wilder allows his actors a good deal of freedom. Power makes Leonard a sympathetic although basically shallow character. Just as Leonard seems incapable of stabbing a defenseless woman, his anguish and confusion during the trial appear symptomatic of an engaging naïveté. Yet he readily gives way to the smug callousness that his acquittal uncovers in him. Marlene Dietrich's Christine embodies the right amount of iciness, mystery, and, in the cockney interlude, low comedy. She does overact embarrassingly when Sir Wilfrid destroys her on the stand and when she finally avenges herself on Leonard. On the other hand, Elsa Lanchester performs at her best as the irritating but loyal Nurse Plimsoll. She shows excellent rapport with Laughton, whether coddling him, berating him, or admiring him.

Witness for the Prosecution nonetheless becomes Laughton's film: his Sir Wilfrid binds all together as he romps through each of his scenes. He bullies and cajoles, grimaces and smirks, assailing the veracity of witnesses by reflecting the glare from his monocle into their eyes. Surely the funniest episode in the film is his cross examination of Janet McKenzie (Una O'Connor), Mrs. French's testy, practically deaf Scottish housekeeper, who hates Leonard for working his way into her mistress' will and thus cheating her out of her share. Sir Wilfrid maintains his owlish dignity when he recognizes that Christine and Leonard alike have thoroughly duped him. Even though he suspected something because the solution turned out too pat, he admits that he never suspected Christine's masquerade. He is aghast after she asks him once again, in her cockney dialect, if he wants to kiss her. Yet he passes over defeat into a new challenge, Christine's defense, for she did not actually murder Leonard—"she executed him" he solemnly tells Miss Plimsoll.

Its surprise conclusion aside, *Witness for the Prosecution* appeals as a well-made, coherent melodrama whose performances engage at least as much as does the plot. It is a handsomely designed production, done almost entirely in interiors, the sets for the courtroom in the Old Bailey and for Euston Station, particularly, giving it a thoroughly London atmosphere. The film was Power's last; he died a year later at the age of forty-four while filming *Solomon and Sheba* (1959), and his scenes were reshot with Yul Brynner. Laughton would make three more films, but in none would he get the opportunity to exhibit the range he does here, not even portraying the wily Senator Cooley in Preminger's *Advise and Consent* (1962), his final role. As Sir Wilfrid, one reviewer noted, "the old ham has found the right platter." Sir Wilfrid plays off excellently against Leonard: he becomes defender, then antagonist, of a killer who has ingratiated himself into a tremendous amount of loyalty from two older women. Mrs. French leaves him her fortune, and Christine sets herself up for a perjury conviction and a prison term in order to ensure his freedom. "The wheels of justice grind slowly," Sir Wilfrid admonishes Leonard at the end, "but they grind finely."

Justice comes unexpectedly through the hand of a spurned woman. Leonard understands his acquittal as a piece of good luck and as the payment due for his bringing Christine out of Germany. Years of marriage have, however, failed to teach him an important thing about his wife, for if he accurately calculates the depth of her loyalty, he fails to reckon with the extent of her jealousy. All sympathy finally goes to Christine, whose acquittal seems assured with Sir Wilfrid by her side.

WILLIAM WYLER

BEN-HUR

Released: 1959
Production: Sam Zimbalist for Metro-Goldwyn-Mayer (AA)
Direction: William Wyler (AA)
Screenplay: Karl Tunberg; based on the novel of the same name by Lew
   Wallace
Cinematography: Robert Surtees (AA)
Editing: Ralph E. Winters and John D. Dunning (AA)
Art direction: William A. Horning and Edward Carfagno (AA); set decora-
   tion, Hugh Hunt (AA)
Special effects: A. Arnold Gillespie, Robert MacDonald, and Milo Lory (AA)
Costume design: Elizabeth Haffenden (AA)
Sound: Franklin E. Milton and M-G-M Studio Sound Department (AA)
Music: Miklos Rozsa (AA)
Running time: 212 minutes

> *Principal characters:*
> Judah Ben-Hur .... Charlton Heston (AA)
> Quintas Arrius .... Jack Hawkins
> Messala ....Stephen Boyd
> Esther .... Haya Harareet
> Sheik Ilderim .... Hugh Griffith (AA)
> Miriam .... Martha Scott
> Simonides .... Sam Jaffe
> Tirzah .... Cathy O'Donnell
> Balthasar .... Finlay Currie

Ben-Hur, as novel, play, silent film, and epic sound film, has set an impressive number of records and precedents. As a novel, it was the first fiction
allowed in a number of American homes and the first to be carried in the
Sears catalogue, outselling everything but the Bible. It has been in print
continuously since 1880. The 1899 stage adaptation set precedents both for
an author's control over the rights to his works (Wallace remarked, in rejecting
an initial offer, "The savages who sell things of civilized value for glass beads
live further West than Indiana") and for his control over the adaptation of
material. A lawsuit against the unauthorized 1907 Kalem film established the
same precedents for film. Wallace insisted, for instance, that Christ not be
directly represented on stage, and his heirs made a similar provision when
selling the film rights to M-G-M. Both the stage version, a monumental
international success for twenty years, and the 1925 epic silent film shared
the distinction of being the first play or film that many Americans were
allowed to see. As "A Tale of the Christ," it was a landmark in breaking
down Puritan prohibitions against fiction, drama, and film.
   The 1959 film version gave rise to so many superlatives as to be almost

overpowering. The M-G-M publicity department was not remiss in providing the public with statistics, from the number of horses to the amount of plaster used in constructing the sets. A roster of distinguished visitors came to the set in Rome together with an impressive number of tourists (twenty-five thousand), and a large number of genuine titled Italians took part as extras in one of the most authentically aristocratic (and most sedate) Roman orgies ever filmed. Most impressive were the five years M-G-M spent in preproduction before a foot of film was shot. Critics were somewhat cynical about the advance publicity. Overall, however, the critical response was favorable, and the picture set a record (still unbroken) for winning eleven Academy Awards.

William Wyler, a director noted for intimate dramas rather than epics, whose distinguished films included *Wuthering Heights* (1939) and *The Heiress* (1949), and who won the Academy Award for Best Direction for *Mrs. Miniver* (1942) and *The Best Years of Our Lives* (1946), took on the project as a challenge to make an "intimate spectacle." He had, in fact, been one of several dozen costumed unit directors among the crowd in filming the 1925 *Ben-Hur*'s chariot race. At first, Wyler wanted to direct only the chariot race in the 1959 film, but producer Sam Zimbalist insisted that he take on the human drama and leave the chariot race to second unit directors Andrew Marton and Yakima Kanutt. Wyler decided to cast the Romans with British performers and the Jews with Americans to underscore the conflict of cultures. Charlton Heston, who had played Moses in Cecil B. De Mille's epic *The Ten Commandments* (1955) and a "heavy" in Wyler's own *The Big Country* (1958), was considered for both Ben-Hur and Messala but ended up with the lead.

Though it is a great oversimplification to call the drama of *Ben-Hur* "Christ and a horse-race," the combination has proved to have surefire box-office appeal. The story is indeed a paradox. It is both a passion play and a bloody drama of revenge, both the timeless story of Christ the healer and of the conflict between Roman and Jew, between two opposite ways of life in the pagan world. Like the novel and the stage version, the film opens with a series of tableaux of the birth of Christ and the coming of the Magi. There follows the sharp contrast of a Roman legion marching into Jerusalem, foreshadowing the fate of both Christ and Judah Ben-Hur.

Messala (Stephen Boyd), a boyhood friend of Judah Ben-Hur returning after some years in Rome, marches with the legion. The two men had been like brothers, and their reunion has a heroic intensity as they compete in hurling spears at the point where two beams cross in the ceiling of the Roman garrison. Judah is a Prince of Judea, wealthy and influential; Messala is on his way up in the imperial service. Judah, his mother Miriam (Martha Scott), and his sister Tirzah (Cathy O'Donnell) receive Messala almost as one of the family, and Judah, foreshadowing the race to come, gives him a valuable Arabian horse that he has admired. Messala in turn offers to advance Judah in the favor of the Emperor Tiberius. But the price is too high. Messala wants Judah to reveal the names of Jewish opponents of Roman rule; rebellion has been brewing. Judah previously has been apolitical, but he will not betray his compatriots and coreligionists. Messala gives him an ultimatum to be with him or against him. The sentiment, if not the words, is "He who is not with me is against me," another allusion to the contrast of Roman and Christian values. When Judah declares that he must be against him, Messala breaks off the friendship with the words "Down Eros, up Mars!"

The new Roman governor arrives shortly thereafter. As Judah and his family watch the parade from the roof of their palace, a tile breaks off when Tirzah leans forward to get a better view, and it strikes the governor on the head. At once, soldiers under Messala's command break into the palace and arrest the entire family. In prison, Judah makes a daring escape from his guards, forces his way into Messala's presence, and threatens to impale him with a spear unless he will free Miriam and Tirzah. Messala counters with a promise that they will be put to death unless Judah surrenders. In frustrated rage, Judah hurls the spear into the wall, recalling the friendly rivalry of the javelins on their first encounter, one of Wyler's many directorial touches reinforcing the dramatic relationships with parallels in action. Messala, who knows that the loose tile was an accident, nevertheless plans to make an "example" of the family to advance his own position.

Needless to say, there is no trial. Judah is condemned to the galleys for life, and his mother and sister are imprisoned. The galley slaves endure a forced march across the desert. Stopping at Nazareth for water, the slaves are permitted to drink only after the soldiers and their horses have finished. The centurion orders that Judah be given no water, but a carpenter quietly defies the centurion's order. It is Judah's first encounter with Jesus of Nazareth.

Opinion differs on the treatment of religion in the film. Certainly no pains were spared for accuracy. Professor Gottstein, Judaic historian of the University of Jerusalem, was one of the technical advisers, and a consultant from the Vatican was also called in. One sample of the technical problems encountered was that none of the experts knew exactly what the cross really looked like. A carpenter on the film crew proposed that the simplest construction was probably the most likely. Wyler concurred—a cross was not, after all, a common means of execution at that time, nor a worldwide symbol—and approved a plain T-shaped cross. Once away from the perhaps stifling tradition of Wallace's stipulation that Christ not be shown directly (the film never shows his face), Wyler presents the events of Jesus' life from the perspective of the time, particularly that of the Romans—as minor events in the life of another Jewish fanatic.

In the galleys, three years pass. Judah is now shackled to an oar of a Roman flagship, and when the new commander, Quintus Arrius (Jack Hawkins), arrives, he orders a demonstration of the rowers at increasingly punishing speeds, set by a sinister hortator hammering relentlessly on a drum. Some oarsmen die of heart attacks; all collapse at the end except Judah, who sits erect and defiant. Arrius is impressed and sends for the slave to learn his history. Though Arrius mocks the Jew's assertion that his God will free him to take revenge on his enemy, Arrius orders that Judah's leg be unchained during the coming battle to give him a chance to survive. When the ship is rammed (a series of gruesome close-ups of the effects of oars smashed and splintered in human bodies provides a less felicitous example of "intimate spectacle"), Judah breaks loose, strangles the hortator, frees his fellow prisoners, and dashes on deck to find the galley boarded by pirates. When Arrius is knocked overboard, Judah dives after him and hauls him aboard some floating planks. The rammed flagship sinks, and Arrius tries in Roman fashion to commit suicide. Judah prevents him, throwing in his face his words to the galley slaves, "We keep you alive to serve this ship. Row well, and live." Thus Judah saves Arrius' life a second time. They are rescued by another Roman ship, and Arrius finds that the fleet has gained the victory.

In gratitude, he adopts Judah and takes him to Rome as his son. Ironically, Judah learns the Roman arts of war that he once rejected and becomes, among other things, an expert charioteer. Although he is devoted to Arrius and has every advantage in Rome, he returns to Judea to look for his mother and sister and to seek revenge. On his return, he finds that Simonides (Sam Jaffe), his steward, has not only saved the family fortune but has increased it to immense wealth, despite his being crippled and nearly killed by Roman torture. Judah falls in love with Simonides' daughter Esther (Haya Harareet).

But he still must locate his mother and sister and gain his revenge on Messala. An opportunity for the former comes first. While searching for his family, he encounters an Arab, Sheik Ilderim (Hugh Griffith), the proud owner of four superb white horses, a team received into his tent like members of the family. Ilderim persuades Judah to drive the horses against Messala in a chariot race. Messala has become a very powerful figure in Jerusalem, but he is apprehensive about Judah's return. He has forgotten the fate of Miriam and Tirzah. The soldier he dispatches to find whether they are still alive in prison is horrified to discover that they have contracted leprosy after years of confinement. He frees them to go to the Valley of the Lepers, but Judah is led to believe that they are dead.

This belief increases Judah's desire for revenge. If he can beat Messala in the race, he will not only shame but bankrupt him, for Ilderim has taunted the Roman into betting his entire fortune. The race is suitably spectacular. Only eleven minutes long, it is a taut and suspenseful sequence that is the best example of "intimate spectacle" in the entire film. Wyler began with a panoramic parade around the ring to display the immense and detailed set. Once the race begins, with a false start for added drama, it is seen largely through a series of close shots which focus on the human conflict. There were very few shots with doubles. Boyd had the most difficult assignment; since a dummy looked fake, the body being dragged around the stadium at the climax of the race, was actually Boyd, covered only by some padding and protective clothing. The race alone took three months to film.

Fully aware of the stakes, Messala has his chariot outfitted with revolving blades at the end of each axle. As the race progresses, he maneuvers his chariot alongside that of one of his chief rivals, and the blades chew the spokes of the wheel. The chariot crashes, and the driver is trampled by the other teams. Messala then tries to repeat the maneuver with Judah and almost succeeds in doing so, but in the last lap of the race, his own wheel comes off. Dragged by his team, trampled and run over by following teams, he is left broken and flayed on the sands. Later, writhing in agony, Messala tells Judah what has happened to his mother and sister and dies gloating at Judah's horror.

Esther has discovered that Miriam and Tirzah are in the Valley of the Lepers and has been taking them food, but she has promised them not to tell Judah. As he searches, Judah encounters a preacher addressing large crowds but does not recognize the carpenter who brought him water at Nazareth. When he finds himself caught up in a mob taking the preacher to be crucified, he is horrified to realize that this is the compassionate young man who gave him water when he was a slave. Again, the audience does not see Christ's face. Judah goes along to Calvary and witnesses the crucifixion. In the darkness and tempest that follow, Miriam, the dying Tirzah, and Esther take refuge in a cave. Lightning flashes reveal that the lepers have been miraculously healed. A spring rain follows, renewing life, and the film ends.

Though it follows the novel in its general outline, the 1959 film departs from it in a number of details. It omits altogether the subplot about Iras, the Egyptian siren who is Messala's lover and who tries to seduce Judah. She is quite expendable, and Heston felt that the love story with Esther could have been cut as well. As Heston portrays him, Judah is older and more mature than Lew Wallace's hero. In both the novel and the 1925 film, Judah sees Jesus as the potential leader of a revolution against Rome, and like a Maccabee, he raises a legion to help him. Not until the end does he realize that Christ's kingdom is not of this world. In the 1959 film, Judah Ben-Hur is not a Jewish nationalist and pays no attention to Jesus until the crucifixion.

Although the screenplay was credited solely to Karl Tunberg, the veteran but not very distinguished scenarist who had written *My Gal Sal* (1942), and *Beau Brummel* (1954), a number of others had a hand in it, including Maxwell Anderson, Gore Vidal, S. N. Behrman, and most importantly and controversially, Christopher Fry, who was called in to work over the script when the cast was actually working on location. Wyler credits Fry with revising the dialogue to add a more classic and flowing tone, altering a line such as "Did you enjoy your dinner?" to "Was the food to your liking?"; Heston called Fry "the principal though uncredited creator of the screenplay." When the authorship came up for arbitration, however, the Screen Writers Guild awarded Tunberg sole credit. He received an Oscar nomination, but his was the only category in which the film did not win.

Heston, of course, won the Oscar for Best Actor and created some stir by publicly thanking Christopher Fry during his acceptance speech. *Ben-Hur* also won Best Picture, Direction, Supporting Actor, Musical Score, Color Costuming, Special Effects, Sound, Film Editing (over a million feet of film were exposed during the shooting), Color Art Direction, and Color Cinematography. In addition, it was named Best Picture of the Year by the British Film Academy and the Hollywood Foreign Press Association. Within the profession, Sam Zimbalist was honored (posthumously, as he had suffered a fatal heart attack two weeks before the conclusion of location shooting in Rome) by the Screen Producers Guild as Best Producer of the Year, and William Wyler was named Best Director by the Screen Directors Guild.

Equally impressive was *Ben-Hur*'s box-office success. It had the largest advance sale to date ($500,000) and made almost $40,000,000 in its first year. Of all M-G-M films, only *Gone with the Wind* (1939) surpassed it in popularity, judging by box-office receipts. On February 14, 1971, *Ben Hur* was shown uncut, on prime time television; viewers gave it the highest rating accorded any movie shown during that period on television; it was telecast again at Easter in 1972 and 1974. Arthur Knight, writing in *The Saturday Review*, observed, "Wyler has proved . . . that taste and intelligence need not be lacking in a film spectacle." It is these qualities that account for *Ben-Hur*'s durability.

THE BEST YEARS OF OUR LIVES

Released: 1946
Production: Samuel Goldwyn for Goldwyn Productions (AA)
Direction: William Wyler (AA)
Screenplay: Robert E. Sherwood (AA); based on the novel *Glory for Me* by
   MacKinley Kantor
Cinematography: Gregg Toland
Editing: Daniel Mandell (AA)
Music: Hugo Friedhofer (AA)
Running time: 172 minutes

Principal characters:

Milly Stephenson	Myrna Loy
Al Stephenson	Fredric March (AA)
Fred Derry	Dana Andrews
Peggy Stephenson	Teresa Wright
Marie Derry	Virginia Mayo
Wilma Cameron	Cathy O'Donnell
Homer Parrish	Harold Russell
	(AA Special Award)
Butch Engle	Hoagy Carmichael

One of the most honored films ever to be made in America, *The Best Years of Our Lives* won a total of eight Academy Awards in 1946. Producer Samuel Goldwyn, who always had a keen showman's instinct, first got the idea for a film about returning World War II veterans in 1944 when he read a story in *Time* magazine. The article suggested that American men might be returning to their jobs and families with mixed emotions, and that life might not be smooth for them. Goldwyn asked novelist MacKinley Kantor to write a story treatment, but Kantor became so fascinated with the subject that his "treatment" turned into a 268-page novel entitled *Glory for Me*. Then playwright Robert E. Sherwood, winner of three Pulitzer Prizes, and speechwriter for Franklin D. Roosevelt, was hired to write the script. The result was both literate and articulate, treating the story of the confused ex-soldiers with honesty and compassion.

Next, director William Wyler was brought in. Wyler had worked with Goldwyn several times before and was one of his favorite directors. He had been in the Air Force for three and a half years and had some understanding of the problems of readjustment to civilian life. Goldwyn and his company were determined that this film would be different, not just another Hollywood product. They spared no expense to assemble the finest cast they could muster, including Fredric March, Myrna Loy, Dana Andrews, Teresa Wright, and Virginia Mayo. The most notable member of the cast was Harold Russell, a young man who lost both hands during the war when a defective fuse exploded while in his grasp. Russell had never acted before, except in a brief training film made by the War Department where he demonstrated his mastery of the prosthetic hooks he used in place of hands. Goldwyn and Wyler were both amazed by Russell's ability, and Wyler went on record to say that Russell was the best natural actor he had ever tested.

The film was shot by ace cameraman Gregg Toland in black and white, with the entire wardrobe of the cast designed in varying shades of black and white to get as naturalistic a look a possible. Sets were built life-sized instead of larger than life, as was common, so that rooms that were meant to look cramped really were small, and characters seemed actually to live in their houses. Other technical innovations included the absence of makeup on all of the male characters in the film, and the revolutionary depth of focus that Toland achieved by strapping down his camera for almost every shot.

Aside from being a well-made film, *The Best Years of Our Lives* is a moving one as well. Wyler has stated that the film in a sense was written by certain events, and therefore the filmmakers had a responsibility not to distort those events. Nothing is overdramatized; human emotions are dealt with in intimate detail and seem to be actually happening and not acted out. The unease and nervousness of people who are reunited with unreal expectations is beautifully shown by small gestures. For example, Milly Stephenson (Myrna Loy) says "I look terrible!" when she first sees her husband; and Homer Parrish's (Harold Russell) mother bursts into tears when she sees his hooks for the first time. The behavior of the characters always arises out of the situation they are in, and by the end of the film, the audience feels as if they know these people very well.

The film opens when three veterans meet on an army plane taking them home to Boone City. Al (Fredric March) is an Army Sergeant returning to his wife, two children, and his job in the Cornbelt Bank. Homer is a young sailor who lost both his hands when his boat was torpedoed, and who has already learned to use his hooks with dexterity. The third man is Fred (Dana Andrews), an ex-Bombardier Captain from the wrong side of the tracks who is anxious to see his beautiful war bride. Their homecomings are mixed affairs. Al's wife and children are glad to see him, but Al, self-conscious, suggests they go out and celebrate rather than stay at home. Fred visits his drunkard father and blowsy stepmother only to find that his wife Marie (Virginia Mayo) has left his father's house and gone to work in a night club. He sets out to find her with mixed emotions. Homer's family treats him with pity—even his sweetheart does not know how to act. All three men meet later in a bar—Al with his wife Milly and grown daughter Peggy (Teresa Wright). Before the bartender closes after sending Homer home to bed, Fred and Al are both roaring drunk. Milly and Peggy drive them home, and put Fred to bed in a guest room.

The next morning, Peggy drives Fred to Marie's new apartment. A certain sympathy has sprung up between them, for during the night, Fred had nightmares about the war, and Peggy, a trained nurse, comforted him. Fred sees Marie and finds her small talk boring after his visit with Peggy's family, but physically she still excites him. The weeks pass and all three men go through the various traumas of adjustment. Al strives to make his work at the bank meaningful; Homer tries valiantly to make a go of his life at home, but he rejects the love of his girl friend Wilma (Cathy O'Donnell) as pity and repudiates her. Fred cannot find a job and finally admits to Marie that they are penniless. He goes back to the drugstore in which he was soda jerking before the war, this time behind the perfume counter for thirty-two dollars a week. Marie becomes disgusted with pinching pennies and the two become more and more estranged. Fred's only relief comes when Peggy drops into the drug store to say hello. One day they go out for lunch and realize that they are in love. When Peggy confesses this to her parents, Al is worried, and seeks Fred out at their favorite bar, telling him to stay away from Peggy. Fred telephones Peggy in Al's presence. He tells her he will not see her again; she is heartbroken.

Later, Fred gets into a scuffle with a customer in the drugstore and is fired. Homer, who was watching, talks to Fred, who wearily advises him to marry Wilma and to take what is good in life before it is too late. When Homer gets home, he removes his hooks in front of Wilma, showing her the harness he must wear. She is neither shocked nor repelled and tells him again that she loves him. Homer, convinced at last of her affection for him, asks her to marry him. Meanwhile, Fred returns to his apartment to find Marie entertaining a man. He realizes that she has been unfaithful to him, and that he is not even remotely in love with her anymore. He tells her to see about getting a quick divorce, and leaves. Jobless and discouraged, Fred decides to leave Boone City, but at the airport he sees hundreds of Flying Fortress planes being dismantled and scrapped. He asks the foreman in charge of the salvaging operation for a job and resolves to start a new life for himself.

Homer and Wilma are married. Al and his family are among the guests and Fred is best man. He greets Peggy coolly, but as the ceremony progresses, they both discover that they are still in love. As the guests crowd around Homer and Wilma, Fred takes Peggy in his arms, and with Al's blessings they decide to face the future together.

As mentioned earlier, *The Best Years of Our Lives* won eight major Academy Awards in 1946; in addition, Samuel Goldwyn won the Irving G. Thalberg Memorial Award primarily because of the film. The acting plaudits were given to Fredric March (who had to be lured away from the Broadway stage to do the film) and to Harold Russell. Russell also received a special award "for bringing hope and courage to his fellow veterans" through his appearance in the film. The critics were rapt; they all felt that this was no ordinary film, but one that had special meaning for the millions of Americans who were living the same situation that they were seeing on the screen. The film is revived frequently in spite of its length, and has lost none of its power or its truth. It is not only quality entertainment, but is an important social document as well.

THE CHILDREN'S HOUR

Released: 1961
Production: William Wyler for United Artists
Direction: William Wyler
Screenplay: John Michael Hayes; based on Lillian Hellman's adaptation of her play of the same name
Cinematography: Franz Planer
Editing: Robert Swink
Art direction: Fernando Carrere; set decoration, Edward G. Boyle
Music: Alex North
Running time: 109 minutes

Principal characters:
Karen Wright .... Audrey Hepburn
Martha Dobie .... Shirley MacLaine
Dr. Joe Cardin ....James Garner
Mrs. Lily Mortar .... Miriam Hopkins
Mrs. Amelia Tilford .... Fay Bainter
Mary Tilford .... Karen Balkin
Rosalie .... Veronica Cartwright

In 1933-1934, Lillian Hellman's prizewinning play about slander and lesbianism, *The Children's Hour*, was a sensational shocker. When Sam Goldwyn's film adaptation of the drama, entitled *These Three*, was released in 1936, it was considerably altered from the stage production. Directed by William Wyler and starring Miriam Hopkins, Merle Oberon, and Joel McCrea, the milder and "safe" screen version had a child accuse a woman of having an affair with a man rather than with a woman.

In 1961, William Wyler again directed an adaptation of Hellman's powerful play, but this time the version was faithful to the original story. Although the theme of slander and lesbianism was still controversial, it was no longer a forbidden subject; but if *The Children's Hour* did not shock audiences of 1961, it was nevertheless a candid and effective drama.

Ironically set in New England, the supposed cradle of liberty and free thought, and entitled *The Children's Hour* (the title of one of Longfellow's best-known poems), this psychological drama deals with two women, Karen Wright (Audrey Hepburn) and Martha Dobie (Shirley MacLaine), who have invested their life savings in an exclusive private all-girls school. As the headmistresses of the Wright-Dobie School, the two find themselves subjected to the lies of one of their students. When twelve-year-old Mary Tilford (Karen Balkin) receives a well-deserved punishment, the evil girl spitefully and irresponsibly accuses the teachers of "unnatural affection" for each other. In spreading the rumor, Mary tells her dowager grandmother, Mrs. Amelia

Tilford (Fay Bainter), one of the town's most influential citizens. The misinformed woman believes the malicious child, and at Mrs. Tilford's urging, the pupils' parents withdraw their children from the school. Soon Martha and Karen are in financial ruin and are forced to close their school.

At the same time, Karen's fiancé, Joe Cardin (James Garner), a promising doctor, begins to doubt his betrothed's word. As their tangled lives and emotions turn into a nightmare, the two women are forced to take drastic action. They bring a slander lawsuit against Mrs. Tilford; but they are unable to prove their innocence in court, and the judge finds them guilty of "a certain kind of repressive moral transgression."

The most tragic ramification of the shattering ordeal is Martha's self-doubt and tortured recognition that she subconsciously did have "those feelings" toward her friend. Feeling guilty in mind, if not in deed, Martha is severely shocked. Though the lie is ultimatedly exposed and the error acknowledged with pleas for forgiveness, it is too late; the devastated Martha commits suicide by hanging herself. In the funeral scene of the film's bitter conclusion, Karen walks silently past Joe, Mrs. Tilford, and all of the other townspeople.

A provocative study sensitively directed by William Wyler, *The Children's Hour* is well acted by its leading players, Audrey Hepburn and Shirley MacLaine, whose personalities and screen presences strongly complement each other. As Karen, Audrey Hepburn is strong and assertive beneath her deceptive softness and frailty. As she walks past the townspeople in the final scene, we know she will survive.

With depth and substance, Shirley MacLaine gains our pity and understanding. Though perhaps Martha's homosexual feelings are exaggerated as a result of the scandal, there are moments in the film where her latent lesbianism is indicated, as in her response to the news that Karen is to be married. Later, Martha says "I never loved a man," and admits that she does love Karen "in the way they said," and "that's what's the matter with me." (Actually, the word "lesbian" is never mentioned during the film; instead, such expressions as "sinful sexual knowledge" are used.)

Young Karen Balkin is fine in her performance as Mary, the child responsible for defamation of character who only dimly understands what she has done; and Veronica Cartwright is well cast as Mary's puppet Rosalie. Fay Bainter is equally good as the well-meaning, if ignorant, grandmother who sets the destruction in motion. Miriam Hopkins (who played the role of Martha in *These Three*) is appropriately despicable as Mrs. Lily Mortar, Martha's simple-minded aunt, the chief court witness who deserts the teachers by refusing to testify in their behalf.

The film, however, does have problems. Written originally as a play, the dialogue-oriented drama is often too wordy for the film medium; and occasionally, its dramatics are too heavy-handed. At times the story strains the viewer's credulity: just what is it, for example, that the twelve-year-old child whispers to her startled, indignant grandmother that causes her to rush to the telephone? Why does no one suspect that the child is lying? Why would parents pull their children out of the school so fast? Why does the court not protect the innocent women? Why does it accept as sole evidence the word of one little girl and the failure of a key witness to appear?

Although *The Children's Hour* is really about malicious gossip and false accusations more than it is about lesbianism, William Wyler did not submit the script to the Johnston Office. Because of the Production Code taboo against any discussion of sexual deviation, the office would not have given its seal of approval. Ironically, however, just after the picture was finished, the Johnston Office reversed itself on the sexual deviation clause. *The Children's Hour* was therefore one of the first films to be released under the relaxed provision of the Production Code Administration.

DODSWORTH

Released: 1936
Production: Samuel Goldwyn for United Artists
Direction: William Wyler
Screenplay: Sidney Howard; based on the novel and play of the same name by Sinclair Lewis
Cinematography: Rudolph Maté
Editing: Daniel Mandell
Art direction: Richard Day (AA)
Running time: 90 minutes

Principal characters:
Sam Dodsworth	Walter Huston
Fran Dodsworth	Ruth Chatterton
Edith Cortright	Mary Astor
Arnold Iselin	Paul Lukas
Major Clyde Lockert	David Niven
Baroness Von Obersdorf	Mme. Maria Ouspenskaya

It is fortunate for filmgoing audiences that Sam Goldwyn was a stubborn man, for without his obstinacy, *Dodsworth* might never have been made. Even though his studio turned out many entertaining products year after year, Goldwyn wanted very much to do movies of importance, and the highly successful Broadway play of Sinclair Lewis' novel was one in which he was particularly interested. Against the recommendations of his advisers, who told him that *Dodsworth* would not have any appeal because it was about middle-aged people, Goldwyn proceeded to pay $160,000 for the film rights and brought Walter Huston, who had played Dodsworth on the New York stage, to Hollywood to star in the film.

Part of the appeal of *Dodsworth* lies in its uncomplicated story. Sam Dodsworth (Walter Huston) is an automobile industry magnate who has retired. At the urging of his wife Fran (Ruth Chatterton), he takes his first trip to Europe aboard the Queen Mary because she wants him to see the world. He is not particularly enthusiastic, and goes more to please her than anything else. The trip, however, becomes a psychologically fatal voyage: after much pain, anguish, revelations of true character, and selfish upheaval, their marriage is ruined. Fran Dodsworth is caught up with the desire to experience "life" before life leaves her behind. She wants the party to go on forever, without her getting old. Because of this, her husband becomes a constantly distasteful reminder that the years are passing; so she turns to younger men, first on the ship and then in cities throughout Europe.

Sam Dodsworth is an uncultured but devoted husband who is ready to stand almost anything once, even adultery, and who cannot rid himself of the deep sense of responsibility he has accumulated in twenty years of marriage. However, he is also human, and while his wife is pursuing various younger men with exotic accents, he meets a genteel, understanding widow, Edith Cortright (Mary Astor), who is capable and willing to give him the affection and company his wife will not. Their relationship is based on living life for the day without expectations on the future, but their idyll is shattered by a phone call from Fran. Rejected by her last suitor and his baroness mother, Fran says that she is ready to go home and settle down. Sam's sense of loyalty and honor leave him no alternative but to go with her; she is his wife, representing the life he has known. As their ship prepares to leave port, however, Fran's shallow repentence for what she has done quickly evaporates and her mean self-centeredness surfaces. It takes only moments for Sam to realize that his wife and the life back home are no longer what he wants. As Edith Cortright stands watching the luxury ship pull out to sea, a small dinghy ties up at the dock with a beaming Sam aboard, returning to the new life he has chosen.

Dodsworth is an extremely well-made and well-acted film. Sam Dodsworth is a man we understand and respect, if not altogether believe for there is a basic improbability inherent in the story, and therefore, in Sam's character; how could he and Fran have been married for twenty years before he realized what a priggish, selfish, vain woman she was? Perhaps all his years spent building his automobile business kept him from really knowing his wife; or perhaps he simply cannot believe that she is the woman he married.

Dodsworth is a very personal story which gives the impression of a film of large scope, mainly because of Walter Huston's portrayal. Since he commanded the role on Broadway for two years prior to the movie, it was a role in which he was as comfortable as any actor could be, and yet the acting is entirely fresh. Huston's Dodsworth is a man of sympathy, humor, irony, and delicacy, and it is sometimes impossible to tell what in Dodsworth is Huston and what is Sinclair Lewis, since the actor fits the character perfectly.

As Fran Dodsworth, Ruth Chatterton creates one of film's most despicable women; her dialogue spews forth venomously and she is consummate in displaying the character's embittered egotism through the way she holds her body, tight and self-conscious, like someone always on display. The character of Edith Cortright is as far removed as possible from the usual "other woman," and Mary Astor plays her with remarkable grace and intelligence. Also adding to the character of the film is the casting of a young man named David Niven as Major Clive Lockert in his first role for Goldwyn, although he had had a contract with the studio for some time.

Although *Dodsworth* is essentially a static and talky film, William Wyler has directed it skillfully in cinematic terms. It easily could have been a visually confining piece, but it is not; the pace flows evenly and is dramatically balanced to sustain the impact of important scenes, then eases naturally back into the expository. The look of the film is grand, expensive, and very Continental, although most of the major shooting took place at the Goldwyn studios in Hollywood. Only a small second-unit was sent to Europe to film the exteriors which give the film such a colorful background.

Goldwyn's insistence that *Dodsworth* was important and thus had to be perfect almost kept *Dodsworth* from ultimately being filmed. Sidney Howard's dramatization of the novel was submitted; according to those involved, it was well-constructed and, in fact, expertly concealed some of the story's basic flaws. Goldwyn, however, brought in another writer, who was then embarrassed because he could find no way to improve upon Howard's adaptation. Over the next two years, Goldwyn hired and fired five more writers and accepted, then rejected, eight different drafts before he finally realized that he could not improve on Howard's version, and that adaptation at last became the official screenplay.

FUNNY GIRL

Released: 1968
Production: Ray Stark for Columbia
Direction: William Wyler
Screenplay: Isobel Lennart; based on her musical play of the same name
with music by Jule Styne and lyrics by Bob Merrill
Cinematography: Harry Stradling
Editing: Robert Swink, Maury Weintrobe, and William Sands
Costume design: Irene Sharaff
Music direction: Herbert Ross
Running time: 151 minutes

> *Principal characters:*
> Fanny Brice .... Barbra Streisand (AA)
> Nick Arnstein .... Omar Sharif
> Rose Brice .... Kay Medford
> Georgia James .... Anne Francis
> Florenz Ziegfeld .... Walter Pidgeon

When the $8.8 million film version of *Funny Girl* had its premiere on September 19, 1968, it succeeded in doing what every reporter, journalist, and columnist had predicted it would—it catapulted Barbra Streisand into superstardom. It also led to an Oscar for her performance as Best Actress of the Year, tying Katharine Hepburn for *The Lion in Winter*. This was only the second time that a tie had occurred in an acting category, the first having been the one between Wallace Beery for *The Champ* and Fredric March for *Dr. Jekyll and Mr. Hyde* in 1931.

Streisand, the ugly-duckling Jewish girl from Brooklyn, had already wooed recording and television fans, and had scored personal acting successes, with her Miss Marmelstein role in Broadway's *I Can Get It for You Wholesale*, and her stage impersonation of Fanny Brice in the Broadway hit version of *Funny Girl*. When the stage version of *Funny Girl* opened at the Winter Garden Theatre in New York City, on March 26, 1964, where it was to run for a total of 1,348 performances, Bette Davis attended the opening night performance and exclaimed afterwards, "The girl has star quality."

Indeed, Streisand's star quality is her greatest asset and her greatest liability. The motion picture version of *Funny Girl* was tailor-made for Streisand's unique personality; most viewers did not care that what remained of Fanny Brice's story was little more than a glossy Cinderella story. The other films which Streisand has made since *Funny Girl* have likewise been tailor-made for her, each capitalizing on her star quality with varying degrees of artistic success, although most have also been box-office blockbusters.

Funny Girl property rights belong to producer Ray Stark, who is married

to Fanny Brice's daughter, Frances, by Nick Arnstein. He had Isobel Lennart
fashion a script for the musical play, to which Jule Styne and Bob Merrill
added music and lyrics, respectively. While the play takes liberty with the
actual facts of Fanny Brice's life, it is an affectionate and nostalgic recalling
of America's Broadway past and a vehicle perfectly suited to the comic talents
of Barbra Streisand. Stark produced the stage version, Garson Kanin directed
it, and Carol Haney staged the musical numbers. When preparing the project
for the screen, additional changes were made to more carefully create a
showcase for Streisand's motion picture debut.

Herbert Ross, who was a former dancer and choreographer and who had
directed Streisand in *I Can Get It for You Wholesale*, was called in to stage
the musical numbers in the screen version; this staging is certainly the most
important ingredient in the film version. (Ross would later direct Streisand
in *The Owl and the Pussycat*, 1970, and *Funny Lady*, 1975, and Anne Bancroft
and Shirley Maclaine in *The Turning Point*, 1977. Curiously, veteran director
William Wyler consented to direct the film, the first time in his illustrious
career (*Wuthering Heights*, 1939, *The Little Foxes*, 1941, *Roman Holiday*,
1953, and *Ben-Hur*, 1959) that he ever tackled a musical. Although a number
of songs from the stage version were cut, Styne and Merrill created three
new songs for the film—"Roller Skate Rag," "The Swan," and "Funny
Girl"—and two longtime standards, "I'd Rather Be Blue" by Fred Fisher
and Billy Rose and "My Man" by Maurice Yvian, were added.

The script for *Funny Girl* covers the early years of Fanny Brice's career
and her marriage to and divorce from Nick Arnstein. The film opens with
Fanny (Barbra Streisand) seated in front of her dressing room mirror in the
Ziegfeld Theatre; as she looks at her reflection, her first words are, "Hello,
gorgeous!" From this point on, the audience is made aware that this is going
to be Streisand's show and nobody else's. The scene next flashes back to the
old days on Henry Street where she fails to get a job at Keeney's Oriental
Palace because she does not look like the other girls. Not one to give up,
Fanny talks her way into a roller-skating production number and wins the
applause of the audience as she hams it up with her comic skating; she also
wins the job. This is one of Streisand's best scenes, putting to use her excellent
talent for comedy and mimicry without being concerned about her "image."
Fanny further pleases the audience with her rendition of "I'd Rather Be
Blue," prompting suave gambler Nick Arnstein (Omar Sharif) to visit her
backstage where he helps her get a fifty-dollar raise.

Fanny Brice soon comes to the attention of Florenz Ziegfeld (Walter Pidgeon), who hires her to appear in a musical "bride" number. Fanny argues
with Ziegfeld that she is not pretty enough for this song, but Ziegfeld insists.
On opening night, still not convinced, Fanny plays the bride with a pillow
under her gown for obvious comic effect. It is a scene which makes excellent
use of Streisand's abilities as a comedienne, even though, in reality, Ziegfeld

would never have tolerated a star of his show getting away with such blatant insubordination. Ziegfeld would also never have had nearly nude showgirls in his Follies, as is depicted in this film.

Nick attends opening night and then accompanies Fanny to her mother's saloon for the after-theater party. Fanny goes on to become a star of the first rank, Nick continues with his gambling and con-artist games, and their paths cross in courtship which leads to love. The film's intermission finds Fanny aboard a tugboat heading to board Nick's European-bound ocean liner and singing "Don't Rain on My Parade."

Their marriage leads Fanny and Nick to a Westchester Tudor mansion, a daughter named Frances, and then bankruptcy and prison for Nick, who gets involved in a phony bond-issue deal. A scene in which Fanny leaves the jail after seeing Nick and faces a throng of loud, pushy reporters, is one of the best in the film, and perhaps Streisand's best on screen. With very little dialogue, she conveys the hurt and love she feels for Nick and the realization that the marriage cannot work out. Eighteen months after going to jail, Nick appears in Fanny's dressing room and kisses her good-bye. This leads to the film's finale in which Fanny tearfully sings "My Man."

Funny Girl is a sumptuous production. Streisand is swathed in exaggerated period costumes designed by Irene Sharaff, and the first-rate technical aspects, as well as settings and cinematography, all aim at making Streisand look good; and she does. What is missing in the film, however, is more story, more characterization, and more directing expertise by William Wyler, whose scenes are underplayed in comparison to the flamboyant musical numbers directed by Herbert Ross. Likewise, the supporting players are so eclipsed by Barbra Streisand that their roles seem insignificant. Kay Medford has a few good moments as Fanny's mother, and Mae Questel is briefly and delightfully seen as the nosy neighbor. The role of Fanny's showgirl-friend is so cut in the final print that actress Anne Francis, who played the role, demanded that her name be omitted from the credits. Even amiable Walter Pidgeon is made short shrift of as Ziegfeld. It is this catering to Streisand that prevents *Funny Girl* from being a good musical biography; instead it is simply superficial glossy entertainment.

THE HEIRESS

Released: 1949
Production: William Wyler for Paramount
Direction: William Wyler
Screenplay: Ruth Goetz and Augustus Goetz; based on their stage adaptation of the novel *Washington Square* by Henry James
Cinematography: Leo Tover
Editing: William Hornbeck
Art direction: John Meehan, Harry Horner (AA)
Set decoration: Emile Kuri (AA)
Costume design: Edith Head and Gile Steele (AA)
Music: Aaron Copland (AA)
Running time: 115 minutes

Principal characters:
Catherine Sloper .... Olivia de Havilland (AA)
Dr. Austin Sloper .... Ralph Richardson
Morris Townsend .... Montgomery Clift
Lavinia Penniman .... Miriam Hopkins

The Heiress is the story of Catherine Sloper (Olivia de Havilland), a plain young woman in her mid-twenties who lives in a grand house in Washington Square, New York City, in the 1850's. She lives with her father, the prominent Dr. Austin Sloper (Ralph Richardson), and his sister, Aunt Lavinia (Miriam Hopkins). The film is an adaptation of Henry James's novel, *Washington Square*. First produced in New York and London as a stage play under the novel's original title, it was not a critical success; consequently, it was not made into a film until several years later.

The Heiress is recognized for many things, including its performances and outstanding art direction. The story takes place mainly in one location, the Sloper home—a limited setting ideally suited for the theater; however, in a screen version it becomes a challenge to keep the audience engrossed and the film visually exciting. *The Heiress* succeeds on both counts. Directed by William Wyler, the excellence of the performances and the intricacies of the character development work to create a film which succeeds through the power of its subtlety. *The Heiress* is a period piece in the true sense; not only the costumes and sets are evocative, but every nuance of dialogue and behavior is consistent with the formality and elegance of mid-nineteenth century New York.

The simple plot revolves around Catherine's love affair with Morris Townsend (Montgomery Clift), a young man whom her father considers a fortune hunter interested only in her inheritance. Since the action is very limited, the success of the story depends upon close attention to detail and complex characterizations. It is essential to get a sense of the drives and needs of each character as they interact within the stifling social regimentation of the period. Dr. Sloper and Catherine form the most complex relationship which gradually unfolds, revealing the raw emotions which lie beneath their façade of propriety. Dr. Sloper is a model of respectability and elegance. The unresolved pain he experienced at his wife's death years ago permeates his life. Ralph Richardson's performance succeeds in creating a character who, without straying from accepted behavior, becomes racked by bitterness and hatred. It is necessary to perceive the poisonous effect of that pain in order to understand the doctor's failure as a father in his relationship with Catherine. His suppressed hatred toward the child that caused his wife's death at childbirth reveals itself little by little, and it is the appearance of Morris which finally brings that hatred to a head.

To Catherine, Morris' arrival in her life is a dream come true. He is handsome and charming and professes to love her. The doctor uses his own low opinion of Catherine in judging Morris' motives, and he is determined to keep them from marrying. In view of Dr. Sloper's attitude towards Catherine, it is easy to see how vulnerable she is and how deeply she yearns to be loved. The first third of the story prepares the audience for Catherine's exploitation. Her starvation for affection is seen in her desperate attempts to please her father; but another side of her character is revealed through her relationship with her aunt, who accepts and loves her. With Aunt Lavinia, Catherine is clever and vibrant and reveals an innate charm; yet a story she amusingly tells her aunt becomes an awkward fiasco when she attempts to retell it to her father. The damage of his influence becomes increasingly evident. When Catherine is first introduced, she still has the spark of what she might be away from her father's emotional domination; the remainder of the story traces the extinguishing of that spark.

The first time Catherine appears in the film she is buying fish, an obvious contrast to the first introduction of Dr. Sloper and his elegant home. Thinking the fish will please her father, she is instead reprimanded for not letting the servant carry the fish. This, like all of Catherine's attempts at pleasing him, is met with criticism and with negative comparisons between Catherine and her late mother. Dr. Sloper's memory of his wife as a beautiful, talented, and charming lady pits Catherine against a ghost to whom she can never live up in his eyes. Catherine has never known her mother except as an ever-present reminder of her own inadequacies. For example, when Catherine wears a red dress because she thought her mother wore one like it, her father responds mainly to its expensiveness, quietly adding that her mother, unlike Catherine, was fair and dominated the color.

Morris Townsend is more the embodiment of all Catherine's dreams than a real man, and to stress this point, he is often photographed in such a way that he is faceless. When he first approaches Catherine at a party, he is a finely dressed torso with a voice; and throughout the film, his face is hidden when the two embrace. The audience sees only Catherine's blissful face against Morris' neck and dark shoulder. Morris convinces Catherine that her awkwardness and shortcomings are charming and lovable to him. Even as his mercenary nature surfaces, Catherine's blindness to his motives is understandable. She is not stupid; she simply wants desperately to believe him. Montgomery Clift as Morris combines good looks with a perfect ability to behave appropriately. His charm is inexhaustible as he skillfully maneuvers his way into the hearts of Catherine and her aunt. Clift's is a difficult role, since he must be slightly shady at the same time that he charms the audience (as well as Catherine) into wondering whether it might not be a good idea that he marry Catherine. His words and behavior are convincing as he deftly counteracts every suspicion directed toward him; but his questionable motives become more evident when he is dealing with Dr. Sloper, with whom his compliments sound false, his promises empty. The doctor and Morris are transparent to each other; their mutual hostility results from the similarity of their feelings towards Catherine. Morris, as a mercenary suitor who desires Catherine's wealth more than her, does not seem any worse than a father who hates his daughter for not being her mother.

The Sloper house is extremely important as a living environment to which each character reacts as if playing against another real character. The house is frozen in time and serves as Dr. Sloper's shrine to his wife; the furnishings are all as she left them more than twenty years earlier, the only change being a visible expansion of the doctor's medical practice downstairs. The most conspicuous furnishing is the spinet, which is introduced as a symbol of everything Mrs. Sloper was and Catherine is not. When first seen, it is being tuned—unnecessarily, since it has not been played since it was last tuned six months earlier; it is religiously kept in perfect shape in memory of its last player, Mrs. Sloper.

To Morris, the house is a lure whose elegance and lavishness are more desirable to him than Catherine. Viewed through his eyes, it is a showplace of wealth and taste, as close-ups are utilized to show off its fine craftsmanship. Morris adapts to the house in a way that Catherine never seems to. He is at home amongst the rich furnishings and is able to sit down at the spinet and play and sing. To Catherine, on the other hand, the house represents the embodiment of her mother's memory. Like the presence of the spinet, the house constantly reinforces her inability to fill her mother's place. There is no evidence of Catherine's presence in the main rooms other than her embroidery loom which eventually becomes an overt object of her father's disdain for her. The house represents enclosure to Catherine; and it will eventually become her prison.

When Doctor Sloper takes Catherine to Europe in the hope that she will forget her marriage plans, Morris is extended the honors of the house by

Aunt Lavinia. He eases comfortably into the rich life as he helps himself to the doctor's cigars and brandy, all the time properly yearning for Catherine. Upon returning from Europe, the doctor realizes he has failed in his attempt to keep Catherine from Morris. He threatens disinheritance and unmercifully confronts her with his feelings that she is dull and unattractive, and desirable to Morris only because of her prospect of thirty thousand dollars a year. His climatic bite is that she does, however, embroider neatly.

Catherine's shock at her father's release of hostility makes her need for Morris more desperate. She meets him to plan their elopment and naïvely tells him of her threatened disinheritance; they plan to leave that night. The scene that follows is certainly one of the most torturous of the film. As Catherine waits for Morris at the front window, it becomes increasingly evident that he will not come. Her aunt, knowing the truth, wishes that Catherine had just been a little wiser and not mentioned the disinheritance. Catherine suffers the harsh realization that she has been deceived and manipulated by those who supposedly love her.

In the time that follows, the doctor falls ill. It is a hardened Catherine who refuses to go to his deathbed. De Havilland's performance excels here as she makes the transition from a naïve and hopeful young woman to a bitter and cynical heiress. When the story picks up five years later, Catherine is an icy, hard woman. Sitting in her own home now, the loom has taken a more prominent place. There is some mystery as to her psychological state at this point. Morris has returned from California after five years and with Aunt Lavinia's help comes to see Catherine. He begs understanding for deserting her, claiming it was in her best interest. His current flattery is as charming as always; he proposes again and seems truly delighted when Catherine appears to weaken and agrees. It is soon evident, however, that *she* is now toying with *him*. He leaves to gather his belongings and Catherine sits down to finish her embroidery. When her aunt realizes that Catherine has no intention of marrying Morris, she asks how she can be so cruel. Catherine's response is that she has been taught by masters. The ultimate revenge occurs as Morris arrives at the appointed moment and futilely bangs on the bolted front door. Catherine once again mounts the stairs, her eyes bright with perverse satisfaction.

The Academy recognized de Havilland's performance in *The Heiress* with the Oscar for Best Actress; the art directors, John Meehan and Harry Horner, also received Oscars for their work. Edith Head received the award for costume design, and Aaron Copland for his musical score. The blend of these talents as well as the direction and script make *The Heiress* a beautiful film which brings to life believable characters from a different time.

JEZEBEL

Released: 1938
Production: Hal B. Wallis for Warner Bros.
Direction: William Wyler
Screenplay: Clements Ripley, Abem Finkel, and John Huston, with assistance from Robert Bruckner; based on the play of the same name by Owen Davis, Sr.
Cinematography: Ernest Haller
Editing: Warren Low
Costume design: Orry-Kelly
Music: Max Steiner
Running time: 104 minutes

Principal characters:
Julie Marsden	Bette Davis (AA)
Preston Dillard	Henry Fonda
Buck Cantrell	George Brent
Dr. Livingstone	Donald Crisp
Aunt Belle Bogardus	Fay Bainter (AA)
General Bogardus	Henry O'Neill
Amy Bradford Dillard	Margaret Lindsay
Ted Dillard	Richard Cromwell

Jezebel has often been dismissed as Warner Bros.' black-and-white version of *Gone with the Wind*, and Bette Davis' Julie as a pale imitation of Vivien Leigh's Scarlett O'Hara. It is true that Warner Bros. originally bid for the Margaret Mitchell novel, intending to star their studio queen Davis. It is also true that Davis tested for the role of Scarlett when David O. Selznick won the screen rights. Having lost the competition all around, Warner Bros. proceeded with their production of *Jezebel*, a period drama set in antebellum New Orleans, its centerpiece a selfish Southern belle.

Such obvious similarities in period and character invite unfortunate comparisons. *Jezebel* cannot compete with *Gone with the Wind* as a romantic Southern epic—the Warners' production lacks the historical scope of Margaret Mitchell's novel and the Technicolor brilliance of Selznick's beautiful film. But in its portrait of prewar New Orleans, *Jezebel* offers a far more realistic appraisal of "the glorious South" so romanticized in American literature.

New Orleans in 1850 prides itself on being "the Paris of the South." It has the grand manner of Southern tradition mixed with the earthy gaiety of its French and Creole heritage. The city's reigning debutante is Julie Marsden (Bette Davis), beautiful and willful ward of General Bogardus (Henry O'Neill) and his wife Belle (Fay Bainter). Julie is engaged to marry Preston Dillard (Henry Fonda), scion of a wealthy banking family. The engagement is long-standing, owing mainly to Julie's mercurial and demanding nature. Although she can command any young man in town, she wants Preston simply because he will not be bent to her will.

This rather trite state of affairs is played out against a fascinating backdrop. The New Orleans of 1850 has been painstakingly re-created with authentic settings, using genuine antiques and perfect copies of period costume. We are treated to a little vignette depicting Southern manners in a bar scene which introduces Buck Cantrell (George Brent), a young gallant and one of Julie's many admirers. Buck and Preston's brother Ted (Richard Cromwell) are drinking in a replica of the famous Long Bar. Buck is holding forth on his usual topics of hunting and horses when another patron comments about the unconventional Julie Marsden. Forestalling Ted, Buck challenges the unfortunate man to a duel because, "No gentleman mentions a lady's name in a bar." We are given to understand that Buck is a veteran of such affairs. He is much admired by the younger Ted as the quintessential Southern gentleman: interested in horses and dogs, gallant to ladies, and eager to defend them against any real or imagined slight to a strict and exaggerated code of honor. The character of Buck has a double purpose here. He serves as an illustration of Southern chivalry while offering a contrast to Preston Dillard.

Preston is a banker. This puts him at odds with his environment because he does not play at his position or apologize for it. He is an earnest businessman, an innovative as well as diligent citizen constantly urging civic improvement upon his complacent, unheeding fellows.

Julie seems at first the ideal match for Preston. She flaunts her rebellion at conventional behavior, arriving late for her own engagement shower dressed in a riding habit, head high, crop swinging at her side. Her Aunt Belle Bogardus is scandalized; but Julie shrugs her shoulders and boldly explains to the assembled ladies that a fractious horse must be made to know its master. Bette Davis does not have to steal this picture—it was meant to showcase her as Julie Marsden. Every character and event in the film revolves around her, reacting to her behavior, acceding to her demands, competing for her attention. This was Davis' first large-scale film, and director William Wyler spared no effort in spotlighting her considerable talents. Davis won the Academy Award for Best Actress for *Jezebel* because the audience, fully aware of Julie's selfish, even vicious, nature, could not help sighing like the young girl at the engagement shower, "I think she's wonderful." Julie is vibrant, exciting, alive.

We see the friction between Julie and Preston when he keeps her waiting in a carriage while he concludes an important business conference. Furious at this slight, she determines to punish him. The highlight of the New Orleans' social season is the Olympus Ball to which all unmarried young women traditionally wear virginal white gowns. Julie obtains a shocking red dress meant for a *demi-mondaine* and, ignoring Preston's ominous objections, wears it to the ball where their engagement is to be officially announced.

In a memorable scene Julie walks into the ballroom and realizes that Preston was right; she has gone too far. The white gowned debutantes and their parents withdraw to the edges of the room, clearing the floor for an agonizing procession as Julie and Preston run the gauntlet of assembled males. Preston stares hard at each man, daring them to comment; Julie stares straight ahead, eyes huge, face frozen. She begs to be taken home; but Preston is adamant that, having ignored his wishes for the last time, she must live with the consequences. He forces her to circle the empty floor with him in a grand waltz.

The waltz for the Olympus Ball is the centerpiece of a beautiful Max Steiner score. In a stiff year of Oscar competition, Steiner lost to *Alexander's Ragtime Band*, and Ernie Haller's cinematography lost to *The Great Waltz*. But the winning combination of Steiner music, Haller cinematography, and Orry-Kelly costume design was established for future Davis pictures at Warner Bros.

The waltz completed, a humiliated and tearful Julie turns to Buck Cantrell who escorts her home. Disgusted, Preston breaks the engagement and leaves to work at the Philadelphia branch of his family's bank. Julie goes into seclusion, retreating from society, certain that Preston will come back to her in spite of Aunt Belle's belief that her ward has driven him away for good this time.

Julie lives on hope for three years. When she learns that Preston has returned, she anticipates that he will marry her and plans a party at Halcyon, her country estate. When Preston arrives Julie greets him in a luminous white gown that appears to be made of spun glass. Kneeling at his feet, she humbly apologizes to him for her behavior. In reply Preston introduces her to Amy (Margaret Lindsay), his wife. Spurned, Julie recovers her old spirit. Assuming a brittle courtesy, she acts the gracious hostess to Preston and his Yankee wife, while encouraging the assembled guests to ridicule Amy's Northern manners.

When Preston repulses Julie's sexual advances, she fabricates an insult and goads Buck into dueling. Preston is called to the city, where a yellow fever epidemic has broken out, and his younger brother, Ted, fights Buck and kills him. As he dies, Buck realizes how he has been used by Julie. The assembled company reviles her, and her aunt and uncle refuse to continue as her guardians. In a telling scene Aunt Belle tells Julie, "I am thinking of a woman who did wrong in the sight of God. Her name was Jezebel." Fay Bainter won an Academy Award as Best Supporting Actress for her portrayal of Aunt Belle. In her faultless characterization of a truly gallant lady, she serves as a perfect foil for Davis' Julie. Her quiet courtesy and grave, gentle manner point up Julie's shallow, selfish nature. When the gracious and staunchly loyal Aunt Belle turns from Julie, so must we all—she is truly a Jezebel.

Quarantined by the epidemic, the uneasy company must remain at Halcyon with Julie, knowing that she is held in contempt by all present, acting as hostess. When word is received that Preston has been struck down by fever, Julie returns to New Orleans, running the blockade by traveling through the swamps. Martial law has been declared in the city. Cannons are fired and torches burned to dispel the swamp air believed to carry fever vapors. Fever victims are heaped onto carts, the living and the dead sent off in boats to Lazerette island, an old leper colony. This is the South's answer to Preston's expressed admiration for the Yankee practice of draining swamps near cities.

Julie nurses Preston day and night. When the militia comes to cart him away she begs Amy to let her accompany him in his wife's place. Speaking the Creole dialect, she argues that she is better able to nurse him, and she swears to send him back to Amy if they survive; in a moving speech she begs Amy for the chance to redeem herself, "to make myself clean again." Julie bumps through the nightmare streets in a wagon, cradling Preston in her lap, traveling with her loved one to probable death.

Besides the astounding artistry of Davis' performance, *Jezebel* is distinguished for its "Yankee viewpoint." John Huston, Abem Finkel, and Clement Ripley fashioned a screenplay that uses the yellow fever epidemic of 1853, which left eight thousand dead, as a symbol of Southern decadence. There are no happy slaves singing on plantations in *Jezebel*; Southern chivalry is portrayed not as a tragic lost ideal but as a senseless nobility that costs a good man his life. Julie Marsden, rather than a charming, self-centered flirt, is a Jezebel who has done wrong and must journey to the hell of Lazarette island to redeem herself. It is this viewpoint that places *Jezebel* outside the category of the standard romantic Southern epic. In this film the perfume of the magnolias is sweetly rotten.

THE LITTLE FOXES

Released: 1941
Production: Samuel Goldwyn for RKO/Radio
Direction: William Wyler
Screenplay: Lillian Hellman, with additional scenes and dialogue by Dorothy Parker, Alan Campbell, and Arthur Kober; based on the play of the same name by Lillian Hellman
Cinematography: Gregg Toland
Editing: Daniel Mandell
Running time: 115 minutes

Principal characters:
Regina Giddens .... Bette Davis
Horace Giddens .... Herbert Marshall
Alexandra Giddens .... Teresa Wright
David Hewitt .... Richard Carlson
Ben Hubbard .... Charles Dingle
Oscar Hubbard .... Carl Benton Reid
Leo Hubbard .... Dan Duryea
Birdie Hubbard .... Patricia Collinge

Lillian Hellman's *The Little Foxes* concerns the Hubbard clan, a ruthless, upwardly mobile family who play out their drama against a backdrop of the South in transition. Crushed by the terrors of reconstruction, the romanticism of the old South gave way to the vitality of industrialism, bringing with it the foxes: the scrappers, the moneymakers. They have nothing but contempt for the old Southern aristocracy whose land and position they covet but whose values they ridicule. The Hubbards have married into this aristocracy because it suits their purposes, but they do not pretend to membership. They revel in their middle-class status.

The leader of the family is the eldest brother Ben. Charles Dingle repeats his stage role, full of joviality, openly proclaiming himself "a plain man, and plain spoken," while hatching devious plots to increase the wealth of the family business and maintain his position as leader. Carl Benton Reid is brilliant as Oscar, the younger brother who has married into the landed gentry at Ben's direction and still follows his lead, vainly attempting to match his ruthlessness and secure a position for his son, Leo. Dan Duryea's performance as Leo is masterful. In his high-pitched whine, he fawns on his uncle Ben's every pronouncement; currying favor on all sides he still manages to put his foot in his mouth every time he opens it. He is constantly curbed by his uncle, whose barbs are explained and softened by his nervous father.

Regina Giddens represents the female of this species. Handsome and clever, she is a match for Ben, fully as ruthless and yet more shrewd. Bette Davis plays her with a reptilian grace that both fascinates and repels. Davis' Academy Award nomination was well deserved, and only the popularity of Alfred Hitchcock's *Suspicion* secured the Best Actress award for Joan Fontaine. Regina's daughter Alexandra seems a role tailor-made for Teresa Wright. She is young and innocent, apparently having no part of the Hubbards in her. We see her with her alcoholic Aunt Birdie (Patricia Collinge), who is gay and charming when she is away from the deliberate cruelties of her husband, Oscar. In the nervous gestures and breathless conversation of her aunt, Alexandra begins to see what might become of her if she remains under the sway of her mother.

The family gathers to entertain Mr. Marshall, a prominent Chicago businessman who plans to build a local cotton gin in partnership with the Hubbards. In an after-dinner scene we observe the Hubbard character. As Birdie and Alexandra play a piano duet Oscar watches his possession perform, Leo surreptitiously catches flies, and Ben tries to interrupt the recital, relentlessly pursuing Marshall with business conversation as the visitor tries to follow the music. Regina silences Ben, stares Leo into dutiful attention, and the recital concludes. She then turns her sexual charms on a receptive Marshall. Marshall asks her to Chicago in an invitation that has obvious sexual overtones. As he leaves, Regina exults to Birdie, "There'll be millions, Birdie, millions." Middle-class riches are not enough for Regina; she craves great wealth and Chicago society.

But Ben puts a damper on her excitement by reminding her that while he and Oscar have put up their third of the money for partnership, Regina's absent banker husband has not made a final commitment. If she does not come up with the cash, she will be cut out of the profits. The Hubbards cannot allow family sentiment to interfere with business.

Regina's husband, Horace (Herbert Marshall), is a heart patient in Johns Hopkins Hospital. Regina determines to send her daughter to fetch him home whether he is well or not, and Alexandra leaves for Baltimore. In the scene at the train station we see that *The Little Foxes* is more successful than most plays in moving offstage. While still relying principally on the playwright's fabrication of character and dialogue, the film manages to re-create the flavor of New Orleans at the turn of the century.

Horace returns home, an ill man, only to be badgered by his wife. In their exchanges we see that he cannot win. Not only his illness but also his character prevent him from besting Regina. He has the wistful despair of the weak aristocrat. He knows what he hates, but lacks the strength of will necessary to fight it. Even his love for his daughter has no vitality; it is genuine but so tinged with his tragic sense of life that it is she who protects and cares for him.

Hellman and her screenplay collaborators, Dorothy Parker and Alan Campbell, made an invaluable addition to the film when they added a character not in the play, David Hewitt (Richard Carlson), a crusading reporter who loves Alexandra. His character provides welcome and necessary relief from the unrelenting despair of Birdie and Horace while competing with the Hubbards in vitality and zest for life. However, in contrast to the Hubbards, David Hewitt's attitude is joyful and energetic, his nature generous. Without Hewitt, Alexandra's character is faced with a choice between the futility of Horace and Birdie and the grasping nature of the Hubbards.

It is in conversation rather than in action that the natures of these characters are revealed. Possibly no American writer can equal Hellman's gift for dialogue. Her speeches are not epigrammatic yet the dialogue of her characters dances along in brilliant counterpoint while remaining grittily realistic. She has a clarity and coherence unsurpassed in American theater.

Horace refuses to invest in the ginning mill. He knows that, like all the Hubbard enterprises, it will become a sweatshop exploiting black labor. The investment deadline approaches and Ben, not wanting any interest in the venture to fall outside the family, convinces Leo, an employee at Horace's bank, to steal negotiable bonds from Horace's strongbox to insure financing for the mill. Regina discovers the theft and plans to blackmail Ben and Oscar into giving her a share of the business. But Horace thwarts her plan by telling Regina that he gave the securities to Leo in order to prevent her from sharing in the mill profits. In a controlled fury Regina turns on him, "I don't hate you. I have only contempt for you. I've always had." She taunts him into a heart attack, and when his shaking hands drop his heart medicine, she watches in silence as he begs her to get the bottle. Horrified at her expression, he tries to rise from his wheelchair and reaches the stairs, gasping. Fascinated, lips compressed in furious concentration, Regina wills him to die. When he collapses she waits a moment and then springs into action calling for help.

Horace on his deathbed uses his last breath to comfort his daughter and urge her to leave with David Hewitt, while downstairs Regina confronts her brothers with Leo's theft and demands seventy-five percent of the mill. They bitterly agree, but Ben suggests that Regina might well be charged with murder. She smiles and defies him to prove it. Alexandra overhears this exchange and in spirited defiance damns them all and vows to leave. She tells her mother,

> Addie said there were people who ate the earth and other people who stood around and watched them do it. And just now Uncle Ben said the same thing. . . . Well, tell him from me, Mama, I'm not going to stand around and watch you do it. I'll be fighting as hard as he'll be fighting, someplace else.

Alexandra leaves, crossing the square in the rain to meet David, while Regina watches from an upstairs window, coldly composed, expressionless, satisfied to remain in the web of her own device.

Although *The Little Foxes* received eight Academy Award nominations, it failed to win in any category. However, Teresa Wright did win the Oscar for Best Supporting Actress for her performance that year in *Mrs. Miniver*. Admittedly, it was a very stiff year in Oscar competition. *Sergeant York*, *How Green Was My Valley*, *Citizen Kane*, *The Maltese Falcon*, and *Suspicion* were only a few of the films in contention. However, more importantly, *The Little Foxes* presented a view of the middle class that was popular with only a minority of the artistic establishment. If Ben, Oscar, and Regina had been peculiar only to their story, the film might have been more successful. But Ben proclaims, "There are hundreds of Hubbards sitting in rooms like this, throughout the country. All their names aren't Hubbard, but they are all Hubbards and they will own this country someday." It is this ugly, unrelieved view of the much maligned merchant class that makes *The Little Foxes* so coldly admired.

MRS. MINIVER

Released: 1942
Production: Sidney Franklin for Metro-Goldwyn-Mayer (AA)
Direction: William Wyler (AA)
Screenplay: Arthur Wimperis, George Froeschel, James Hilton, and Claudine West (AA); based on the novel of the same name by Jan Struther
Cinematography: Joseph Ruttenberg (AA)
Editing: Harold F. Kress
Running time: 135 minutes

Principal characters:
Kay Miniver	Greer Garson (AA)
Clem Miniver	Walter Pidgeon
Carol Beldon	Teresa Wright (AA)
Lady Beldon	Dame May Whitty
Mr. Ballard	Henry Travers
Foley	Reginald Owen
German Agent's Voice	Miles Mander
Vicar	Henry Wilcoxon

The sentimental stories of the Miniver family had first appeared in serial form in *The London Times*, and were later published in book form in the United States, where they had considerable popular and commercial success. At a time when America was still neutral and when the film industry's pro-British bias was under investigation by a congressional committee, producer Sidney Franklin had the courage to persuade M-G-M to purchase the screen rights to *Mrs. Miniver* and to assign the scripting to the staunchly pro-British writing team of Arthur Wimperis, George Froeschel, James Hilton, and Claudine West, who, individually and collectively, were responsible for a number of films depicting Hollywood's view of British heroism and stoicism, including *Goodbye, Mr. Chips* (1939), *Random Harvest* (1942), *That Forsyte Woman* (1949), *The White Cliffs of Dover* (1944), *Forever and a Day* (1943), and *Waterloo Bridge* (1940). *Mrs. Miniver* was written as a starring vehicle for Greer Garson as a follow-up to her success in *Goodbye, Mr. Chips* and to continue her teaming with Walter Pidgeon, which had begun with *Blossoms in the Dust* (1941). Although *Mrs. Miniver* went into production prior to Pearl Harbor, the United States was firmly involved in the world conflict by the time of its release, and the film's success was assured.

Despite its tremendous success both in the United States and in England, *Mrs. Miniver* presents an idealized view of English life. Its central characters represent upper-middle-class English people, who suffered little hardship and privation during World War II as compared to other classes of society living in British cities. German bombers nightly made devastating raids on cities such as London, Hull, Coventry, Bristol, and Birmingham, causing tremendous damage and loss of life. These industrial cities were their targets; the Germans would never have wasted bombs on a small village such as that inhabited by the Miniver clan. The suggestion that the Minivers spend their nights in a cramped Anderson air-raid shelter, or the fact that the village church, which in *Mrs. Miniver* looks more like a cathedral, is deliberately destroyed by bombs, is simply unrealistic. It is obvious almost forty years later that the Hollywood producers and scriptwriters realized that to win sympathy for their cause they would have to depict a war which hurt the upper-class family and destroyed beautiful buildings, rather than a war which ravaged working-class slums and destroyed homes which should have been condemned as unsanitary years before.

The film opens with Kay Miniver (Greer Garson) guiltily buying a foolish little hat while on a shopping spree in London, while her husband Clem (Walter Pidgeon) is equally guilty, buying a new car. Both realize that their expenditures are a little extravagant, but both eventually agree that they are two lucky people to have so much. On the way home, the kindly old station master tells Mrs. Miniver that he has grown a particularly beautiful rose, and he asks if he may name it the "Mrs. Miniver Rose" in her honor.

The Minivers live in a house with the lyrical name of Starlings, and here the family—husband and wife, son and daughter—gather to welcome the eldest son, returning home from Oxford. In an England at peace, the biggest commotion concerns the village's annual flower show, where the "Mrs. Miniver Rose" has been entered in competition against a rose entered by Lady Beldon (Dame May Whitty), the lady of the manor. Lady Beldon's family has, apparently, been growing flowers since the days of William the Conqueror, and no one has dared to question their supremacy until now. To add to the controversy, Lady Beldon's granddaughter Carol (Teresa Wright) is in love with the Miniver's eldest son, and she worries that Lady Beldon will disapprove of the match because of the success of the "Mrs. Miniver Rose." A considerable amount of time is spent on the flower show and its implications, for, as one critic at the time pointed out, it is as if the film's producers are saying, "If battles aren't for gardens and roses and neighbors, old and young, gathering at a country fair, what are they for?"

Next morning, the Minivers attend church, and the vicar (Henry Wilcoxon), the local representative of the Church of England, which, in turn, represents England's strength and heritage, announces that the country is at war.

The war changes life, but at the same time life remains unchanged. The eldest son joins the R.A.F., but is stationed at a local airfield. Mrs. Miniver is still a pillar of society, a representative of English motherhood at its best. She seems to embody the idea that the English are indomitable be it in capturing a German airman who tries to hide in her house or in comforting her children as they take cover in the air-raid shelter. Then, she and Lady

Beldon's granddaughter are caught in an air raid while driving home from the first flower show of the war—the flower show at which Lady Beldon has recognized the superiority of the "Mrs. Miniver Rose," just as she has allowed her granddaughter to marry the Minivers' eldest son; the car is hit by machine-gun fire and her daughter-in-law is killed.

Mr. Miniver also proves his determination in the face of enemy action, as he and the other men of the village fetch their boats and sail to Dunkirk to rescue the stranded British soldiers. Whatever they do in *Mrs. Miniver*, this average, ordinary English family seems rather extraordinary.

At first it appears as if the film will end on a tragic note. Mrs. Miniver's daughter-in-law is dead, the village is in ruins and the church roof shattered. But the vicar, like Mrs. Miniver a symbol of enduring strength, courage, and faith, gathers his congregation together. In a speech intended as much for the American moviegoer as for the villagers, the vicar says, "This is the people's war! It is our war! We are the fighters! Fight it, then! Fight it with all that is in us! And may God defend the right." As the Miniver clan stands, a formation of R.A.F. planes is seen in the sky through the bombed roof of the church, and the choir breaks into "Onward Christian Soldiers." The ending is either inspiring or pure kitsch, depending on one's viewpoint.

As an interesting aside, director William Wyler and actor Henry Wilcoxon apparently found the vicar's speech as written too palid and rewrote much of it. President Roosevelt was so impressed that he had the speech printed on leaflets to be dropped over German-occupied Europe.

Mrs. Miniver is what is best described as a polished production, impeccably made and impeccably acted, but lacking any warmth or genuine emotion. The camerawork, for example, is good, but so uninspired that it is amazing that Joseph Ruttenberg should have received an Academy Award for Best Cinematography for his work on the film.

However, *Mrs. Miniver* was highly honored on its initial release. It received six Academy Awards, including Best Picture, Best Actress, and Best Direction. It broke box-office records during its ten-week run at New York's Radio City Music Hall. Radio City Music Hall was also the site for the New York premiere of a 1950 sequel, *The Miniver Story*, filmed in England, which reunited Greer Garson, Walter Pidgeon, Reginald Owen, and Henry Wilcoxon from the original cast in the adventures of Mrs. Miniver following VE Day. That film ended with the death of Mrs. Miniver.

THESE THREE

Released: 1936
Production: Samuel Goldwyn for United Artists
Direction: William Wyler
Screenplay: Lillian Hellman; based on her play *The Children's Hour*
Cinematography: Gregg Toland
Editing: Daniel Mandell
Running time: 93 minutes

Principal characters:
Martha Dobie .... Miriam Hopkins
Karen Wright .... Merle Oberon
Dr. Joseph Cardin .... Joel McCrea
Mrs. Mortar .... Catherine Doucet
Mrs. Tilford .... Alma Kruger
Mary Tilford .... Bonita Granville
Rosalie .... Marcia Mae Jones
Evelyn .... Carmencita Johnson

These Three is a powerful, deeply moving, and sensitively acted and directed film. Indeed, its mounting tension and culminating tragedy at times
make it almost too painful to watch as it explores the effects of malicious
gossip on the lives of three people. Although the film has a nominally happy
and romantic ending, Lillian Hellman's well-written screenplay leaves no
doubt in the viewer's mind that the lives of "these three" have been irrevocably
changed. Nothing will be quite the same for any of them again.

Martha Dobie (Miriam Hopkins) and Karen Wright (Merle Oberon), two
intelligent and ambitious college graduates, discover that their graduation
day is not a happy one because they have no family and friends, no jobs, and
little money. On an impulse, Karen suggests to Martha that they open a
private girls' school in the old farmhouse she has inherited from her grandmother. Upon their arrival at the farm, they find that the house is completely
dilapidated, with holes in the roof, windows boarded up, and the grounds
overgrown and neglected. Discouraged, they are preparing to leave when
they meet Dr. Joe Cardin (Joel McCrea), who likes to spend his free time
from the hospital puttering about the place. He encourages them to stay and
repair the old house and offers to help them fix it.

Although the two women first think the task is impossible, they gradually
grow accustomed to and finally enthusiastic about the idea. While they are
still repairing the house, Karen meets wealthy and influential Mrs. Tilford
(Alma Kruger) and her granddaughter Mary (Bonita Granville). Mrs. Tilford
offers Karen help in starting the school. By sending her granddaughter Mary
to it and also urging her friends to send their children, Mrs. Tilford ensures

the initial success of the school. In the midst of the preparations for opening the school, Martha's aunt, Lily Mortar (Catherine Doucet), arrives. An egotistical, insensitive woman, she expects to be given a job at the school teaching elocution because she was once a stage actress. Martha is dismayed but unwilling to turn her away.

While working closely with Martha and Karen in repairing the old house, Joe has fallen in love with Karen and she with him. Both are oblivious of the fact that Martha is also in love with Joe. In fact, no one suspects except Lily Mortar, who uses her knowledge to torment Martha.

For a short time all goes well. The school is successful, and Karen and Martha are tired but happy. As the children study and play, there is no suggestion of the trouble to come, although all the causes of the catastrophe have been established: the dishonesty and selfishness of Mary Tilford, the meanness and meddlesomeness of Aunt Lily, and the unrequited love of Martha for Joe.

One winter evening Joe comes to see Karen, but since she is in town buying supplies, Martha invites him to come up to her room to help her paint a table while he waits. Exhausted after his busy day at the hospital, Joe throws himself down on a couch and goes to sleep; but Martha, not realizing this, begins talking about her unhappy childhood with Aunt Lily and why she became a teacher. Being young was so hard for her that she wants to make it easier for other children, she says. When she sees Joe is asleep, she puts out the light, sits down in an easy chair and gazes sadly and longingly at him. In this crucial scene we realize how deeply Martha feels about Joe. Joe awakens suddenly, knocking over a glass of milk and making enough noise to bring Aunt Lily to the scene. After Joe leaves, Lily makes her usual sarcastic comments designed to hurt Martha, who turns away, sobbing. Unknown to them, however, there is another interested observer of the scene. Young Mary Tilford, Amelia Tilford's granddaughter, is watching and listening from the corner of the stairway.

Mary, a pathological liar and a bad influence on weaker, more malleable girls, is a problem for Karen and Martha, particularly since her grandmother has so much influence in the community. Their problems with her come to a head when Karen confronts Mary with one of her lies. Mary then pretends to have a heart attack and fakes a fainting fit, forcing Karen to call Joe to examine her. When Joe tells Karen there is nothing the matter with the girl, Mary becomes hysterical. Afraid of Mary's bad influence on her roommates, Karen orders them to move out of Mary's room, further infuriating Mary, who decides to return home to her grandmother.

Before leaving, however, she forces her roommates, Rosalie (Marcia Mae Jones) and Evelyn (Carmencita Johnson), to tell her what they heard while eavesdropping at the door when Martha was quarreling with Aunt Lily. Karen had asked Martha to get rid of Lily, fearing her bad influence on the students, but when Martha offered to pay for her trip to England, Lily angrily accused Martha of wanting to get rid of her because she knew that Martha was in love with Joe and did not want him to marry Karen. She also reminds Martha that she once saw Joe leave her room late at night. Lily's angry accusations are overheard by the two girls, who repeat them to Mary.

Mary does not want to return to the school, so when her grandmother insists that she go back, Mary tells her what Lily has said to Martha. Realizing that her grandmother may not believe her, Mary has brought Rosalie home with her to support her story. Having accidentally discovered that Rosalie had stolen another girl's bracelet, Mary is able to force Rosalie to do what she tells her by threatening her with exposure and jail. Mrs. Tilford is at first incredulous at Mary's story, but when Rosalie supports it, she promises Mary she will not have to return to the school. Mrs. Tilford then calls all her friends to tell them the story, and all the pupils are taken out of the school.

Karen and Martha watch the exodus uncomprehendingly, still unaware of what has caused the disaster until a gossipy chauffeur enlightens them. Together with Joe, they decide to confront Mrs. Tilford since both their self-respect and their livelihood are at stake. They persuade Mrs. Tilford to let them see Mary and almost succeed in breaking down her story. At the crucial moment, however, a terrified Rosalie backs up Mary's story, and the three leave, having no further recourse but a libel suit.

They lose the suit and afterwards are mocked and laughed at by the hostile spectators. Their reputations ruined and their lives shattered, Karen and Martha return to the deserted school. Joe has been asked to leave his post at the hospital because of the unsavory publicity and decides to go to Vienna for further study. He asks Karen to marry him and go with him, but the lie has also poisoned their relationship. Despite his protestations that there has never been anything between him and Martha, she no longer believes in him and sends him away alone.

Martha is distraught when she learns what has happened and confesses to Karen that, although she has loved Joe from the first, he has never been interested in her and the rumors are completely untrue. When she is unable to convince Karen, Martha decides to leave with Aunt Lily, who has returned from England, after waiting until the trial ended so she would not have to testify.

On the train, Lily casually mentions the story of the bracelet to Martha, who realizes its significance. Martha gets off the train and goes back to the town where she confronts Rosalie and persuades her to go to Mrs. Tilford and confess. When she hears the confession, Mrs. Tilford offers to make a public apology and to assist Karen and Martha financially, but Martha replies that it is too late to mend the damage to their lives. She tells Mrs. Tilford that her punishment will be the greatest, for she must live with Mary for the rest of her life, not knowing when to believe the girl. Martha merely asks

Mrs. Tilford to carry the message to Karen that she return to Joe, and then leaves. In the final scene Karen and Joe are reunited in Vienna for a nominally happy ending.

The central character in *These Three* is Martha, and an important element of the film, which becomes part of the tragedy, is Martha's concealed and unrequited love for Joe Cardin. Her love is revealed by small but telling details. Early in the film she begins to tell him about an old newspaper story she has discovered while stripping off layers of old wallpaper at the farmhouse, but he leaves her abruptly when Karen calls to him. Martha's face registers her pain and disappointment. In a later scene, she reveals the depth of her feelings as she gazes at him longingly and hopelessly while he is sleeping on a couch in her room. Martha's innate dignity and compassion are seen throughout the film. She does not even turn away Lily although we see from the first that Lily is a selfish, malicious woman who will cause mischief. When the three confront Amelia Tilford, it is Martha who tells her that they are human beings, not paper dolls to be played with.

Besides Martha, the other key character is Mary Tilford, the malevolent child whose lies create such havoc. Not only does she willfully wreck the lives of Karen, Martha, and Joe, but also the lives of her grandmother and Rosalie. At first we see that she is selfish and spoiled; later we realize that she is also evil, vicious, and a compulsive liar. The film does not, however, dwell on the reasons for her behavior but rather on the effect of her lies. The ultimate impact is chilling as we see the destructiveness of Mary's original lie to her grandmother spread in ever widening circles, in the manner of ripples after a stone is dropped in a pool of water, until it overwhelms all it touches. Especially tragic is the lack of defense the others have against Mary's machinations.

The film is based on Lillian Hellman's 1934 hit Broadway play, *The Children's Hour*, in which the two teachers are accused of lesbianism. Producer Samuel Goldwyn knew that the lesbian theme was too daring to be filmed in the 1930's, but he wanted the necessary adaptation to be as good and as faithful to the spirit of the original as possible, so he asked Hellman to adapt her own play. Since she saw the play as being not about lesbianism but about the evil that lies and malicious gossip can cause, she was able to adapt the script so that it retained all its original intensity and was still acceptable to the censors.

Although many critics thought the changes would lessen the dramatic impact of the play, *These Three* was greeted upon release by almost universal critical acclaim and was found to retain its poignancy and power. Further evidence of the intelligence of the adaptation came in 1962 when the play was filmed with the original lesbian theme under its original title. The result was not as powerful as *These Three*, and Hellman herself reportedly prefers the original film version.

Hellman's idea for the play came from an actual trial which took place in Scotland in 1810. Two teachers at a Scottish boarding school were accused of lesbianism by the false testimony of a sixteen-year-old girl whose grandmother believed her and persuaded the parents of the other students to withdraw them from the school. The teachers brought a libel suit which dragged on for ten years and destroyed them both economically and socially. The character of Mary was drawn from Hellman's own childhood experiences. Mary's fainting fit, fake heart attack, and her bullying of other girls were all based on "the world of the half-remembered, the half-observed, the half-understood which you need so much as you begin to write," Hellman has commented.

Under the sensitive direction of William Wyler, the actors all deliver fine performances, particularly Miriam Hopkins as Martha, the most varied role. Hopkins ranges from tense, angry confrontations to relaxed, intimate conversations, and her performance provides beautiful nuances and is expressive throughout. Merle Oberon is also memorable as Karen, particularly in the final scenes, in which her suspicions finally surface. Joel McCrae is appropriately strong and supportive as Joe, and Bonita Granville is credible and generally effective as the vicious, selfish Mary.

These Three is a powerful, intense film whose theme retains all its dramatic impact. The sensitive, carefully constructed script, well-written dialogue, sharply etched characters, and moving performances of the actors, all artfully controlled and balanced by director William Wyler, combine to create an intelligent, complex, and often brilliant film.

THE WESTERNER

Released: 1940
Production: Samuel Goldwyn for United Artists
Direction: William Wyler
Screenplay: Jo Swerling and Niven Busch; based on a story by Stuart N. Lake
Cinematography: Gregg Toland
Editing: Daniel Mandell
Art direction: James Basevi
Music: Dmitri Tiomkin and Alfred Newman (uncredited)
Running time: 100 minutes

> *Principal characters:*
> Cole Hardin .... Gary Cooper
> Judge Roy Bean .... Walter Brennan (AA)
> Jane-Ellen Mathews .... Doris Davenport
> Caliphet Mathews .... Fred Stone
> Southeast .... Chill Wills
> Wade Harper .... Forrest Tucker
> Chickenfoot .... Paul Hurst
> Teresita .... Lupita Tovar
> Lily Langtry .... Lillian Bond
> Hod Johnson .... Dana Andrews

The Western had flourished in silent films with such stars as William S. Hart, Tom Mix, and the young Gary Cooper, and with epic productions such as James Cruze's *The Covered Wagon* (1923) and John Ford's *The Iron Horse* (1924), and it continued to do well through the earliest years of sound films. For some unaccountable reason, however, it fell into a decline between 1931 and 1939, during which time the genre lapsed into B-class productions or serials. During that interval, only four major studio productions were Westerns: King Vidor's *The Texas Rangers* (1936), Cecil B. De Mille's *The Plainsman* (1937), Frank Lloyd's *Wells Fargo* (1937), and James Hogan's *The Texans* (1938). But in 1939, the genre underwent a spectacular revival with such big-budget films as *Jesse James*, *Stagecoach*, *Dodge City*, *Union Pacific*, and *Destry Rides Again*. In that year, John Wayne finally became a star, and Henry Fonda, Errol Flynn, James Stewart, and Tyrone Power each made his first Western. The Western continued to flourish until World War II, when war dramas preempted almost all other action films.

After the blockbuster success of 1939's Westerns, most studios and stars were eager to get into the act, and in 1940, Samuel Goldwyn made *The Westerner*, his sole talking Western and only his second film in the genre. Goldwyn's only previous Western, *The Winning of Barbara Worth* (1926), was Gary Cooper's first featured film. Although Cooper made an impressive debut, Goldwyn let him go, observing that his studio did not make Westerns and Cooper seemed typed as a Western star. Cooper then moved to Paramount, and Goldwyn did not get him back until 1935.

Actually, although Cooper is the quintessence of the Western star, he did not play primarily in Westerns. From 1926 to 1931, eight of his films were Westerns, but during the next nineteen years, he made only four Westerns (in addition to playing a cowboy in *The Cowboy and the Lady*, 1939, which is not a Western) and played a great diversity of roles.

Nevertheless, the Western and Cooper put an indelible stamp on each other. Lean, laconic, soft-spoken, steely-eyed, wryly humorous, quick on the draw, and a superb horseman, Cooper epitomizes the image of the Westerner. He starred in *The Virginian* (1929), the prototypal Western novel and the first talking Western made, and entered legend with his portrayal of Wild Bill Hickok in *The Plainsman*. He was therefore the only possible star for a film called *The Westerner*. No other actor, not even John Wayne (who at that time had just emerged from a decade of B pictures), could qualify for that title.

Though Cooper is the star, *The Westerner* is primarily the story of Judge Roy Bean (Walter Brennan), a scruffy Confederate veteran who is self-appointed judge and boss of the scratchy, sun-baked hamlet of Vinegaroon, Texas. Bean runs the saloon, which doubles as a kangaroo court where he dispenses vigilante-type justice as the only law "west of the Pecos." (The actual town, on the Mexican border, is only about ten miles west of the Pecos River.) A hanging judge, Bean is less interested in evidence, legality, and justice, than in the cash in his victims' possession or the value of their horses and outfits. To be accused is to be convicted, and Bean confiscates the victim's money and possessions for "court costs." Into his lair comes Cole Hardin (Gary Cooper), a rootless drifter captured by Bean's men and unjustly accused of stealing a horse. This is a hanging offense, and the undertaker gallops up with his hearse, ready like a vulture for its prey. During the jury's deliberations, Jane-Ellen Mathews (Doris Davenport), daughter of a homesteading farmer, comes to town to denounce the judge for having his cattlemen harass the homesteaders in the area. She condemns Bean's travesties of justice and sympathizes with Hardin's plight, but believes he is as good as dead.

Meanwhile, Hardin discovers Bean's one soft spot, an idolatry of Lily Langtry (Lillian Bond), the British actress known as the "Jersey Lily" and the reigning beauty of the day. In her honor, Bean has renamed the town "Langtry." Hardin persuades Bean that he knows Lily personally and that he has a lock of her hair, which he will give to Bean, but that he unfortunately does not carry the lock with him. Accordingly, although the "jury" has convicted him, Bean postpones the execution. Sizing up each other, the two men develop a grudging admiration for each other, and Bean celebrates their temporary alliance with a bottle apiece of a local rot-gut whiskey called "Rub of the Brush." The next morning, they are horribly hungover, but Hardin manages to get up first and ride off. Fearful of being betrayed and losing

Lily's lock, Bean gallops after him, leaps onto Hardin's horse, and knocks him sprawling into the sand. Fortunately, Hardin has taken the precaution to steal Bean's revolver, and he persuades him that he has merely gone to get the lock of hair, though his real plan is to move on to California.

Hardin's first stop is at the Mathews farm, where Jane-Ellen is startled to see him alive. Her father induces her to persuade Hardin to join the farmers in their fight against Bean's cattlemen. She is embarrassed to have to flirt with him, but they are genuinely attracted to each other. Wade Harper (Forrest Tucker), her frustrated suitor, denounces Hardin as a spy for Bean and forces him into a fist fight, which Hardin wins. He agrees to help the farmers and rides back to town to reason with Bean. Baited once more by the lock of hair, Bean promises to have the cattle rounded up and removed from the homesteaders' farms. Pretending he wants it for himself, Hardin snips off a lock of Jane-Ellen's hair and gives it to the Judge. Bean, however, breaks his promise and has his men burn the farmers' homes and fields. While trying to put out the fire, Jane-Ellen's father is killed, and the men turn against Hardin for allegedly deceiving them with false promises of peace.

Realizing that Bean must be stopped, Hardin has himself deputized, gets a warrant for the Judge, and goes to arrest him. He discovers that Bean has gone to Fort Davis to see Lily Langtry, who is there on tour. Wanting Lily all to himself, Bean has bought out the entire house. He is dressed in his Confederate uniform, takes the best seat, and waits eagerly for the show to begin. After the overture, the curtain rises to reveal Hardin on stage with his guns drawn. "I'm coming for you, Judge," he says. "Come a-shootin'," says Bean. As the orchestra dives for cover, the two men shoot it out in the empty theater. Bean is mortally wounded, but before he dies, Hardin takes him backstage to meet Lily Langtry. Bean kisses her hand, falls to the floor, and dies happy, his last vision being of the Jersey Lily.

Except for the conflict between the homesteaders and the cattlemen, *The Westerner* avoids most clichés of the genre. Most previous Westerns were shoot-'em-up action films designed for the adolescent mentality. Goldwyn and director William Wyler were determined to make a sophisticated, adult, psychological Western for a change. *The Westerner*, therefore, stresses characterization rather than action; the fist fight, the burning fields, and the final shoot-out provide some excitement, but audiences looking for another slam-bang adventure were disappointed. Director William Wyler had done his share of two-reel silent Westerns during his apprentice days, but *The Westerner* was his first major work in the genre (his only other Western was *The Big Country* in 1958). He directed at a deliberate pace, maintaining tension in the relationship between Hardin and Bean. René Jordan says Cooper was discouraged by his initial look at the screenplay, in which he would merely have been providing star assistance to Walter Brennan, who indisputably had the central role as the fabled Judge Roy Bean.

Brennan congratulated himself on having the juicier part, for which he won his third Academy Award as Best Supporting Actor. It is a mistake, however, to dismiss Cooper. Not only is his role the longer of the two, but also in *The Westerner*, he gave one of his most subtle performances. What makes the film work is the chemistry between Cooper and Brennan. Cooper underplays with a wry sense of humor that provides a necessary foil to the more flamboyant Judge. Without his contrasting role, the story becomes merely the history of a colorful but insignificant eccentric. When John Huston made *The Life and Times of Judge Roy Bean* in 1972 with Paul Newman in the title role, the project misfired, largely because Bean was magnified into a mythological figure. There was no normal protagonist for balance, and there was no central plot to hold his career together; instead, the narrative consisted of a series of vignettes spanning a generation. Newman's Bean became a symbol of authentic justice and of a West when there were giants in the earth. By contrast, William Wyler opted for an unglamorous realism. Brennan's Bean is a whiskey-voiced, stubble-bearded, vinegary old goat who spends most of the time in a flannel undershirt and baggy pants held up by suspenders. What passes for justice in his saloon-court is of the vigilante variety. He is more than a little mad, and there is a manic gleam in his eye. His redeeming traits are a crackerbarrel sense of humor, a feistiness, and his devotion to Lily Langtry. The latter has all the quality of courtly love; like a knight-errant with his lady's scarf on his helmet who challenges all comers to concede that she is the fairest in the world, Bean adores the "Jersey Lily" with a platonic purity and hangs anyone who dares suggest the slightest disrespect towards her. The incongruity of knightly veneration from such a scruffy source is part of the humor which makes up a good deal of the film.

Cooper likewise contributes a more quietly humorous characterization; the scene in which he snips a lock of hair from the farmer's daughter and the later one in which he reluctantly parts with it to the eager Judge are masterpieces of comic underplaying. If Brennan's Judge Roy Bean is a legendary figure, so too Cooper's Cole Hardin is an archetypal Western hero—like Shane, he has no past, comes from nowhere, owns only his horse and outfit, and becomes involved only reluctantly with the settlers who are trying to put down roots. Cooper plays Hardin with consummate assurance; a decade later, when Clifton Webb was to do a Cooper imitation in *Dreamboat* (1952), he asked Cooper what film to study, and Cooper advised *The Westerner*.

Cooper and Brennan made such an effective team that they did six films together; the others are *The Cowboy and the Lady* (1938), *Meet John Doe* (1940), *Sergeant York* (1941), *Pride of the Yankees* (1942), and *Task Force* (1949), but they were at their best together in *The Westerner*, where Cooper's quiet reserve and perceptive understanding of human nature balanced Brennan's garrulous and basically childish Judge. It is the combination of appealing and appalling traits in Bean and the friendship/antagonist relationship between him and Hardin that gives the film its tension and provides a richly ambiguous texture. The Old West itself was simultaneously colorful, adventurous, dangerous, dingy, and dull; and *The Westerner* captures this paradox as few films have done.

William Wyler's direction constructs an authentic blend of legend and unglamorous realism. The secondary players lend admirable support. Stage actor Fred Stone and newcomers Forrest Tucker and Dana Andrews are in their movie debuts; and as Jane-Ellen, Doris Davenport (in her only film role) is appealing, with a mixture of wistful shyness and spunky indignation. In too many Western films the heroines were spoiled by wearing thick lipstick, elegant gowns, and fancy coiffures; for instance, Calamity Jane in *The Plainsman* never has her lipstick smeared, even when being tortured by the Cheyenne Indians. Doris Davenport, however, is refreshingly free from makeup and is dressed like a working farm girl. None of the men wears a fancy costume; they are all dressed in working clothes that show hard wear. The details throughout were so authentic that James Basevi's art direction was nominated for an Academy Award. Stuart N. Lake was also nominated for his original story. Gregg Toland contributed strikingly artistic cinematography, but Wyler was dissatisfied with Dmitri Tiomkin's score and had Alfred Newman rewrite it, though Tiomkin received sole credit. Perhaps because of its minimal action and offbeat humor, *The Westerner* was less successful than the big-budget Westerns of 1939, but it holds up better and is one of the most durable classics in the genre.

WUTHERING HEIGHTS

Released: 1939
Production: Samuel Goldwyn for United Artists
Direction: William Wyler
Screenplay: Ben Hecht and Charles MacArthur; based on the novel of the same name by Emily Brontë
Cinematography: Gregg Toland (AA)
Editing: Daniel Mandell
Interior decoration: James Basevi
Running time: 102 minutes

> *Principal characters:*
> Cathy .... Merle Oberon
> Heathcliff ....Laurence Olivier
> Ellen Dean .... Flora Robson
> Edgar Linton ....David Niven
> Isabella .... Geraldine Fitzgerald
> Earnshaw .... Cecil Kellaway
> Hindley .... Hugh Williams
> Dr. Kenneth .... Donald Crisp

It was during Laurence Olivier's third period in Hollywood that he played Heathcliff in *Wuthering Heights*. He had been on holiday with Vivien Leigh, driving through the south of France. It was the beginning of summer, 1938, and he had been working hard all the previous season at the Old Vic, and she had just finished her ninth film, *Sidewalks of London* (known in England as *St. Martin's Lane*), playing with Charles Laughton and Rex Harrison.

When they checked in at their hotel in Agay on the French coast, there was a cablegram awaiting Olivier, asking if he would be interested in a Goldwyn film of *Wuthering Heights* in which he, Vivien Leigh, and Merle Oberon would play the leading roles. Shortly thereafter, the screenplay arrived, written by Ben Hecht and Charles MacArthur. Hecht had suggested Olivier to director William Wyler as the only choice for the role of Heathcliff. Olivier admired the *Wuthering Heights* screenplay, but he had not been happy in either of his previous two adventures in Hollywood, and when he found out that Oberon was already cast for Cathy and Leigh was wanted for the secondary role of Isabella, he turned down the whole proposition.

William Wyler was in London when they returned from their holiday, and he did his best to persuade Olivier to accept the role; but Olivier seemed adamant. He still liked the script and he liked the role of Heathcliff enormously, but unless Leigh were part of the deal, he was not interested, and she had reaffirmed that she would accept only the role of Cathy. Olivier signed to do a melodramatic prewar film, *Q Planes*, and Wyler made a test of Robert Newton for Heathcliff; but the Newton test was no more favorable than a previous one with Douglas Fairbanks, Jr. Once again Olivier was approached by Wyler, and once again he declined. At this point, Leigh stepped in, realizing that they could not keep turning down offers on the grounds that there were not roles for both of them in the same picture, and she persuaded Olivier to reconsider; he did and signed a contract with Goldwyn to play Heathcliff.

Olivier's first days in Hollywood filming *Wuthering Heights* were a nightmare. He was not only homesick for London and Vivien Leigh, but also he had problems with Merle Oberon, with Goldwyn, and with Wyler himself, who had done everything to get him signed for the role. He muttered his way through rehearsals and sulked his way through scenes, but Heathcliff is a sulky man, and this behavior was decidedly in character. After tempers flared and there was a showdown, a turnabout slowly came; temperaments cooled, and personalities became more compatible. Relationships on the set actually became amiable.

Olivier and Leigh had parted in London with misgivings, knowing that their separation would last for a full three months at least. In spite of the fact that she was scheduled to begin rehearsals for a production of *A Midsummer Night's Dream*, she flew on an impulse to Hollywood for a few days to visit Olivier. During her visit, Leigh met David O. Selznick; he ordered a test of her to be made by George Cukor for Scarlett O'Hara in *Gone with the Wind*; and the ultimate result was that she got the most coveted role in Hollywood, one she had dreamed of playing. Thus Olivier and Leigh were able to work in Hollywood at the same time, if not in the same picture.

Wuthering Heights opened the pathway to stardom for Olivier and he earned a nomination as Best Actor at Academy Awards time, although the award went to another Englishman, Robert Donat, for *Goodbye, Mr. Chips*, over not only Olivier, but also Clark Gable for *Gone with the Wind*.

The story of the deathless romance of Cathy (Merle Oberon) and Heathcliff (Laurence Olivier) is told in retrospect, through the narration of Ellen Dean (Flora Robson), the housekeeper at Wuthering Heights. It is a bitter night on the Yorkshire moors, when a lone traveler, Dr. Kenneth (Donald Crisp), seeks refuge at the Heights. Grudgingly, he is given a room, and he prepares himself to spend the night. The wind is howling ferociously, but over it the traveler hears a woman's voice calling desperately, "Heathcliff! Heathcliff!" He goes to the window and peers out at the howling storm. There seems to be a movement in the wind, and the panes rattle as if someone were knocking on them. Impulsively, he puts his hand outside, and it is clutched almost immediately in an icy grasp. Startled, he flings himself backward with a cry. Ellen Dean hears his cry and takes him downstairs for a warm drink, and when she learns what has happened, she reluctantly begins to tell him the tale of stark passion, revenge, and terror that had taken place not so long ago in this same desolate house.

Earnshaw (Cecil Kellaway), who owned Wuthering Heights, was a widower with two children to rear, a daughter named Cathy, and a son, Hindley (Hugh Williams), who, although he was the favored young master, was thoroughly disliked by the household. One day Earnshaw returns from a visit to Liverpool, bringing with him a young gypsy boy, a waif who had attached himself to him in the wintry Liverpool streets. From the beginning, young Hindley loathes the intruder, calling him "gypsy scum," but young Cathy is fascinated by the young Heathcliff, which is the name given him by Earnshaw. The children mature, and the fascination between Heathcliff and Cathy grows into a fast, deeper emotion, even as the enmity of Hindley is fired by the sight of his sister's friendliness toward a dark stableboy from nowhere.

Even when they are grown, Cathy and Heathcliff have a royal time alone together on the moors, and one day they make their way to the nearest lodge, Thruschcross Grange, where a big party is being given. They climb the wall so that they may look upon the dancing couples, but Cathy has an accident and falls, arousing the dogs as well as the guests. Cathy is recognized and carried into the house, but Heathcliff is rudely dismissed and sent back to Wuthering Heights.

Cathy becomes fond of Edgar Linton (David Niven) and his sister Isabella (Geraldine Fitzgerald), the young heirs to the Grange, and she stays several weeks with them until her injuries are mended. She is brought home in style, wearing borrowed finery, a changed young lady. She has had a taste of society and worldly living and tries to goad Heathcliff into going away and making a gentleman of himself so that she might be seen in his company. Heathcliff overhears her deriding him, saying that it would degrade her to wed him, and in a rage he runs away. Edgar woos Cathy; she is flattered. Heathcliff has become only a memory, and Cathy and Edgar are wed.

The years pass, and then, with no warning, Heathcliff returns from America, which is where he says he has been. He has now returned with a considerable fortune. Hindley has turned into a brooding, ill-tempered drunkard, and Heathcliff wins the little fortune Hindley possesses, including Wuthering Heights. Hindley dies in bitterness. Heathcliff's helpless fury on finding that Cathy has become the wife of Edgar turns to nightmarish revenge when he uses Isabella as his pawn; he marries her and then treats her abominably, neglecting her entirely. Isabella knows no happiness in her marriage, nor has Cathy found any lasting pleasure in becoming the wife of Edgar. She knows that there is only one man for her—Heathcliff—and he has abandoned her out of revenge.

The moors become a scene of tumultuous, twisted passions, as the frustrated lovers yearn hopelessly for each other. Cathy sickens, and when Heathcliff learns that she is dying, he rushes to the Grange, forcing his way up to her room. The ensuing scene in which they plan an enduring love, and he carries her to the big window where she may look out on the moors she loves as if they were her sea and she a star-crossed maiden, is unforgettable.

With her death, the scene returns to Ellen Dean ending her narration. An embittered Heathcliff enters the room; he has aged and is half-mad. When he learns that the lonely, lovely ghost of his Cathy has come back to Wuthering Heights crying his name, a look of anguish crosses his face, and he rushes out into the wind and storm to claim her as his own.

Wuthering Heights became Goldwyn's favorite of all his personal productions, although during its shooting he often spoke of it with aggravation as "a doubtful picture." He withheld it for a long time from television release, preferring to reissue it for theatrical viewing in new prints. It remains one of the great love stories of all time.

Wuthering Heights remains Merle Oberon's finest piece of work in films. After playing Heathcliff, Laurence Olivier played several other moody heroes, such as Max de Winter in *Rebecca* (1940) and Lord Nelson in *That Hamilton Woman* (1941). He was a stunning Mr. Darcy in *Pride and Prejudice* (1940) before he went on to play the great Shakespearean roles that have made him the premier actor of our time. Geraldine Fitzgerald, a newcomer as Isabella, won a nomination as Best Supporting Actress for the year; Flora Robson was superb as Ellen Dean; and the whole production has sterling values in every category. *Wuthering Heights* was refilmed during the 1960's by American-International, but that production had none of the haunting beauty of this first dramatization of Emily Brontë's passionate love story.

GREAT DIRECTORS

ALPHABETICAL LIST OF FILMS